D1880347

TRADE IN THE EASTERN SEAS

TRADE IN THE EASTERN SEAS
1793-1813

By

C. NORTHCOTE PARKINSON
M.A.; PH.D.; F.R.HIST.S.
Fellow of Emmanuel College Cambridge
Julian Corbett Prizeman

KALPAZ

©Reserved
All rights reserved. No part of this work may be reproduced, stored, adapted, or transmitted in any form or by any means, electronic, mechanical, photocopying, micro-filming recording or otherwise, or translated in any language, without the prior written permission of the copyright owner and the publisher. The book is sold subject to the condition that it shall not, by way of trade or otherwise, be lent, resold, hired out, or otherwise circulated without the prior publisher's written consent in any form of binding or cover other than that in which it is published.

The views and opinions expressed in this book are author(s) own and the facts reported by them have been verified to the extent possible, and the publishers are not in any way liable for the same.

ISBN: 978-93-5128-461-1(HB)

First Published in 1937
Indian Reprint in 2017

Published by

Kalpaz Publications
C-30, Satyawati Nagar,
Delhi – 110052
E-mail: kalpaz@hotmail.com
Website: kalpazpublications.com
Ph.: +91-9212142040

CONTENTS

ILLUSTRATIONS

PLATES

MAPS AT END

PREFACE

MARITIME HISTORY has never yet taken its rightful place as a subject for investigation. We have, on the one hand, the economic historian, who tells us much about imports and exports but very little about shipping. We have, on the other hand, the student of nautical archaeology, who tells us much about ships but very little about trade. Somewhere between these two types of scholarship, and largely unheeded by both types of scholar, lies the true history of the sea. Maritime history I have called it, and this would seem to be its only possible name. In the text-book of economic history we learn of goods being sent overseas to this country and to that. We have the facts given us, together with such columns of figures as may serve to enliven the tale, and with that we must be content. Is not this, however, a little remote from human activities as we can picture them? Abstract statements about imports and exports do very well for the counting house, but there is that in most of us which demands more concrete information. We wish to visualise the quayside, the ships and the bales of goods. In books again of a different kind we may read of the speed and beauty of clipper ships; but here we are often disappointed by our failure to learn what the ships carried or even why they were in a hurry. It is the task of the maritime historian to bridge the gulf between these two types of work, avoiding equally the abstract and the anecdotal.

It is my contention that there is much in English history which cannot be understood without its maritime context. It is also my belief that naval history, as now studied, is far too apt to lack its economic background. Were naval history treated as an aspect of maritime history it would itself become more intelligible, while at the same time fitting more easily into the general story of mankind. The object of this work, as originally written, was to describe a naval campaign in what I hold to be its proper historical and geographical setting. Treated thus, the subject became too vast for a single volume, and I decided to deal with it in two separate books, the one maritime and the other strictly naval. The present work is the first of these. The second I hope to write in the near future.

The twofold undertaking, from a part of which this book has developed, was entitled "Trade and War in the Eastern Seas, 1803–1810". It was a thesis submitted to the University of London for the degree of Doctor of Philosophy, and consisted of two distinct parts, the one dealing with trade and the other with war. Only a portion of the first half is here reproduced; and of this the greater part has been re-written. It has also been expanded and lengthened so as to cover the longer period 1793–1813. The epoch chosen is that of the French Wars, omitting the years 1813–1815 on account of the partial abolition in that period of the East India Company's monopoly. Although, however, certain limits are set in point of time, it is necessary to warn the reader that there is here no attempt to chronicle the maritime occurrences of the period so defined. This book is a description of conditions, not a narrative of events.

It will be found that I have used no footnotes; and this, to some readers, will prove the unsoundness of any views I may have advanced. To them, my plea must be that footnotes serve but two useful purposes, and that each of these purposes may be achieved in another way. There is the footnote which conveys some additional information; and there is the footnote which refers the reader to some authority. Here the notes of the first type are collected at the end of the book, while those of the second type are concealed in the text itself. However laconic, these references are mostly to be understood when taken in conjunction with the bibliography, which, for that purpose, is arranged by chapters. Many authorities are quoted in full, so that the most exacting reader has little occasion to verify the context. I have never seen the merit of paraphrasing what might just as well be given in the original words.

Although alone responsible for the many shortcomings of this book, I should like to thank all who have helped me to produce it. First I must express my gratitude to Professor A. P. Newton, of London University, under whose experienced direction my original thesis was written. I am indebted to him for much valuable help, and not least for his suggesting the title. No pupil of his could be in any doubt as to how much I must necessarily owe to his scholarly guidance. At the same time, I have a debt of older standing to Mr E. Welbourne, of Emmanuel College. Such knowledge as I have I owe mainly to him. It is my hope that Mr Welbourne himself will not refuse to acknowledge this book as the offspring, however unworthy, of his own most stimulating thought. I also wish to express my gratitude to Sir Herbert Richmond, Master of Downing College, for much valuable criticism; to Mr J. C. Lockhart for his advice; and to Mr Carrington and Mr Kendon, of the University Press, for their unfailing tact and patience. To the Council of the Navy Records Society I am indebted for permission to reproduce certain passages from their publications. I cannot thank individually all those, particularly among the staffs of the India Office and the British Museum, who have been of assistance to me; but I cannot refrain from thanking Mr M. S. Robinson of the National Maritime Museum for kindly helping me with the illustrations. Like a great many students of naval history, I am already deeply in his debt.

C. N. P.

Emmanuel College
Cambridge
1937

Chapter I

THE INDIA HOUSE

THE new India House, which was opened in April 1800, was an austere building, severely classical, stone built and plain; but it was not entirely unadorned. The façade was relieved by pilasters and crowned by a pediment; and the pediment contained figures in high relief, much admired at the time, which were supposed to indicate the nature of the business transacted within. Even had this masterpiece survived, which it has not, it is doubtful whether the casual observer would have grasped the point of the allegory. A point, however, there was, as the following quotation will show:

DESCRIPTION OF THE PEDIMENT

Commerce, represented by Mercury, attended by Navigation, and followed by Tritons on Sea Horses, is introducing Asia to Britannia, at whose Feet She pours out her Treasures. The King is holding the Shield of Protection over the Head of Britannia and of Liberty, who is embraced by Her—By the Side of His Majesty sits Order, attended by Religion and Justice. In the Back Ground is the City Barge etc. near to which stand Industry and Integrity—The Thames fills the Angle to the Right Hand, and the Ganges the Angle towards the East.

One is loath to spoil the effect of such a description. Yet, here is an epitome of nineteenth-century England, firmly carved on the walls of Leadenhall Street almost before the century had begun. With the exception, perhaps, of the Tritons on Sea Horses, every figure was significant, prophetic and unconsciously revealing. 'Order, attended by Religion and Justice....' What Religion? What kind of Justice? For the present purpose, however, it is with Commerce that we have to do; with Commerce, and with the treasures Asia has been induced to outpour. For this part of the allegory is highly characteristic of nineteenth-century England in general and of the City in particular. It was a period and especially a place, wholly self-deceived in the matter of its own prosperity. There was a theory abroad, and it grew in strength, that England owed her power to merchants and industrialists, to hard work and self-denial, shrewdness and sobriety. At no time was this altogether true, and in 1800 it was not true at all. William Cobbett once rose in the House of Commons to congratulate the Legislature on having made the remarkable discovery that England's greatness depended solely on the work of little girls in Lancashire. He was himself inclined to give some of the credit to the Navy, among other institutions; but this doctrine was not well received then, nor is it well received now. The merchants and bankers triumphed, and, in the main, they triumph still. It was in some such spirit, and fostering the same delusion, that East India House was adorned with figures representing Commerce, Industry and Integrity. To judge from such sculpture, one would suppose that the United Company of Merchants of England trading to the East Indies was in fact what its name would suggest. There would be nothing manifestly reckless in concluding that India House sheltered a body of English merchants trading with India. Nevertheless, such a conclusion would be wrong: the men within were not merchants, and they were not trading with India. One might add, a little unkindly, that they were not always united, and that they were not all English.

How was the East India Company controlled? By the Government. What was its object? To collect taxes. How was its object attained? By means of a large standing army. What were its employees? Soldiers, mostly; the rest, Civil Servants. Where did it trade to? China. What did it export from England? Courage. And what did it import? Tea.

Plate I. The East India House
From the engraving by J. C. Stadler after T. H. Shepherd

An East India director of 1800, if closely questioned as to what the Company did, would probably have muttered something about commercial enterprise. He might have spoken about bringing the benefits of civilisation into India. To be just to him, he would not have described the Company's business as being purely philanthropic. Still less, however, would he have explained the truth, that in India the Company represented the Sword; that its chief business was to govern at a profit; and that its surplus revenues were brought home in the form of tea. Had the directors been in the habit of enlightening mankind as to the nature of the affairs they directed, they would hardly have decorated their front door with the figures of Commerce, Industry and Integrity.

Originally, of course, the Company had been engaged in Commerce. But, with its growing territories, its interests had shifted. The turning point was Lord Clive's treaty of 1765. By this agreement with the Mogul and the Nabob of Bengal, the Company became tax-farmer of the Bengal provinces. From that time onwards the collecting of taxes or rents was the Company's primary concern. At first the revenues amounted to a clear £1,700,000 a year. Rather over a million of this was spent in governing and protecting the ceded provinces. The rest was profit; or, as some would say, a fair return for the invisible import of good government. This situation lasted from 1766 to 1777. It is worthy of note that the Company did not raise the rents or taxes, whichever they were, due to it from the inhabitants of Bengal. This was found to be impossible. Neither, of course, did it lower them. From the natives' point of view the situation was not greatly changed. The great certainty of life, the tax-collector or land-agent, remained a certainty. Formerly, half this fixed revenue went in the expenses of governing Bengal; and half was paid into the treasury at Delhi. It is not clear what happened to it after that. It was either hoarded or spent. And now, under the Company, the taxes remained the same. More, however, was collected through the Company's taking into its hands the monopolies of salt and opium. The expenses of administration were not much increased, but more had to be spent on the army, not for the coercion of the natives so much as for defence against France. Then, as time went on, more territories were absorbed. Each province acquired brought with it a surplus revenue. Indeed, the Company's servants seldom reckoned land in acres or square miles. They measured land in terms of revenue. And the more land they conquered the more revenue there would be—lessened, however, by the interest to be paid on the sums spent in conquest.

It was never the declared policy of the East India Company to enter into wars for the sake of acquiring territory. But its soldiers were rather difficult to control at so great a distance. Some of them took to reporting conquests instead of proposing them, at which others of the Company's servants were terrified. Indeed, to the end, there was a good deal of opposition; partly from those who were behind the times to the extent of thinking in terms of trade; partly from those who saw that some of the later conquests were less profitable than the first. Lord Cornwallis, for instance, was one of these. He was at one time appalled at the prospect of having to take Seringapatam, and went about moaning 'Good God! What shall I do with this place?' Views such as his were usually based on a calculation that the revenues of the land to be acquired would not equal the cost of defending it added to the interest payable on the loans raised to pay for its capture. Few of the Company's servants thought about trade. Although ranking as writers, factors, junior and senior merchants, the civilians were nearly all in reality either magistrates or tax-collectors.

It appears, then, that the figure of Asia pouring out wealth at the feet of Britannia was by no means misleading. So far the allegory holds good. And even Order, attended (at a respectful distance) by Religion and Justice, had some right to appear. But why Commerce? And why Industry and Integrity?

As regards industry, the Englishman in the East was never noted for it. And in business ability he was continually outdone by the Oriental. He could make no headway in a town he did not rule, such as Rangoon. In those days Rangoon was the Alsatia of the East. It was under native government and open to all the world. There were to be found there fugitives and insolvent debtors from every part of Asia. The Exchange at Rangoon swarmed with a motley collection of people of every colour, French, English and Portuguese mingling in free rivalry with the Asiatic. And the whole wealth of the town came automatically into the hands of the Parsees and Armenians. The same tendency was apparent at Muscat and even at Bombay.

It is not clear that the East India Company had any great reputation for integrity. Edmund Burke once undertook to prove that the Company had betrayed every ally it had made from the Himalayas to Cape Comorin, and had broken every single treaty it had concluded. This was in the course of his speech on Fox's East India Bill of 1783, in which the following words occur:

> In effect, Sir, every legal, regular authority in matters of revenue, of political administration, of criminal law, in many of the most essential parts of military discipline, is laid level with the ground; and an oppressive, irregular, capricious, unsteady, rapacious, and peculating despotism, with a direct disavowal of obedience to any authority at home, and without any fixed maxim, principle, or rule of proceeding, to guide them in India, is at present the state of your charter-government over great kingdoms.

This was a topic on which Burke may have been guilty of exaggeration, yet his remarks suggest that some events in the Company's past were not immediately recognisable as fruits of integrity. The Hindoo could probably ponder the idea of integrity without instantly calling the Company to mind.

The figure of Navigation had, perhaps, some right to a niche, but even this was begging the question, for, neither in the broadest or the narrowest sense, had navigation much to do with the European discovery of the East. When Vasco da Gama first reached India he not only found a broker from Tunis speaking fluent Portuguese; he also found some local seamen who knew more about navigation than he did. When he tried to impress them with his navigational instruments, they instantly produced their own, which he found to be similar but quite obviously superior.

Judging merely by knowledge of navigation and shipbuilding, there was nothing whatever to have prevented Asiatic seamen from sailing round the Cape and discovering Europe. As far as mere physical possibility goes, it must be remembered that a Chinese junk was once sailed to Europe; although it took a European to do it. It was through Courage that Europeans, and especially Englishmen, found their way to the East. And, once there, it was Courage that they had to sell. And if the English eventually managed to exclude their rivals from India, it was not through business ability or hard work or honesty, but through fighting; and especially fighting at sea.

The East India Company came, then, not to trade but to collect tribute. The Company was, in the first instance, willing enough to trade. But the difficulty was to find anything to export. There were many things in India which Englishmen desired, but the Hindoo desired nothing.

> The Hindoo, born and desiring to pass his life in the same country...whose food is rice, whose drink is water or milk, to whom wine or strong drink is an object of abomination, and who, if he strictly acts up to his religious principles, would sooner lay down his own life than put any living creature to death or permit a morsel of animal food to enter his mouth, whose warm climate renders any clothing, beyond what decency requires, intolerable, and whose light clothing is made by himself and his family from

the cotton produced in his own fertile fields, whose customs and religion, to which he adheres with the most inflexible constancy, render utterly inadmissable many articles of enjoyment and comfort, which our habits have rendered almost necessary to our existence, can never have any desire to acquire the produce or manufactures of Europe....

David Macpherson, the author of this paragraph, wrote on the eve of a great discovery. He was shown to be a false prophet almost before he had finished uttering his prophecy; and yet, all his facts were correct. The Hindoo was such as he described. Macpherson's only failure was in not grasping the significance of one of the facts which he actually stated; the fact that the Hindoo wears cotton garments. The garments may have been home-made, but it was soon found that they were more easily produced in Lancashire. They may have been scanty, but then the Hindoos were so numerous that the total demand could not be small. In 'Mr Lee's Calculation' it was shown that an English cotton-spinner, with mule spindles, could produce as much as forty, perhaps as much as sixty Indian spinners. With this discovery of how to sell cotton cloth to the people of India came the end of an epoch in Anglo-Indian relations. For two centuries and more the problem remained unsolved. The Hindoo apparently wanted nothing. A solution at one time seemed in sight when it was found that some of the peasants had a weakness for scarlet cloth; but they would not buy it for fear of being thought rich and having their rents raised. The turning point, after which the problem ceased to be a problem, was the year 1813. Macpherson had the singular misfortune of publishing his prophecy in 1812.

The problem so soon to be solved was still apparently insoluble during the period with which we are concerned. And the result was that the Hindoo who would not buy was compelled to pay just as if he had. Or, to put it another way, the native who would not buy goods was coerced into buying services, political, military and legal services; not all illusory but all expensive.

The chief burden laid on the native taxpayer was the expense of saving him from the French. For this essential service his gratitude may have been only moderate. He nevertheless had to pay for the exclusion of the French in the past, their continued exclusion in the present and their proposed exclusion in the future. His burden under this heading is easy to underestimate. For it might seem, at first sight, that the troops destined to exclude the French were equally useful in keeping order among the natives of India themselves. That they did, to some extent, keep order, is undeniable. But their disposal was in accordance with a scheme of defensive strategy and their number far in excess of what was needed for police work.

The cost of maintaining armies was a serious burden and the natives felt the weight of it; but so did the Company. However heavy the rents or taxes, the Company paid no sensational dividend. Money might seem to pour into the treasury, but it only trickled out again into the shareholders' pockets. Nearly all the profits were absorbed in the process of government. The Company might be compared to an enormous and highly intricate machine, pounding and roaring in the most impressive manner, and yet, somehow, requiring almost the whole of its energy to overcome the friction of its own mechanism.

Now, this spectacle of a strangely unprofitable machine is not unknown in the history of joint-stock enterprise; and especially so in the history of monopolistic enterprise. And the cause is seldom far to seek. The Company which absorbs profits is being guided to suit the convenience of its servants. The men it employs are managing the whole business and sharing the proceeds. Instead of paying dividends it is paying unnecessarily large salaries and pensions to a crowd of idle officials. Nowadays, this process can be hidden from the shareholders by the technical nature of the work in hand.

Chemists and engineers and accountants can between them produce a report and balance-sheet proof against the most careful inspection. Technicality and complexity silence most inquirers. Few are bold enough to demand a translation in English.

To shield the shareholders from loss, a joint-stock company has a board of directors. The board is composed of shareholders and elected by shareholders. That, at least, is the theory. And its object is to safeguard the shareholders' interests. But those interests will be safeguarded only so long as the directors are representative of the shareholders and quite distinct from the paid management. As soon as one of the directors has secured a salaried post for his son, as soon as a retired servant of the Company has become a director, the board has to that extent become unrepresentative. And once this kind of thing becomes common, the board ceases to fulfil its purpose. It no longer represents the shareholders. Its interests are identical with those of the staff. The dividends will dwindle as the salaries increase.

The East India Company was managed in this fashion. Its affairs were concealed in part by technicality but more by distance. India was too far away for effective control. There was this difference, however, between the East India Company and any other company, that even the shareholders had been in their turn seduced. In a sense, there were no shareholders; none, that is to say, much interested in the joint-stock enterprise as such. Those interested at all must have been few and unimportant. In a sense, there was no Company; for it had become a mere name to cover the operations of groups and individuals. East India stock was bought for the patronage it conferred. Few of those who held it had any desire to reduce 'overhead expenses'; for what the Company lost its servants gained, and among the servants was numbered the shareholder's son or nephew, brother or friend. To one whose son was making a fortune, it mattered little what dividend the

Company might pay. No sensational profit could arise in any case. Dividends were limited by law to 10½ per cent., which might represent as little as 3½ per cent. on the market value.

Who, it may be asked, are the East India Company? The people of Thibet having heard their name frequently mentioned, inquired whether the Company was a *man* or a *woman*. It is not to be wondered, that the people of Thibet were ignorant on this subject; since many are ignorant who have much better opportunities of being acquainted with it.

The East India Company is composed of a great number of persons, each of whom, in general, devotes to the common object of it only a small part of his fortune. All therefore possessed of the moderate amount of stock, which serves as a qualification for voting, may interfere in its concerns, though each acquires only a weak interest in the general prosperity of them. The rich individual is inclined through indifference to abandon this little fragment of his property to chance; seldom feeling a case of mismanagement or speculation as of moment enough to call for his exertions. Proprietors of this description, with all those who love their ease and tranquillity, or who are placed at a distance from the scene of action, rarely take part in the controul of the Company's affairs: unless to vote for *friends* at the election for Directors, or upon *political* occasions.

But there is a numerous body of proprietors of a far different complexion, who have views of interest to pursue, and whose great object in having a share in the stock of the Company, is to serve THEMSELVES. They have no solicitude about the dividend on their qualification, whether it be 6 per cent. or 8 per cent.: they have a private concern of far greater amount, which goes to thousands and ten thousands a year, besides immense patronage. In short, they do not join in the cause to abide the issue of it; but, like contractors and vultures, they follow the camp for prey. However the Company may decline, they are sure of prosperity; and, in some cases, in exact proportion to that decline. A qualification to vote in the Company's affairs is so easily bought, and many of those who propose to benefit themselves in its employ, are so wealthy, and have so many wealthy friends, that a multitude of votes become easily at their command. Power, when once established, generally begets power. As the immense extent of the Company's affairs presents lucrative objects in every quarter, each candidate for favor seeks for effectual support: influence is bartered for influence; and a combination arises from it, capable of accomplishing every thing. Directors are chosen by virtue of it; and these Directors feel a gratitude for their patrons, which is the more natural, as they have to seek for votes again at the end of every four years....Hence we see rich servants, and a poor Company; hence the interests of the Company are made a secondary object, and the possession of posts and emoluments becomes primary; and though Parliament and the Court of Directors or of proprietors, now and then, make an effort towards a reform, things sooner or later shew the strongest tendency to a relapse....

Fiott, the author of the above, was a man with a grievance. It does not appear, however, that he exaggerated the tendency of the East India Company to defraud itself for its servants' benefit. He was, for that matter, far from alone in commenting on it.

The East India Company was ruled by a Court of Proprietors and a Court of Directors. The principal function of the Court of Proprietors was to elect the members to serve on the Court of Directors. To be a qualified proprietor, entitled to vote, it was necessary to hold £1000 stock and to have held it for at least a year. Those with only £500 stock could vote on a show of hands, but not by ballot. Those with upwards of £2000 stock might become candidates for election to the Court of Directors. Those with larger investments had two or three votes and a holder of £10,000 stock had four, which was the maximum. 'Three stars in India Stock to her name, begad!'—thus did Thackeray's Major Pendennis describe an heiress. In 1799 there were eighteen hundred and twenty-four qualified voters. Of these nearly fourteen hundred lived in London or within easy reach of it. Of the forty-nine proprietors holding upwards of £10,000 stock, forty-six lived in London or in the immediate vicinity. On the most important occasions, there would not be many more than a thousand proprietors at a General Court. The normal attendance might be four or five hundred.

The Court of Directors is thus described by Montefiore:

> There are twenty-four directors, including the chairman and deputy chairman, who may be re-elected in turn, six each year for four years successively, by rotation. The meetings or courts of directors are to be held at least once a week, but are commonly oftener, being summoned as occasion requires.
>
> Out of the body of the members are chosen different committees, who have the peculiar inspection of certain branches of the company's business, such as the separate committees of correspondence, of buying, of treasury, of warehouses, of shipping, of accounts, of law-suits, a committee to prevent the growth of private trade, and, under stat. 33 Geo. III. c. 52, a committee of secrecy.

The directors each served for four years, six retiring each year to make room for others. Those thus retiring were not eligible for re-election until the following year. During their enforced holiday, they were said to be 'out by rotation'. If this system was designed to prevent the Direction from becoming a profession, it scarcely attained its end. Despite free and open elections, the Court was, and always remained, very largely co-optive. It revealed a tendency to become even hereditary. The same surnames were apt to recur, so that the Court rarely lacked a Baring, a Thornton and an Inglis. After one has seen a list of directors for 1780, the list for 1800 cannot but seem vaguely familiar. Apart, moreover, from periodical spells of retirement, the same man might remain a director over a very long period of years. To take two years at random, nine who had been directors in 1802 were still directors in 1810; while there are three other surnames to be found in both lists. Turning to an individual case, Charles Grant, first elected in 1794, was chairman in 1805–6, in 1809–10, and again in 1815–16. He was a director, in short, for almost the whole of his life after his return from India. Nor was it thought in any way exceptional that this should be so.

The elections at India House were hotly contested and not without a great deal of intrigue, especially in the election of the chairman and deputy. Those who sought election were nearly all wealthy City men, financiers, bankers and the like. Some had made their fortunes in India. There was even an occasional retired sea captain among them. They had houses in Bedford Square, Portland Place or Harley Street. Some were baronets and some—to Cobbett's intense disgust—had country houses in Surrey. It was not unusual for some of the directors to be in Parliament; in 1809 eight directors and ex-directors had this distinction. An average Court might be expected to include four or five members of the Lower House. Men who thus divided their energies between Leadenhall Street and Westminster would often take up a strategic position by living in the vicinity of Russell Square, midway between the two. Political and East Indian affairs intermingled, indeed, in more ways than one. It was by no means unknown for the Ministry to lend its influence to one candidate or another in an India House election. When Charles Grant first stood for a vacancy in the Court of Directors, it was at Dundas's suggestion and with Pitt's support. And it is worthy of note that this ministerial recognition was of sufficient weight to overcome an opposition of 'astonishing strength'.

For their services the directors were rewarded with a moderate salary of £300 a year each. This in itself would hardly account for the eagerness with which candidates pressed forward; still less for the fact that voters were sometimes fetched in a carriage-and-four. What exactly a directorship was worth it is difficult to say. According to Lindsay 'the general opinion of the day seems to have been (and this opinion was frequently expressed) that the worth of each directorship amounted to no less than 10,000 l. per annum, in one form or another....' No authority is given for this statement. On the other hand, there is nothing inherently improbable about it. Judging from the sums of money said to have been spent in the elections, judging from the opportunities open to the directors, one can hardly think £10,000 a year a gross overestimate. It is clearly impossible, however, in the nature of things, to compute the value of anything so unsubstantial as patronage. What a directorship was worth in credit and prestige must have varied enormously with the circumstances of the individual. What it was worth in money must have varied still more enormously according to the individual's honesty.

Once in office, a director had the right to appoint in rotation to many posts in the Company's service. Governors and councillors had to be appointed to the Indian Presidencies, and in the filling of such important offices a director's influence might be sought and, in some form, paid for. There were posts in the Civil Service worth from £4000 to £6000 a year. There were cadetships and writerships and posts as assistant-surgeon, chaplain, solicitor, barrister or pilot. There were three armies to be officered and the Company's navy as well. So that, altogether, the patronage was considerable; and the more so in that men often died almost as soon as they landed in India, leaving their posts to be filled again. The chairman and deputy each enjoyed double the patronage of an ordinary director. It was said, moreover, that to the chairman alone belonged the right to fill vacancies in the establishment at Canton. Whether the chief post in that favoured service had ever been worth its rumoured value of £20,000 a year may be doubted, but half that income, easily earned in a healthy climate, constituted a sufficiently valuable appointment. That it should be given to a relative of the chairman was more or less inevitable.

On the subject of patronage the following passage is enlightening, especially on the extent to which the President of the Board of Control might share in it. That official's duties will be described on a later page. His position was briefly, that of a cabinet minister entrusted with the supervision of the Company's political affairs.

> The patronage arising from the annual appointment of youths to the service of the Company, is, as was explained in a former chapter, equitably divided among the Directors. In the continual intercourse, for which there is occasion, between the President of the Board of Controul and the heads of the Court of Directors, mutual habits of personal cordiality are of course formed, and, indeed, are, on public grounds, highly proper. It certainly, therefore, would not be unnatural to expect that the President might occasionally obtain an appointment in the service. Such an appointment, however, would be the personal and, possibly, the private gift of an individual Director...the most advisable plan seems to be, that the Court, in their collective capacity, should avowedly allot to the President of the Board of Controul a certain limited portion of their annual mass of patronage. This plan is now usually adopted. The amount assigned to the President of the Board never exceeds the share of the Chairman or the Deputy Chairman, which again never exceeds, and sometimes fails to reach, double the share of an ordinary Director. So that, if we suppose the patronage for a given year divided into twenty-eight equal lots, two of these lots, at the most, would be the quota of the minister in question. This custom, it should be observed, has not been embodied in any compact or written regulation; but depends, for its existence, on the pleasure of the Court of Directors.

This passage was written in 1813 by Robert Grant, two years before his father, Charles Grant, entered on his third term of office as chairman, so that it may be said to have been written with a full knowledge of how the directors managed their affairs. The author goes on to point out what exactly a twenty-eighth part of the Company's patronage would amount to. He gives the average number of writers appointed each year as thirty, the average number of cadets as a hundred and thirty. Thus, under this head alone, neglecting the appointment of surgeons, chaplains, law officers and the rest, any director would have four or five vacancies to fill each year.

The obvious way in which a director could enrich himself was by selling appointments. It is difficult, however, to determine to what extent appointments were actually sold. There had been a time, twenty or twenty-five years before the period with which we are concerned, when the sale of writerships had been as much a matter of common knowledge as the corruption at Parliamentary elections. It was, for example, in 1765 that Lord Sandwich was said to have given a seat in Parliament and another in Trinity House in exchange for a writership—his nominee being his own illegitimate son by the famous singer, Martha Ray. Latterly, however, the influence of directors like Charles Grant (a member of the Clapham Sect) had brought about a change for the better. The traffic continued, if at all, in secrecy. In 1809 a Parliamentary Committee discovered that one of the directors had, during the preceding three years, given three writerships to a relative, who had sold them. Although acquitted of any connivance in the sale, the director was not re-elected. And again, in 1810, the Court of Proprietors resolved that 'sixteen young gentlemen, whose nominations had been procured by corrupt practices, should be dismissed'. It may be remarked that these examples were made at about the period of Grant's second term of office as chairman. It may also be said, and with truth, that the rending of an occasional scapegoat is not incompatible with a generally low level of conduct.

For the less scrupulous directors there was another form of corruption, and one less liable to detection. This consisted in maintaining a secret connection with firms and individuals—and especially shipowners—with whom the Company had business dealings. The relationship between the Court of Directors and the 'Shipping Interest' was sometimes a great deal too close. It was this which made the Company appear so blind to its own interests.

The East India Company, then, must be visualised as a ring of men actually in office as directors; a larger group of those who had been in office or hoped soon to be elected; a still larger group of voters living in London and in close touch with directors and candidates; and, lastly, a negligible outer circle of proprietors living elsewhere, nearly half of them foreigners. Of these four groups, only the last consisted of shareholders considering themselves as such. The first three should rather be considered as electors and elected; and these, who used their votes actively, made more, perhaps, by voting than was paid them in dividend.

Patronage was the chief concern of the East India Company in its London aspect. For the rest, the directors managed the Company's commercial and maritime concerns. The military and political side of the Company's affairs, which was far more important than the commercial, was mainly outside their province. They made their appointments, but the men appointed, once in India, were subject only to orders which had been approved by the Board of Control. This Board, established by stat. 24 Geo. III, sess. 2, c. 25, was a Committee of the Privy Council, which existed, in practice, only in the person of its President. To him the India directors had to submit all their minutes, resolutions and correspondence of a political nature. And if he saw fit to alter their orders, he might do so. He might reverse the sense of their decrees, which had nevertheless to go forth with their signature. Through him, the Government fixed the strength of the Indian armies. And apart from this, the Government's approval was necessary for the policy followed in India. It might, moreover, through the King, recall any of the Company's servants from the Governor-General downwards. Sir George Barlow's appointment was, in this way, revoked in 1806.

The Government, in practical control of the Company's political and military affairs—so far, at least, as they could be controlled from England—had no particular interest in the Company's financial stability. If so inclined, the ministers might use the Indian armies for imperial ends, regardless of the directors' protests. The directors themselves, as we have seen, had more to gain from the Company's extravagance than from its solvency, since a more economical system would have lessened their patronage. The proprietors, in their turn, were more eager to share the plunder than prevent it. So that it was, in fact, nobody's interest to insist on a sound financial policy. And, while all connected with the Company were evidently prosperous, that curious abstraction the Company itself was always drifting towards disaster.

As early as 1783 Edmund Burke pointed out that the interests of the Company, as such, were the concern of nobody. The following passage is taken from his speech on the East India Bill, delivered in December of that year:

> ...there is none who hears me, that is not as certain as I am, that the Company, in the sense in which it was formerly understood, has no existence. The question is not, what injury you may do to the proprietors of India stock; for there are no such men to be injured. If the active, ruling part of the Company, who form the general Court, who fill the offices, and direct the measures, (the rest tell for nothing) were persons who held their stock as a means of their subsistence, who in the part they took were only concerned in the government of India for the rise or fall of their dividend, it would be indeed a defective plan of policy. The interest of the people who are governed by them would not be their primary object; perhaps a very small part of their consideration at all. But then they might well be depended on, and perhaps more than persons in other respects preferable, for preventing the peculation of their servants to their own prejudice. Such a body would not easily have left their trade as a spoil to the avarice of those who received their wages. But now things are totally reversed. The stock is of no value, whether it be the qualification of a director or proprietor; and it is impossible that it should. A director's qualification may be worth about two thousand five hundred pounds—and the interest, at eight per cent., is about one hundred and sixty pounds a year. Of what value is that, whether it rise to ten, or fall to six, or to nothing, to him whose son, before he is in Bengal two months, and before he descends the steps of the council-chamber, sells the grant of a single contract for forty thousand pounds? Accordingly the stock is bought up in qualifications. The vote is not to protect the stock, but the stock is bought to acquire the vote; and the end of the vote is to cover and support, against justice, some man of power who has made an obnoxious

fortune in India; or to maintain in power those who are actually employing it in the acquisition of such a fortune....

As Burke perceived, the Company's tendency was towards financial ruin. As if doubly to ensure that this should be the case, there was a clause inserted in the charter, as renewed in 1793, by which the Government was to share in the Company's profits, should they prove excessive. The Company, under 33 Geo. III, c. 52, was not to pay more than 10½ per cent. dividend. Were a greater profit made, half a million sterling was to be paid out of it into the Exchequer. As a fact, only one such payment was ever made, for war-time conditions absorbed the expected surplus. Had events been different, however, this limiting of the dividend (which was by no means the first measure of the kind) was hardly calculated to revive any languid interest the proprietors may have had in their investments. Most of them, it must be remembered, had bought their shares at about double their nominal value, so that the dividend was not particularly high when considered as interest on their capital outlay. Before 1793 the Company's dividend had fluctuated considerably, from as little as 6 per cent. in 1755–66 to as much as 12½ per cent. in 1770–72. Only 8 per cent. was paid in 1787–89, and it is somewhat strange that the dividend should ultimately have become fixed at so high a rate as 10½ per cent. There were not wanting critics of this state of affairs. One pamphleteer, writing in 1813 and veiling his identity under the pseudonym of 'Common Sense', was careful to point out that speculation in India stock had given way, of necessity, to place-mongering:

> Making the dividends fixed, and independent of loss and gain, is wrong and absurd. No effort can increase the dividend, no extravagance or negligence can lessen it, and it cannot be concealed, that from such a state of things it necessarily arises that patronage is the only bonus on India stock. There is some connection either with ship-builders, sail-makers, or the furnishers of stores, officers, secretaries, clerks, or appointments abroad.

It is true the connection is circuitous, and the patronage difficult to trace, but the fact resolves itself to this, that however it may be divided amongst them, the whole of the patronage of places and profits, at home and abroad, civil and military, is vested in the Directors and Proprietors, and that patronage is of an amazing amount and extent....

What the effect would be of any measure to deflect the Company's surplus profits into the Exchequer was predicted by Adam Smith:

It might be more agreeable to the Company, that their own servants and dependants should have either the pleasure of wasting, or the profit of embezzling, whatever surplus might remain, after paying the proposed dividend of eight per cent. than that it should come into the hands of a set of people, with whom those resolutions could scarce fail to set them, in some measure, at variance. The interest of those servants and dependants might so far predominate in the court of proprietors, as sometimes to dispose it to support the authors of depredations which had been committed, in direct violation of its own authority. With the majority of proprietors, the support of the authority of their own court might sometimes be a matter of less consequence, than the support of those who had set that authority at defiance.

That this prediction would have been fulfilled, supposing there had been no war, seems more than probable. But the actual course of events was such that the Government had actually to subsidise the Company to keep it afloat at all—the subsidy being disguised as repayment for the services rendered by the Company during the war. So far was the Exchequer from profiting that William Cobbett was able to write in 1806 that,

...not one penny (since the *first* year) has the Company ever paid into the Exchequer of the stipulated half million a-year; and, what is still more glaringly unjust, and more galling to the burdened people, two millions of our taxes have already been granted to this Company, wherewith to pay the dividends upon their stock; and, such has been the management, and such is now the state, of the Company's affairs, that we need not be at all surprised if another million be called for from us, during the present Session of Parliament....

It may be wondered how the East India Company contrived to exist for so long, despite annual deficits and the 'negligence, profusion, and malversation' which Adam Smith believed it to encourage. Here we must remember that, whereas few were interested in the East India Company's corporate prosperity, many were interested in its continued existence. When actual collapse threatened, efforts were made to avert the catastrophe. And outside criticism was at all times hotly resented. An attack on the Company's monopoly was enough to unite all the conflicting interests and factions which sheltered behind its imposing exterior. Whatever the deficit, however large the debt, the Company had to be supported. To propose winding up its unprofitable concerns was to disturb a hornets' nest.

It was mainly this fear of extinction that saved the finances of the Company. But there were other factors tending to check leeway. One was the stupidity of some who could never be brought to understand the Company's affairs, and who still thought in terms of trade. Another was the instinct of honesty from which few of the directors were entirely free. And yet another was the capacity shown at times by the Company's servants in India. By themselves, these factors could not avert final shipwreck; but they could and did postpone it.

Some attempt has been made to describe the general character of the India House; as also the character of the men whose carriages stood at the door. There remains to describe how the Company's business was transacted; how, in short, the machinery worked. And perhaps the best approach to this subject is through some slight knowledge of the India House itself.

The ground floor of the building was chiefly occupied by Court and Committee rooms. Of these the largest was called

'The General Court Room'. This was where the proprietors met periodically, and where the Company's imports were sold by auction. The room was a sort of theatre, with tiers of seats formed in a semicircle, facing a railed enclosure. Within the enclosure was a long table at which the directors sat when the Court of Proprietors met. The chairman sat in the middle and it was to him that all speeches were addressed. When the room was used for an auction, a single director represented the dignity of the Court.

Next in size to 'The General Court Room' was 'The Court Room'. It was here that the Court of Directors met. This was an impressive chamber, decorated with portraits and having, as its principal object of furniture, a horse-shoe shaped table for the convenience of the directors. Of the various Committee rooms, the 'Finance and Home Committee Room' was the largest. Finally, also on the ground floor, there were the private rooms of the directors.

Now, much has been said of the privileges and profits of the directors. It is now but just to explain that a directorship, whatever it might be worth, was very far from being a sinecure. The Court of Directors met, it may be, two or three times a week. It could meet as seldom as this because most of its business consisted in ratifying the decisions already reached in committee. It acted chiefly on reports laid before it by its committees. Only rarely were these reports rejected. The normal procedure was for a resolution to be passed in the exact wording of the appropriate committee's recommendation; and probably, in minor matters, without discussion. The real work, in fact, was done in committee, not in Court. There were such things as committees of the whole Court, but these were less important than the thirteen or fourteen specialised committees into which the twenty-four directors were grouped.

According to seniority, the directors were, first of all, divided into three unequal groups. The senior group, which included the 'Chairs'—that is, the chairman and deputy—attended, in the first instance, to all major questions of policy. For this purpose, they formed three committees; one known as the Secret Committee, the second as the Committee of Correspondence, the third as the Committee of Treasury. The Secret Committee had only three members, the chairman, deputy, and one other. Its functions are thus defined by M'Culloch in a note appended to his edition of Adam Smith's *Wealth of Nations*:

> The principal powers of the court of directors are vested in a secret committee, forming a sort of cabinet or privy council. All communications of a confidential or delicate nature between the board of control and the company are submitted, in the first instance at least, to the consideration of this committee; and the directions of the board, as to political affairs, may be transmitted direct to India, through the committee, without being seen by the other directors. The secret committee is appointed by the court of directors, and its members are sworn to secrecy.

Through the Board of Control, and the normally docile Secret Committee, the Government's power of directing the Company in its political aspect was all but complete. That there were limits to the directors' complaisance was discovered in 1806. In that year the Ministry, having decided on Barlow's recall, determined that Lord Lauderdale should succeed him. Not anticipating any opposition, the ministers allowed their decision to be known before even consulting the Court of Directors. This high-handed treatment, the occasion of the revolt which followed, was clearly the outcome of many years of subservience on the part of the Company. The Secret Committee, with its small membership, must have been more easily coerced than the Court could ever be. Its wide powers, therefore, were useful, chiefly, to the Government.

The Committee of Correspondence dealt with the reports received from the civil and military authorities in India. By drafting the replies and instructions for the approval of the Court as a whole, this committee exercised considerable powers. Its proposed replies, however, required the sanction of the Board of Control as well as that of the Court of Directors. The committee's responsibilities were not, therefore, as heavy as might at first be supposed. More impressive, perhaps, than its authority was the mere volume of business it had to transact.

The Committee of Treasury scarcely requires explaining. It was, in some sort, the connecting link between the Company's commercial and political affairs. It necessarily played a part in all major decisions of policy.

The same senior group of directors, apparently about eleven in number, which formed the above three committees, had also to provide two committees of lesser importance; the Committee of Lawsuits and the Committee to control the Military Fund. The same men, of course, sat on the various committees. Some, nevertheless, may have become specialists to a certain extent; and the attendance, at any given meeting, and especially the attendance of the chairman, would depend, doubtless, on the agenda. The chairman and deputy were members of all committees. Each committee was of course attended by a permanent official, the head of the department concerned; the principal officials being the secretary and the treasurer.

Below the senior group of directors was an intermediate group of six, entrusted with the strictly commercial affairs of the Company. The Committee of Warehouses, the Committee of Accounts, and the Committee of Buying; each of these dealt with a special branch of the business.

The Committee of Warehouses was responsible not only for the storage but also for the sale of the Company's imports. To the Committee of Buying was entrusted the purchase of two of the staple exports, woollens and lead. From the same group of directors was also formed a fourth committee, the business of which was to look after the India House itself, the upkeep of the building and the efficiency of the servants.

The remaining directors, forming the junior group, had control over the Company's shipping. The Committee of Shipping, however, had to do more than receive tenders and sign charter-parties. It had also, for no very obvious reason, to purchase all exports other than woollens and lead. There were three subsidiary committees, all more or less concerned with the shipping. First, the Committee of Private Trade, which had to supervise the private investments, both outward and homeward, of the Company's commanders and officers. Second, and rather oddly separated from the previous committee (the result, possibly, of a panic measure), the Committee for Preventing the Growth of the Private Trade. Lastly, the Committee for Government Troops and Stores, which had to arrange for the embarkation of such of the King's regiments as might be sent to India, and also for the sending out of military stores, which the Company conveyed gratis.

The standing committees already described may be tabulated as follows:

Group 1 (11 members):
- Committee of Secrecy or Secret Committee (3 members).
- Committee of Correspondence.
- Committee of Treasury.
- Committee of Lawsuits.
- Committee of Military Fund.

Group 2 (6 members):
- Committee of Warehouses.
- Committee of Accounts.
- Committee of Buying.
- Committee of House.

Group 3 (7 members):
- Committee of Shipping.
- Committee of Private Trade.
- Committee for Preventing the Growth of Private Trade.
- Committee of Government Troops and Stores.

A certain amount of confusion is apt to arise from the way in which contemporary authorities make use of the terms 'Committee of Secrecy' and 'Secret Committee'. These terms were used indifferently to denote the same body. 'Secret Committee' is the more correct, as it is thus worded in the Statute of 1793, 33 Geo. III, c. 52. Still further to confuse matters, there existed another Secret Committee, chosen from the senior group, the sole function of which was to discuss with the Admiralty all questions relating to convoys, signals and places of rendezvous. The Secret Commercial Committee, yet a third body, was not appointed until 1815.

Working at India House, and under the orders of the different committees, was an office staff numbering between 350 and 400. The rooms where all these clerks worked were apparently on the upper floors. The first floor housed the library and the museum as well as the principal offices. The upper part of the House can have had little of the magnificence to be seen on the ground floor. Charles Lamb, who spent thirty-five years of his life in the accountant's office, apostrophised the building as:

> ...thou dreary pile, fit mansion for a Gresham or a Whittington of old, stately house of Merchants; with thy labyrinthine passages, and light-excluding, pent-up offices, where candles for one half of the year supplied the place of the sun's light; unhealthy contributor to my weal, stern fosterer of my living....

To judge from this account, the less public parts of the India House were ill-designed to accommodate the horde of clerks which the business of the Company required. The following figures include secretaries, assistants and clerks, but exclude the extra clerks, a numerous but perhaps fluctuating body, abounding in some departments, unknown in others. The figures are for 1802:

Secretary's Office	56
Office of the Examiner of Indian Correspondence	21
Auditor's Office	10

Register Office for Indian Books	4
The Indian Book Office (Library)	4
Treasurer's Office	17
Under Committee of Lawsuits	3
Under Committee of Military Fund	3
Under Committee of Warehouses (including auctioneers, cryers, etc.)	9
Under Committee of Buying	6
Under Committee of Accounts	39
Transfer Office	12
Under Committee of House (including doorkeepers, firemen and watchmen)	34
Under Committee of Shipping:	
Pay Office (including 2 Inspectors of Recruits, 1 Inspector of Small Arms, 1 Inspector of Locks, 1 Agent for Recruits in Ireland, 1 Examining Surgeon)	40
Master Attendant's Office	10
Under Committee for Preventing the Growth of Private Trade	1

In addition to the office staff, the Company employed a small army of workmen:

Under the Committee of Warehouses:	
Warehousemen, elders, deputy-elders, writers, labourers	3170
Under Committee of Buying:	
Cloth-workers, packers etc.	138
Under Committee of Private Trade:	
Freight Office	100
Watermen	12
Under the respective Committees of House and Warehouses:	
Workmen, painter, carpenter, plumber, cabinet-maker, tallow-chandler etc.	15

Altogether, allowing for extra clerks and casual labour, there may have been at times as many as four thousand people employed by the Company in London, including a clerical staff of four hundred. In addition, the Committee for Government Troops and Stores had agents at Gravesend,

Deal, Dover, Portsmouth, Bristol, Dartmouth, Torbay, Plymouth, Falmouth, Cork, Limerick, Venice, Vienna, Constantinople, Grand Cairo, Aleppo and Bussorah. The officers and seamen of the Company's ships have not been taken into account; but these, it must be understood, were not directly employed by the Company.

Altogether, it will be seen that the Company's affairs, even in England, were on an enormous scale. This fact in itself, when we allow for what Adam Smith called 'the fraud and abuse, inseparable from the management of the affairs of so great a company', must convince us of the Company's inherent instability. To support such an edifice, the foundations had need to be of the solidest. But those of India House were far from that. The House was doomed through its essential defects. Monopolies nevertheless have their virtues. At the India House there was generosity shown to even the humbler servants. Much, surely, may be forgiven those magnates who pensioned Charles Lamb so long before his life was done. Truly, this was 'the kindness of the most munificent firm in the world'. Here at least was magnificence not thrown away.

Chapter II

BRITISH INDIA

As seen from the invader's standpoint, India consists of an immense and fertile river valley, with mountains to the north of it and uplands filling the peninsula to the south. The river valley is all-important. The rest of the country matters not at all. The river valley, the basin of the Ganges, is worth conquering and the rest is not. This at any rate was true in 1800, and is very probably true now.

To reach the basin of the Ganges from Europe, there are several possible routes—three at least—each of which is beset by different obstacles. Those to the westward, however, involve the crossing of intermediate and worthless lands, whereas that solitary entrance to the eastward opens full upon the plain itself. The best method, therefore, of invading India is to begin operations at the eastern gate. And for this it is necessary to come by sea. The gate is not easy of access, as we shall see, for the coast is guarded by shallows. There is but a single harbour and that most difficult to enter under sail. But the invader who succeeds in landing there comes at once into the plain he wishes to subdue. He wastes no time in conquering territory he does not want. He pierces instantly to the heart of the country.

The English gained their first foothold in India as early as 1639. This was Fort St George on the Coromandel Coast, the situation of which was determined by political accident rather than deliberate choice. As if to repair the mistake, an attempt was made immediately afterwards to secure a footing in Bengal, at the eastern entrance to the Ganges basin. Although without a thought of conquest, the pioneers showed a very proper instinct. Despite initial setbacks, the foothold was gradually gained, and by 1697 Fort William had come into being on the banks of the Hooghly. England had now, as it were, a foot inside the door. So had the French and Dutch; but the English were stronger at sea, and, at the crucial date 1765, they secured the province of Bengal by force of arms. They also promised tribute to the Mogul—a tribute which they subsequently neglected to pay. Henceforth, Bengal was their most valued possession; for the rent formerly paid into the treasury at Delhi was now so much clear profit for the Company in England. This, as we have seen, was the basis of the Company's fortunes.

Fort St George had never been quitted, and Bombay, on the other side of India, had been acquired by treaty from the Portuguese in 1662. So that there were, from the end of the seventeenth century, three separate forts in India belonging to the East India Company; Fort St George, Bombay Castle and Fort William. There were other footholds and outposts, but these were the three seats of government. Fort William, otherwise known as Calcutta, inevitably gained an ascendancy over the other two; for once the Company had taken to landowning as its principal concern, the other two strongholds had ceased to matter as sources of profit. Neither of them stood in that fertile plain which yielded revenue; indeed, they neither of them included a river valley at all. From 1765 onwards, Fort William was the heart of British India; the key to prosperity; the one thing that mattered. After 1773 the other two Governments were made subordinate to it.

Fort William, or Calcutta, lies nearly a hundred miles inland, up the Hooghly, the western branch of the Ganges. This is too high up for big ships, as a general rule. At the period with which we are concerned, it was usual for men-of-war to lie forty or fifty miles downstream at Kedgaree or Diamond Harbour; and it was at the latter place that the regular Indiamen would moor, refit and take in their cargoes.

Ships would come in from the sea at a prodigious speed during the South-West Monsoon. Wind and tide would hurl them into the river like corks in a millrace, at a speed perhaps of eighteen knots. The larger and more valuable vessels, drawing twenty feet of water or thereabouts, might have not only a pilot aboard but a pilot brig ahead to signal the soundings with flags or a lantern. Smaller ships, with lesser draught, took a pilot on board and left the brig to await fresh customers. There were as many as twelve pilot vessels in the English service, besides a Dutch and a French vessel in time of peace. These English brigs or snows were stout and handy craft, the newer ones built at Bombay and pierced for sixteen guns. They could be used as sloops-of-war in an emergency. During the North-East Monsoon the pilotage was easier. It was merely a long beat to windward, assisted by the flood tide. But the channels are narrow, and a ship might have to go about every ten minutes, on finding herself in four and a half fathoms. There was only seven fathoms in mid-channel.

Smaller ships going up to Calcutta itself had to hire native rowing boats to do the towage and especially to drag the ship's head round as need arose. In those swirling and eddying tides a heavy ship would need a dozen of these boats to keep her off the James and Mary shoals. Thus attended, she would make her way from Kedgaree up to Diamond Harbour. Here were provided mooring buoys with huge fixed anchors, at which vessels could ride during the ebb. And here also were English port officials, a large bakehouse, a shambles, a market and a hospital—not to mention prostitutes and mosquitoes.

So far there was nothing much to see except low-lying jungle-covered shores, sandbanks and islands and the reddish brown waters. So that Calcutta, concealed until the last moment by the windings of the river, seemed all the more impressive by contrast with its drab approach. This view of the fort, the town and of Garden Reach was deservedly famous. The following is a foreigner's description:

Fort William, the finest fortress that exists out of Europe, presents itself immediately to the sight, which it astonishes by its grandeur and the splendour of the buildings that are seen above its ramparts. The houses, which form the first front...are so many magnificent palaces, some of them having a peristyle of four-and-twenty pillars. All these structures, disposed in an irregular line through a space of more than a league, form an inconceivably striking prospect, and give to the town a most noble and majestic appearance....

This is from Grandpré. There is also another passage in his work in which he refers to Calcutta as the 'capital of the East, the metropolis of the English empire in Asia, and the finest colony in the world'. And he does full justice to 'the gardens and sumptuous palaces' and their 'costliness and elegance' which all went to denote 'the opulence and power of the conquerors of India and the masters of the Ganges'. He might have added that it also went to explain what was wrong with the East India Company's balance-sheet.

Here is another description:

At Garden Reach the most striking and beautiful prospect presents itself to the view. The banks of the Hoogly, which is here about twice the breadth of the Thames at London, are covered with a verdant carpet to the water's edge, and decorated with numerous villas, or rather palaces....

'Calcutta', wrote the Rev. Daniel Corrie, afterwards Bishop of Madras, 'strikes me as the most magnificent city in the world....'

All accounts agree in conveying this impression of magnificence, and the fact is significant.

The mouth of the Ganges is, as we have seen, the gateway into those plains from which the English revenues were derived. And Lord Clive's first business, after securing Bengal, was to shut out future invaders, to lock the door in the face of any who would imitate him. The door was the Hooghly, the lock was Fort William. That is why Calcutta is just where it is; and that is why the name Fort William defines more exactly the nature and function of the place. The native name, however, has prevailed.

The writer has not forgotten that the Fort existed long before the Battle of Plassey. Exist, in a sense, it did; a pitiful affair, which the Nabob stormed in 1756; a small fort and a straggling village at its gates, the whole half-hidden in the jungle. But Fort William as it was known to the generation alive in 1800 was Clive's creation; the padlock of Bengal. Both fortress and city had grown up since 1765.

Fort William was a remarkable achievement. English military engineers, firmly prevented from exercising their art in England, are sometimes given a free hand elsewhere. Their long-suppressed energies found, in this way, a splendid outlet on the eastern bank of the Ganges. The Fort took years to make, and it cost about two million pounds. But it was worth it. It was, as Grandpré observes, the finest thing of its kind out of Europe. As a soldier and a Frenchman he loved it. Fort William was an octagon following the first plan of Vauban; it had salients, bastions, a counter-guard, orillons, retired circular flanks and an inverse double flank at the height of the berme, a mined glacis also and a master-gallery behind the counter-forts of the revêtement. If it had a defect, it was that the water supply was undrinkable throughout the hot season. But this was no great matter, for there was nothing inside but barracks, grass plots and piles of cannon balls. The troops were mostly stationed elsewhere, and there was little likelihood of a siege.

The fortress lay a quarter of a mile downstream from the town, the intervening space being called the Esplanade. Overlooking it was the new Government House, just completed for the Marquess Wellesley; an Ionic building with a rusticated basement and long colonnades, the gates to which were adorned with sphinxes and other patriotic emblems. The expense involved was enormous. Near this palace were other houses in a similar style, occupied by the higher officials. The other public buildings included the town house, law courts, writers' buildings and two Anglican churches.

The Black Town lay to the northward, a mass of houses built of mud, bamboos and mats, intersected with narrow crooked streets, for the most part unpaved and filthy. There were Portuguese, Greek and Armenian churches with numerous Hindoo temples and Moslem mosques. The population of the White and Black Towns taken together might amount to half a million, mostly Hindoos.

> The European society in Calcutta is numerous, gay, and convivial, and the fêtes given by the governors-general splendid and well-arranged. Each of the principal officers of government have their public days for the reception of their friends, independent of which not a day passes, particularly during the cold season, without several large dinner parties being formed of from 30 to 40....
>
> The usual mode of visiting is in palanquins, but many gentlemen have carriages adapted to the climate....It is universally the custom to drive out between sunset and dinner.... (Hamilton.)

The standard of living among the English inhabitants was extremely high. An average official might have a household of thirty or forty. A prosperous attorney's servants might number sixty. A hundred servants scarcely sufficed for a Member of Council. Salaries were on a lavish scale. The Governor-General himself had £25,000 a year with which to maintain his semi-regal state. The three Members of Council—senior civilians of at least twelve years' service—had each a salary of £10,000 a year. The Chief Justice earned £8000 and his three colleagues £6000 a year each. Senior merchants and the higher ranks of the Civil Service generally may have made anything from two thousand to four thousand a year. Military pay was in proportion, a General being about equal in status to a Member of Council, field officers corresponding to senior and junior merchants and factors, captains and subalterns being on a level with writers. The only sufferers were young men compelled to live beyond their means. An ensign, for example, could not live on his pay. To obtain the scarlet cloth, nankeen, linen, hats, feathers, soap, hair powder and pomatum he needed—not to mention the daily pint of Madeira he was expected to drink—he too often had to borrow from a native moneylender. The rate of interest was high. From the moneylender's point of view it was a speculation on the young officer's chances of survival and promotion. Those who had been extravagant in youth might never be free from debt for the rest of their lives.

As a direct result of the high salaries paid by the Company, the physicians, barristers, attorneys and tradesmen were correspondingly wealthy. So were merchants, shipowners and sea captains, but this was but a reflection and result of the officials' wealth, for Calcutta was essentially a fort and a garrison and a seat of administration. Trade was incidental, not vital. The town had grown up round the fort.

The essentially political character of Calcutta is shown both by the strength of its army and the defects of its anchorage. The writer has found no exact information as to the white population of Bengal alone. But, taking India as a whole, in 1805, the total number of British-born men and women numbered about 31,000. Of these, twenty-two thousand were soldiers, and two thousand, civil servants; seamen forming the bulk of the remainder. There were not many white women. The point to notice is that the number of merchants was trifling. They can scarcely have outnumbered the lawyers.

Calcutta, in fact, was a garrison, and it had much of the discipline of an army even outside its military circles. No one, to begin with, was allowed to go to India without the permission of the Company. There was more than one method of evading this regulation, but the interloper gained little by his ingenuity. Except to officials, professional men, and men with capital, British India was practically closed; and this not only from policy but also by the business ability of the natives. No white man could hope to exceed the Hindoo in dishonesty.

The entrance of white people was thus controlled both by law and by the nature of things. But even those actually in residence were under a kind of martial law. The Governor-General could send anyone back to England by a stroke of the pen, without a hint of legal proceedings, and, if he chose, without explanation. It was in this way that Lord Mornington controlled the Press. A critical or indiscreet editor soon found himself on the way home. With so large an army, military methods infected civil life.

The armies—for each of the three Governments had its own—were by English, by eighteenth-century standards, enormous. So far, only the number of Europeans has been given for the year 1805. Owing to the Mutiny of Vellore, this number had increased slightly by 1808. But the total strength was reduced, the Mahratta War having come to an end. The peace establishment, after this reduction had been made, allowed for 24,500 Europeans and 130,000 natives; or a total of 154,500 men. These figures include the King's regiments in India, as well as the Company's own troops. The forces were distributed as follows: 64,000 men in Bengal, as many at Madras, and 26,500 at Bombay. And it must be remembered that there was, in addition, a small navy at Bombay in the Company's service; which must be added to the total strength of fighting men. These figures show plainly enough the nature of the Company's business in India.

Had Calcutta been designed for a seaport and a place of trade, it would not have been where it was and is. The anchorage was too bad and the water too shallow. The current, rapid at all times, became violent when the snows melted in the mountains in July and August. It may still do so, but modern ships have chain cables. In 1800 the mass of shipping—mostly native craft—huddled opposite the four or five mile waterfront of Calcutta depended on coir or hempen cables. Under the strain and impact of the current, cables would snap and the whole crowd of shipping would break adrift. At night especially, the result was chaos. And even at ordinary times ground tackle was subject to a considerable strain. Of the Company's ships, only the smaller came up as high as Calcutta. Nevertheless, the yearly loss in anchors and cables came to nearly £3000. A European vessel could lose five anchors in three weeks. The Company's port officers, with their native divers and rowboats, were expert at recovering lost cables; but they sometimes preferred to do so in an unostentatious manner, with no audience at hand. They occasionally made fortunes by selling these anchors and cables —often, perhaps, to the original owners themselves. This is enough to show that Calcutta was not designed, first and foremost, as a seaport. The origin of its being was, first and foremost, political.

Now, before discussing the other English settlements and the special function of each, it is necessary to dwell shortly on what was the more general function of all. For between Fort William and the other English Governments there was an essential difference; the difference between profit and loss. Calcutta was a paying concern. The other Presidencies were not.

It was suggested on an earlier page that Indian taxpayers were chiefly burdened with the cost of excluding the French. The truth of this is only apparent when it is realised that Madras, Bombay and Penang were all governed at a loss. Useless and expensive in themselves, they existed to protect Bengal against French invasion. And it was by the taxpayers of Bengal that a part of their expenses was borne.

Fort St George, or Madras, owed its birth to historical accident and its survival to strategic necessity. An expedition against India by sea would almost certainly arrive during the South-West Monsoon, for it was then that the passage was shortest to the Bay of Bengal. This is supposing that the expedition came by sea from Europe and had the east side of India for its object. To meet such an expedition by sea, it was obviously desirable to base the naval defence on a port to windward of the bay. Without such a base the defending squadron would be thrown hopelessly to leeward from the start. Thus, Bengal River was useless in its own defence. And it was, for that matter, too unhealthy to be used as a naval base. It could be defended from the Coromandel Coast, and from nowhere else.

This fact is very fully illustrated by the history of Anglo-French campaigns in the Indian Seas. There was seldom a strong English squadron stationed in India before 1757, and there was no general action with the French until 1758. The action then fought, on 29 April, took place between Fort St David and Pondicherry on the Coromandel Coast. The eastern seas saw eight other naval actions between the French and English during the remainder of the eighteenth century. Every one of them was fought in the same waters; somewhere between Madras, that is to say, and Point de Galle. And every one of them, without exception, was fought during the South-West Monsoon. It was more than a coincidence that all the fighting should take place between April and September in a strip of water about three hundred miles in length.

Here, then, was one reason for having an English settlement on the Coromandel Coast: to provide a weatherly naval base for the defence of the Bay of Bengal. Unfortunately, the whole east side of India provides only one natural harbour, and that is Trincomalee. And to this place, throughout most of the eighteenth century, there were two objections; first, that it belonged to the Dutch; second, that, even supposing it to be captured, there was here no hinterland from which to draw supplies. The only real harbour being thus, to some extent, ruled out, there was little to choose between one place and another on the Coast. All the roadsteads were bad; and Madras, the place already held, was no worse than the rest.

There was also a military reason for retaining Madras: for to occupy that coast was the most effective way of preventing the French coming there. Come they certainly would, if an opening was left for them. Once there, they would threaten Bengal. Already they held Pondicherry, but this was a weak fortress and one which could be neutralised by a place of greater strength planted to the northward, between it and Bengal. Just such a place was Madras. And herein lay its military importance. Madras, with its inland territory, kept the French capital in check. In point of fact, whenever the French fortified Pondicherry an English army promptly stormed it and carefully demolished the works.

In external appearance, Madras was a smaller edition of Calcutta. It consisted, that is to say, of a citadel and a large native town built at a respectful distance. It differed, however, from the chief English Presidency in having no 'white town' outside the fort. Here, as there, the military engineer had been at work. But whereas Fort William was wholly executed in the early manner of Vauban, Fort St George was a masterpiece in which several styles had been blended. No two aspects were alike. The north-east front was in the Italian tradition of Sardi. The opposite side was strictly in accordance with the ideas of the Chevalier de Ville. From other angles no method was apparent, but only a series of inconsistencies. However, Grandpré, who stood aghast at these defects, had to admit that it was very complete in its way. There were bastions, ditches, lunette and counter-way, barriers, palisadoes and a counter-mined glacis. Moreover, even if it lacked caponiers and tenailles, it had actually sustained a siege in 1758.

Although owing so much to foreign ideas, and something, perhaps, to having been at one time in French hands, Fort St George had contrived to remain characteristically English in one respect. For the English, having yielded to convention up to a point, had ultimately succeeded in defying it. The fortifications, which had cost more than a million and a half sterling, were intended to shelter the whole white population, but the English drew the line at this. They would pay for a fort, if there had to be one; but they resolutely refused to live in it. And, on this principle, they had all gone to live somewhere else.

For the above reason, Fort St George contained only the offices in which business was transacted between the hours of eleven and three. During the rest of the day, the English inhabitants, including the Governor himself, were to be found at their garden houses, scattered in the vicinity. The Mount Road, a principal place of resort for their carriages in the cool of the evening, was five miles from the Fort.

> Even the theatre is in the country; so that the ground to a considerable distance round Madras presents to the view a multitude of gardens, spread over an extent so great, as to prevent persons who reside at the opposite extremities from visiting each other, unless on horseback or in carriages; the palanquins in many instances would be insufficient for the purpose. Some of these gardens are extremely beautiful, and the houses are in general elegant....
>
> ...The Black Town exhibits only a spectacle of filth and dirt.... There are several pagodas in the town, some mosques, an armenian church, and a portuguese one, of which the service is performed by Capuchins....
>
> The approaches to Madras are uncommonly magnificent, particularly the great road to the west of Fort St George: the avenues, planted with four rows of trees, majestically announce the residence of no inferior power....

The nominal power was a puppet sovereign, the Nabob of the Carnatic. In its capacity as ally and protector, the Company had built him a splendid palace close to Government House, and the Nabob was occasionally to be seen driving about in the carriage provided for him.

The population of Madras was over 300,000, nearly all natives. The exact number of the Europeans can only be guessed at. In 1808, out of an army of 64,000 some 11,000 were Europeans—a far higher proportion than at Fort William, where there were only 7000. This was probably due to the recent sepoy mutiny, and can be regarded as exceptional. By 1811 the army had been reduced to 50,000 and the proportion of Europeans had probably by that time been reduced. However, even then, there were some thirteen hundred officers drawing between them over half a million a year in pay, while the civil servants, numbering rather over two hundred, to which must be added a numerous band of minor assistants, cost almost as much again; £470,000, to be exact. The merchants at Madras were very few in number—the European merchants, that is to say. But the public buildings in the Fort included an Exchange, the central hall of which, decorated with portraits of Lord Cornwallis and General Meadows, found many admirers. Including the merchants, then, and a few sailors, Madras may have held two or three thousand white inhabitants. Most of the troops were, of course, stationed elsewhere.

Besides Government offices, an arsenal, storehouses, a national lottery and the offices of the merchants and of two local newspapers, the Fort also contained the church. It stood in a sort of central square, into which the palanquins would flock on Sunday morning, and where carriages would wait until the service was over. As at Calcutta, the Governor was treated with a good deal of ceremony. The following is Wathen's description of the Governor's attending church:

> Soon after we were seated, a band of military music was heard, announcing the approach of the Governor, Sir George Hilaro Barlow, Bart. K.B., escorted by his guards, and accompanied by his aides-de-camp, the latter in full uniform. On their entry into the church, the band ceased, and a voluntary was performed on the organ, while the Governor took his seat on a chair of state under a canopy. The ladies occupied the centre of the church; on one side the Company's naval officers were ranged, and on the other the military officers, all in complete uniform. In the course of the

service the 104th Psalm was sung by about forty charity children, neatly dressed in white jackets....

Although Wathen may seem to describe a sufficiently formal and official act of worship, of which the casual observer might suppose the Governor to have been the object, it was actually a very great improvement on what had gone before. On this point, the evidence of Mr, afterwards Bishop, Corrie is of value. The following observation of his dates from 1806:

The state of society among our countrymen here is much altered for the better within these few years. The Marquis Wellesley openly patronised religion. He, on every possible occasion, made moral character a sine qua non to his patronage, and sought for men of character from every quarter to fill offices of trust. He avowedly encouraged, and contributed to, the translation of the Scriptures into the native languages, and, wherever he went, paid a strict regard to divine worship on the Sunday.

There were thirty-six chaplains altogether in India and fifteen on the establishment of this one Presidency, but the conversion of the natives was not considered a part of their duties. Some doubted whether it would be advisable to convert them, in case they should be given ideas above their station. Those, on the other hand, who had made the attempt, doubted whether it was possible. Missionary enterprise was therefore restricted, in the main, to the attempted conversion of the Portuguese Catholics; to which end, the chaplains had to learn Portuguese. They did not have much success among these half-breeds, who remained loyal to a mulatto bishop living at St Thomas—a suffragan of the see of Goa. Few, probably, of these chaplains spent their outward voyage like Bishop Heber in learning the native tongue.

From the maritime point of view, Madras was far from ideal. There was no shelter, and the water shoaled so gradually that large ships had to anchor two miles from the shore. There they would lie, rolling and straining in the heavy swell and cut off from the shore by a belt of surf which only native boats could cross. To these craft passengers had to entrust themselves; and even these sometimes upset—a serious matter in those shark-infested waters. The surf varied. On some days it was literally impassable, even for the native boats; and then a flag was hoisted at the beach house and all communication with the shore cut off. Yet, despite these difficulties, Madras roads were frequented by ships of all kinds during one half of the year. And they even made shift to land cargoes there and ship such goods as the town produced.

The roadstead was never satisfactory, owing to strong currents, a high surf even in the calmest weather, and the risk of a gale such as covered the beach with wreckage in 1811. Apart from the erection of warehouses close to the shore, and the public provision of masullah boats and catamarans, the only improvement it was found possible to make was the erection of a lighthouse on the roof of the Exchange. To render the roadstead safe was impossible, all that could be done was to discourage ships from entering it at the worst time of year. Accordingly, the flag-staff, by which vessels took their bearings before anchoring, was struck each year on 15 October, and was not erected again until 15 December. All ships entering the roads, or indeed coming anywhere within soundings during this period, vitiated their insurance; and most were so debarred over a longer period of time. The same rule applied to the whole coast from Point Palmyras to Ceylon.

The Coromandel Coast, henceforward to be referred to as 'the Coast', as was the custom of the time, contained few places of importance besides Madras. There was Negapatam, a trifling place with as heavy a surf as that of Madras. Then there was Masulipatam and Vizigapatam, neither of much value. Coringa, on the other hand, is worthy of notice in having something which might, in moments of enthusiasm, be called a harbour. The river there, unlike those at Madras and Pondicherry, which served only to enliven siege operations, was almost navigable. Small craft could take shelter there, and but for a bar of mud across the river mouth, it might have been of use to medium-sized merchantmen. An enterprising private individual had constructed a wet dock on the river bank; the only dock on the whole coast. Hopes were entertained of removing the mud barrier. And had this proved possible, Coringa would certainly have become of the greatest importance. It might even have superseded Madras as a naval base. But, for various reasons, nothing came of it. The *Albatross* brig and the frigate *Wilhelmina* were successively docked there, being dragged through the mud by main force. Other captains, however, refused to take the risk; and so the place fell into disuse as far as the Navy was concerned.

The Presidency third in rank was Bombay, on the west side of India. Like Madras it was, economically speaking, parasitical. The function of this town is sufficiently expressed in the obvious derivation of its name. It derived its importance from its harbour; the only good harbour to be found on the mainland of India. Situated on the east side of a narrow island running parallel with the coast, it faced a large and tolerably sheltered bay, opening to the southward. In 1805 a causeway was completed, joining the Island of Bombay to the neighbouring Island of Salsette.

Second only in importance to the good anchorage was the considerable rise and fall of the tide. Without such a rise and fall, it was, until the advent of steam, impossible to construct docks. The difference between high and low tides at Bombay varies from fourteen to seventeen feet, which was quite adequate for the purpose. The docks, which were considerably extended between 1803 and 1810, were the property of the Company. Ships of the Royal Navy made use of them for repairing, but only on payment of a monthly rent.

Bombay, both town and castle, was of Portuguese origin and had not, at this time, lost its Portuguese character. The architecture of the houses within the fort was especially reminiscent of the former régime. This was partly due to the fact that the English residents all lived in the country, as at Madras. In the main, they kept their Ionic columns for their country houses, and left the town much as they found it when it was handed over in 1662, only adding a church, law courts and docks. The population was estimated at about 165,000 in 1812. Besides Hindoos and Moslems, there were three or four thousand Jews and some eight thousand Parsees. The Portuguese also were numerous, being mostly half-breeds, as elsewhere in the East, and treated by the English as natives. The army based on Bombay was far smaller than the armies of Madras and Bengal. In 1808 there were 6500 Europeans and 20,000 natives serving in the territories administered from Bombay Castle. Some 550 military officers, the total employed in 1811, drew between them over £171,000 a year in pay. The higher civil servants, numbering seventy-four, with their minor officials, cost over £174,000 between them. With an average salary of perhaps £2000 a year, they were considered poverty-stricken in comparison with the civil servants of Bengal and Madras. Indeed, the third Presidency was considered inferior in every way to the other two. The European society was, for one thing, less numerous, the white residents not exceeding seventeen hundred. A good criterion by which the relative position of Bombay may be judged is provided by the great voluntary subscription of 1798, for the prosecution of the war. The residents in Bengal subscribed about £160,000, those at Madras £75,000, those at Bombay £38,000. The status of the respective Governments is indicated by the fact that the Governor-General at Fort William had to be an earl or a marquis, the Governor at Fort St George a courtesy lord or at least a baronet, while the Governor of Bombay was, as often as not, a simple esquire.

Although supporting a comparatively small army and a comparatively modest civil establishment, Bombay was not inexpensive to maintain. For it was here that the Company stationed its navy. There were the vessels to be built and repaired, the crews to be paid, and a dockyard maintained. This navy was called the Bombay or Company's Marine, and consisted of some fifteen cruisers, besides a few armed advice boats. In 1800 there were seven ships, mounting from ten to twenty-two guns; two brigs, with ten or twelve guns; four ketches similarly armed; and two schooners rather more lightly equipped. The European officers numbered about a hundred, exclusive of volunteers or midshipmen; the seamen can hardly have been less than a thousand in number.

The Marine was ruled by a superintendent, a master attendant and a commodore. The first was paid a little less than £4000 a year, the other two respectively £3000 and £2500. Captains and commanders were paid from £300 to £500, but had other sources of profit. They probably, for instance, received certain fees from the merchantmen they convoyed. After ten years' service an officer, usually by that time a captain, was allowed three years' furlough on full pay. After twenty-five years' service, he might retire on a pension. The pensions were not very large, but the senior officers, who held in rotation the lucrative post of commodore at Surat, usually retired with ample private means. In the regulations as to precedence, the commodore of the Bombay Marine was the equal of a colonel in the land forces. A captain, although ranking as a lieutenant-colonel or major, was considered inferior to the commander of a regular Indiaman. The superintendent was almost but not quite equal to a Member of Council.

The objects for which the Company's Marine existed were five, or so it was held at the time: first, the protection of the coastwise trade against pirates; second, the defence of the Company's trade and possessions in time of war; third, the transporting of troops; fourth, surveying; and fifth, the carrying of the overland mail. As regards the primary object of defence against pirates, it is to be remarked that the Company had long since discovered that the pursuit of pirates is a task for trained specialists. The Royal Navy, with obvious wisdom, seldom showed either taste or talent for it. As in the China Seas to-day, special craft were required, and it was more important that the officers should have local knowledge than that their vessels should be heavily armed. It was not a task for men-of-war. The pirates to be dealt with were principally those on the Malabar Coast and at the head of the Arabian Sea; a region to which piracy had been familiar since, at any rate, the time of Alexander the Great. At the end of our period, there was talk of extending the operations of the Marine to the other two pirate-infested regions, the Malay Archipelago and Canton River. Little, however, came of these proposals until after 1815. Between 1803 and 1810 the Company's cruisers were mainly confined to the west side of India. If they passed Cape Comorin, it was usually to cruise off the sandheads.

The Company's Marine was of very little use against European enemies. The cruisers were not big enough; they were useless against all but the very smallest privateers, and occasionally fell a prey to the larger ones. All survey work, of course, was more or less suspended in time of war. And the vessels were only very occasionally wanted for the transport of troops. The carrying of the overland mails, in short, was infinitely the most important of the functions enumerated.

The overland mail is a subject in itself. It is enough, however, for the purposes of this study, to know its effects. Briefly, then, there was a system established by which dispatches to and from Europe could be sent overland. The news, for example, of the Battle of the Nile came to Fort William via Aleppo, Baghdad, Bussorah and Bombay. At a later period the more urgent dispatches went through Cosseir and Cairo. Mainly to safeguard this process, there was a Residency at Bussorah which cost £5000 a year; money well spent, for in the delivery of news, even a few days saved might be of vital importance. As a matter of fact, the speed of delivery was not enormously increased by this mode of postage. The dispatch sent overland would not arrive much sooner than a dispatch sent simultaneously by a fast frigate round the Cape, but it was of course cheaper than sending a frigate specially for the purpose, and it was far quicker than the ordinary post, carried by Indiamen and subject to every species of delay. While, however, the dispatches from England came tardily in any case, the overland mail justified itself in another way, for news came by it from the south of Europe. The letters from Constantinople or even Vienna would come quite quickly. The latest of Napoleon's crimes might be known in India within three months of its occurrence; whereas the most urgent message from Whitehall or Leadenhall Street would take about four months to arrive, and all ordinary correspondence would take six. Such was the overland mail. Whether it came by the Red Sea or the Persian Gulf, the journey was always begun or finished in one of the Company's cruisers.

However usefully employed in this respect, the Bombay Marine seems to have attracted its fair share of criticism. What exactly was wrong with it does not appear, except that the vessels were largely manned by natives. As early as 1795, Admiral Rainier was commenting on the fact that their crews were more than half composed of lascars, and that, of the Europeans, less than half were English. In 1801 he repeated this assertion, saying that the Company's cruisers were not to be relied upon; but there was more in it than that. In 1805 the Governor-General, the Marquess Wellesley, wrote to Admiral Pellew lamenting that the 'constitution of the Marine Establishment' was 'extremely defective'. He added that neither the Court of Directors nor the Government in India had the power to reform it. It would be natural to suspect that the defect complained of was the Marine's independence of the Governor-General. It might be supposed that the Marine was under the control of the Governor of Bombay, and that Wellesley had only the most indirect powers over it. This, however, was not the case, for his condemnation of the Marine's management was only the prelude to a proposal to transfer two of the Company's vessels to the Royal Navy. His power over the Marine can hardly have been incomplete if it allowed him to sell the ships composing it. Whatever his grievance may have been, it is worthy of note that Sir Edward Pellew entirely agreed with him.

The attitude of naval officers towards the Bombay Marine was rather unreasonable. Always short-handed themselves, they grudged the Company even such few English seamen as it employed. On the other hand, they were by no means in favour of abolishing the Marine altogether. Instead, they frequently demanded its co-operation and showed no inclination whatever to take over its duties. They were in the position of wanting it to exist without the means of existence.

One source of endless trouble was the question of impressment. It was at first thought, by captains in the Navy, that men might be impressed from the Company's Marine whenever the need was urgent. This was, in the main, their attitude in Admiral Rainier's time. The Governor of Bombay strongly objected, claiming that the seamen of the Marine were exempt from impressment under any circumstances. The question was complicated by the fact that deserters from the Navy occasionally found their way into the Marine. They were sometimes harboured by captains who knew very well where they came from. Naval officers naturally claimed that they had at least a right of search where they had reason to suspect that deserters from the Navy were being so harboured.

The matter was still under dispute when Sir Edward Pellew took over the Command. When a specific case arose on which he had to decide, he referred the matter to the

Admiralty. Until the Admiralty's decision should arrive, he forbade the impressment of men from the Company's cruisers, and also forbade his officers to search them without the permission of the authorities at Bombay; in which he anticipated the Admiralty's attitude fairly exactly. But, while yielding so far, he maintained that it was not within his power to refuse men who volunteered for the King's service. Men did occasionally volunteer from the Marine, as a result of ill-usage in particular vessels; and Pellew held that it would be illegal for him to refuse the protection of the flag to any seaman who should claim it. The Bombay Government denied that their seamen had a right to volunteer. They were serving by contract and were not free to break their agreement on a merely patriotic pretext. This was a question on which the Admiralty would not commit itself. Pellew was merely told that he was not to encourage such men to volunteer. The victory, for all practical purposes, lay with the Bombay Government.

Before quitting the subject of Bombay, some further mention must be made of the Parsee inhabitants of that town. They numbered eight thousand on the island itself; and the Presidency was thought to contain the whole body of them which had been driven from Persia. That they should have come to own nearly the whole of the island will seem natural enough to any who are at all acquainted with the Parsee character. It was the more natural in this instance in that no European was allowed to become a landowner in any part of India. The English might own their own houses, apparently, but it would not always pay them to do so. Although chiefly engaged in trade, some of the Parsees were expert shipwrights. The whole business of the dockyard was in their hands, and in shipbuilding they probably taught the English far more than they learnt from them.

Less than two hundred miles to the north of Bombay is Surat, which was said to be the most populous city in India, being slightly larger than Calcutta itself. Its trade was still, at this time, considerable, although it had declined with the growth of Bombay. Surat was nominally ruled by its Nabob, but had actually been controlled by the East India Company since 1800. Being in the Presidency of Bombay, it can be regarded as an appendage of that settlement. Actually, it was Bombay that was the offspring of the older city, the trade of which it had attracted, but to which it remained greatly inferior in size. It was from Surat that Bombay had recruited its Parsees, as also its tradition of shipbuilding.

Bombay was acquired, like Madras, through an historical accident. The Portuguese had made England a present of it. The heavy annual loss which the Company incurred in governing it may suggest a possible explanation of why they did this. In its function, Bombay again resembled Madras, for its primary purpose was to occupy a coastline which would otherwise be occupied by the French. It was to the one side of India what Madras was to the other. In addition, it had a good harbour which, imperfect as it was in some respects, marked it out as the inevitable naval base on the Malabar Coast; and consequently the only base during six months of the year. And, besides providing a badly needed dockyard, it was a military post guarding the western entrance into the valley of the Ganges. In the early nineteenth century, Bombay and Madras were both held as outposts for the defence of Bengal against French invasion.

The next English possession to consider, Prince of Wales Island, was also financially dependent on Bengal. But it existed rather to defend trade than territory, and should be considered, first and foremost, as the halfway house on the voyage between India and China. The position was not ideal, since it commanded only the one route by the Straits of Malacca. It had not the strategic value now enjoyed by Singapore. On the other hand, it was useful as a place at which to refit and water, as a trading station and as a minor naval base from which to protect English interests in the Malay Archipelago. First acquired by Captain Light, for the East India Company, it was rented from the Rajah of Quedah from 1786 onwards. The island is situated in the Malacca Straits, close to the west coast of the Malay Peninsula. The harbour is formed by the narrow strait between it and the shore. The anchorage is good and sheltered completely throughout the year. The island, some fifteen miles long and seven or eight miles broad, is mountainous in the centre and was originally thickly wooded. In 1800 a strip of the mainland was acquired and added to the territory comprised in the settlement. The native name, Pulo Penang, has since prevailed over the English name.

Fort Cornwallis, the English garrison, was placed on the north-east point of the island in a singularly ill-chosen position. Constructed badly in the first place, large sums were wasted in various attempts to improve it. Eventually it was found that nothing could be done, since the construction of a proper glacis would involve the demolition of about half the town which had rapidly grown up round it. Neither was it possible to follow Colonel Arthur Wesley's advice and move the whole place somewhere else. However, its apparent strength, although illusory, had a proper effect on the native imagination. The ten thousand inhabitants of 1800 had increased to fourteen thousand by 1805. By another account the increase was from sixteen to twenty thousand. This growth was at the expense of Malacca, the ancient Malay capital, which, after being in Portuguese and Dutch hands for some three hundred years, fell to England in 1795. Malacca was retained, but it was hoped that all its trade and capital would be transferred to Penang; as indeed it very largely was.

The town which had grown up round Fort Cornwallis differed from the other English settlements in that it was planned with wide streets crossing each other at right angles. George Town was the official name for it; Panjang Panaique was what it was called. The local amenities included a Government House, a church, a jail, and a pier fitted with water pipes for the convenience of shipping. Within the fort was an arsenal, magazine, barracks for the garrison and storehouses in which to keep provisions in time of siege. Not that a siege was very likely, since it was thought that a single frigate could have bombarded the town with impunity; while a ship of the line could have sailed up within pistol shot of the fort and rendered it untenable. These facts, however, were successfully kept secret. Prince of Wales Island was used as a place of exile for convicts from Bengal, a species of settler to whom it owed an excellent set of roads and bridges. The other inhabitants were Dutch, Portuguese, Armenians, Arabians, Parsees, Chulias, Malays, Buggusses, Burmans and Javanese. The Chinese predominated among the merchants of the place, the Malays among the cultivators.

> In 1805 the Court of Directors, having taken into their consideration the position of the island, its fertility, its harbour, its produce of large timber, its contiguity to Pegu, which contains the most abundant teak forests in Asia, and which had long pointed it out as an acquisition of very great importance in a commercial and political view, being placed in a most favourable situation for an emporium of commerce in the Eastern seas, and for becoming a commanding station for the rendezvous, refitting, and supply of that portion of His Majesty's Navy required for the protection of the Company's possessions and affairs in the Eastern parts of Asia, had resolved to new model the government, and to place the island under the same form of government as the Company's other settlements in India enjoyed; when the Board of Admiralty laid before them a plan for the building and repairing His Majesty's ships, which gave a new and high degree of importance to the subject, and rendered the projected reform of government absolutely indispensable. Accordingly the island was formed into a regular government....

This process put Fort Cornwallis on a level with Fort St George and Bombay Castle. There was now to be a Governor, Members of Council, master-attendant, collector of customs, secretary, chaplain and so forth—not to mention ten writers, two surgeons, accountants and auditors. The salaries ranged from £9000 a year, or rather more, in the case of the Governor, to 900 dollars in the case of the schoolmaster. A staff of twenty-seven cost about £43,000 a year in salaries. Over and above all that could be raised locally, the settlement relied on an annual subsidy of close on £100,000 sent from Bengal.

This transaction is described at length not as particularly important in itself but as eminently characteristic of the East India Company. The idea of making Prince of Wales Island a Presidency evidently originated from the Admiralty. It was clearly connected with the 1805 arrangement by which the East Indies Command was divided in two. As a division of the squadron was henceforth to remain constantly on the east side of India, without being able to resort to Bombay, it was necessary to create a new base for it. So the East India Company was ordered to enlarge their settlement at Prince of Wales Island. The man responsible for the scheme was Henry Dundas, Viscount Melville, First Lord of the Admiralty, who had been President of the Board of Control as lately as 1801; and, by a really remarkable coincidence, the first Governor of Fort Cornwallis was Mr Philip Dundas.

The object of all this extravagance at Prince of Wales Island was twofold. It made possible the division of the Command, which was looked upon, first and foremost, as a means of punishing the existing Commander-in-Chief for his political views. It also enabled the Court of Directors to appoint to a number of newly created vacancies; a duty to which the Court always submitted without much reluctance.

Unfortunately, no attempt had been made to ascertain whether Prince of Wales Island did, in fact, enjoy all the advantages with which it had been credited. The timber supply, for instance, proved something of a disappointment. The local timber was found to be mostly unsuitable for the building of men-of-war. The contiguity of the Pegu teak forests had, of course, been pointed out. But a closer inspection of the map sufficed to show that Rangoon and Penang are well over seven hundred miles apart; not perhaps a great distance, but quite far enough to make the process somewhat expensive. Worse still, the climate was found to be less healthy than had been supposed. In this connection, the First Lord's plan to provide for Mr Philip Dundas may be said to have succeeded only too well. Coming out in 1805, he was dead by 1807. All the Members of Council died shortly afterwards, which greatly simplified the task of a new Ministry in reducing Prince of Wales Island to its former status. The wisdom of this policy was evident, as the reunited Command required no second base to the eastward. There might, incidentally, have been some difficulty in filling the vacancies in the Government. Penang had hardly, so far, earned its reputation for the salubrity of its air. There were doubts, indeed, whether the title of 'the Montpellier of India' had not been too hastily bestowed.

Setting aside the extravagant claims that had been made for it, this settlement was genuinely useful in more ways than one. Especially was it useful as a base for potential operations against the Dutch. This was noted by Colonel Arthur Wesley in 1797. Calling there with a force bound for Manilla, but which was recalled before it arrived there, he made certain observations and afterwards embodied them in a Memorandum:

> Pulo Penang, from its position in the Straits of Malacca, and from the advantages which it possesses, is so capable of giving assistance, and of being of service to the trade between the eastern and western parts of India, that it ought to be encouraged and preserved. It is likewise of considerable importance to the Company in its military operations to the eastward....Another advantage which attends Pulo Penang is the stillness of the water, which enables ships to shift their cargo, and to perform numberless operations, which, in other places, are rendered impossible by the violence of the sea....Another circumstance is, that at all times,

and with all winds, there is neither difficulty nor danger in getting in or out of this harbour.

Penang would have grown more rapidly had the Company come to an earlier decision with regard to it. In those days, any fortification of a sufficiently impressive type would attract settlers in the East. But there were doubts as to whether Fort Cornwallis might not be razed and abandoned sooner or later; doubts which the fluctuations of policy seemed to justify. It was partly for this reason that Malacca held its own during this period; partly also because of its antiquity and the unwillingness of the wealthier inhabitants to leave it. The fort there was demolished in 1807: 'A most useless piece of gratuitous mischief, as far as I can understand the subject' (Lord Minto); but it was found that much of the trade of the old Malay capital could not be deflected. Stamford Raffles, the assistant-secretary at Prince of Wales Island, on whom most of the work of that settlement fell, warmly advocated the retaining of Malacca, if only to prevent the town falling into the hands of another power. It was accordingly retained.

Another settlement which declined with the growth of Prince of Wales Island was Bencoolen, or Benkulen as it is now spelt. This had been a place of some importance previous to the acquisition of Penang. It owed its importance, in part, to its position near the Straits of Sunda; in part, to the trade in pepper. As a result of a decline in this trade, Bencoolen lost its government in 1801. Henceforward, Fort Marlborough had only a Resident and four assistants; and it was made immediately subject to the Governor-General.

Until the time of Napoleon's exile, St Helena also was a minor possession of the East India Company. It was useful as an occasional port of call. The civil establishment there comprised a Governor, deputy, counsellor, secretary, and over fourteen subordinates, including a chaplain, surgeon, paymaster and judge-advocate.

The last of the Company's establishments requiring detailed treatment is the Committee of Supercargoes at Canton. This was the only port in China at which the Chinese Government allowed Europeans to trade. The Russians were an exception, but only because they were similarly confined to Kiatcha on the borders of Siberia. The English, Dutch and Americans were less fortunate, however, than the Portuguese, who had their own settlement at Macao. There they had a senate, a bishop, thirteen churches, three monasteries and a convent. They had held the town since 1586, but were still subject to occasional Chinese oppressions and exactions. The Portuguese there numbered about four thousand. These, with a garrison of half-breeds and blacks and some seven thousand Chinamen, made up the population of this singular town. And it was here, for most of the year, that the English representatives lived.

The chief difficulty felt in dealing with the Chinese was due to the latter people's complete ignorance of geography. Knowing nothing of the rest of the world, the Chinese visualised China as the centre of the earth, surrounded by an awestruck circle of tributary nations, of which England was one. With such invincible ignorance it is difficult to cope. Nothing short of a prolonged bombardment was likely to make any impression; and such violence, although obviously inevitable, could hardly be attempted in the midst of a European conflict. A mere demonstration of force had no effect, for the Central Government, with the Emperor, lived too far inland to see it. And the authorities at Canton had long ago acquired a more accurate notion of their foreign relationships; a notion which they dared not transmit to the Emperor, even had they wanted to—which, as a fact, they did not. The situation had grown up through the Viceroy at Canton concealing from the Emperor the number of European ships frequenting the port. This he had found it necessary to do as early as 1789, and probably much earlier. To have given a true report would have occasioned alarm at Pekin. This might produce an order to eject the Europeans which, if practicable, would have ruined the Viceroy's private emoluments: for the customs paid by the European and American ships were heavy, and the concealment of their number had of course necessitated the retention by himself of the bulk of what was paid. Certain of the high officials at Pekin were in the secret and, incidentally, in the Viceroy's pay; but betrayal was exceedingly unlikely. To have explained the whole situation to the Emperor would have required a certain courage. Besides, he would probably have refused to believe it.

Little was done to enlighten the Chinese until 1827. In the meanwhile, the East India Company had to submit cheerfully to rules and regulations, exactions and indignities. Because of these, the ships trading to Canton found China, in Charles Reade's words, as difficult to enter as Heaven and as difficult to get out of as Chancery. There were consolations, however: the profits were enormous.

While the stranger might trade only at Canton, only certain of the natives might trade with him. These privileged Chinamen were the Hong merchants, and they numbered about a dozen. By a system to which there are medieval European parallels each foreign ship was put under the care of a particular Hong merchant, who made himself responsible for it in every way, controlled the trade and fixed the prices. Apart from these monopolists, foreigners met only custom-house officials, brokers and small tradesmen, being forbidden even to enter Canton itself. For this reason the foreigner seldom gained a very favourable impression of Chinese character. The 'subtle, intellectual, doll-faced, bolus-eyed people' may have looked like forked mushrooms at first sight, but they proved more than equal to the foreigner in business capacity. 'The people of Canton', remarked Captain Eastwick, 'are more shrewd than their unintelligent faces would lead a stranger to suspect....'

For the purpose of wrangling with the Hong merchants and the Viceroy, the Company maintained a factory at Canton. It was a long courtyard surrounded by warehouses and other buildings, situated among the other and similar foreign factories on the river bank. Between it and the beach was a railed-in quay or promenade called the Respondentia Walk, where the various foreign merchants and ship captains would stroll up and down after dinner during the busy season. These foreign factories, which the Chinese called hongs, were outside the city walls. Each one flew its national flag. This is Wathen's description of the East India Company's hong:

> The Factory belonging to the Company is erected within a hundred yards of the bank of the river, and is a very handsome building, of a mixed kind of architecture, partaking of the European style in its internal construction, with that of the Eastern in some respects; and externally having an elegant veranda, from which the views up and down the river are open and uninterrupted. The beach is covered with an immense quantity of merchandize; teas, silks, nankeens, cotton, etc. continually shifting from country-boats to the wharf and from thence by other boats to the ships waiting for their lading at Wampoa. The great room where the supercargo and other officers belonging to the Company dine, is a large and handsome apartment, appropriately furnished, and decorated with some original pictures, and portraits of the King and Queen. Three noble cut-glass lustres depend from the ceiling, and add much to the elegance of the whole....The Factory also boasts a spacious library....
>
> There are factories at Canton belonging to other European nations, as well as one to the United States of America; but the trade of all the rest united, dwindles into insignificance when compared to that of the English East India Company....

One critic, writing anonymously in 1812, was rather bitter about it on the score of expense:

> ...The factory erected by the Company at Canton is, no doubt, very costly and splendid; and it has been made the means of provision for the sons, and other immediate relatives of the Directors: for the appointments on that establishment are retained

specially for those persons, and handed down as a sort of heirloom from one set of Directors to another. With this view, a palace, rather than a warehouse, has been built; and a princely institution founded, for the maintenance of which, a suitable revenue has been assigned. And for what, we will ask, is this expensive and luxurious institution created? Why, to enable the Company's supracargoes to pass, in easy and convenient state, the progress of the *trading season*—the permitted period of *the Fair*—whence we are to see them banished the moment their stalls are taken down; when they are glad to find a shelter for their heads in the hospitality of the Portuguese, on their island of Macao.

It has been pointed out on an earlier page that few of the Company's servants were engaged in mercantile affairs, and that the Company traded, not to India but to China. The supercargoes at Canton were nearer being merchants than most other officials employed by the Company. They had, that is to say, no territory to administer, no troops to command. Apart from diplomatic functions, and the control of English shipping in the river, they were free to devote their entire attention to trade; to the sale of woollens and the purchase of tea. As they could buy tea only when there was tea on the market to be bought, they were not greatly inconvenienced by the Chinese regulation which compelled them to retire to Macao at the end of the season. The factory at Canton, if in some respects a palace, was in other respects a prison. They would not, in any case, have wanted to spend their months of comparative idleness in a place from which Chinese law forbade them to emerge except by water.

The executive staff of the factory usually numbered about twenty. One or two supernumeraries, such as the librarian, slightly increased the total of Europeans. In the earlier part of the period under review, the supercargoes numbered twelve, the writers, eight. The three senior supercargoes, with the President or "Tyepan", formed the Select Committee. This group of four discharged the diplomatic duties entrusted them. In purely commercial matters, the supercargoes acted as a whole. The writers had no voice either in commerce or policy and little remuneration except in the prospect of becoming supercargoes in their turn. In this favoured service, however, the prospect of rising to the higher rank was reward sufficient.

The supercargoes and their assistants were not paid a regular salary but were given a commission on the sums of money which passed through their hands. They shared in the commission according to a steeply graded scale. What exactly the commission amounted to it is not easy to determine. By one account, perhaps exaggerated, some £80,000 was shared among the staff each year, the President receiving no less than £20,000, and a junior supercargo no more than £1500. In 1810 there seems to have been a mild effort to reform the establishment at Canton. This was the result, presumably, of the discreditable part taken by the supercargoes in the fiasco following the occupation of Macao in 1808–9. A new President was appointed, and it is probable that the scale of remuneration was simultaneously revised; perhaps in answer to critics who wished to know why unsuccessful diplomats should be so grossly overpaid. At any rate, a Parliamentary Paper printed in 1812 gives the probable average amount of the commission as £68,000, of which nearly £66,000 would be shared among the staff, the President receiving £8550 and the other members of the Select Committee £7124 each. As part, possibly, of the same reform, the supercargoes in that year apparently numbered fifteen, whereas the number of writers had been reduced to two. Two surgeons, an inspector and assistant-inspector of teas completed the establishment.

It was the privilege of the Chairman of the Court of Directors to appoint to vacancies at Canton. When, as must frequently have happened, the Chairman had no son or nephew to provide for, he evidently made some sort of bargain or exchange of patronage with some other director. Three out of the four members of the Select Committee of supercargoes in 1812 bore the surname of some former Chairman of the Court. Of the other names on the list at least nine are also the names of directors, either then or recently in office. Altogether, the conclusion must be that the family connection between Leadenhall Street and Canton must have been very close indeed.

The Company's servants in China were thought to be better paid than those in any other branch of the Company's employ. Their prosperity was the more enviable in that it bore no relationship to the services expected of them. Throughout much of the year they had little or nothing to do; and, during their few months of activity, their work was neither hard nor perilous. They ran no risk from battle or disease. And indeed the climate of China was considered so healthy that the well-to-do civilians in India would sometimes send their children to Macao at the age when their modern successors send their children home to England. This was not a common practice, if only because most of the children in question were half-breeds; but that it was done at all is sufficient tribute to the Chinese climate.

It might be supposed that it was for their skill that the supercargoes were rewarded so lavishly. But it does not appear that there was much mystery in the buying of tea. It was, at least, an art which American sea captains could master in addition to the proper duties of their calling. It would be equally wrong to imagine that the supercargoes had any special knowledge of the country and its language. They could know little of either while it was the official Chinese policy to thwart the curiosity of the foreigner. This policy was not in any degree relaxed until about 1801, when the Chinese ceased to discourage all attempts on the part of foreigners to learn their tongue. After that year, indeed, the young gentlemen of the factory began to study Chinese, but it was long before those who had so studied could take the place of those who had not. In the meanwhile, and until the older men should see fit to retire, business was conducted, as hitherto, in a barbarous dialect known as 'pigeon' or 'pidgin' English. This mixture of English, Portuguese and Chinese is said to be spoken to this day. Except among those accustomed to it, 'pidgin' English was hardly more intelligible than Chinese itself. So the most elderly of the supercargoes cannot have been altogether unskilled. The change from this strange jargon to Chinese, as the language of commerce, probably took place about 1810. Captain Hall, who was at Canton in 1816, speaks of this reform as recent:

> Until very lately, all business was transacted by the British Factory in this most absurd language. Of late years, however, the Company's servants at Canton have made themselves acquainted both with the written and spoken Chinese, and everything material now passes in the language of the country. The natives themselves, whose principle it is to discourage all assimilation, sometimes lament this newly acquired power of communicating, and look back with regret to the times when the supercargoes drank a great deal of wine, and spoke not a word of their language. 'Now', as I heard one of the Hong merchants say, with a sigh and a shake of the head, 'the English speak Chinese as well as I do, and drink nothing but water.'

Even after it became necessary to learn Chinese, the supercargoes can hardly be thought of as ill-paid or overworked. It is not clear, moreover, that their knowledge of the language was as complete as Captain Hall's remarks would lead one to believe. At any rate, even in 1812, a comparatively junior member of the factory staff received a salary of £500 a year, over and above his ordinary income, as 'Chinese Interpreter'. This fact being taken into consideration, it is possible that a certain allowance should be made for the courtliness of Hall's interlocutor. And, in that case, his statement concerning the abstemious habits of the supercargoes need not be taken too literally.

The chief hardship the supercargoes underwent was in exile, in a more or less irksome confinement, and in being restricted to each other's society for the greater part of the year. It is not to be supposed that they would mix very much with the Catholic Portuguese, and it does not appear that they were often much more than civil to the American consul. They found what solace they might in their library and awaited the return of their countrymen with the China fleet. Their boredom, recompensed so highly, may not have been intolerable.

Returning to the Indian scene, some account must be given of Ceylon. This English possession, acquired by conquest in 1795 and retained at the Peace of Amiens, has been left to the last as being totally distinct from the other possessions in the East. It was distinct in being a crown colony, having no connection with the East India Company and owning no allegiance to the Governor-General.

Held successively by Portugal, Holland, France and England, Ceylon had never been thoroughly conquered. Its importance was strategical and consisted wholly in the possession of Trincomalee. Unfortunately, this fine harbour lies on the side of the island farthest from the fertile part of the coast where the capital is necessarily situated. The harbour was therefore difficult to defend, being in a barren land, far from Colombo, the centre of population and the seat of government. Apart from these two places, Colombo and Trincomalee, the only other garrison was at Galle, a small harbour on the south coast of the island. Colombo, it may be remarked, had no harbour at all, but only an open roadstead. In the early nineteenth century these three garrisons were connected with each other by a strip of territory along the coast. The interior was ruled by the King of Kandy, who was impregnably situated at his capital in the middle of an unhealthy jungle. So far from being a pleasant hill station, Kandy was then a legendary stronghold in the jungle, the mere whereabouts of which was doubtful.

Trincomalee, 'from its centrical position, and the easy

ingress and egress which it affords at all seasons, is better adapted for being made a marine depot, and a rendezvous for his Majesty's squadron, than any other station in India'. This opinion, expressed by Milburn, had been expressed often enough before. Portuguese, Dutch and French had been discussing for centuries the possibilities of Trincomalee. The vital importance of the harbour was fully recognised. Nevertheless, it was continually changing hands by capture, and this for the simple reason that the vicinity afforded insufficient supplies. In that barren land it was difficult or impossible to maintain a garrison sufficient for the defence of the place.

The view of Trincomalee from Back Bay is striking and beautiful. On one hand stands a projecting cliff, rising in many places perpendicularly from the sea upwards of 100 feet, and the broken hill above it is elevated about 200 feet more. The flagstaff is placed near to the outermost point of the rock; and along the summit and declivities of the higher ground are situated the bungalows of the officers, and barracks of the private soldiers. On the other hand, a line of native villages are shaded amidst groves of cocoa-nut trees. The great body of the fort and town of Trincomalee is situated at the bottom of the rock, and joined to a narrow neck of land, running parallel to the sea, and separating the harbour from two adjacent bays, one of which lies on each side of the promontary.

The guns of Trincomalee command both bays, the former on the south, the latter on the north side of the fortified rock. Fort Ostenberg protects the mouth of the harbour; that fortress stands upon a mount three miles west of Trincomalee. One chain of batteries surrounds the base, and another the summit of the hill. The greater part of the works of both these forts was built by the Government of Portugal. Some additions were made to it by the French during the short time they had possession of this place: but little or nothing was done by the Dutch. Seventy-two pieces of cannon are mounted on the ramparts of Trincomalee, and 50 on those of Ostenberg....

If little or nothing was done by the Dutch, as Milburn states, apart from finding a name for the fort, less than nothing was done by the English. It might seem desirable that the Royal Navy in India should not depend entirely on the hospitality of the East India Company, and to this extent the direct government of Ceylon might seem reasonable. But there can be no doubt that it would have been governed a great deal more competently by the Company; if only in being subsidised from Fort William on a more lavish scale than it would ever be subsidised from England. Under Wellesley's control, the fort might have been rendered impregnable. Considering its position on a steep narrow-necked promontory, this would not have been difficult. As it was, most of the buildings were in ruins. The roof of the garrison church having fallen in, the edifice was used as a tennis-court. The fortifications as a whole were in a very bad state of repair. It was known that the place could not stand a siege. Had the French sent a strong squadron into the Indian Ocean, this fact would have had immense influence on the strategy of the English defence.

As a naval base, Trincomalee had the advantages of complete shelter, at all times of year, in one or other of its two bays; the protection of the batteries; and an ample supply of water and fuel. To set against this, there was not enough rise and fall of the tide to admit of the construction of docks, and, above all, there were no provisions. Fresh beef and pork could be had only in very small quantities. There were sometimes a few fowls, but never any vegetables or salt provisions. Communications with Madras and Bombay were very slow during the North-East Monsoon. In Colonel Wellesley's Memorandum of 1801 the following remarks occur:

> Refreshments at Trincomalee are scarce, and the little that is to be got, very bad. The troops belonging to the garrison live upon salt provisions and fish, in general; and the latter is scarce when a large armament is collected in the harbour.
>
> During the months of October, November, December, and to the 15th of January, the weather is very bad...the communication may be said at times to be entirely stopped. A letter from Colombo

is sometimes a fortnight on the road; one from Madras three weeks....

...I conclude that Trincomalee is useful as a port only....

The conclusion here advanced was just. Trincomalee was indeed useful only as a port and as a rendezvous for men-of-war. And Ceylon was of use only as an appendage to Trincomalee. That, probably, is the explanation of why Ceylon was a crown colony.

Under the Dutch, Ceylon had not been a source of profit. Expenditure had exceeded revenue, and only the profits of trade had saved the Dutch from actual loss. During the first years of English rule the island was thrown into hopeless confusion and became accordingly a drain on English resources. This was due to the wild administration of the first Governor, the Hon. Frederick North. Starting in the sanguine hope of great trade expansion and mistaking altogether the nature of the island's importance, North produced nothing but chaos. He was superseded in July 1805 by Sir Thomas Maitland. Much damage had, however, been done in the meanwhile. In particular, as the last of a series of expensive blunders, North had gone to war with the King of Kandy. The Kandians had the best of it, and, during part of the period with which we are dealing, the situation was at once dangerous and comic. The anxiety felt by English naval officers on account of Trincomalee was heightened by the knowledge that such troops as there were for its defence were embroiled in North's futile campaigns in the interior.

Maitland, who was a soldier, stopped the war as soon as he arrived. 'War in this climate!' he exclaimed, and the fighting came to an end. He did not make peace, but simply cancelled operations and ignored the enemy in future. The King of Kandy did the same, so that a nominal state of warfare existed for years. Under the rule of this surly and despotic Scotsman, the Government's deficit turned into a balance.

But this was only possible through the insufficiency of the garrison. In those years Ceylon contained no more than twelve hundred white soldiers, a regiment of sepoys and a regiment of Malays. The loyalty of the sepoys was very doubtful. Of the attitude of the Malays there was no doubt at all. In the Kandian War most of them had fought on the other side, subsequently returning to barracks and demanding their pay; which they obtained.

Maitland was under no delusions as to his function at Colombo. He was fully aware that Ceylon was only useful as an outpost of India, and that, without a sufficient garrison, it could be of no use whatever. He wrote of 'the total neglect that had hitherto been shown to put the island in a decent, far less a formidable, state of defence'. Of Trincomalee itself he reported that its defences stood 'exactly where they did in the year 1781, with this essential difference, however, that the trifling works then in decent order are fast mouldering into decay'. He pointed out that Trincomalee is 'the real key by the possession of which alone you can hold the naval superiority of India'. 'So long', he admitted, 'as we are supreme at sea it does not matter; but directly a hostile squadron with four or five thousand men makes its appearance, we shall lose all that we have paid so much for during so many years.' His final conclusion was that 'if we are not prepared to fortify Trincomalee not only adequately but formidably, we may as well give up Ceylon altogether'. Despite these remarks, and the complaints of successive Admirals, nothing was done to strengthen Trincomalee. Had there been another campaign like those of Suffren and Hughes, the English squadron would have been tied to this port like a mastiff chained to its kennel.

Chapter III

TRADE TO THE EAST

WHAT DID the East India Company export to India? It has already been suggested that the answer to this question should be 'Courage'. Perhaps it would be more correct to give 'Men' for an answer. Whichever reply is the more exact, it is at least clear that the Company could find little to export in the form of merchandise, and that the little it exported brought in but a scanty profit even when it did not occasion an actual loss. Whereas the men sent out, who mostly did not return, were the true means by which the wealth of Asia was procured. These men were mostly boys, and it was their sole merit that they did not run away in battle. In this quality of not running away, the East India Company had a monopoly which was secure just so long as the French could be excluded from India. It was Cobbett who, in 1808, observed 'how abominably cowardly our language respecting the French is. We appear to be more afraid of six Frenchmen than of thirty millions of Indians....' And in this observation he scarcely went beyond the bounds of truth. Without French help, the native armies could do very little against the Company's troops, officered as they were by young Englishmen and stiffened by a few English units. It was not so much a matter of superior equipment or knowledge; still less of superior tactics. The native troops were beaten because their discipline broke down under fire; they ran away. And the people who will not fight sometimes end by paying tribute to the people who will.

Of the Company's export cargoes, then, the human part

was always the most valuable. It consisted of cadets for the Company's forces, recruits for its European units and soldiers for the King's regiments serving in India. The cadets were mainly English, the recruits very largely Irish, and their surgeons almost invariably Scotch. From the point of view of health, it would perhaps have been wiser to leave the surgeons at home and rely for medical aid on Portuguese half-breeds who knew something of the climate. But on this point convention was too strong to be defied.

Technically speaking, the Company's chief export was 'invisible'. It would be a mistake, however, to suppose that it could not be seen. The difference between the numbers of those sent to India and those returning was sufficiently obvious to those who allotted cabin space on board the outward and homeward-bound Indiamen. Europeans did not live very long in India and it required a steady flow of recruits to keep the numbers up to strength. From Parliamentary Papers printed in 1813 it appears that, between 1793 and 1808, the total number of writers sent to India amounted to 635, the total number of cadets to 4254. Perhaps a clearer notion, however, of the outward flow would be conveyed by giving the yearly averages for the period 1803–12. The following figures represent approximately the numbers which would sail for India in an average year:

Writers	34	18 to Bengal 9 to Madras 5 to Bombay 2 to Penang
Cadets	263	119 to Bengal 105 to Madras 39 to Bombay
Surgeons	33	
Free Merchants	3	
Free Mariners	33	

To arrive at statistics as to the numbers of recruits sent to the Company's armies, of seamen sent to join the Bombay Marine, and of cadets destined for the same service, is not by any means easy. Nor do there seem to be available any figures regarding the migration to India of such private persons as lawyers, servants and ladies; people neither in the Company's service nor to be described as merchants. If 500, however, be accepted as the average yearly number of recruits, and fifty as the number of seamen together with otherwise unclassified passengers, there will probably be nothing wildly amiss. Adding these numbers to the numbers previously given of the Company's servants, the grand total comes to over 850. Allowing for the maintenance in numbers of a not inconsiderable white population which had arrived in India without the Company's invitation, it might be allowable to take the figure of a thousand as representing the average annual outflow of Europeans other than those in the King's forces.

An estimate of the number of soldiers sent out each year to join the King's regiments in India must be somewhat misleading. For such an average would seem to represent as a steady flow what was, in fact, the least regular of migrations. Whole regiments would be dispatched in the course of one year and scarcely a man during the year following. It would probably be true, however, to say that a rough average of two thousand fresh troops each year would be the minimum required to keep the forces in India up to strength. This total, taken in conjunction with the total arrived at for the recruitment of the rest of the white population, gives three thousand as the average annual number of Europeans sailing for India; roughly, ten for each hundred of the existing white population.

What proportion of those who sailed for India ever returned to England? As far as the cadets are concerned, the answer would seem to be about one in four. This, at least, is the conclusion reached by one scholar after a careful calculation covering the period 1760 to 1834. But it seems very doubtful whether, of the soldiers, anything like this proportion lived long enough to make the homeward voyage. A few references to 'invalids' show that a few soldiers made their way home from time to time. Were it not for these, one would question whether any survived.

As an initial loss, a certain number of men died on the voyage out from England. The *Scaleby Castle* Indiaman, on a passage to India in 1799, lost a hundred and eighty men from malignant fever, most of those who died being soldiers of the 34th Regiment. This was certainly exceptional, but the proportion lost during a normal voyage was quite considerable. Of 4707 men, embarked in 1792, 86 died or were drowned before India was reached. In the following year, 62 were lost out of 3817; and in 1794, 40 out of 1877. Once the troops were landed in India, campaigning, disease and heat began to thin their ranks. If they fared better than the sailors of the East Indies squadron, it is as much as can be said for their chances of survival.

The civil servants, it is clear, ran fewer risks than the officers in the army. But it is evident that most of them, nevertheless, died in India. James Forbes, returning to England in 1784 after exactly eighteen years spent in India, found that he was the only survivor of those who had sailed with him in 1765:

> ...nineteen passengers had embarked from England in the same ship with myself, full of youthful ardour, and eager to obtain their respective situations in the civil, military, and marine departments of the Company's service....Of the nineteen youths with whom I thus commenced my juvenile career, seventeen died in India many years before my departure; one only besides myself then survived; with whom I formed an early friendship, which continued without interruption to his death, for he also has since fallen a sacrifice to the climate, and I have been for nearly ten years the only survivor!

That Forbes outlived his contemporaries was chiefly due to his retiring at the age of thirty-five. Very few of the boys who went to India, even though some were as young as fourteen and few much older than twenty, could afford to retire at so early an age. Almost as fortunate as Forbes was G. F. Grand, who wrote that ten died out of the eleven writers with whom he sailed for India in 1766; the one who survived being William Makepeace Thackeray, the grandfather of the novelist.

The mortality among the European population in India must have been almost high enough to counterbalance the annual influx. Allowing for the returning invalids and 'East India Plunderers', it would probably be fairly accurate to estimate the yearly average of deaths as within a few hundred of the yearly average of arrivals. Comparatively little notice was taken in England of this dreadful waste of lives. That most of those who returned were wealthy somehow obscured the fact that very few returned. Criticism there was, but it was directed rather at the upstarts who, as Cobbett said, would 'thrust the gentry of the country from their paternal domains, and introduce into the villages of England the haughtiness and insolence exercised over the sooty slaves of Hindostan'. A slow realisation of the fact that the one or two million pounds brought home each year 'to build big white houses on the tops of hills' came ultimately from the English tax-payer diverted attention from the graveyards of Bengal.

Why did Englishmen die so quickly in the East? Some, it is clear, died from premature responsibility. Cadets sent to Ceylon, for example, were immediately given employment as revenue collectors in the more remote districts. Many of them died in consequence, insane from loneliness. The East India Company, however, seldom made this mistake. The cadets intended for the Company's service were lodged in barracks of a more or less monastic type, where they lived under proper supervision. The barracks, indeed, tended to turn into a school; and would have done so had not a faction in what Lord Wellesley termed 'the most loathsome den of the India House' combined to prevent it; chiefly with the object of annoying that nobleman himself. Being, then, neither overpaid nor given any great responsibility, the boys did not die; not, at any rate, immediately.

The mortality was not so much among boys as among young men. To the question as to why they died, the official reply was that the climate disagreed with them. Of most of them, it would probably have been more exact to say that they died of dissipation. Young men in India were, as Burke remarked, full grown in fortune long before they were ripe in principle. Many suffered through the excesses of their premature power. Some seem to have exposed themselves needlessly to the sun, but the liver complaint, which was the commonest disease among the well-to-do, had a closer connection with Hodgson's pale ale, claret and sangaree. The supply of Madeira, for that matter, was on a scale hardly conducive to the health of the English community in Bengal, to which the bulk of it was consigned. In 1805, for instance, six thousand, two hundred and sixty pipes of this wine were imported into India, at a cost of about £44 each pipe. The pipe was equal to about forty dozen bottles, so that this was not a very expensive wine, except when bought ready matured. Nevertheless, an annual wine bill which includes the cost of well over three million bottles of one wine is not unimpressive, considering the comparatively small number of people in a position to drink wine at all. Claret, a more expensive wine, was not imported so extensively. There were wo kinds of claret, one called 'English' and the other 'French'. The 'English' claret was a French wine doctored with brandy and other unspecified additions in England so as to make it stand the climate. It cost about 6*s.* 3*d.* the bottle. The 'French' claret came direct from Bordeaux and cost only about 3*s.* 4*d.* the bottle. It had the disadvantage of not keeping much longer than seven months. If not drunk at once it was apt to go 'sharp' and become bad for the bowels. Statistics as to the quantity of liquor consumed may not wholly account for the high death-rate among the English residents in India, but they throw light on the problem. If they do not solve it, they suggest the lines on which the solution might be attempted. There are other forms of excess besides drink.

Next in importance to the Company's human exports was the supply of military and naval stores. Political activities in India were apt to consume considerable quantities of ammunition and ordnance stores. The armies were large, and muskets, cannon, uniform clothing and equipment went out to India, never to return. With these exports can be classed the goods required for the comfort of the English community: books and pamphlets, boots and shoes, furniture, cutlery, carriages, grocery, hardware, glass, haberdashery, hosiery, paint, perfumery, saddlery, harness and plate. Nor is the list complete without ale and porter, hock, claret, port, rum, cognac, brandy, geneva and hollands.

Last of all among the Company's exports must be reckoned the goods intended for the natives of India. Under this heading the chief item was woollens. The Company was compelled to send out a certain quantity of woollens and did so somewhat unwillingly. The sale in India was slow and uncertain, and the goods were mostly sold at cost price. The loss was not appreciable in that the freight was trifling. The ships were going to India half empty and might as well carry cloth as nothing. The only articles of export on which a profit was made were metals. English and Swedish iron, copper, and tin for China, would always realise a profit. Other metals exported were lead, red lead, brass wire and vitry. In 1811 three thousand, seven hundred and sixty tons of British iron were sent out, two thousand, two hundred tons of lead and fifteen hundred tons of copper. These proportions may have been affected by the Company's obligation to export certain quantities of the products of English mines. The bulk, probably, of these metals was used in shipbuilding.

The export of Manchester cotton cloth, which was to provide the ultimate solution to the problem of the trade with India, had hardly begun during this period. Both French and English had attempted to sell imitations of native goods, especially in the region of the Red Sea. But there were difficulties to overcome. Even when the pattern was copied identically, dealers could tell the difference by the feel and smell. And in India the Company was hampered by certain scruples as regards the livelihood of the native weavers. Nevertheless, the trade was growing with various parts of the East, and the goods so exported were valued at about £100,000 in 1812. The sudden rise in exports following the partial abolition of the Company's monopoly was attributed solely to the merits of private enterprise. It gave rise to free-trade rejoicings for half a century. The suppression of monopoly in that particular form was looked upon as a principal factor in nineteenth-century prosperity. This view was not wholly mistaken; but, at the same time, the increase was at least as much the result of changed conditions, among which must be reckoned certain technical improvements in England. Neither must it be forgotten that the opening of the trade was almost coincident with the end of the war; and that some of the effects attributed to the former event may have been rather due to the latter. If, moreover, the Company checked the growth of the industry in any perceptible degree, it was not so much from lack of enterprise as from a desire to protect the Indian weavers. These weavers were at once subjects and serfs, and for their welfare the Company was thus doubly responsible.

The last of the Company's exports was that always referred to, with pedantic inaccuracy, as bullion. Where exports are considered, this word must be taken to mean silver. The bullion brought from China, on the other hand, was gold. An official love of ambiguity prevented the mention of the words gold and silver. This was unfortunate; partly in that it involved the use of the same word to describe two quite distinct metals; partly in that a part of the silver came in the form of specie. That is, it was in Spanish dollars, the general currency of the East. It is true, however, that most of the dollars in circulation had come the other way round the world. The silver exported from London, although from the same mines, was mostly in the form of bullion.

In its trading days the Company had been compelled to export silver in considerable quantities, to the intense alarm of contemporary adepts in political arithmetic. It was latterly spared this necessity to some extent, chiefly owing to the growth of its invisible exports, but also owing to an increased export of merchandise. The export of silver was tending to die out altogether, although it cannot be said that there was an equivalent increase of merchandise. During the war of 1793–1802 the annual value of the exports varied in the region of two million sterling, of which rather more than half a million was in silver. By 1800 the total had risen to nearly two and a half million without a proportionate increase in the amount of silver. Peace altered the situation largely, so that of the total of about four millions in 1802, the silver amounted to nearly a million and three-quarters. Dropping to less than a million out of three million in 1803, it rose in the following year to about half the total of nearly four millions. Then, with the outbreak of war, the volume of exports dwindled considerably, while the proportion of silver died away altogether. Of two and three-quarter millions exported in 1805 rather over a half-million was in silver. In 1806 no silver was exported. There was very little in 1807, and none again in 1808 or in the two years following. Meanwhile, the value of the merchandise, after rising slightly in 1806–7, kept at a level well below two millions. More than a million of this was in woollen goods, the bulk of which was consigned to China.

It will be seen from the above figures that the Company exported very little to India. This did not prevent the importation of goods from that country, for, as already noted, Bengal produced a considerable amount of surplus revenue. Out of that surplus a deficit had to be made up at the various outposts, Madras, Bombay and Penang. What was left after these overhead expenses had been met could be removed from the country in the form of goods. A reason advanced for taking tribute in the form of goods was that India would otherwise be drained of the precious metals. That there was any serious risk of this may be doubted. What decided the question was the fact that part of the revenue was paid in the form of goods, and that Indian goods were acceptable in England and elsewhere.

It was through monopolies that the Company raised revenue in kind, and of these monopolies the two most important were those in saltpetre and opium. The other absolute monopoly, that in salt, falls into a different category as being more in the nature of a direct tax. But the monopoly in the manufacture of cotton and raw silk, if not established by law, was virtually complete. These monopolies worked in different ways. Saltpetre, the principal ingredient of gunpowder, was a biological product of Bengal villages, and cost little to produce. The Company had merely to meet, out of revenue, the expenses of collection. Apart from a single washing, which was all that Indian saltpetre needed to arrive at a crystalline state, no process of manufacture was needed. Refinement and the blending with sulphur and charcoal was done in England. The nitrate of potash exported from India was in an impure state. The monopolies in opium, silk and cotton, on the other hand, were managed differently. Each of these articles involved extensive employment of labour. With cotton weavers and silk winders the Company dealt directly through its agents. By a process of making advance payments to the workmen and thenceforward keeping them perpetually in debt to the Company, a form of serfdom was produced. This enabled the Company to pay the producers anything from 15 per cent. to 40 per cent. below the market price, while preventing them either quitting the trade or working for another employer. Compulsion was occasionally used, though not officially. There was also said to be a certain amount of oppression involved in the cultivation of poppies for the manufacture of opium. This article was obtained from Bahar and Benares and was very jealously monopolised. It was upon opium and raw cotton that the Company relied for much of its revenues.

Revenue was drawn from India in the form of goods, which were paid for out of the taxes or else delivered in payment of them. How large was the sum available for investment in this way, after the expenses of the various Governments had been met? In Lord Cornwallis's first administration, when 'normal' conditions had prevailed, the available surplus amounted to a clear million sterling each year, after paying all expenses and the interest on a debt of ten millions. Since then there had been continual warfare both in India and Europe, enough in itself to absorb the surplus revenue.

It was a sound instinct in the English governing class which led to the appointment of the Marquess Wellesley as Governor-General. Whereas many still talked of India in terms of commerce, an Irish landlord could be relied upon to recognise a landed estate when he saw one. Wellesley not only recognised the essential character of the Company's possessions but also applied to them the governing principle of landowning; the principle that more land means more rent. Unfortunately for his calculations, which were perfectly sound, the wars in Europe continued for a length of time he did not anticipate; so that the return to normal conditions, which should have meant a larger surplus revenue from a larger landed estate, was indefinitely postponed. Meanwhile, the wartime conditions produced a debt which swallowed up the increase in revenue.

The revenue from all parts of India, which had been about

eight millions in 1797, had risen to fifteen and a half millions in 1805. But military expenditure, due as well to the wars in Europe as to those in India, had increased in proportion. This continued expense, together with the interest on an additional twenty millions of debt, borrowed at Oriental rates of from 8 per cent. to 12 per cent., produced an actual deficit. And even after peace had been made in India, the available surplus was no more, even in theory, than it had been in 1797. While in fact, there turned out to be no surplus at all, owing to continued war conditions; this, in spite of the drastic and dangerous economies of 1806.

As a result of the unexpected prolongation of the wars, which upset all of Wellesley's calculations, the Company's finances were in a bad state during most of the period with which we are dealing. The expenses in India in 1805 exceeded the receipts by two and a half millions. Peace being made with the native powers at that time, all military expenses were reduced. This gave Bengal a surplus of well over two millions in 1808. Under normal conditions, this would have been enough to put the Company on a paying basis once more, but the French wars combined with an accident to produce yet another deficit. The interest on war debts and the upkeep of the still considerable armies did away with some of the profit and the shutting of the Continental markets swallowed part of what remained. The accidental cause which brought about an actual loss was the foundering of ships in the course of 1808 and 1809. No less than fourteen Indiamen were lost in two years, mainly owing to stress of weather; a catastrophe without either precedent or repetition.

From one cause or another there was continued loss and the contraction of fresh debt down to 1811–12. So that, during much of our period, the theory that the Company's imports should be paid for out of the surplus revenues of Bengal was a theory only. For there was no surplus beyond what was absorbed by the other Presidencies. Throughout these years however, goods were imported at a steady rate by a process of running more and more deeply into debt. One result of this maintenance of imports was that the Company's warehouses were said in 1808 to contain unsold goods worth seven million pounds.

The general course, then, of the Company's trade was outwardly unchanged by the mere fact of its being run at a loss. Normal times would return, it was thought, and the Company flourish again. Moreover, it is clear that few men cared much whether it flourished or not. So long as they were individually prosperous, the servants of the Company and all those connected with it were much at their ease. The East India Company was an abstraction, a figment of the mind, and what it should earn or lose was nobody's concern. It was only honest but stupid men like Sir George Barlow who lost any sleep from contemplating the balance-sheet. More intelligent men of equal honesty realised that the Company's days were numbered in any case. Lord Wellesley, for instance, foresaw that India would eventually come under the crown. If annoyed at finding his calculations apparently disproved, he was not stricken with remorse whenever India was mentioned. The Company, whatever the amount of its debt, was obviously but a temporary arrangement.

By virtue of a real or imaginary surplus revenue, and through the monopolies retained in its own hands, the Bengal Government had yearly to dispose of certain quantities of goods. These goods consisted chiefly of opium, cotton cloth, saltpetre, silk, indigo, sugar and rice. Part of this tribute was sent straight to England, part went to China and elsewhere. In the latter category opium was the only important item. It was a source of profit to the Company, but the actual carrying of it to China was left to private merchants who bought it at public auctions held by the Company. There remains to be considered the goods sent to England, the various kinds of which need treating separately.

First of all, there was cotton cloth, otherwise known as piece goods. This was the biggest item. The growth of the industry in England, the output of which increased ninefold between 1797 and 1810, tended to narrow the market for Indian cottons. But the demand was also on the increase, especially in England, where calicoes and muslins were becoming the chief article of ladies' dress, annihilating the manufacture of some of the lighter kinds of woollens and worsted stuff. What was even more important, India had still a superiority in the finer kinds of cotton. This was the age of muslin in England. 'Nothing else is worn in gowns by any rank of people,' wrote Lady Newdigate in 1797, from Brighton, 'but I don't know that I can get them cheaper here, but great choice there is, very beautiful and real India.' It was still the fashion in 1811. Jane Austen's correspondence is full of references to spotted, checked and cambric muslin, bought at anything from seven shillings to three and six a yard; while some of her heroines paid as much as nine shillings and upwards. Mr Henry Tilney, in *Northanger Abbey*, boasted of buying a gown for his sister: 'I gave but five shillings a yard for it, and a true Indian muslin.' The point to observe about this and the former quotation is the emphasis on the genuineness of the stuff. For this shows that there were imitations on the market, and it suggests that the counterfeit was not easy to recognise. When, largely through the efforts of Mr Robert Owen, the counterfeit had become impossible to recognise, the day of the true Indian muslin was over. But that day had not yet arrived, and the East India Company could still import quantities of piece goods. Between 1793 and 1810 those from Bengal alone sold altogether for nearly fourteen and a half million pounds.

The Bengal manufactures of muslins, whether plain, striped, or worked with gold and silver, were mainly at Dacca, in the northern part of the province. There also they made doreas, terrindans, cossaes, nainsooks, gurrahs and balla-sores. To these must be added the chintzes of Patna and the carpets of Barampour. The Company had also its own manufactories near Calcutta, chiefly for what were called printed linens.

Saltpetre, the next product of Bengal to be considered, was of very great importance from a political point of view. Although used in the preserving of meat and the manufacture of glass, its chief use was in the making of gunpowder. For this reason, saltpetre was hedged about from the earliest times with careful legislation. It was never looked upon as a mere article of trade. The earliest laws concerning it date from Queen Anne's reign, but only the Act of 1791 need now concern us. By that Act of the 31 Geo. III, c. 42, the Company was compelled to put up at its sales, each half-year, five thousand bags of saltpetre more than the quantity sold on the average of the last four years, and also to supply the Board of Ordnance with five hundred tons at the average price. This Act was passed because the Company was thought to have imported less than was needed in the past, and also because the English powder manufacturers were attempting to supplant the Dutch in supplying powder to the rest of Europe.

Attempts to fix the price of saltpetre were not successful, for the market price fluctuated violently during time of war. According to Tooke, the price was highest in 1795, when it stood at between £8 and £9 per cwt. That the price varied with the scale of hostilities on the Continent and at sea is shown by its falling to a little over £2 in 1796, and then rising again to nearly £5. But the chemical discoveries at this time which enabled the French to dispense with a foreign supply, combined with the increased importations from India with which England flooded the rest of the Continent, brought about a permanent decline in price after 1798. Although it sold in that year at over £7, it was never again as high as £5, except during the speculations caused by the brief campaign of 1815.

Despite new agreements with the Government, such fluctuations tended to involve the Company in difficulties. With all the roads of Europe covered with the marching columns, and all the hills echoing with the sound of the guns, there was no telling how much saltpetre would be used in each campaign. During one month the guns would be thundering everywhere and next month all would have died down again. Each puff of smoke meant a reduction in the available supply of nitrates, but none could predict how many shots would be fired next year. Fortunes might be made by those who guessed correctly. By 1808 the East India Company was agreeing to supply the Government with six thousand tons at £50 per ton. By 1810 the quantity had more than doubled, while the price had risen to £65 per ton. Between 1793 and 1809 the Company imported 24,752 tons, for which the Board of Ordnance paid rather over a million pounds, an unprofitable transaction, as the cost price, with freight, had come to nearly a million and a half.

Naval history has recently been written in terms of timber. Sooner or later it will become necessary to write it again in terms of gunpowder. For there can be no doubt that one factor in the English success at sea was the good quality of the powder used. It was pointed out in a letter to the *Moniteur* that the powder burnt in the French fleet at the Battle of the Nile was adulterated by more than 25 per cent. This was naturally, perhaps rightly, attributed to the dishonesty of contractors and the venality of commissaries. Yet an exhaustive experiment at Bombay in 1808, with the powder used on each side in the action between the *San Fiorenzo* and *Piedmontaise*, proved that the English powder was better, almost in the proportion of six to five—seven to six, at any rate—which seems to suggest that there must have been some basic difference. It is hard, at least, to believe that all the dishonest contractors were on one side. And this suggests, again, that English powder may have owed its quality to the purity of Bengal saltpetre, of which England had a complete and permanent monopoly. The raw material was peculiar in the ease with which it was prepared for export, and perhaps it had other merits.

Contemporary experts considered that powder depended for its quality on the exact proportions of the ingredients used. And if stress was laid on any one ingredient, it was charcoal. If the making of the charcoal held any mysteries, they are mysteries still and so will probably remain. The proportions used, however, which were fixed, traditional and different in each country, are known. From these it might be possible to reach some conclusion as to the respective qualities of the kinds of gunpowder in use. And it would be no very difficult experiment to determine whether and in what respect Indian saltpetre differs from Spanish and also from the synthetic kind. The subject seems worthy of study, for with solid missiles, the velocity is a vital matter quite apart from the question of range.

Of silk and indigo it is unnecessary to say very much. The latter product was almost as important as opium. The former, in its raw state, was the produce of an industry fostered by the Company itself. Garments of silk were not in as great demand as formerly, but the trade continued. This was probably due to the continued wearing of silk stockings. Exports of silk were hardly more than a quarter the value of the exports of piece goods.

The Company sometimes brought sugar to England. The value of the sugar so imported in 1805 was about the same as the silk. It was known at the time that very much more might be produced but for the discriminating tariff designed to protect the West India planters. It was believed that, despite the higher freight, the East Indies could undersell the West. The fact that the Company could import sugar at all in the face of such a tariff is the proof of it. But the West India interests were strongly represented in Parliament—by ninety members it was at one time said—and the preferential tariff remained. The 'East India Plunderers' may not have had as much weight as the 'West India Floggers'; but this is a point on which it is difficult to feel certain. The difficulty is the greater in that the bigger financiers clearly had a foot in both camps; the Barings, for instance, were in this position. But, apart from the weight of the interests concerned, there were certain considerations at stake which concerned the national welfare. One of these was stated by Colonel Wesley in his *Memorandum on Bengal.* In this he pointed out that the West India trade was a much better school of seamanship than the East, the seamen gaining more experience and being exposed for a shorter period to the dangers of a tropical climate. This being so, there was perhaps some reason for protecting West India sugar.

Rice is the last of the products of Bengal to be considered. It was usually referred to politely as 'grain'. The first exports of rice from Bengal to England seem to have taken place in 1795. In that year, owing to successive failures of the English crops, there was a serious shortage of food in England. The Company was thereby induced to assist in relieving the situation by importing some twenty-seven shiploads of rice. The shortage persisting to some extent in succeeding years, these importations were continued, although on a much smaller scale. Royal and official appeals urged all possible economy in the use of bread, so that patriotism demanded a resort to substitutes; it became an act of virtue to eat rice. The element of self-sacrifice would be less striking had the English at any time discovered how to cook it. But as nearly a century and a half of experience has brought no enlightenment, a change in this respect is hardly to be looked for.

It is now necessary to deal with the Company's affairs at Madras. That Presidency, as already noted, helped to swallow up the surplus revenue of Bengal. Over the period 1792 to 1809 the expenses of Fort St George exceeded the revenues by over eleven millions. The annual deficiency at the end of this period was something under half a million. The budget was made up from Bengal, mainly through an adverse balance of trade against Madras. Whereas Madras supplied Bengal with salt, cordage, and re-exported naval stores, Bengal supplied Madras with rice to a very much greater value. The rice was carried thither by private merchants trading from Calcutta, who were probably paid largely in bills drawn on Fort William.

The Company exported to Madras, from England, a quantity of woollens, lead, iron, copper and naval stores; this in addition to the supplies for the English community there. From Madras the Company imported piece goods and little else. It also exported from Madras to China a certain amount of piece goods, with a little cotton; while sugar and saltpetre passed through Madras on the way to China and England. Altogether, the trade there was not considerable.

Bombay, which must next be dealt with, was more expensive than Fort St George. The annual deficit, to be made up from Bengal, amounted to about a million. This was partly done through an adverse balance of trade with Madras, from whence Bombay obtained grain, pepper, fruit and naval stores, sending in return chiefly treasure and cotton. Despite the expense involved, however, Bombay was of greater commercial worth to the Company than Madras. For it exported something of very great importance; and that was cotton. The Bombay cotton was not exported in the form of cloth. It was the raw material, grown in the Guzerat, partly in the Company's territory which was extended in 1802, and partly in lands farther inland. Most of it came down the various rivers emptying into the Gulf of Cambay, and so drifted naturally into the warehouses at Bombay. It was not a Government monopoly, and more was exported by private individuals than by the Company. Had it been sent to England on a large scale, the Company would have had a monopoly, as none but the Company's ships might round the Cape of Good Hope. Some of the cotton did indeed go to England. This was the cotton from the factories, and was as good and clean as any from Brazil or the Levant. But it would only sell in England when Arkwright's machinery had outrun all other supplies. Normally, the freight was too heavy to allow the India cotton to compete. That brought in the Company's extra ships had to pay a freight working out at about 3⅜*d.* per pound. The freight from Surinam, Demarara or Berbice was only 3*d.*, from Grenada 2¾*d.*, and from St Lucia and Nevis but 2½*d.* Moreover, the southern territories of the United States were already beginning to grow cotton with a success which would soon lead to expansion. Bombay was farther from Liverpool than any of these places and was conceivably handicapped by a comparative absence of slavery. The Company seems occasionally to have compelled people to work, but its subjects were nominally free and had to be paid; so Bombay could not send cotton to Liverpool. Instead, it had what was almost a monopoly in a market of its own at Canton, an oriental Liverpool, and there it sold cotton for well over a million sterling nearly every year.

It is curious that the Company did not monopolise the carrying of raw cotton to China, and the more so in that the private merchants occasionally overstocked the market and so lessened the profit made on the Company's investment. The sale price of the cotton crop, with cost and freight deducted, would have gone a long way to pay for the upkeep of Bombay Castle. But it was the Company's policy to leave most of the carrying trade of the East in private hands; a policy which was thought very creditable to it as an institution, but which was perhaps rather less creditable to its servants as individuals.

At Canton, the raw cotton from Bombay was added to the woollens from England, the tin from Cornwall, the cotton and piece goods from Madras, and the opium from Bengal; and the whole was sold to the Hong merchants. But only a small part of the cotton belonged to the Company, and the opium—which was contraband—was all private property. In the latter article, however, the Company may be said to have shared; for the whole crop had been grown by the Company, mainly with a view to a sale in China, and was now in other hands merely for the sake of decency or safety. Of the goods actually exported by the Company to Canton, woollen goods formed the bulk. The total value in 1809 was well over a million sterling, of which nearly nine hundred thousand was in woollens—cloths, long ells and camblets. The remaining hundred thousand represented the value of cotton, piece goods, lead and tin.

With what was paid for the woollens and the rest, the Company bought tea. Any other imports from China shrank to nothing in comparison with the tea, on which the whole of the Company's trading activities centred. Only with China could there be any real exchange of commodities. In India the Company governed and took tribute when it could. Its trade was with China, and it was a trade in tea.

China teas are of two kinds, black and green. Those imported by the East India Company were mostly black, the green teas going, for the most part, to the United States. Nearly all the black teas were grown in a district north-east of Canton called Fokien. The quality of the tea depends on the time of year at which it is picked. The younger the leaf, the stronger the tea. So the most highly flavoured, and for that reason the most valuable, teas are those picked in the spring. Pekoe, the most expensive kind of black tea, consisted of leaf buds, picked before they could expand. This was also called 'white-blossom' tea. From the same plants, three more crops were taken; one at the beginning of May, one about the middle of June, and one in August. The last crop, consisting of large and old leaves, was thought very inferior. When left unsold at the end of the season, it was mixed with tea from Woping, a district of Canton, and was then called Bohea. The second and third, the intermediate crops, were called Souchong and Congou. The green teas were similarly graded, in ascending order, as Twankay, Hyson skin, young Hyson, Hyson, Imperial and Gunpowder. The Souchong and Congou teas were sometimes mixed with a little Pekoe, to improve their quality, and were then distinguished as teas of 'Pekoe flavour'.

Before sending to market, the teas had to be dried. And an essential difference between black and green teas was the method of drying. Green tea was carefully dried in iron vessels over a fire. Black tea was left to dry under sheds in the open air throughout the summer. When completed, the tea was packed in chests and the chests made up into parcels, each marked with the name of the district and the grower. These were sold to the tea merchants.

The tea merchants were a numerous body of small dealers who worked in connection with big capitalists at Canton, from whom they received advance payments. The tea, when sold to them, was put into little single-masted boats, each carrying perhaps a hundred and fifty chests. Manned each by about a dozen men, these small craft brought the tea from the interior down to Canton. The earliest would arrive some time in the middle of October, but the bulk was delivered for sale in November, December and January. The sales might continue until March, but the prices had always fallen by then, for the change of the monsoon prevented any further export during the rest of the spring and summer. And tea soon deteriorates, especially in a hot and damp climate. Last year's tea was virtually unsaleable, except in the hands of the more plausible kind of liar. When mixed with new tea it could be sold, but only at a low price.

It was the duty of the supercargoes to buy tea for the East India Company. These twenty men cost the Company between sixty and eighty thousand pounds a year. In return for this sum, they bought tea; and the point of their existence was that, being resident, they could buy it, if need be, before the ships arrived. The best of the crop could be bought up and warehoused before there was a single Indiaman there to put it in. Owing to the supercargoes, the foreign buyer could gain nothing from any delays the Company's ships might experience on the outward voyage. This was certainly an advantage. But it is not surprising that critics were to be found who asserted that the same end might have been gained more cheaply.

The supercargoes were supposed, of course, to be expert in the selecting of tea, which chiefly meant the avoiding of stale teas left over from the year before and offered as new. It is to be doubted whether the skill needed was of a very high order. The name of the grower was probably the chief thing to know. It is to be supposed that the books of the factory embodied a working knowledge of the honesty or otherwise of most of the growers and dealers; and from this past experience a certain technique may have been evolved. There were frauds to be detected and prices, besides, to be fixed. The art must have consisted more in fixing the price than in selecting the tea. For the bulk of the black teas offered for sale was bought for the Company in any case. The supercargoes would reject tea that appeared from nowhere suspiciously early in the season. Otherwise, they had little choice. They must have bought nearly all that came on the market.

Perhaps the best account of the tea buying is that given in the evidence of Mr Marjoribanks before the Select Committee of the House of Commons in 1830, and quoted in John Phipps's *Practical Treatise on the China and Eastern Trade*. It refers to a somewhat later period than that now under review, but there is no reason to suppose that the system had radically changed during the intervening years:

Mode in which the Teas were bought for the Company—how they were examined, as to their quality, and their prices arranged.

[From the Evidence of C. Marjoribanks, Esq. 1830.]

The most considerable portion of the Company's tea investment, is contracted for by the Company with the Hong merchants, in the season previously to that in which the teas are delivered to them. The Hong merchants enter into engagements with the tea merchants, and make to them advances upon those contracts. The tea when it is brought to Canton is submitted to the inspection of the Company's inspectors there; and, indeed is subjected to every scrutiny which is supposed to be desirable to ascertain its quality. The Company have, I believe I may say, every leaf of black tea at their option; I mean every parcel of black tea of any value is first offered to the Company, and is submitted to their inspection previously to its reception....

The contracts are concluded annually with the Hong merchants in the month of March, for teas to be delivered in the ensuing season. The amount [and] quantity varies according to the varying demand; the prices are not fixed until the teas are delivered: the teas are generally paid for in the course of the season, sometimes earlier, sometimes later.

The reports of the tea inspectors are made to the Select Committee; the members of that Select Committee are present in the hall where those examinations take place; they hear the reports of the tea inspectors, and are principally guided by their reports; but the tea inspector has nothing whatever to do with the settlement of price of tea; that rests entirely with the Committee... the price is not established by any old standard, but by the real merits of the tea itself.

The teas examined at the Tea Hall were sample chests, forwarded there as each boatload arrived in Canton. A chest was sent out of each chop—a chop of black tea consisting of about 600 chests. The inspector of teas, who was paid from £2000 to £2500 a year, aided by the assistant-inspector, then applied various tests to the tea. After a 'most vigilant examination' he made a report in writing to the Select Committee. One of the frauds against which the inspector had to guard was the offer of old and valueless tea treated with imported Prussian blue so as to look fresh. Another was the offer of tea adulterated with the leaves of other plants. It was said that 'no means are left untried which the unparalleled cunning and ingenuity of a Chinaman can devise to impose on foreigners'. One of the simplest tests applied by the inspector was that of the magnet—to detect the presence of iron filings.

Although only samples were examined in the first instance, another inspection took place when the tea was weighed for shipment. The receiving officer selected one out of every twenty chests at random, and made certain that its contents tallied with its description. If it did not, it was still possible for the Company to reject the whole chop.

The competition of foreign buyers varied a great deal. Swedish, Danish, Prussian, Hamburger, French and Dutch purchases of tea in the season 1802–3 amounted altogether to between a seventh and a sixth of the English investment. Most of these buyers disappeared altogether at the renewal of war. Between 1804 and 1808 there were occasional small purchases by the Swedish, Danish and Dutch. Then these stopped, and from 1808 to 1811 the English were the only buyers, apart from the Americans. The exact figures relating to American importations do not seem to be known for every year. But it was said that they entered the market for the first time in 1785, and that their trade increased with the decline of the trade of other neutrals, from 1793 onwards. Between 1806 and 1808 they shipped nearly a third as much as the East India Company, but after that their trade was thought to have decreased.

England was always the best market for the sale of tea. Heavy duties during the middle part of the eighteenth century had restricted the demand and encouraged smuggling. The reduction of the duties to 12½ per cent. on the sale price in 1784 had appeared to double the amount consumed—partly because much now passed through the customs which had previously been smuggled across the North Sea from Hamburg or Ostend. The actual consumption doubtless, however, increased at the same time with the fall in prices. It had become stationary by 1798 and remained so until 1815, when it rose a little, rising more steeply from 1822 onwards.

It was presumably between 1784 and 1798 that tea 'may literally be said to have descended from the palace to the cottage'. It became at about that time the breakfast of practically the whole population. It was also drunk at other times, which led Raynal to remark that tea had done more for English sobriety than any laws, sermons or moral treatises could have done. Other and native authors regarded it in a different light. Cobbett made horrified guesses at the probable effect of hot water on the human interior, and Arthur Young blamed the poor for their wicked extravagance in buying it. Growing poverty made tea increasingly essential to the lower classes as ale was put beyond their means. Tea and bread became the labourer's diet in many parts of the country.

The steadiness of the demand for tea pointed it out as a suitable source of increased revenue. The duties were increased to 25 per cent. in 1795, and further raised in 1797, 1798, 1800 and 1803, reaching 96 per cent. in 1806, and 100 per cent. in 1819. Tea was found to have a very high resistance to taxation. These heavy duties had practically no effect on the amount consumed, and produced only a slight tendency in favour of the cheaper qualities. At least half the sugar imported was consumed in tea, and this also was taxed. It was calculated in 1812 that, directly and indirectly, the State gained five millions a year on tea.

It may be supposed that an article subject to these duties, added to the profit made by the East India Company, added to the expensive freight and the cost of the factory at Canton, was not sold cheaply. The bulk of it was Congou and Souchong, the wholesale price of which varied according to quality between 2*s.* 10*d.* and 6*s.* 10*d.* per pound. Bohea was the cheapest kind, and sold for less than half-a-crown. The expensive brands might be sold retail for 16*s.* or 18*s.* per pound.

Plate II

The *Windham* and *Wexford*. East Indiamen unloading in the homeward bound East India Dock.

Drawn and engraved by C. Turner, published in 1807 and dedicated to Robert Wigram, Esq., M.P., F.R.S.

With such prices, it may seem odd that any tea should have found its way into the labourer's cottage. The explanation seems to be that a moderately low price was arrived at by a process of illegally adulterating the tea. There were a number of ways of doing this. One was to mix the tea with sloe leaves, liquorice leaves, used tea leaves or leaves of the ash and elder. To make the deception complete the added rubbish had to be coloured with Terra Japonica, copperas, sugar, molasses, clay or logwood. The resulting substance was then used in a very sparing fashion. Even middle-class families were careful in this respect; more so, in all probability, in that they used the more expensive blends. As a proof of their economy, there survive numberless mahogany teacaddies, all carefully made, with compartments inside for different teas. Most of them are, in shape, vaguely reminiscent of Napoleon's tomb. The point, however, to notice about them is that they all have efficient brass locks. The object of these was to prevent the servants from stealing the best tea. Servants were allowed tea, of course, but not the same tea as was used above-stairs.

Tea, then, at one price or another, had become the universal drink of all classes in England. Perhaps in recognition of this fact, and of the serious consequences likely to follow on a temporary stoppage of the supply, the East India Company was compelled to keep a year's requirements in stock. The disadvantage of this was that no tea was sold until it had deteriorated with keeping. After a voyage lasting five or six months, the tea would be brought into London River, landed and taken to one of the tea warehouses. There, under the care of Messrs Stockwell and Saunders, either in Fenchurch Street, Haydon Square, Cooper's Row, Jewry Street or Crutched Friars, the tea would lie for eleven months at least before being put up for sale. It so happened that the Company was never forced to use all its reserves. Ships were lost fairly frequently, but, by good fortune, the China fleet as a whole never failed to arrive. The China ships were very nearly lost in 1804, and they were very nearly prevented from sailing in 1809. In either event, the importance of there being a year's supply in hand would have become sufficiently apparent.

One result of this policy of keeping ample reserves was that the amount of tea sold in any given year bore no relation to the amount of that year's importation. The quantity imported might vary with the state of the crop in China and with the number of ships lost by shipwreck or capture. But the quantity sold varied very little, while the total sale price varied still less. Between 1801 and 1810, the average amount of tea sold each year was about twenty-four million pounds. Throughout that period, the amount never fell as low as twenty-two million and never rose much above twenty-seven million.

A principal factor governing the quantity of tea sold was the care taken by the Company not to overstock the market. The supply was often deliberately limited in order to keep up the price. It was through the Company's yielding to this temptation that the tea was sometimes kept in the warehouse for fourteen months at a time. The temptation was strong in that the amount consumed annually was more or less constant. The demand, if certain, was limited. The effect, therefore, of flooding the market was not so much to increase the sales as to lower the price. And the additional supply was more probably bought by speculators than by the public. More tea, in short, could be sold but no larger profit could be made. Twenty-seven million pounds of tea were sold in 1803 at a price of nearly four and a quarter millions sterling. In 1808 the same price was paid for twenty-five million pounds of tea.

The comparative importance of the various articles imported by the Company is shown by the following approximate figures: From 1793 to 1810 the total sale amount of India and China goods was a hundred and three millions sterling. Of this sum more than half—fifty-five millions, to be exact—was the sale price of tea. Twenty-five millions was paid to the Company for piece goods, muslins, chintz and the rest. Raw silk from Bengal and China accounted for seven millions, and the rest of the sum was made up from the sales of sugar, indigo, nankeens, saltpetre, pepper, chinese crockery, coffee and spices. The yearly sale amount on all these goods was remarkably steady, as was also the apparent profit. During the period 1801–11 the total cost of the goods each year, with freight and customs included, would be between four and four-and-a-half millions, the sale amount usually close on six millions, the apparent profit averaging about a million and a half. Out of this sum the yearly dividend was paid, after administrative expenses had been met.

The profits are described here as 'apparent' because they were more than counterbalanced by the deficit in India. Dividends were paid, none the less, and the annual deficit in India was allowed to mount up and add to the Company's debt. The only effort made to check this process, apart from a series of ill-judged economies in India which saved about a million a year and almost procured the downfall of the English power in that country, was an appeal to the Government for the repayment of sums owing to the Company. This was in 1805, and produced a million pounds in that year and another million in the year following, as a compensation to the Company for military expenses incurred by order of the Government and for national ends. As a matter of fact, these expenses had been wholly incurred in defence of the Company's possessions, but this was a circumstance which only radicals noticed. There was already a budding imperialism abroad which blinded men to the cost of conquest.

Chapter IV

THE EASTERN SEAS

THE INDIAN OCEAN, the setting for much that is to follow, is a world by itself, with winds peculiar to it and but few ways by which it may be entered. In the years with which we are concerned these winds were of greater moment and the entrances fewer than they are now. From the westward the route round the Cape was the only gateway. Of the entrances from the Pacific only four or five at most were used. Between these narrow doors and northwards about the lands to which they lead, all maritime trade and war was dominated by the winds; peculiarly so, in that the winds tend to be both constant and predictable. Without a knowledge of these winds there can be no understanding of Eastern commerce or naval strategy in the days of sail.

In the Eastern Seas the year is divided into two seasons according to the direction of the prevailing wind. From April to October is the period of the South-West Monsoon. The effect of this wind may be said to extend between the Equator and the Tropic of Cancer, and from the east coast of Africa to the Sea of Japan; beyond the Philippines also, as far to the eastward as long. 145° E. The North-East Monsoon prevails throughout much the same area from October to May. These monsoons, however, are limited in two respects; in time, that is to say, and in space. For, out of the six months during which a monsoon is said to blow it can be relied upon for only four, there being an intermediate period at the change of the monsoon. And, again, there are certain regions more or less exempt from the monsoons' effects, notably the Red Sea, the Persian Gulf and the Straits of Malacca.

South of the Equator and north of parallel 28, between Madagascar and Australia, the South-East Trade-wind blows throughout the year. In the vicinity, however, of Mauritius, there is what has sometimes been called a northerly monsoon, productive of hurricanes, especially between December and March. Further south still the prevailing winds are westerly at all times of the year.

Having indicated the main tendencies, it is necessary to warn the reader that the above account of the winds is greatly simplified. The system of winds is actually complicated by a host of exceptions and local variations, which cannot be wholly omitted. The best method of dealing with these, together with other factors in the navigation of the Eastern Seas, will be to describe how the different voyages were governed by the winds, beginning with that from England to the Cape of Good Hope.

In the North Atlantic the prevailing wind is south-westerly, and ships often began their voyage with a struggle in the Channel itself. Whether they did so or not, they were fortunate if they did not meet contrary winds during the first ten days at sea. On leaving the Channel, it was normal to set a course for Madeira, passing just within sight of the coast of Galicia. With southerly winds it would take about a fortnight to reach Madeira from Portsmouth; otherwise, seven or eight days. Were no call made at Funchal, opportunity was nevertheless taken to check the ship's position by a sight of the island; and vessels which carried chronometers were enabled in this way to verify their rates. Soon after leaving Madeira, when in the latitude of the Canary Islands, the navigator might expect to feel the North-East Trade-wind, often in this latitude blowing from within a very few degrees of due east.

Once in the Trades, a course was steered so as to pass to the westward of the Cape Verde Islands. Some preferred to pass within this group, but the usual course was to the west of the

7-2

islands and barely in sight of St Anthony. From this point navigators were torn between the desire to steer their course and the desire to keep the Trade-wind as long as possible. In the hope of keeping the Trade-wind, some ships kept well to the westward. More, however, aimed at crossing the Equator between 18° and 23° W.

On losing the Trade-wind, to the north of the Line, the ship was in the region of Variable winds and calms, a belt varying in breadth from 150 to 500 miles, which must be crossed before the South-East Trade-wind could be picked up. The Variables, with their unsteady breezes, long calms and heavy rain, varied at times by dangerous squalls, were a trial even to experienced seamen, while they were said to drive young navigators almost out of their senses. To pass through this troublesome region quickly required considerable skill—or perhaps luck—and theories abounded as to how it could be done. Here, it was thought, the difference appeared between the scientific navigator and the merely practical seaman.

Once the Variables were overcome, whether by experience, science or chance, the ship would encounter the South-East Trade-wind. It now became the main object to get as soon as possible into the region where westerly gales might be expected. So long as progress was made to the southward, it mattered little that the ship was pushed over towards Brazil; and all vessels, in fact, came fairly near that coast. Some even called at Rio de Janeiro. Captain Hall's remarks on this subject are worth quoting:

> On first encountering the south-east Trade, an outward-bound ship is obliged to steer much more to the westward than she wishes to do, in consequence of the wind blowing so directly towards the equator, and not along it, as some of the books will insist on....So that if she be a dull sailer, she may have some difficulty in weathering the coast of Brazil about Cape St Roque. As she proceeds onwards, however, and makes a little more southing, the wind will haul more and more round from the south to the south-east, and eventually to east at the southern limit of the

Trade-wind. An inexperienced sailor, on first entering the south-east Trade, is very apt to be too solicitous about making southing; whereas, he ought rather to keep his ship off a little, give her a fathom or two of the fore and main sheets, and take a small pull of the weather topsail and top-gallant braces, to ensure making good way through the water. Indeed, many officers go so far as to recommend flanking across the south-east Trade with a fore-top-mast studding-sail set.... In this respect, it may be remarked, that the scale of navigation on every Indian voyage is so great, and the importance of getting into those parallels where favourable breezes are certain to be met with, of so much more consequence than the gain of mere distance, that two or three hundred miles to the right or left, or even twice that space, is often not to be regarded. Accordingly, in cutting or flanking across the south-east Trade-wind, the object, it should be remembered, is not to shorten the distance, but to reach those latitudes where strong westerly gales are to be met with, by help of which five hundred or a thousand miles of lost distance are speedily made up, and the rest of the passage secured.

These westerly gales might be found in latitude 30° or 40°. Ships bound for China direct, having once gained this latitude, would stay in it until they had gone half round the world. One enterprising commander, in 1794, sailed right round Tasmania and made a sweep into the Pacific as far as 171° E. before heading for Canton. The usual course, however, was to the northward of Australia.

Ships bound for St Helena, it may be remarked, steered a different course altogether, keeping nearer the African coast and sometimes reaching 10° S. before encountering the Trade-wind. Ships bound for the Cape of Good Hope, on the other hand, would use the westerly winds to run down their easting and eventually approach the Cape from the south, or even south-east, so as to allow for the current setting to the westward on the Agulhas bank. Ships bound for India and not intending to call at the Cape would often check their position by getting into soundings on this bank.

To sail from England to the Cape, whether calling there

or not, might take a couple of months. It might take six weeks or less, and again it might take five months with bad luck or bad management. From the Cape, there were several alternative routes leading to various parts of the East and varying according to the season and according to the knowledge and courage of the navigator. In sailing for the Mauritius the tactics were roughly the same as for making the Cape—a sweep to the southward until nearly in the meridian of the island itself. In sailing for Java also, it was usually necessary to go as far south as latitude 35° or 36° and then make North-West Cape, New Holland, before heading northwards. Captain Hall again deserves quotation. The following remarks refer to a passage of his own in 1816:

> ...Better weather might have been obtained by keeping nearly in the latitude of the Cape; but it is essential to the success of a passage from thence to Java, or to any part of India, to run to the southward as far sometimes as 40 degrees, in which parallel the wind blows almost invariably from the westward all round the globe. The requisite quantity of easting is thus easily gained, although at the expense of some discomfort, for the weather is generally tempestuous. This point once accomplished, the ship's head may be turned to the northward, and all sail made to reach the south-east trade, which, now that the ship has gone so far to the eastward, proves a fair wind; whereas, had the limits been approached sooner, it would have been directly unfavourable.
>
> On a knowledge of such particulars the success of Eastern navigation essentially depends: for so great is the regularity of the Phenomena, and so rigorously obedient to known laws, that an experienced navigator, if he sail at a proper time of the year, can calculate with tolerable certainty upon having fair winds nearly all the way from Madeira to Canton. To sailors accustomed only to the confined navigation of the Atlantic or the Mediterranean, these bold stretches out of the direct course seem, at first sight, an unreasonable prolongation of the voyage; and it does, in fact, require considerable resolution to steer, as it were, away from the port for many hundreds of miles in search of a wind....

The penalty awaiting the mariner who turned northward too soon, and before he had run his easting down, was to find

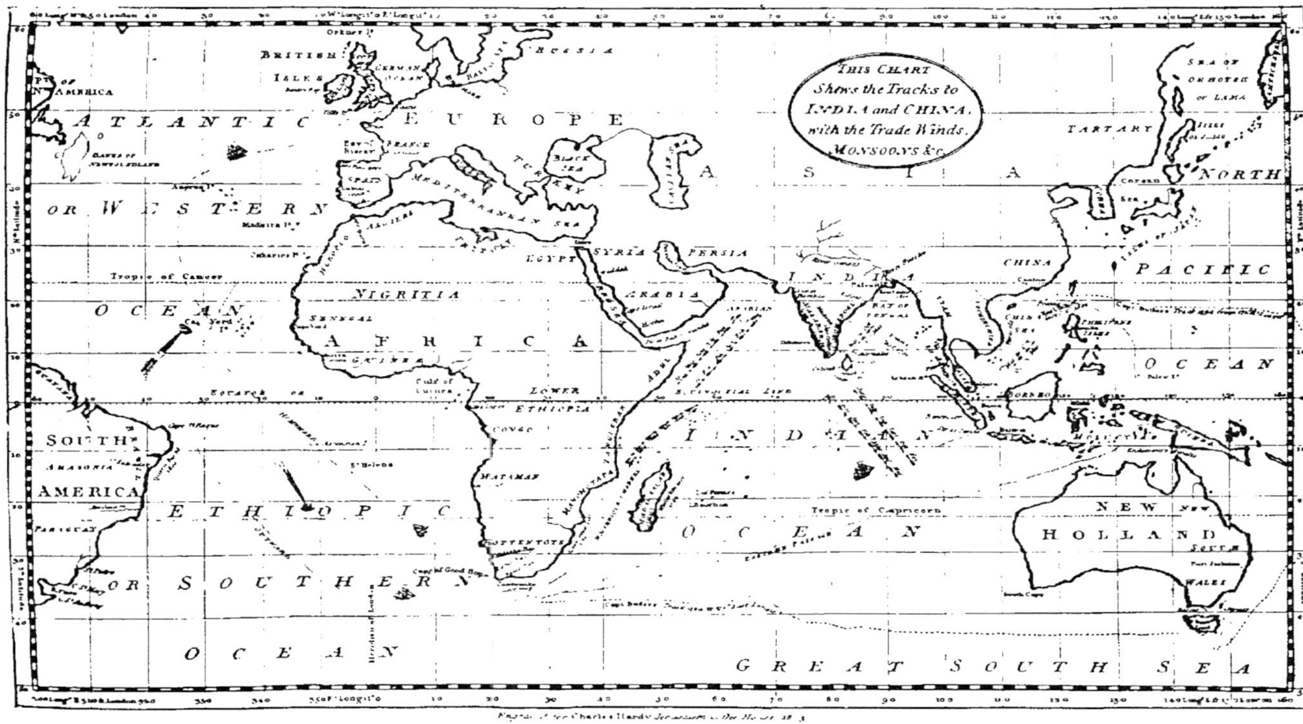

Plate III. Chart showing the courses usually steered on the voyages to India and China.

the Trade-wind scant and be forced to seek higher latitudes again. An error of fifty miles might waste a fortnight.

Ships bound for the Malabar Coast had the alternative of sailing to the east or west of Madagascar. Both routes were complicated by the fact that the Archipelago to the north-east of Madagascar was very badly charted. So were certain other parts of the Eastern Seas. And this compels us to face the historical difficulties caused by the geographical mistakes of the past. While it is essential to realise what the conditions really were, it is equally necessary to grasp what they were thought to be. The maritime affairs of the past have as their background an array not merely of physical facts but of facts imperfectly understood. It is not enough to know the facts. One must also discover the extent to which the facts were known. Ignorances and delusions are no less the facts of history for being errors in geography. Old maps and charts are all the more important for being wrong.

Now, at first glance, the maps of 1800 betray no startling degree of ignorance with regard to the Eastern Seas. Navigation was by no means in its infancy, and the maps convey what is, on the whole, a just notion of the surrounding shores. The map of New Holland, indeed, seems less misleading than the contemporary map of Scotland. Africa, although the words 'Nigritia' and 'Lower Ethiopia' account for most of the interior, has very much the shape to which one is accustomed. And even the outline of Tasmania is not wildly amiss. A closer inspection, however, will lead to the conclusion that some parts of these seas had never been surveyed, and that some of the shores were but little known. These semi-unknown regions may be said to have numbered five: first, there is Japan; second, the Philippines and the Moluccas, Borneo and the Celebes; third, the east coast of Africa; fourth, though in a lesser degree, the Red Sea and Persian Gulf; and fifth, these islands between Madagascar and Ceylon.

These different regions will be dealt with separately, but

it must be noted from the outset that these areas have something in common. For they are all places that should have been well known. It would be natural to expect that the uncharted regions would be those which had been discovered last. Yet it appears that the areas ill-represented in the atlas are almost precisely those which had been discovered first. The shores most vaguely indicated are those of lands which Europeans had frequented since the Middle Ages or the sixteenth century.

It seems clear that certain parts of the Eastern world, originally ill-charted from ignorance, were latterly kept unsurveyed from policy. Where they existed, the charts were kept in manuscript and jealously guarded. The origin of such a policy is not difficult to understand. The English, comparatively late-comers on the scene, had fought their way to the heart of the Indies. The original invaders, the Portuguese and Dutch, were left in precarious tenure of the fringes, retaining, nevertheless, the solid advantage of having arrived there first. The Portuguese, for example, had a settlement in China, a town of their own; the English had only a factory. The Dutch, almost as impotent in arms as the Portuguese, had a factory in Japan; the English hardly knew where Japan was. Even the French had their preserves in Madagascar and the Seychelles. Hence it was that the Englishman, although in the ascendant, could still be made to feel a new-comer. Whether he liked it or not, he found himself using Portuguese words and Spanish currency. What he found more difficult to obtain was a Portuguese or Spanish chart.

Now, as regards the islands between Madagascar and the mainland of India, the south-western groups were, it is evident, well known to the French, and perhaps to the Portuguese. It was among these that the French had their outposts, Mahé, Praslin, St Anne and Cerf; while some of the names are Portuguese. But the English charts, based on hearsay and legend, were, and were known to be, utterly unreliable. They represented the bank of Mahé, for example, as far less extensive than it is. And the local French traders in 'black ivory' did not become communicative on the subject of navigation until after the conquest of Mauritius. Until then they dared not show the English their charts. Men had been guillotined for less.

In a state, then, of conscious ignorance with regard to the exact position of many of these islands and shoals, English navigators were cautious in their approach to this region. It is not to be wondered at. Even the better-known Maldives and Laccadives were treated with respect; and, indeed, they were never properly surveyed until 1835. Tradition, as repeated to Linschoten and Marco Polo, gave the number of the islands as eleven or twelve thousand. To be more exact, Marco Polo gathered, both from the conversation of eminent mariners and from the writings of those acquainted with the Indian Seas, that these islands numbered exactly twelve thousand seven hundred. If this is an overestimate, it is at least true that the navigation of those waters requires considerable care. And it required more at a date when the most expensive chronometers were liable to considerable error. Making the Cape of Good Hope in 1801, Flinders, who was specially equipped for exploration, was at fault in his reckoning by three leagues or four miles according as to whether he trusted in his timepiece or his lunar observations. Other navigators had obviously to work with a much wider margin of error.

Under these conditions, the possible routes from the Cape to the Malabar Coast were reduced to two. The first, and the one commonly followed, was the Inner Passage. This led through the Mozambique Channel and then through either the Eight-Degree or the Nine-Degree Passage. This route was usually, though not always, adopted during the South-West Monsoon; from March, that is to say, until about 15 August. Ships passing the Cape after that date, or at any rate after 1 September, could not attempt the Mozambique Channel on account of the calms, variable weather and feeble or else contrary winds which they would be liable to encounter at that time of year. Instead, they went by what was known as the Middle Passage, which was possible at any season. Discovered originally by Boscawen in 1748, it was frequented from about 1750 onwards. But the French had improved on the original discovery. It was not until 1811 that the English knew of the Degree-and-a-Half Channel, which saved nearly a thousand miles. They would not have found it then but for a naval officer happening to obtain a manuscript chart in the Seychelles. The Middle Passage was not a single route, for it included a number of alternative passages among the islands. But, whatever the variations, this passage always entailed passing to the eastward of Madagascar; and the final approach to India was the same as that for the Inner Passage. It was possible, following either of these routes, to pass to the westward of the Laccadives and steer straight for Bombay or Surat; a course which might, however, entail a rougher passage than might be made under the lee of the islands.

Ships bound for the Malabar Coast would normally take care to arrive in the Indian Ocean during the South-West Monsoon. At that season the passage from the Cape could be made in five or six weeks. In July and August a fast ship might do it in a month. This was the best time of year to arrive, as the change of the monsoon takes place in September. It was only after 1 September that the Malabar Coast was considered safe. Even then, safety was only comparative, for the great storm of 1799, which wrecked over a hundred sail, occurred on 4 November.

Nevertheless, the danger of remaining on this coast during the South-West Monsoon was perhaps exaggerated. Bombay at least seems nearly always to have offered fairly adequate shelter at this season. All movement, however, along the coast was hazardous, and voyages from thence to the westward, to the Red Sea or Persian Gulf, were almost precluded. Such voyages entailed a Southern Passage; a detour, that is to say, as far southward as the Equator, which would occupy forty days if the vessel were bound for Muscat and at least two months if she were bound for Bussorah. It was always better to wait for the changing of the monsoon, even if bound for the Cape or Mauritius.

The South-West Monsoon was, on the other hand, favourable for the passage from Malabar round to the other side of India. Here, perhaps, the *Bombay Calendar* may be quoted:

> To the other side of India, on the contrary, it is now the most advantageous period of departing. From the middle of April even to the middle of August, a voyage to Madras may be made in about twelve or fifteen days; to Bengal, from fifteen to twenty days; after this time it becomes excessively tedious, from the necessity of keeping to the eastern side of the bay to avoid the violent weather on the Coromandel coast: for the same reason the south-west monsoon is eligible to leave Bombay for any of the ports in the Gulf of Bengal, or the Straits of Malacca:—hence also it is the season for sailing to China; after the 20th of August, however, what is called the direct passage to China becomes very precarious, with much probability of finding blowing weather in the China seas.

The South-West Monsoon being favourable only for voyages to the eastward, the natives of the west coast of India had a tradition that this season was not favourable for anything. This was natural because their outlook had always been towards Arabia and Persia and the old route to Europe. It was the custom for the native merchants to lay up their ships throughout the rainy season, from about 28 May to 1 September. The custom was an ancient one, based on experience, but latterly hedged with superstition, shared by all but the Parsees. It was remarked that none of the country trading vessels would put to sea before the festival which marked the end of the rainy season. The ceremony then performed consisted chiefly in throwing a gilt and decorated coconut into the sea. Only after this oblation was the sea regarded as navigable.

It is clear that the tradition just described was weakening by the beginning of the nineteenth century. Nevertheless, the Europeans could not altogether resist the weight of local prejudice. Imbibing something of it, they may have accorded the South-West Monsoon a little more respect than it deserved.

The season favourable for the voyage from the Cape to Malabar was also, of course, the best time of year for the passage to India from the Red Sea and Persian Gulf. The voyage from Muscat might take ten or twelve days, from Mocha twenty days and from Suez about a month. The Red Sea, however, allowed of no egress after the beginning of September. Ships detained beyond that date were said to have lost their passage. They had to remain there until the change of the monsoon.

> The south-west monsoon is also the most favourable season in which a passage may be made from Batavia or any ports to the eastward, through these southern straits; from Batavia to Bombay in particular, a passage may be made in about thirty-five days. From Madras and Bengal, during the south-west monsoon, it is necessary to make the southern passage in order to reach Bombay; this will require in a passage from Madras from thirty to forty days, and from Bengal from forty-five to sixty days, from the necessity of working out of the river and beating down the bay to clear Acheen-head; from the straits of Malacca it is an arduous task to sail for this port, or even to any one on the Peninsula of India, owing to the difficulty of working round Acheen-head.

To illustrate the difficulty experienced in reaching the Malabar Coast from the opposite side of the Peninsula, even as late as September, it may be said that a fast and well-manned frigate could scarcely be expected to perform the Southern Passage in less than a month. Yet, in general, the importance of these weather conditions was, for the most part, felt by merchantmen. In emergencies, a fast-sailing cruiser might sail for Bombay in the teeth of the monsoon. A merchantman would not even attempt it. In the first place, such heroics cost too much in wages, victuals, wear and tear. In the second place, ships were precluded by their insurance policies from touching on the Malabar Coast between 1 May and 1 September. Such luxuries as a Southern Passage were not within the merchant's means.

The North-East Monsoon lasts on the Malabar Coast from about 15 August to 15 April. With all India as a breakwater, the coast was then security itself. This was the season for a voyage to the westward. Muscat could be reached in a fortnight, Bussorah in less than a month. Between the middle of February and the middle of March was the time to sail for the Red Sea. The passage to Mokha might then take eighteen days, that to Suez, twenty-five. The voyage could not be delayed too long as to sail in April was to risk losing one's passage.

> Between the 15th of August and the 15th of September, it may be considered favourable to sail to Madras and Bengal; but after this time the season is suspended, owing to the setting in of the north-east monsoon on the other side of India, which closes the ports on the coast of Coromandel, Golconda, and Orissa, between the 15th of October and the 15th of December...this season may be deemed unfavourable to the coast of Pegue and the straits of Malacca; but for the straits of Sunda, Batavia, for example, it is the best adapted; a passage thither may be made in thirty-five days.

Ships sailing from Malabar for Europe would take the Inner Passage during the North-East Monsoon. This route became uncertain towards the end of the season, about February. Thenceforward, the Outer Passage was adopted, which led 'eastward of Roderigue and all the other islands situated in the western part of the Indian Ocean'. The best-known Sailing Directory, Horsburgh's, warned navigators against attempting the Middle Passage during the South-West Monsoon.

With reference to the Red Sea and Persian Gulf, it has already been remarked that these regions were but imperfectly charted. In the *East India Directory* revised by Samuel Dunn in 1780, the following advice is given to those sailing from Mokha to Jidda:

> The navigation up the Red Sea, from Mocha to Judda, is the mid-channel, the shores being incumbered with many islands and shoals; among which however there are safe channels, through which trankeys sail to Judda; but these channels are unknown to Europeans....A good look-out, both night and day, is very requisite in this track; for there are seldom soundings, and the shoals are so steep, that a ship will have 10 or 15 fathoms on rocks under one end of the ship, and no ground under the other at 60 fathoms.

Horsburgh, who wrote long afterwards, is not less gloomy nor more explicit when dealing with the Red Sea and its perils. He gives the exact position of Jidda, which had been ascertained in the course of the expedition of 1800–1. And he also mentions a particular reef in the vicinity of that town, the position of which had been ascertained at about the same time; but not before an English frigate had been totally wrecked on it. He describes a complicated system of winds and currents and ends by advising the navigator to procure a native pilot.

The navigation of the Red Sea was not wholly neglected, for reasons to be considered on a later page, but there was a tendency for trade to the westwards to fall into the hands of the merchants of Muscat. It is remarkable that this should have been the case, for Portuguese, Dutch, French and English had all at one time or another frequented both Arabia and Persia. The Portuguese, in particular, had been the masters of these seas during the period following their seizure of the Island of Hormuz in 1507. But trade had dwindled, and with it much traditional knowledge of that region.

Returning once more to the Cape, there is next to be

described the route to and from the east side of India and the Bay of Bengal. This voyage to India would normally be contrived in such a way as to allow of an arrival during the South-West Monsoon. The following account of this, which was called the Outward or Outer Passage to India, is taken from Johnson's narrative of the *Caroline's* voyage in 1803. This ship took her departure from the Cape in August:

> To ensure strong breezes after leaving the Cape, we steered to the southward as far as 38 S. latitude; in which parallel we ran down most of our longitude. This was by far the most unpleasant part of our voyage: the weather being dreary and cold, with constant gales of wind from the N.W.... Our daily progression... was from 250 to 266 miles a day, steering due east. Vide-Chart.
>
> Having got into the 70th parallel of east longitude, we shaped our course to the northward, and left this stormy latitude.... We soon got into the S.E. trades, and had no more disagreeable weather; a fine breeze wafting us along two hundred miles a day, till on the night of the 4th of September we saw the fires on the mountains of Ceylon, after a passage of one hundred and four days.

The *Caroline* was bound for Bengal. After a call at Madras, she sailed from thence early in September, near the breaking up of the South-West Monsoon, and had a tedious passage along the Coromandel Coast. Nevertheless, this was well under the average time for the voyage to India. It usually took five or six months altogether. The passage from the Cape to the Coromandel Coast might take from two to three months. Ships arriving during the North-East Monsoon had to make a detour to the eastward, as far as 89° or 90° E., if bound for Madras; and ships bound for Bengal might even pass to the eastward of the Nicobars and Andamans.

In sailing for Europe from the east side of India, the Outer Passage was followed. In the South-West Monsoon it was necessary to keep well to the eastward. But the best time for sailing was January or February. At that time of year a course could be steered for the Cape almost the same as that steered from the Cape during the South-West Monsoon. Ships would pass to the east and south of Mauritius, make the Natal Coast and round the Cape with the help of the current from the Mozambique Channel. From the Cape to England, the course lay fairly close to Africa and ended with a circuit to the westwards, passing to the west of the Azores. This return voyage would take about six months as a rule, and it usually involved a call at St Helena. There were instances of ships making the passage in a considerably shorter time. The *Medusa* frigate, for example, made a record-breaking passage in 1805–6. She sighted the Lizard eighty-four days out from the Hooghly. As she had spent two days at anchor in St Helena Roads, she was only eighty-two days under sail; and in that time she travelled thirteen thousand eight hundred and thirty-one miles—an average of over a hundred and sixty-eight miles a day. But such a feat was, of course, exceptional; and, until that time, unheard of. A passage of four months would be thought very creditable and a passage of five months would be described as good.

The navigation of the Bay of Bengal was not complicated by lack of knowledge. The difficulties arose, rather, from the nature of things. First of all, it must be noted that the Coromandel Coast is a lee shore throughout the North-East Monsoon; a shore, moreover, without a single natural harbour except for Trincomalee in Ceylon, which is a refuge, although not on the coast itself. During this monsoon, therefore, the Coromandel Coast was to be avoided. All interest was confined to the other side of the bay at this season. Ships from the southward bound for Bengal would then keep close along the Malay Coast. Ships might enter or leave the Hooghly throughout the year, but it was during the North-East Monsoon and especially towards the end of the season that ships preferred to sail from thence.

From the middle of March, southerly winds tended to retard vessels sailing from Bengal; nor did sailings again become frequent until the beginning of August. The period of the South-West Monsoon, however, was the time for navigating the Coromandel Coast. Without a single sheltered anchorage during one season, the whole coast was a kind of roadstead during the other. Shelter from the monsoon is derived partly from the mainland of India, partly from the Island of Ceylon. It was during the South-West Monsoon that ships could ride safely at anchor in Madras Roads; and it was then that ships would touch there on their way up to Bengal.

The goal of most navigators of the bay is and has always been the entrance to Bengal River; the Hooghly. Although not altogether unlike the Thames Estuary, the Hooghly is still more reminiscent of the Elbe. And, like the Elbe, it has its dangers.

> The entrance into the river Hoogly is allowed to be the most difficult of any river in India; and is the terror of strangers....
>
> The S.W. monsoon, in the bottom of the Bay of Bengal, always brings in thick weather, with drizzling rain, and prevents observations (at times) for many days; by which strangers are much at a loss, and afraid to run in for Point Palmiras....

So Elmore hints at the dangers of the river. And it may be noted that, whereas the approach to the Hooghly during the South-West Monsoon is often complicated by thick weather, it is also the approach to a lee shore. During the North-East Monsoon, on the other hand, it was a great deal more difficult, even if a little less dangerous, for it entailed beating to windward in a very narrow channel.

To the dangers arising from weather one must add those arising from shoal water, sandbanks, and the lowness of the coast. The water shoals so gradually that a ship may be in ten fathoms while still twelve or more leagues from the river mouth, and while still out of sight of the land. A seaman in doubt as to his exact position would be aware that, somewhere ahead of him, the sands encumbering the river mouth stretched far out seawards. Their position, in the complete absence of landmarks, might be ascertained by constant sounding, by sighting the buoys which marked the channels; and, again, by running hard aground.

Once discovered, the various channels were sufficiently buoyed, and there was, and had long been, an efficient pilot service—the more essential in that the sands are continually shifting. Special brigs and snows were constantly stationed at the ten-fathom line, ready to conduct ships into the river. And no pilot who had wrecked an Indiaman was ever employed again. Even so, bad luck or bad seamanship might produce disaster. The great sandbanks curve south-eastward like the prongs of a gigantic fork; the Western and Eastern Braces, Barabulla Sand, Long Sand and the Eastern Sea-Reef—much like the Scharhorn Reef or the Grosser Vogel Sand familiar to Hamburgers, except that their seaward ends are safely covered. Where these hard flats come to an end, some seven leagues out, is the region called the Sandheads.

During the North-East Monsoon the passage from Bengal River to the Coromandel Coast might require five or six days. The same passage, during the South-West Monsoon, might take five weeks or more, except at the beginning and end of the season, when a fortnight might suffice. To work against the monsoon, a good ship was needed and a knowledge of the currents.

The contrary passage up the bay is well described in the *East India Vade-Mecum*:

> ...the voyage from Madras to Bengal will depend, in regard to duration, entirely upon the season. If the southerly monsoon prevails, Point Palmiras, which is at the southern boundary of Balasore Roads, may be made in from three to seven days: during the northerly monsoon, it is usual, experience having confirmed what accident probably first suggested, to stretch over to the opposite side of the bay upon a wind, and then to run obliquely across on the other tack, so as to arrive in soundings off the mouth of the Hooghly, where the tides will speedily convey a vessel up to

any place on the river, notwithstanding the wind's direction. During the passage, under the former prevalence, the land is not, in general, seen until the water becomes obviously discolored with sand. In the first instance, the course is made directly from Madras Roads, to gain a good offing, whereby the dangerous shoals of Pulicat, about five miles north of Madras, may be avoided: the land all along the coast being invariably low, and the shallows projecting, in some places, full ten miles seaward, it is prudent to keep rather towards the middle of the bay, and from a N.N.E. course, to change latterly to a N.N.W.; rounding in, when the latitude directs, until Point Palmiras may be from four to six leagues distant....

At the change of the monsoon in October, there is generally a gale on the Coromandel Coast, which ships might escape only by standing out to sea, and, as on the other Coast, insurance companies and underwriters did not lose sight of the fact. It was understood that no policy covered ships on the Coast, from Cape Comorin to Point Palmiras, between 16 October and 15 December. Gales also occur, though not so regularly, at the other change of the monsoon. In May 1811 there was a storm in which a hundred and twenty vessels were lost in Madras Roads, driven ashore or foundered at their moorings. This was quite exceptional. But even at normal times, the coast had certain disadvantages. Immense shoals stretch from Tranquebar up to the Ganges. Such ports as there were, Pondicherry, Cuddalore and Negapatam, situated opposite gaps in this barrier, were few and far between. It must be remembered, too, that, except for the smallest craft, there is no passage between Ceylon and the mainland. This made the coast, when a lee shore, all the more dangerous, Palk Strait, with its reefs, being a trap rather than a means of escape. Moreover, even at Madras itself, and at the most favourable time of year, there is a heavy surf which often made landing difficult or impossible.

From Bengal to China, the natural route lies between Cape Negrais and the Andamans and so through the Straits or

Malacca. For this voyage the best time of year was the end of the North-East Monsoon. A ship might then have a following wind through the straits and reach the China Seas in time to have the first of the South-West Monsoon to take her up to Canton. A quick return voyage could be made on the same principle. From the Coromandel Coast, the route to China might also lead through the Straits of Malacca, by way of the Ten-Degree Channel.

The normal course from Europe to China or from the Malabar Coast to China led through the Straits of Sunda. This route might also be taken from Madras. The alternative straits to the eastward, used sometimes in time of war, were those of Lombok and Bali. The other straits had hardly been explored, and indeed the two mentioned above were very ill-charted. As late as 1789 the East India Company's hydrographer was endeavouring to discover the exact longitude of the Straits of Allas, Lombok and Bali. 'The charts of Java', he wrote, 'differ several degrees in its extent from west to east, and there are no observations that have come into my hands, competent to determine the exact situation of the east end of Java.' The H.C.S. *Vansittart* was ordered to reconnoitre the eastward straits, and also to find out whether the passage to the east of Banca Island would be preferable to the better known passage to the west. Captain Lestock Wilson's success was only moderate, it seems, for the *Vansittart* was wrecked and the eastward straits remained unsurveyed. Captain Beaver, R.N., passed through the Straits of Bali in 1811 on his way from Mauritius to Batavia. These are his remarks: 'We are now running through the Straits of Balli, all my charts of which resemble it just as much as they do the Sea of Marmora, and no more.' The Straits of Sunda were better known, but no part of this region had been thoroughly surveyed. This was evidently the result of Dutch jealousy; in which connection the following remarks of the Dutch Rear-Admiral Stavorinus are enlightening:

It is really to be lamented, that so powerful a body as the [Dutch] East India Company, and whose prosperity so much depends upon the safe and prosperous voyages of the ships, should trouble themselves so little with the improvement of navigation in general, and the correction of their charts in particular. I could adduce many instances of their faultiness, both with respect to the Indies, and to the coast of Africa. Other nations pursue this object with indefatigable assiduity, especially the English, whose maps are, in general, infinitely preferable to ours....

Much stress is laid, among the Company's servants, upon the great danger of the navigation to the eastward of Batavia, which may possibly be encouraged underhand, for political reasons, by persons in power; but I did not, in fact, find it so bad, at least as far as Celebes, or Macasser, as is pretended. It would be well if the charts of these parts, which the Company give to their vessels, were correct; it is this that makes the navigation so dangerous. None of the islands which I met with, except the group called the Hen and Chickens, are laid down in their true latitudes....This inaccuracy not only renders these charts useless but likewise extremely dangerous; for instead of being, as they ought, the surest guide and dependence of the navigator, they mislead him and become his bane. It is not impossible but this may be purposely left so, and that it is an adopted opinion, that it is better to expose a few ships to the danger of shipwreck, than to correct errors, which might operate to render the navigation towards the Spice Islands difficult and hazardous for other nations; for it cannot be pretended that this notorious faultiness is unknown to the Company....

There are other reasons for supposing that the Dutch made a secret of everything connected with the Spice Islands. But their navigational methods did not, in any case, tend to produce very reliable observations. In steering a course, they were said to keep within a quarter of a point, and attempt no greater degree of accuracy. They heaved no log and made no allowance for the sun's declination when on a different meridian from that for which their tables were calculated. Often more than ten degrees out in their reckoning, it is not to be wondered at if their hydrography was at fault.

The passage from, say, Ceylon to the Straits of Sunda might

take a month or five weeks. From England, the passage to the southward, passing near St Paul or Amsterdam and checking position again by North-West Cape in Western Australia, would probably, as a rule, take about five months. But it could be done in a shorter period. The *Alceste* frigate in 1816 made Java Head ninety-two days out from Spithead, not counting the time she spent at Rio Janeiro on the way; fourteen thousand miles covered at an average speed of over a hundred and fifty miles a day. As if to illustrate, however, the unsurveyed state of the Dutch East Indies, she was wrecked on an unknown rock between Banca and Pulo Leat while on her homeward voyage from China.

Most of the routes to Canton converged in the South China Sea. From there to the Bocca Tigris there were two alternative routes, the Inside and the Outside Passages. By the former, a ship passed to the westward of the Paracel Shoal, by the latter to the eastward. The Inside Passage was more generally used.

The China Seas themselves were dominated by the monsoons even more than was the Indian Ocean. Few ships attempted to make headway against the North-East Monsoon in the China Seas. Occasionally, however, ships would circumvent it by what was called the Eastern Passage, which led south of the Moluccas, north of New Guinea and well to the westward of the Philippines. Captain Wilson, of the H.C.S. *Pitt* had discovered some such possibility in 1758. The *Earl Talbot* Indiaman was lost while attempting this feat in 1800. Mention has already been made of Captain Butler's passage in 1794; this also was a method of evading the monsoon, although his object was more probably the evading of enemy cruisers.

Those sailing to or from China were usually careful to avoid being at sea in those regions at certain periods of the year which were thought especially liable to bad weather. The Typhoon, which was then spelt either as Tuffoon or Ty-Foong, was especially to be feared at the autumnal equinox. It was then, in September 1802, that the *Nautilus* of Calcutta was lost near the Lema Isles at the same time as a Spanish frigate. Ships caught in a typhoon near the China Coast were thought fortunate if they escaped with dismasting.

Since the expulsion of the Portuguese, Japan was known only to the Dutch. It was not until 1804, when two Russian exploring vessels visited Nagasaki, that the exact position of that port was known. An English frigate called there in 1808. Before that date the English knew practically nothing of Japan beyond the mere fact of its existence and that the Dutch traded there.

Before quitting the subject of Navigation and the Winds, it is necessary to warn the reader that the facts here stated concerning the winds are only very approximately correct. Fixed and traditional rules existed, which many seamen were content to follow: this voyage was possible only at this season, that coast denied approach at that time of year. But there were other seamen who had begun to study not only the rules but also the exceptions; who had begun to discover how the impossible might be done.

> There is no part of the world of coasts, continents, oceans, seas, straits, capes, and islands which is not under the sway of a reigning wind, the sovereign of its typical weather. The wind rules the aspects of the sky and the action of the sea. But no wind rules unchallenged....

So wrote Joseph Conrad. And while some navigators were shocked and angry to find the sway of a prevailing wind less absolute than they had believed it, a few took note and discovered a rhythm in the eccentricities of the weather. And such discoveries were valuable. Here is an example, a remark made by a certain Captain M'Intosh:

> Although the Southerly winds commence with March on all the Indian Shores *presenting a front to the East*, and prevail also in the Northern parts of the different Bays, Yet this Monsoon seldom

becomes general on Malabar much before June, is as late as May on the East side of the Bengal Bay and it is even July before it attains strength on the East part of the Chinese Sea: and although the circumstance escapes common notice we find in fact this periodical wind nearly exhausted in one quarter while on the other it is only acquiring strength, thus presenting facilities to commercial or other Enterprize hitherto but little availed....

Marco Polo, writing concerning the Sea of Chin, in which the Island of Zipangu is situated, remarked that 'so extensive is this eastern sea, that according to the report of experienced pilots and mariners who frequent it, and to whom the truth must be known, it contains no fewer than seven thousand four hundred and forty islands...'. He goes on to add, before quitting the subject, that 'in these regions only two winds prevail; one of them during the winter, and the other during the summer season...'. Whatever may be thought of Marco Polo's statistics, they at least convey a right impression of navigational complexity. But his account of the winds is all too simple; later seamen were to find that the monsoons were not the only winds to reckon with.

Chapter V

EAST INDIAMEN

NEARLY every Indiaman was built at one of perhaps a dozen shipyards in the Thames. There were only twenty-two shipbuilding firms of any size in 1814, and there can hardly have been as many in 1800. Of those then existing only a limited number were capable of building a 1200-ton, or even an 800-ton ship. So that, in practice, most Indiamen, large or small, came from one or other of the eight or ten principal yards. At the beginning of the century the leading firms were Randall's, Barnard's, Perry's, Pitcher's and Wells's; and it was mainly at these yards that the larger ships were built. Some were launched at Batson's, Melluish's or Clevely's. Others, especially at the end of the period with which we are dealing, were built by Dudman and Co., S. and D. Brent, or Curling and Co.

Pitcher and Sons had two yards, one at Blackwall and the other at Northfleet. Barnard's, which later became Barnard and Robarts's, was at Deptford. Curling and Co. had their establishment at Rotherhithe. Perry's yard was at Blackwall, Dudman's at Deptford. All these yards were of great size, capable not only of building the largest ships but of building several of them simultaneously. All, too, engaged largely in repairing and refitting ships; a more profitable business, it was said, than constructing them. Randall's, which later became Randall and Brent's, and, later still, Brent's, had in the end no less than seven building slips, two double and one single repairing dock, and so might, at least in theory, have work proceeding on a dozen ships at once. There were five launching ways at Dudman's, and two double docks. Altogether, in 1814, there were in the Thames forty-one building slips and sixty-two berths for repair in dry dock.

It would be interesting to discover where exactly the old Thames shipyards stood. The sites of some of them are now, presumably, lost in the immensity of the more recently constructed wet docks; but of others it is possible to give the approximate position. The Deptford yard of Dudman's, for example, is easily traceable. It lay between Grove Street and the river, just at the point where Windmill Lane connects Grove Street with the Lower Road. The site is bounded on the south by that of the still existing Royal Victualling Yard, and the basin remains to be seen almost opposite Millwall Pier. Randall and Brent's yard was in Lower Queen Street, Rotherhithe, a highway now absorbed in Rotherhithe Street at its eastern end. This yard must have been almost directly opposite the present West India Docks Pier. Mr Batson's yard was on the other side of the river, just south of Limehouse Hole. Mr Wells's, one of the larger yards, was in Lower Trinity Street, Rotherhithe. This was the name then given, it seems, to Derrick Street and its continuation northwards as far as Trinity Road; so that Wells's must have been a little north of the Commercial Docks Pier. Very nearly opposite to Shadwell Dock was Mestaer's, a small firm, the yard of which probably stood near the present entrance to Albion Dock and not far from Rotherhithe Tunnel. Builders' yards were thus to be found all along the river from the Lower Pool to Blackwall, and at Blackwall was the yard still known during most of our period as Perry's.

Of all these yards, Perry's was perhaps the most interesting. It is cited not as being typical but as the yard about which most is known. It was founded about 1588 as 'The East India Yard' and was owned originally by the Company itself. The Company's arms were over the gate and the East India chapel adjoined the yard, which was completed by about 1612.

Henry Johnson, a cousin of Phineas Pett, was builder there throughout most of the seventeenth century and built men-of-war impartially for Cromwell and Charles II. Passing at some period into private hands, the yard was the property of the Perry family by 1693. During our period there were two partners in the yard, the reigning Mr Perry, who had been the head of the firm since 1776, and his former apprentice and son-in-law, George Green. On John Perry's death in 1810, the Perry shares were bought by Sir Robert Wigram. Green lived until 1849, and under him and two of Wigram's sons the Blackwall yard became almost a national institution, outdistancing competition in a special branch of the trade.

Unconscious of its destiny, the Blackwall yard was but one of several rival yards in 1793. Indeed, it was not yet known as the Blackwall yard. It was still merely Perry's. The peculiarity of Perry's yard was that it comprised a wet dock, the Brunswick Dock, begun in 1789; a large double basin with a masthouse at one end. The masthouse was a prominent and well-known landmark in the Thames, and the dock was probably used chiefly for masting and re-rigging the Company's ships. It was not used, as far as one can judge, for loading or unloading anything but provisions and stores, for it was not walled. The basins now form the East India Export Dock.

The process by which an Indiaman was built began with the acceptance of the tender from the prospective managing owner, who had previously come to an agreement with one of the building firms. The terms of the agreement would depend on the level of wages and the price of timber; and the cost of building may be said to have increased fairly steadily throughout the war. An 800-ton ship could be built for £14 per ton in 1793. The rate had risen to £21. 15*s*. 6*d*. by 1801, and was later to rise further still.

The firms which built the Company's ships also contracted to build for the Navy whenever the opportunity was given them. Their doing so was a check on the building of other vessels; a check, one result of which was to prolong the 'life' of the existing Indiamen. The maximum of six voyages was increased to eight, at the Government's instigation, in 1803; and increased again indefinitely in 1810. There was a respite in 1801, when the naval building programmes were curtailed as a result of the Peace of Amiens. As a consequence, eight Indiamen were launched in that year, and sixteen in 1802. The Addington administration, meanwhile, in which Earl St Vincent was First Lord of the Admiralty, had set its face against contract-built men-of-war. This policy, which drove the Thames builders back to the building of merchantmen and which was very largely responsible for the spate of new Indiamen in 1802, aroused a great deal of opposition. The builders, with their friends on the Navy Board, were behind most of the clamour. Pitt seized the occasion to enlist these interested parties in a campaign to overturn the Government. Popular fears were easily worked upon, and Addington and St Vincent accordingly went out of office in 1804. John Perry and Robert Wigram, who obtained his baronetcy from Pitt in 1805, were prominent supporters of Pitt in this campaign and must be included therefore in 'the corrupt band of detected speculators' who had to do with Addington's fall. The new cabinet of 1804 thus came in committed to the policy of building by contract. This told inversely on the building of Indiamen. Six ships were launched for the Company's service in 1804, two only in 1805, one in 1806 and none in 1807. Not many more were built before 1811.

It has been stated that nearly all Indiamen were built in the Thames. None, probably, had been built elsewhere—of the regular ships, that is to say—before 1786; and but few were built elsewhere even after 1796. Those built subsequently to that date at other English ports were mostly ordered by new managing owners who had no connection with the Thames builders. Several of these came from Yarmouth, Liverpool and Buckler's Hard. One or two were launched at more unexpected places like Chester and Topsham; and one, in 1817, at Ipswich. Fiott, who had one ship built at Itchenor, near Chichester, said that he might as easily have ordered it at Southampton, Bursledon or Harwich. Apart from those built elsewhere in England, a few Indiamen were built in India, the first of these being built as early as 1735. These ships, built almost invariably at Bombay, were sometimes owned by the Company itself. There were two of them in 1801, and others were built later, without their becoming, however, much more numerous. Through accidental circumstances one was built at Penang. Until the end, however, of the Company's day, and even after that day was over, the East India ships continued to be built, for the most part, in the Thames. During the period 1794–1813 ninety-eight Indiamen were launched in the river. These included nearly all the big ships of the 1200-ton class—which mostly came, indeed, from one or other of the half-dozen leading firms.

It was usual for the managing owner to appoint the captain before even tendering his ship and long before the vessel was either laid down or named. This was because every tender had to be in a particular form as laid down in the Company's regulations, and because the captain's name was supposed to appear in this document. It also, of course, saved the managing owner from the spate of petitions he might otherwise receive. Captains sometimes had the opportunity of supervising the construction of their future ships, but this was not the object of the regulation enforcing early appointment, as the average captain would be at sea during the time his next ship was built.

Although normally absent during the construction of his ship, the captain was usually present at the launch. The launching of an Indiaman was a formidable affair. Galleries were built for the friends of the captain and the owners, and other spectators would come down the river in boats. Workmen from the yard and casual onlookers would crowd on both banks. And when it was all over there would be a banquet, at which popular singers would render songs about Hearts of Oak and the Death of Nelson. The cost of these banquets was borne by the owners and 'Launching and survey dinners...£70' formed a regular item in any building estimate. After the launching of the *Union* and the *Lady Castlereagh* in 1803, from Mr Randall's shipyard at Rotherhithe, three hundred and seventy persons dined in the modelling loft at 4.30. At 6.0 the ladies retired to take tea at Mr Randall's house, and in the evening there was a ball, with dancing till midnight. Then there was supper, and the party finally broke up at 2.0 a.m. On another occasion:

> The Northampton East Indiaman, of 542 tons, was lately launched at the King and Queen Dock, Rotherhithe. At the top of the tide she turned off the stocks very finely, the launch being gradual. At the turn of the tide, yesterday, she was taken into dock to finish her coppering....Captain Barker, the owner, provided a very elegant dinner at the London Tavern, for three hundred persons; it was set out in the loft (i.e. workshop) where 180 ladies took their seats: in the evening the tables were removed, and the scene concluded with a ball....(1801.)

Even the smallest of the Company's ships evidently made something of a sensation. They did not consider a 542-ton ship small in those days. The two following reports date from the same prolific period of building as the first:

> November 21. A new ship, built for the Honourable East India Company's service, of 800 tons burthen, called the Baring, to be commanded by Captain Meadows, was launched from Messrs Barnard's yard, Deptford...after which a most elegant cold collation, provided from the London Tavern, was given to upwards of four hundred ladies and gentlemen, at which Robert Charnock, Esq., the owner, presided. Dignum, and some other vocal performers attended upon the occasion.
>
> November 23. An East Indiaman, to be commanded by Captain Alexander Nash, but in his absence by Captain John Locke, was launched from Messrs Randal and Brent's yard, Rotherhithe, and named...Marchioness of Exeter.

The report which follows refers to an 'extra ship'—a vessel freighted by the Company for a single voyage, or for two or three voyages, but not admitted to the regular service:

> ...A new ship, called the Retreat, of the burthen of 548 tons, has lately been launched at Liverpool. She was built by Robert Wigram Esq. and is engaged by the Directors of the East India Company to proceed to the Presidency of Bengal, for a cargo of gruff goods.

Robert Wigram was not, of course, the builder; although this account might seem to indicate that he was. The 'Esq.' after his name is accurate and the word 'by' should read 'for'. 'Gruff goods' were imports from India of small value in proportion to their bulk: cotton, rice, sugar or saltpetre. Goods of this description were often entrusted to the smaller ships, and particularly 'extra ships', because these were thought especially liable to capture and so unfitted to carry a more valuable cargo.

The managing owner of a ship usually engaged with the Company to have the vessel launched by a certain date and 'afloat', that is, ready for lading, by another date. Sometimes, however, the day for launching had to be postponed; in some cases because of a strike among the shipwrights. The builders and owners were so notoriously in league with each other that they had no real ground for complaint when they found a powerful trade-union organisation among the men they employed. This did not, however, prevent them complaining; and it is from their complaints and excuses offered to the Committee of Shipping that one learns of the 'unprecedented and notorious combination of the shipwrights in the River' which brought work to a temporary standstill in the summer of 1802. Mr Henry Bonham it was who used this phrase in explaining to the Committee why the *Lord Melville* was not launched at the appointed time. And he enclosed with his letter an enlightening communication from the builder, Mr Dudman, in answer to his repeated requests on the subject:

Deptford, 11th June, 1803.

Sir

In answer to your letter of the 9th instant, requesting that I will explain the cause of the delay in launching the ship, Lord Melville, I have to state that although I had contracted to launch the ship the last spring tides in December, 1802, in which case she would have been afloat the 23rd January last, it proved to be absolutely impossible for me to do so, from causes which were not in my power to foresee or prevent; for, on the 10th May, 1802, the whole body of sawyers on the River formed a combination, and refused to work but on their own terms, which were so exorbitant, that not only the ship builders, but every other tradesman employing sawyers was, for the good of the community, obliged to resist it; and it was not until the 29th July that they returned to their duty: and I am sorry to state, that no sooner had we got the better of this combination, than another of a more serious nature broke out, which was that public and notorious combination of the shipwrights and caulkers, who also positively refused to go on with the work they had agreed to perform on your ship, as well as others: and I beg leave further to state, that this combination was so strong, as to baffle the united endeavours of the ship-builders to break it; and I am fully persuaded, that it would not have been accomplished in time to have fitted out the East India ships of that season, had not the principal ship builders, in July last, waited on Jacob Bosanquet, Esq. to make known the alarming situation in which the East India shipping stood, and to request he would be pleased to use his interest with the Honorable Court of Directors to make application to the Lords Commissioners of the Admiralty to grant them assistance, by permitting the workmen of His Majesty's dock-yards to come out and work on the East-India shipping in the merchants' yards: which request was complied with on the 9th July, by a letter directed to Even Nepean Esq.; and on the 20th orders were issued from the Admiralty to the officers of His Majesty's dock-yards, to supply one hundred caulkers; and on the 28th July, as the caulkers were coming up from Chatham, they were met by the River people, and grossly insulted and forced back to their respective homes, and threatened to murder them, if they dared to return again; and on this being made known to the Lords of the Admiralty, their Lordships were pleased to direct the Diligence sloop of war to take in the men, and proceed to Deptford: and on the 9th August, the sloop arrived off the yard, and on the 10th landed the men, and set them to work on the several ships. On the 23d, a supply of shipwrights was sent up in one of His Majesty's gun-brigs, and on the 26th I was then enabled to get up the ship's stem, and not before. On the 27th crossed some floor timbers: and on the 31st arrived another gun-brig with a further supply of shipwrights and caulkers. And I have the pleasure to state, that this very great exertion, on the part of Government, began to work a good effect on the minds of the people of the River, and brought them a little to a sense of their duty; but their behaviour was so unsettled, that no dependance could be placed in them: and it was the month of November before the King's people were all returned, and His Majesty's sloop Diligence detained until February last, to enforce obedience.

Although highly skilled, the Thames shipwrights were a turbulent body of men with ancient family traditions and a strong corporate feeling which showed itself in jealousy of the outsider. Especially in building men-of-war, they were often accused of idleness and dishonesty; and often, no doubt, with reason. The shipping system of the East India Company, which is still to be described, had therefore this to be said for it, that it provided each ship with an owner a great deal less remote than the Company itself. Many a shipwright capable of cheating an abstraction like the Government would hesitate to cheat Mr Wigram or Captain Barker.

It remains to describe the Indiaman. The inevitable way of doing this is by comparison with the man-of-war of the period. And here, at the outset, one is faced with the difficulty caused by different methods of tonnage measurement, and by lists of dimensions in which length between perpendiculars is confused with length of keel or length over-all. All figures relating to tonnage must be treated with the utmost caution. A correspondent wrote to the *Naval Chronicle* in 1799 to point out that merchantmen, designed as they were with a view to evading a heavy tax on tonnage, had a greater burthen than they measured; and that ships-of-war had, for some reason, a lesser burthen than they measured. In this way, the *Hindostan* East Indiaman was rated at 1248 tons but actually carried 1890 tons; while the famous 100-gun ship, H.M.S. *Victory*, was rated at 2143 tons and carried only 1839. From this it would appear that the Indiaman was the larger ship of the two by fifty-one tons. No very definite conclusion can be drawn from a statement of this kind as no authority is given for the figures. Nevertheless, it is certain that the method then used for measuring tonnage had important and mischievous results on the design of the ships.

The method of calculating tonnage was to multiply the length of the keel by the extreme breadth, multiply the product by the half-breadth and then divide by ninety-four. Into this calculation the depth of the hold does not enter, and owners were consequently tempted to increase the depth without increasing the other dimensions in proportion. More especially were they inclined at all costs to avoid increasing the breadth. The tendency, then, was to produce a long, deep, and crank vessel, far too narrow for her size. It was in breadth that the East India ships were markedly inferior to ships-of-war, which had always to be broad enough to allow for the recoil of their guns.

Too frequently the mistake has been made of regarding Indiamen as equivalent to frigates. Actually, few of them seem to have resembled frigates very closely except in the number of their guns. An 800-ton ship might perhaps have been mistaken for a frigate, but the 1200-ton Indiaman, while manned with as few men as a sloop, looked far more like a line-of-battle ship. The 1300–1500-ton Indiamen were not easily to be distinguished from 74-gun ships.

Although the table of dimensions given on the following page affords but an imperfect means of comparison, it may serve to indicate the main difference between men-of-war and Indiamen; the difference in the proportion of length and beam. As the proportion of 1 : 3 was held to be the most desirable, it is clear that this difference was wholly in favour of the men-of-war. The smaller Indiamen, moreover, departed still further from this rule of proportion. In this and the following table, length between perpendiculars and length on the gun-deck may be taken as equivalent.

Name	Guns	Length between perpendiculars	Length of keel	Length of gun deck	Extreme breadth	Depth in hold	Tons	Built
H.M.S.		ft: in.	ft. in.	ft. in.	ft. in.	ft. in.		
Culloden	74	—	138 11	170 0	47 8¼	20 1	1638	1783
Powerful	74	—	138 1	168 6	47 ¾	19 8½	1627	1783
H.C.S.								
Hope	34	194 0	144 0	—	43 6	17 5	1498	1797
Cumberland	36	184 0	144 0	—	42 8	17 2	1352	1802

The 1200-ton Indiamen, as distinct from huge 1400-ton ships like the *Arniston*, *Ceres*, *Coutts* and *Hope*, closely resembled 64-gun ships, as the following table will show.

Name	Guns	Length between perpendiculars	Length of keel	Length of gun deck	Extreme breadth	Depth in hold	Tons	Built
H.M.S.		ft. in.	ft. in.	ft. in.	ft. in.	ft. in.		
Belliqueux	64	—	131 6½	160 0	44 4	19 0	1376	1780
Lancaster	64	—	144 0	172 2	43 0	17 6	1416	1796
H.C.S.								
(Unknown)	38	165 6	134 0	—	42 0	17 0	1257	1804

The Indiaman here cited is no particular ship. The dimensions given are those of an average 1200-ton ship as represented by the plans in Steel's *Naval Architecture*. The 800-ton Indiaman was a much shorter vessel, perhaps resembling a two-decked 50-gun ship more than a frigate. Such a ship might measure about 150 feet between perpendiculars, 116 feet on the keel, and 35 feet broad; or perhaps 118 feet along the keel and 36 feet broad. A 600-ton ship might measure 125 feet between perpendiculars, 100 feet on the keel, and 34 feet in breadth. A 500-ton ship might measure 102 feet on the keel and 31 feet broad. It was, on the whole, the 800-ton ships which most violated the canons of proportion, some being as much as 10 feet longer than was warranted by their breadth. The 1200-ton ships also exceeded the proper proportion, but not in the same degree.

More illuminating than figures is the impression made on the beholder. Captain Marryat, in his novel *Newton Forster*, begins a descriptive paragraph with the words: 'The Indiaman was a 1200-ton ship, as large as one of the small seventy-fours in the King's service....' Again, when the French Admiral Sercey, with a squadron of six frigates, met as many homeward bound China ships off the north end of Java in 1797, he took them for two sail of the line and four frigates and fled accordingly. Admiral Linois made a similar mistake in 1804, when he credited some of the China fleet with sixty-four guns each. There were instances, too, of French privateers going in chase of English 74-gun ships under the impression that they were Indiamen. Since some of the larger Indiamen could mount as many as sixty guns, and, when brought into the Navy, as some of them were, actually did so, this sort of error was not easily avoidable.

Among the biggest Indiamen afloat towards the end of the war were the *Royal Charlotte*, *Walmer Castle*, *Arniston*, *Hope*, *Cirencester*, *Coutts*, *Cuffnells*, *Glatton*, *Neptune* and *Thames*. The first of these had, it was said, an extreme length of 194 feet, and was therefore a great deal longer than any ordinary third-rate. Some of the later ships, like the Earl of Balcarres, were hardly distinguishable from three-deckers except by the absence of poop.

Although built by contract, an Indiaman was, in a sense, under the Company's eye from the moment its keel was laid. The Committee of Shipping had under its direction several departments, including the Shipping Office, the Pay Office and the Master Attendants' Office. It was through this last institution that the builders were, to some extent, controlled. The master attendant and his chief surveyor of shipping were two important officials, who had under them four assistants, ten inspectors, thirty-nine surveyors and a proper number of clerks and menials. It was the duty of this swarm of people to see that the ships built were all exactly as specified in their contracts. It is probable that they succeeded in doing this; otherwise the builders would not have turned so eagerly to build ships-of-war. A ship of the line was, it is true, somewhat more expensive than an East Indiaman; costing, as it did, from £25 to £31 a ton. But it was also a little more expensive to build. Judging from results, it would seem that the Government surveyed less strictly than the Company, either from lack of experience or lack of honesty in the men it employed. To detect bad workmanship or unseasoned timber in a ship on the stocks may well have been a business as highly skilled as it was dangerous.

Besides the surveyors employed by the Company, there were eight more surveyors employed by the owners. These were probably concerned more with repairs than with building. It was presumably their object to oversee the refitting of ships and prevent peculation at the expense of the owners.

Two thousand loads of oak, a hundred tons of wrought iron and thirty tons of copper might go to the making of one of the larger Indiamen. It was not surprising, therefore, that alarm was felt concerning the supply of timber for the Navy. Of copper there does not seem to have been any serious shortage, although the Company probably drove the price up against the Navy Board, so that it was altogether desirable that Indiamen should be made to last as long as possible. The introduction of copper sheathing about 1780 had lengthened the effective life of shipping in general, and it enabled the Company to retain ships for six voyages instead of four; that is, for about twelve or fourteen years instead of eight or ten. The period of service, latterly extended more or less indefinitely, might, of course, be longer or shorter according to the state of the ship's timbers. It was customary to give each ship a very thorough examination and repair at the end of her third voyage. After that, she would normally last for another three voyages. If then found to be worn out she passed out of the Company's service.

Once an Indiaman was sold she was almost always broken up. None but the smallest Indiaman could be used in any other trade. The difficulty was one of manning so large a ship. There would have been little difficulty in selling an Indiaman in India, where native seamen were cheap and plentiful. But the ship which went out of the Company's service almost always did so in the Thames, after returning there with cargo. And, once there, she could not return to India without infringing the Company's monopoly.

One effect of the timber shortage was to bring about several great improvements in the construction of the East India ships. The want, more especially, of crooked or compass timber, of which there was not enough even for the Navy alone, led the East India Company to resort to iron knees, standards, breasthooks and crutches. This was a distinct advance; and although there were bad results occasionally from using inferior iron, the practice was eventually to become universal. Ships so constructed were cheaper and stronger, and the iron knees took up less space between decks and in the hold. The Indiamen also attained a degree of superiority over the King's ships through contact with India, where the art of shipbuilding was in some respects more advanced than in any part of Europe. In this connection the career of Mr Gabriel Snodgrass is of great importance. Sent out as a young man to Bengal, as shipwright to the East India Company, he returned to England and became one of the Company's surveyors in 1757. As chief surveyor, he was still in office as late as 1796. With the knowledge acquired in India and the prestige of his long period of service, he was enabled to bring about a number of important alterations in the design of the Company's ships. He explained his ideas to Committees of the House of Commons in 1771 and again in 1791, with a view to the same reforms being introduced into the Navy. His efforts had some vitally important results, though at a rather later period and after overcoming much official opposition.

The obstructiveness of the Navy Board is reflected in his essay *On the mode of improving the Navy* addressed to the Rt Hon. Henry Dundas in 1796. He writes with a sigh: 'It is upwards of twenty-four years since I first introduced.... It is now more than seventeen years since I brought into use....About twenty-seven years ago....I have made it a practice for many years....' He advocated, among other things, iron knees, better methods of seasoning timber, round-headed rudders, four-inch bottoms, capstans with iron spindles and pawls, wood sheathing under the copper, and shifting boards in the hold. All these improvements had been introduced into the Company's service by altering the requirements laid down in the contracts. But these were details; the substance of his gospel was contained in two major alterations affecting the general design of ships. One was the abolition of the 'tumble-home' top side, the other was the introduction of the flush upper deck.

In advocating a nearly vertical side, Snodgrass was probably drawing on his experience in India; and he was certainly here on very firm ground. Such a side to a ship was easier to build, gave a greater beam and, for that reason, a greater spread to the shrouds. A vessel constructed on this plan was stronger, roomier, stiffer and more seaworthy than a ship with its least breadth on the upper deck. In this connection, Snodgrass showed startling originality in deriding the French models which it was the fashion to venerate. He thought the French men-of-war if anything worse than the English in everything except size, being slighter, weaker, drawing more water and tumbling-home more absurdly. 'It must appear very extraordinary', he wrote, 'that there are several Line of Battle Ships and large Frigates now building for Government from Draughts copied from these ridiculous Ships....' Snodgrass was a bold man, but he was not bold enough to sum up his advice by urging the Government to build each future man-of-war as nearly as possible like a Bengal rice-ship.

Snodgrass was by no means alone in advocating the flush upper deck. Here he was more in line with the other theorists of the age. In fact, he only differed from them in that he acted as well as talked. While the open waist was subject to criticism in the King's service, it was abolished in the Company's. The theory of the flush deck was penetrating the Navy but only in a half-hearted fashion. The tendency was to reduce the waist by widening the gangways and then filling in the remaining space with gratings. This was done in frigates even before the French wars began, but the resulting upper deck was a flimsy affair, forming no integral part of the vessel's structure. The upper decks of the new Indiamen, on the contrary, involved a radical alteration in design. Both quarter-deck and forecastle were absorbed in one firm upper deck, strong enough to mount guns amidships and extending forward from the break of the poop.

The importance of the flush deck is obvious. A ship with a deep waist was bound to take in water on the main deck every time it shipped a sea, and water so trapped between decks was difficult to get rid of. The ship might easily capsize in the meanwhile. With a strong well-cambered flush deck, the hatches had only to be battened to make the ship proof against this danger. The sea that came on board would go as quickly as it came. This was a vital improvement and one which the East India Company had the credit of introducing. It justified Snodgrass's complacent boast:

> In the first place, I take the liberty of asserting (and from experience), that the East India Company's Ships, as now constructed, are the first and safest Ships in Europe....If the improvements adopted in those Ships were extended to the Navy, much labour and expense would be saved to the Nation....

This was true enough; but emphasis should be laid on the words 'as *now* constructed' and also on the words 'in *Europe*'. These reservations are significant. Snodgrass did not say 'in the World' because it would not have been true. There were better ships in India, there may even have been better ships in America; and, in saying 'as now constructed', he excluded a great number of the older Indiamen, many of which were extremely defective in every way.

The difference between the old type of deep-waisted Indiaman and the new 'three-decked' kind was demonstrated in the tragic losses of 1809; and from the contemporary comments it appears that deep-waisted ships continued to be built after 1800, despite Mr Snodgrass's efforts. On that occasion, as soon as the losses by foundering were known, the Court of Directors instituted inquiries, more especially by obtaining the opinion of former Directors who had also been East India captains. One of these, in his written reply dealing with the probable causes of the disaster, remarked that most of the missing ships were deep-waisted:

> ...it is not to be disguised, however, that these were of a very defective class of ships, over built aloft, and too deep below for their breadth, defects acknowledged by every builder, and felt by every experienced commander: the extreme breadth of their floors, too, is carried so far aft, that they have rudders given them like a west country barge, and when the sea strikes the rudder in a

gale of wind, the helm is not only held with difficulty, but the seamen are frequently thrown round the wheel. These are serious evils, for which no savings can compensate, because they endanger the ultimate safety of ship and cargo....

The saving of expense here mentioned had clearly little to do with the cost of construction. The narrowness of the ships was obviously a defect due to the faulty system of tonnage measurement. George Millett, the author of the above letter to the Joint Committee of Warehouses and Shipping, proved his point by comparing the log-books of two ships that survived, the *Sovereign*, of three decks, and the *Huddart*, of two decks, with a deep waist and poop. The former was found to have suffered not at all. The *Huddart*, on the other hand, came very near to foundering. On first shipping a heavy sea, this ship was laid over on her starboard side and her crew could only right her by throwing overboard the starboard guns. Later, another heavy sea came over the starboard quarter, laying the ship on her beam ends. This time she was on her larboard side, and 'what lee guns could be gotten at' were thrown overboard but without effect. The ship was finally saved only through the gale abating.

The foregoing comparison has been made for the purpose of shewing the danger of deep-waisted ships; the Sovereign weathered the gale with ease, but had it been of much longer continuance, the fate of the Huddart would, in my opinion, have been inevitable. The situation of the Sir William Bensley has already been shown; the Indus also suffered, threw some of her guns overboard, and cut away some of her anchors; the Harriet laboured, and shipped so much water, that with all her pumps going she had two and a half feet water in the well the greatest part of the night; whilst the three-decked ships, Northumberland, Euphrates, and Sovereign, were making exceedingly good weather of it. The conclusion is clear, that the deep-waisted ships, when laden, are but ill calculated to encounter gales of wind.

From such accounts as this, it appears that the flush-decked ship was slow to supersede the older type of Indiaman;

though it is very probable that the catastrophe of 1809 considerably hastened the process. Although, however, the flush-decked ship had the virtues here claimed for her, it was none the less true that she had, and developed, faults of her own. To understand this it is necessary to follow the steps by which the three-decked ship evolved.

The old type of Indiaman of the middle of the eighteenth century had two complete decks, a forecastle and poop. The waist was open with a gangway on either side and gratings laid between them. The long boat was stowed beneath these gratings on the upper or main deck. Great care was taken to keep the upper part of the ship as light as possible. In general, such a ship fairly closely resembled a frigate; except that it had no orlop deck. Then, in about 1769, two flush-decked ships were built, the *Granby* and *Queen*. The difference between these and the old ships lay in the disappearance of the waist. The forecastle and poop, themselves built more substantially, were, in this new type, joined to each other by a strong upper deck; the gangways and gratings giving way to solid beams and planks. The ship so constructed had three whole decks, upper, main or middle, and lower; and the long boat was now carried on the upper deck, which had to be strengthened accordingly.

Now, the advantages of having a flush upper deck have already been described. The disadvantage was in the raising of the centre of gravity. Here was a great weight added to the upper part of the ship, and something had to be done to compensate it. The builder of the *Granby*, a 786-ton ship, allowed for this by reducing the ship's length and adding to her beam. That ship measured 110 feet on the keel and was 36 ft. 8 in. broad; the proportion almost exactly of 3 : 1. The result was entirely satisfactory and the *Granby* 'performed well to the last'.

Had the later ships of the 800-ton class been built with proportions like those of the *Granby* and without other material alteration, the potential disadvantages of the flush deck would not have turned into actual defects. We have already seen, however, that the tendency was for Indiamen to become too long for their breadth. We have also seen what temptation there was to increase the depth of hold. All these tendencies were apparent in the *Royal Admiral*, built in about 1776; a crank ship, requiring a great deal of ballast. As if these growing defects, all working towards one end, were not enough, yet another fault began to appear. The three-decked ship had, from the start, to have a poop built over the upper deck. This was necessary for the accommodation of passengers. But the forecastle, in these earlier flush-decked ships, was very properly dispensed with. Now, with the building of the *Royal Admiral*, the forecastle began to reappear. It assumed, in that ship, but a rudimentary form; a platform, merely, raised two feet above the upper deck, built well forward and covering the cables and manger. It saved space below and served to accommodate the ship's livestock. With the building of the *Boddam* in 1787 came in the fashion to have this embryo forecastle four feet above the upper deck. And now, to the sheep-pens and hogsties was added the ship's galley. The convenience of this was that it lessened the risk of fire and left more room below for the troops which had often to be carried during the American War and the succeeding years. As the need for conveying troops became even more acute after 1793, the rule was made in 1799 that the galley was so to be placed in all the Company's ships built thereafter. To preserve the ship's appearance the sides were raised amidships to the height of the forecastle. Finally, from 1787 onwards, the top timbers had to be strengthened considerably to allow of carrying additional guns; the guns themselves each becoming heavier by 4 cwt.

Captain George Millett, remarking on these tendencies in a letter to the Court of Directors in 1809, complained that 'the weight has been constantly augmented upon the upper part of our ships, the length of the keel and depth of the hold increased out of all proportion to the breadth'. Referring especially to the 800-ton ships, he gave the following dimensions as typical:

118′ 0″ Keel for tonnage
36′ 0″ Breadth
14′ 9″ Depth in hold
6′ 2″ Height between decks

He goes on to comment:

Now here is a class of ships, more numerous than any other, of 800 tons burthen, having all the accumulation of weight upon her upper deck, already described, with a keel 10 feet longer than three times her breadth. This really outrages all proportion, and I do most sincerely hope, will be remedied in future.

It appears that Millett's protest was not without effect. Previous to his making it, the advertisement for tenders to build a 1200-ton ship at Penang had specified that 'the cook-rooms, sheep-pens, and hog-sties' were 'to be built upon the upper deck, in the manner which has lately been practised in ships built for the Company's service'. The month after his letter was written, on the other hand, the managing owner of the *Cirencester* was asking permission to relieve that ship 'by taking off the high forecastle, and placing the galley in the usual situation on the gun-deck'. A month later, moreover, a similar request came from the owners of the *Arniston*. As both these applications resulted from proposals made by the surveyor, it may be supposed that they indicate a change of policy.

Although improvements might be made in detail so as to lighten the upper works of the Company's ships, as soon as their top-heavy tendency was admitted, their basic defect was their inadequate beam. As late as 1822, the reviser of Steel's *Naval Architecture* could write:

...For, when we examine the East India Company's ships of the largest class, built according to their present methods...we must pronounce them in every respect unsafe, and ill adapted for any other purpose than that of carrying at a great sea-risk, a large cargo with comparatively small tonnage, and this advantage arises only from the present faulty and imperfect method of casting the tonnage of ships.

John Knowles, the author of the above, thought Indiamen unsafe less because of their proportions than because they lacked the diagonal framing which Sir Robert Seppings had by then introduced into the Navy. Nevertheless, the proportions had clearly remained unaltered even to as late a period as that.

Before quitting the subject of shipbuilding, something must be said about the 'extra ships'. Mention has already been made of their numbers and their tendency to supersede the small class of regular Indiaman, but no attempt has been made to describe them or define their status. The difference between the regular and extra ships was this: that the former were taken up for six, and latterly for eight or more voyages, whereas the latter were taken up for a single voyage, or three or four voyages, and had no guarantee of further employment. The following is a typical announcement of the period:

[1800] March 7. A Court of Directors was held at the East India House, when the following ships were taken up for one voyage, to bring home sugar, cotton, saltpetre etc. from Bengal:

			Builder
New Ship	580	Tons	Mr Mangle
" "	600	"	Mr Wilkinson
Melville Castle	806	"	Hamilton & Co.
Rockingham	798	"	Mr Wigram
Herculean	637	"	Lyatt & Co.

The 'New Ships' referred to are, of course, vessels which had not yet been built or named. The 'builders' are those for whom the vessels were built; that is to say, the owners.

In theory, an extra ship was one hired in an emergency, not designed for the service therefore and readily employable in any other trade. In practice, nearly all extra ships were specially built for the purpose; and they came, many of them, from the same yards as the regular ships. The same owners might be interested in both regular and extra shipping, and the officers were also to some extent interchangeable. The gulf fixed between regular and extra ships probably became less pronounced after the abolition of 'hereditary bottoms'. An extra ship which had been repeatedly taken up had a sort of footing in the service; but for certain differences in the uniform of the officers, such a ship was hardly to be distinguished from a regular vessel of the same tonnage. Most extra ships were of from 500 to 600 tons. A few were larger, but these were not supposed to exceed 800 tons in burthen. The usefulness of extra ships lay in the fact that they could be discarded at will. They represented the elasticity of the Company's shipping. By a manipulation of the numbers of extra ships taken up each year, the total tonnage of shipping could be made exactly equal to the expected demands on it. When, for example, it was decided to save England by importing rice in 1800–1, this additional quantity of goods was brought home in extra ships sent out from England as well as in private ships specially licensed in India. Without counting the Indian shipping, the extra ships for that year numbered thirty-seven. Perhaps not half of these had been built for the East India trade. Of the rest, no less than sixteen were tendered by a single firm, Messrs Prinsep and Saunders. It was only by extending and contracting the list of extra ships that emergencies like this could be met. A study of the lists cannot fail to suggest that some of the extra ships were employed almost continually. Such vessels, regular ships in all but name, must not be confused with ships freighted at a time of crisis. For these last must have been built for some other purpose. Additional ships like those tendered by Messrs Prinsep and Saunders must have been deflected from some other trade, then temporarily at a standstill.

The numbers of extra ships varied a great deal, as will be

supposed. There were fourteen in 1786. From 1793 to 1800 perhaps ten or twelve such ships were taken up each year. After that the number seems to have risen, apart from the exceptional numbers of 1800–1. There were twenty or more in 1802, and at least seventeen in 1804–5. The smallest Indiamen, those of the 500-ton class, both regular and extra, were employed in the carriage of 'gruff goods' for the most part. They were laden with cotton, rice, sugar, saltpetre or hemp. They might sometimes carry pepper, indigo or bale goods, but the rule was that they should carry whatever was least valuable. Ships of this class, measuring up to 610 or even 643 tons, were about a hundred feet long on the keel, a hundred and twenty-four to a hundred and thirty-two feet long, and thirty-two to thirty-five feet broad. Captain Millett gave it as his opinion that extra ships proved far more expensive to the Company than regular ships. This was partly because they were sometimes taken up as an afterthought and dispatched too late in the season. The demorage, upon twenty-seven extra ships which arrived in 1807, amounted because of this to over £91,000. However, apart from this, such vessels could not be a cheap form of transport. They were theoretically more liable to capture than were the larger Indiamen, and yet had a much larger crew in proportion to the amount of cargo they carried.

In the matter of proportion, the 500-ton Indiamen seem to have been better designed than those of 800 tons. Those, on the other hand, with two decks and a poop, were open to certain objections; while those with three flush decks had the defects of the 800-ton class. With regard to extra ships especially, Millett wrote as follows:

> Some of the three-decked ships carry their guns below, and are hardly ever able, when laden, to keep their ports open at sea, which not only renders them defenceless in general; but it being impossible for their ports to be fitted tight enough to keep the decks sufficiently dry for the preservation of the cargo, damage frequently

ensues. Some of them, too, are burthened with poops and high forecastles, which makes them extremely crank, leewardly, and less seaworthy: others have more the form of chests than ships, and detain every thing they are in company with....

In advertising for tenders of extra ships, the Company did not make any stipulation as to whether they should have two or three decks. Captain Millett, however, writing in 1809, commended the three-decked ship, provided she were not encumbered with poop or forecastle and provided her guns were mounted on the upper deck. A two-decked ship, he pointed out, had no room for troops, and was less likely to keep her cargo dry. A ship of this tonnage was not, of course, designed to carry passengers, and so could the better dispense with poop and forecastle.

To compare the three classes of Indiamen, it is necessary to know their comparative cost, and the fluctuation, or rather the steady rise in the cost of building as the war went on.

Rates per ton for building 800-*ton ships in the Thames*

	£	*s.*	*d.*		£	*s.*	*d.*		£	*s.*	*d.*
1781	14	14	0	1793	14	0	0	1799	15	15	0
1784	12	12	0	1795	16	13	0	1800	19	10	0
1792	12	10	0	1798	17	10	0	1801	21	15	6

The following figures illustrate the rise in prices occasioned by the renewal of war in 1803, while also specifying the principal items of expense in building, equipping, storing and provisioning an East Indiaman for fourteen months. The first example is that of an 800-ton ship with a crew of a hundred and ten:

	1802	1803
	£	£
Hull	16,267	17,600
Copper	2,570	2,699
Masts and yards	1,907	1,910
Cordage	2,380	2,987
Sails	1,544	1,634
Total (including stores, provisions, etc. etc.)	33,445	36,378

The second example is that of a 1200-ton ship with a crew of a hundred and thirty:

	1802	1803
	£	£
Hull	25,600	27,600
Copper	3,105	3,262
Masts and yards	2,838	2,725
Cordage	3,160	3,970
Sails	1,834	1,943
Total (including stores, provisions, etc. etc.)	47,673	51,621

The figures given below show the rising prices, while they also show the expense incurred by the owners of an Indiaman in repairs and fitting out for later voyages. The period is April–June 1804.

Estimate of the expense of building and fitting out a new ship, of 550 tons burthen, and 50 men, for six voyages, at the present prices:

1st Voyage	2nd	3rd	4th	5th	6th
£23,552	£5464	£6058	£10,553	£5384	£5629

Estimate, as above, for 800-ton ship:

1st Voyage	2nd	3rd	4th	5th	6th
£36,520	£10,785	£12,053	£17,975	£10,619	£13,246

Estimate, as above, for 1200-ton ship:

1st Voyage	2nd	3rd	4th	5th	6th
£50,810	£12,498	£13,928	£24,465	£14,008	£15,590

By 1805 a 1200-ton ship cost about £67,347 to build and equip for her first voyage, and the expenses for subsequent voyages were proportionately increased. An 800-ton ship in that year cost £47,396 for the first voyage, with a proportionate increase for the later voyages. It will be observed in the above figures that the fourth voyage involved considerable outlay in repairs. After about 1806 a still more extensive repair followed the sixth voyage so as to make the ship last for two or more additional voyages. For this purpose, the copper and sheathing were stripped off and the sides of the ship doubled with three-inch oak plank from the lower port sills down to two feet below the floor heads. The chains, too, were lengthened down so that fresh holes could be made for the chain plates; the ship being strengthened at the same time by additional iron riders, breasthooks, standards, ballast beams, knees and copper bolts.

Prices fell somewhat in 1806. A 1200-ton ship cost £61,859 in 1807, the hull amounting to £33,000. By 1808 the cost was estimated at £64,580. But in that year prices steadied, so that the estimate for a 1200-ton ship in 1809 was £64,133. An 800-ton ship in that year would cost about £45,826, the ship's hull accounting for £20,800 of that sum. On subsequent voyages she would cost her owners between thirteen and fifteen thousand pounds each voyage and over twenty-one thousand pounds for the fourth or repairing voyage. It will be remarked that the cost of a ship as launched was half or less than half the total cost. The following estimate, slightly different from that given above, is for a 1200-ton ship in 1809. It shows the proportionate expense of the various items:

Total cost, building and first voyage	£63,068
Chief items:	
Ship's hull	£34,400
Cordage	£5,194
Sheathing	£4,459
Masts	£3,000
Beef, pork, suet and lard	£2,220
Sails	£2,200
Interest on money paid to builder in several instalments	£1,282
Kintledge [ballast], including cost of shipping	£1,092
Guns	£990
Bread	£907
Anchors	£798
Minor items:	
Block-maker	£531
Gunpowder	£515
Water-casks	£472

Butcher [fresh meat for use in the river]	£378
Smith's bill	£335
Pilot	£300
Gunsmith [presumably for small-arms]	£293
Captain's sundry disbursements	£285
Distiller [rum]	£226
Boat-builder [long-boat, cutter or yawl, and jolly-boat]	£206
Firehearth	£182
Firewood	£182
Brewer	£179
Rigger	£135
Carpenter's stores	£129
Oilman	£109
Launching and survey dinners	£70

In this list, the expense of the cordage may seem very high. It includes, however, not only the rigging but also the cables. Of these an Indiaman carried at least six, with a voyal, hawser and towline in addition. The term cordage also included a boarding netting. From the mast-maker there came not only masts but also spars, together with spare topmasts and yards. Including topgallant masts and topsail yards, an Indiaman carried eleven spare spars, as well as sixteen stunsail booms. Sails were an expensive item. An Indiaman needed two complete suits, one half-worn and the other new, and several spare sails as well. All the vessels were ship-rigged, and a complete suit of sails, including seven staysails, six studding sails, spritsail and sprit-topsail, might number twenty-eight items. The anchors carried numbered five or six; usually a sheet anchor, best bower, small bower, stream and kedge. One item which needs explaining is that regarding the interest on money paid in advance to the builder. Agreements between owner and builder may have varied, but the following may be taken as typical: 'In the agreement for the building of the *Tottenham*, drawn up between Robert Wigram, Esq. of Crosby Square, London, and Thomas Haw, builder, of Stockton in County Durham, dated March 6th 1801, the payment stipulated for is fourteen pounds per ton.'

Now, the *Tottenham* measured 102 ft. 6 in. on the keel for tonnage and 31 ft. in breadth. Her tonnage was therefore very much what it was listed as; namely, 517 tons. The builder thus received £7238; a great deal less than a London builder would have demanded. Payment was to be by instalments; £400 within fourteen days from signing the agreement, £1000 as soon as the keel was laid, £1000 as soon as the floors should be crossed, £1000 when the frame should be finished, £1000 as soon as the lower deck beams should be in, £1000 when all the decks should be caulked, and the remainder by the time of the vessel's completion. The owner had thus to pay £5400 before the ship was even launched, and the whole sum of £7238 before she was fit for service. As about fifteen months were to elapse between the first payment and the last, a large sum of capital was for a considerable period prevented from earning the normal rate of interest. In the case especially of the larger ships, this loss of interest on the capital outlay was a serious item of expense. It may be remarked that the £14 per ton paid for the *Tottenham* did not cover the cost of equipment, and cannot therefore be compared with the £21 or £22 per ton which Wigram would have had to pay at one of the big yards on the Thames.

In considering the question of expense, one fact is bound to strike the reader, and that is the comparative cheapness of the larger ships. A large proportion of the cost of a vessel was, as we have seen, in such items as masts, copper, cordage and sails. Under many such heads of expense—cables, spars, boats and anchors, for instance—a small ship cost almost as much as a large one. A 500-ton ship cost nearly half as much as a 1200-ton ship but was very far from carrying half as large a cargo. The crew, moreover, of a 1200-ton ship was not very much larger than that of an 800-ton ship, so that there was no great difference in the cost of provisioning them; and yet the difference in carrying capacity was enormous. All comparison of cost was altogether in favour of the larger ships.

Nothing so far has been said about the arming of the Company's ships beyond the fact that the guns of a 1200-ton ship would cost nearly a thousand pounds. It will be shown later how one argument used in favour of the new class of Indiamen introduced in 1786 was that these ships would serve both for trade and war. It was suggested at the time that ships of this class should mount guns on the lower deck. Thomas Newte and others strongly objected to this proposal, pointing out that cargo carried on the lower deck would be damaged by water entering the ports, and that the ports could not, in any case, be opened in bad weather, as they could not be far enough above the waterline. It was found that fifty-six guns could be mounted on the middle and upper decks and that a greater number was not to be desired. The intention was to carry 9-pounders on the middle or gun deck in time of peace, exchanging them for 18-pounders on the outbreak of war. Other ships at this time often seem to have mounted 6-pounders, 9-pounders and 12-pounders—sometimes in considerable numbers. The owners of the Nottingham were proposing in 1796 to equip her with twenty-eight 12-pounders on the gun deck and fourteen 18-pounder carronades on the upper deck, making forty-two guns in all.

During the period 1793–1801 seven Indiamen were captured. The Court of Directors, evidently regarding these losses as excessive, proceeded to take steps to safeguard Indiamen for the future. Among the experts consulted by the Committee of Shipping was Captain Joseph Cotton. The gist of his advice was that Indiamen should have heavier guns, to enable them to open fire at five hundred yards range.

It certainly is not the business of the Company's ships to court an action, but to avoid one, or render it decisive in their favour, by disabling the enemy if possible, before he comes near; hence all light ordnance will be defective: and to wait for an enemy of the same force, or a superior one, without using their best endeavours to escape, by firing at him directly he is in within reach of the guns, may constitute bravery, but it is not the precaution the Company require in their commanders....

Joseph Cotton
20th Aug. 1801

Cotton had a certain prestige as a former East India captain who had become a director. On occasions of dispute about any maritime question his written advice would come from Layton, Essex, as inevitably as that of George Millett would come from Wallwood House, Leytonstone. On this occasion, Cotton's ideas were almost instantly acted upon.

At a Court of Directors, September 23, 1801

...On reading a report from the Committee of Shipping, dated the 22nd instant;

Resolved, That it is highly expedient that the guns of all the ships in the Company's service should be of one calibre.

That, as neither light guns with a conical bore, nor carronades, whatever may be their calibre, are calculated for a ship's principal battery, and have therefore been discarded from those situations in the navy, they be not permitted to be carried in the Company's ships.

That ships of about 1200 tons burthen should carry thirty-eight pieces of ordnance, the whole of which should be eighteen pounders. That not more than twenty-six of these pieces should be mounted on the principal battery, the remainder be carried on the upper deck....

The object of thus insisting that certain proportion of the guns should be on the upper deck was to provide a nucleus of men to resist any attempt at boarding. It had been found that the crews, largely composed as they were of foreigners, showed little inclination to come on deck to repel boarders. To defend the upper deck it was essential to have men stationed there from the start. In 1805 Robert Wigram proposed that 500-ton ships should mount all their guns on the upper deck so that 'all hands will be together to fight the guns, to work the ship, and resist boarding'. By dispensing with ports on the middle deck, he argued, there would also be much less risk of water damaging the cargo. The Committee of Shipping, however, decided against this plan; probably on the ground that it would make the ship top-heavy. Other reforms dating from 1801 and due to Cotton's advice were the introduction of the lock and chamber and also of Gover's patent gun carriages. The effect of the new gun carriages, for which the Company itself had to pay, was to lessen the number of men needed in each gun crew. The men thus set free were to work swivels and musquetoons in the tops. Each ship was also in future to have a master-at-arms to instruct the seamen in musketry, while each gun captain was to receive a gratuity of three shillings a month as an encouragement.

The resolution of the Court of Directors that 'it is highly expedient that the guns of all the ships in the Company's service should be of one calibre' is not to be taken too literally. It was not intended to apply to the 500-ton ships, and the change was only gradually brought about among the others. As then established, however, the light 18-pounder gun was to be the only weapon used in the ships of the two larger classes. The 1200-ton vessels were to be armed as follows:

On the gun-deck: twenty-four 18-pounder cannonades, 6′ 6″ long, weighing 28½ cwt. Two 18-pounder cannonades, stern-chasers, 8′ long, weighing 30 cwt.

On the upper-deck: twelve 18-pounder carronades, 4′ long, weighing 14 cwt.

Total: 38 guns.

The 800-ton ships were to be armed as follows:

On the gun-deck: twenty 18-pounder cannonades, 6′ long. Two 18-pounder cannonades, stern-chasers. Weight, 26 cwt. and 30 cwt. respectively.

On the upper-deck: ten 18-pounder carronades, 3′ 6″ long, weighing 11 cwt.

Although no mention was made of the 500-ton ships in the resolution of 23 September, 1801, it became usual to word the advertisements for tenders in such a way as to secure ships armed as follows:

500-ton ships: sixteen 12-pounder carronades,
600-ton ships: eighteen 12-pounder carronades.

The Committee of Shipping was to decide in each case whether the guns should be mounted on the upper or middle deck. When the vessel had only two decks and a poop, the Committee usually had the guns placed on the upper deck. In a three-decked ship the Committee would insist on the guns being mounted below. This was a policy of doubtful wisdom, for the 12-pounder carronade was only four feet long and could scarcely be run out of a 'tween-deck port without some risk of blowing off the port lid as soon as the weapon should be elevated.

The number of guns actually mounted by Indiamen did not always correspond very exactly to their establishment as laid down in 1801. Ships had their peculiarities and exceptions had to be made. So far from it being possible for all ships to carry guns of one calibre, it was soon found next to impossible to compel individual ships to carry guns of the same calibre. As late as 1804 the *Royal Charlotte*, of 1252 tons, had 12-pounder guns in her principal battery, with two 18-pounder cannonades as stern-chasers. Driven to allow variations both in number and calibre of guns, the Committee of Shipping was resolute on two points. The one was that 'although it is not practicable, at present, to have the whole of the guns in a ship of the same calibre, yet the Committee cannot admit of two different calibres being on the same deck'. The other was that 'it is indispensably necessary that the stern-chasers should be long guns'. The assumption was that guns of different calibres, if on the same deck, would inevitably be served with each other's ammunition. There was also a dark suspicion that this would happen in any case so long as there were two sizes of shot to be confused. The long stern-chasers were intended to cripple pursuing enemies, though it does not appear that they often did so. It may be doubted whether an Indiaman's gunnery was equal to bringing down an opponent's topmast at long range. These stern-chasers were mounted in the aftermost ports, not the stern ports. When required, they could be heaved round and run aft, and thus brought to bear on a pursuer.

The number of guns an Indiaman would carry might vary, to a certain extent, with the ideas of the owner. Occasionally permission was asked of the Company to mount additional guns. This was a request which the Shipping Committee was usually willing to consider, and the result was that some ships were much more heavily armed than others. John Pascal Larkins, Esq. put ten extra 18-pounder guns on board the *Walmer Castle* in 1803, in the expectation of her sailing without convoy. This 1200-ton ship must therefore have mounted over forty guns. In 1804 the owner of the *Winchelsea* armed that ship with thirty 18-pounders on the gun deck and ten carronades of the same calibre on the quarter-deck. Similarly, when the *Warren Hastings*, of 1200 tons, was taken in 1806, her captor described her as mounting forty-eight 18-pounders.

The smaller Indiamen also often carried a greater or lesser number of guns than was planned for them. In a convoy sailing from Madras to London in 1806 there were nine ships of from 500 to 600 tons. Six of them had sixteen guns, one of them had twelve, another eighteen, and the last, for some reason, twenty-six. In the same convoy, of six 800-ton ships, five mounted thirty guns and only one the established number of thirty-two. A similar convoy in 1808 included five of the small class, three with sixteen and two with eighteen guns. Of the four 800-ton ships one carried thirty guns and another, thirty-two; but the remaining two carried only twenty-six. It is evident that ships varied considerably in gun power. There is a model of an 830-ton

Indiaman in the Science Museum, South Kensington, which mounts thirty-four guns, twenty on the gun deck and fourteen on the upper deck. Formidable as such a ship would look, many 800-ton vessels looked more formidable still. They were pierced, many of them, for many more guns than they ever carried. A sheer draught of one of these, a ship of 818 tons, given in Steel's *Naval Architecture*, shows a broadside of thirty ports. Had all these been filled—an impossible condition—the ship would have mounted twenty-six guns on the middle deck, twenty-four on the upper deck, and ten on the poop; making a grand total of no less than sixty guns and carronades. Such a vessel might easily have passed for a 50-gun ship.

An Indiaman like that just described would not, of course, mount more than thirty-two or thirty-four guns at most. The two after ports on the middle deck would be empty, as also all the forward ports on the upper deck. No guns were mounted on the poop. A more typical 800-ton ship, like the *Marquis Wellesley*, would have only eleven ports a-side on the middle deck, and perhaps as many on the upper deck. The after port being empty, there would thus be twenty guns on the middle deck; and, of the ports on the upper deck, five a-side might be filled, making a total of thirty. It made no difference whether a ship was flush-decked or deep-waisted, except that the guns in the latter type of vessel were said to be mounted on the quarter-deck. A ship of this class looked very much like a 36-gun frigate.

The 1200-ton Indiaman differed from the 800-ton ship in being a potential man-of-war. The theory was that these ships, when supplied with additional carronades from the arsenal at Bombay, together with an exceptionally large crew and some soldiers to act as marines, would be equivalent to ships of the line. On a sudden outbreak of war, there would always be sufficient of these in the East to enable the Indian Governments to improvise a squadron for the protection of trade.

This was actually done in 1793, when the Indian Ocean was all but devoid of English ships-of-war. Three Indiamen, the *Triton*, *Royal Charlotte* and *Warley*, co-operated with a solitary frigate at the taking of Pondicherry. In 1795 seven of the larger Indiamen were bought into the Navy and equipped as ships of the line. The *Bombay Castle*, *Exeter* and *Brunswick* were present at the first capture of the Cape of Good Hope. Similar services were repeatedly rendered by these big China ships, and two of them actually took a French frigate in 1800.

The ordinary 1200-ton ship would show fourteen ports a-side on the middle deck and thirteen ports a-side on the upper deck. As in the case of the 800-ton ship, only a proportion of these were filled under normal circumstances. Of the upper deck ports five a-side might be filled and thirteen a-side of the lower, leaving the after port empty. Pierced as they were for over fifty guns, these 1200-ton ships usually mounted only thirty-six or thirty-eight, and some no more than thirty. When, however, an owner wished his ship to bristle with artillery, he could send forty-eight guns on board without altering the vessel in any way. And this, as we have seen, was occasionally done.

All Indiamen, of whatever size, were supposed to carry at least thirty rounds for every gun and carronade on board. An inventory of stores for a 500-ton ship in 1804 includes the following items: 400 round shot, 100 double-headed bar shot, 40 grape shot, and 56 barrels of cannon powder. As compared with naval weapons of the day, an Indiaman's guns were not thought very effective. The 'cannonade' or medium 18-pounder was a poor weapon, if we are to believe James, the naval historian. And, according to Sir Robert Wigram, the carronades 'almost invariably upset on being fired'. Some of the extra ships seem to have mounted long 6-pounders as chase guns, together with their 12-pounder carronades, and these can scarcely have been very formidable. There was a minor reform when 'sliding carriages' were introduced in 1804; probably in order to prevent the carronades upsetting. And there was another minor reform, apparently in 1803, as a result of which 'the proper charge of powder' was to be 'marked on each gun'.

For defence against boarding, an Indiaman carried nettings and small-arms. A 550-ton ship, in 1806, was expected to have boarding nettings which could be run up 'half mast high', made of 1½ in. rope and strengthened by three horizontal chains. This vessel, an extra ship, was also to carry 'a stand of arms and cutlass for every man on board, and also twenty boarding pikes'. An inventory for a 500-ton ship in 1804 is rather more detailed. The ship was to carry

2 Arm chests
6 Iron Musketoons
50 Muskets
50 Bayonets
50 Boarding Pikes
20 Scabbards for ditto
25 Pistols
50 Cutlasses & scabbards
25 Pole axes
30 Hand Grenade Shells
5 Half Barrels of Musket Powder
1 Drum

For a ship which carried but fifty men this is an impressive list. On the other hand, the small-arms supplied were sometimes of a poor quality. Seamen, moreover, were not easy to drill, so that in some ships the arms chests were never opened.

The smallest Indiaman was, at least in theory, a ship to be reckoned with. Few of the Company's ships, however, could successfully encounter a French corvette, even though mounting the same or a greater number of guns. A merchant ship would seldom attempt to fight a ship-of-war. But the assumption was that an East Indiaman was proof against privateers and pirates. Admiral Rainier wrote to the Governor of Madras in 1804: 'I cannot help remarking to your Lordship, that it has always been presumed in War time, that your ships are adequate to their own defence against the Enemy's Privateers....' As a general rule, this theory was justified. An Indiaman could beat off the average French privateer; supposing, at any rate, that she were given time to clear for action. As for native pirates, it was but seldom that any such dared to come within range of an Indiaman's guns.

In attempting to discover how formidable the Indiamen were, the prints and paintings of the period are apt to be somewhat misleading. Towards the end of the wars especially, after Indiamen had adopted the 'Nelson chequer', it was the custom to paint a row of ports to correspond with the lower battery of a man-of-war. The Company's ships mostly had a lower deck, but it is extremely doubtful whether it was, in any instance, pierced for cannon. Cargo was stowed on the lower deck. To have made genuine ports would have exposed the goods to damage from sea water. And, supposing that any guns were mounted there, it would have been impossible to serve them for two reasons. In the first place, they would have been too deeply embedded in cargo; and, in the second place, they would have been too near the waterline. Pictures of Indiamen must therefore be treated with caution. Illustrations of the *Earl of Balcarres*, for instance, an Indiaman built at the close of the war, credit her with a number of ports which, supposing all to be genuine and filled, would give her a total of about ninety-two guns. Similarly, there are pictures of the *Essex*, another ship of the 1816 period, from which one might gain the impression that she mounted at least eighty guns. As neither of these ships carried more than about a hundred and thirty men, barely sufficient to man one battery of a 38-gun ship, it is scarcely necessary to point out that the lower-deck ports were counterfeit and most of the upper-deck ports empty.

So far were most Indiamen from mounting as many guns as

there were ports to fill, that captains sometimes struck some of their guns below, even in war time. The *Brunswick*, at the time of her capture, had six of her guns thus disposed of, to make room for cargo. Moreover, even when this was prevented, the guns were often so buried in stores as to be practically useless. The temptation to do this was the greater in that the ships were frequently undermanned, with too few men to serve the guns, even had these not been hidden among hogsheads of potatoes and butts of water. When the question of manning is considered, it is well to remember that there was a difference in this respect between the outward- and homeward-bound ships; a difference applying in some degree to all classes of the East India fleet. The outward-bound ship was fully manned, if partly with foreigners and landsmen, and often carried either soldiers or recruits. Being half-empty, she was far less likely to be encumbered with stores on the gun deck. The homeward-bound ship, on the other hand, which was far more likely to be attacked, being a great deal more valuable, had far fewer men for its defence. All the best seamen had, as a rule, been impressed into the Navy, the gaps being filled up by lascars and Chinese. Of the remaining European seamen, some would very likely be ill. A few might have died from disease or been drowned by accident. If any soldiers were carried—and a China ship would have none—they would all be worn-out invalids. The hold, being crammed with tea or muslin or indigo, would have little room for water or provisions, which would consequently be stowed, in part, between the guns. In these circumstances, the only way to clear for action was to stave in most of the waterbutts; a process neither rapid nor even possible when there was no chance of immediate replenishment.

Indiamen were, as we have seen, occasionally equipped as men-of-war. And the question naturally arises as to how many guns they mounted when so equipped. As regards those fitted out in India, the answer would seem to be, very few more than were ordinarily carried. When the two 800-ton ships, *Calcutta* and *Lady Castlereagh*, were armed for war in the year 1804, they mounted only forty guns each. Fully to man a vessel so heavily armed required at least two hundred men. Some Indiamen had ports for fifty guns or more, but there can never have been the men available to serve so many cannon. It is probable, therefore, that the *Earl Camden*, *Wexford*, *Brunswick* and *Exeter*, with other 1200-ton ships fitted at different times for war, mounted no more than forty or forty-eight guns. And indeed those purchased into the Navy seldom seem to have carried more than fifty-four or fifty-six. These last, although fitted with 32-pounder carronades instead of 18-pounders on the upper deck, found little favour in naval officers' sight. The only exception was the *Glatton*, which was given a freak armament of 68-pounder carronades on the gun deck and 32-pounder carronades on the upper deck. So equipped, she proved exceedingly formidable at short range. It will be observed, however, that no attempt was made to give these ships a lower battery and so convert them into two-decked men-of-war. The original idea, first propounded by Gabriel Snodgrass in 1786, that an Indiaman could be made a potential 64-gun ship, had clearly proved erroneous.

With regard to the speed of the East India ships there has been a great deal of misconception. Writers on maritime subjects have noted how long they took to make their passages and jumped to the conclusion that they were all slow ships. Nor have they found difficulty in accounting for this. Ships with such bluff bows, it has been asserted, could not travel fast. Now, it is fairly clear that such reasoning is unscientific. Criticism of 'apple-cheeked' sailing ships may appeal to the imagination and carry conviction to the general reader, but the naval architect knows that the problem is not as simple as that. The fine hollow bow of the clipper ship certainly gives an impression of speed, but it has little to do with the rapid passages made. It has, in fact, been discarded by the modern racing yacht. The fact seems to be that the improvement in sailing ships after 1815 has been largely misrepresented. Increased speed was only partially the result of altered design. Another factor must be considered, and that is the factor of motive.

Why then was the Indiaman so long on the voyage? The answer is, because she was not in a hurry. There was no competition. Nor was there any merit or profit in arriving there first. The China clippers of a later period raced homeward with the object of an early market for the tea. We have seen what the East India Company did with the tea when it came—put it in a warehouse for twelve months. The later nineteenth-century ship, again, was run on an economic basis. She had to make a profit in a world of low freights and feverish competition. If she stayed too long at sea, the wages would consume the gains. Little details like wages were hardly noticed by the East India Company; its affairs were on too vast a scale. In the present century it is too readily assumed that speed is everything. Yet, even to-day, no one supposes that an ordinary railway train is allowed to travel as fast as it can. The possibilities of speed were explored at a comparatively early stage in the history of railways, and it was found that a low speed was in many ways preferable. Only under the pressure of competition will this policy be reversed.

In the same way, with the East Indiaman, other considerations were put before speed; one consideration was safety, and another was comfort. Safety was regarded by a cautious handling of the ship and the taking in of sail on the least appearance of danger. Both safety and comfort lay in the prevailing custom, which the Company encouraged, of making all snug for the night by taking in royals and even topgallants. No India captain, in blowing weather, would crack on sail in the hope of breaking a record. The process of carrying on until just before 'God Almighty takes them in for him' was unknown in the Company's service. The ships were too valuable for such heroics. Besides, the more influential passengers disliked it. In general, there was no need to hurry and every motive for proceeding at a comfortable rate.

The difference between the actual speed and the speed of which the ships were capable was shown after the partial throwing open of the India trade in 1813, when competition began to lend an interest to the matter. There was a mild sensation when an American schooner reached England from the Mauritius in sixty days, in 1817. This was probably changed to something like alarm when an American merchant vessel came from China in a hundred and eight days. But the East India Company had already felt the spur of competition, and the professional jealousy of its seamen had already been aroused. That very year, in 1817 that is to say, the voyage from Ceylon to England was performed by an English transport in seventy-seven days. But this feat was eclipsed when the China fleet—thirteen heavily laden Indiamen—swept into the Channel only a hundred and nine days out from Canton River. This was, as journalists claimed,

> ...a triumph of mercantile navigation, a combination of nautical skill with good fortune, of which there is no record of an equal exertion; to cut through 15,000 miles of ocean in that short time, is, with so many vessels, without example in marine experience. With *similar* passages we ought to communicate with our Asiatic Presidency at Calcutta within *six* months, instead of *once* in twelve or fifteen months, as is now the loitering and *dilatory* habit of that important intercourse. The Americans of New York and Washington will soon exchange letters and *products* with Bengal in five months! The only early account *we* had of the victory of Waterloo being heard of at Calcutta was from New York.

The point to notice about this is that the Indiamen who performed this feat were the same ships, very largely, that were making their dilatory voyages between 1800 and 1813. They were the same ships and the same men, but after 1815 they were for the first time in a hurry. The difference in speed was brought about simply by carrying more sail, and caring less about splitting it. This may have entailed having an extra spare suit of canvas. It certainly seems to have entailed setting a number of additional sails. The *Essex* Indiaman, in 1816, is said to have set as many as sixty-four sails—royals, skysails, moonrakers, cloudscrapers, stargazers, sprit-topsails and upper topgallant stunsails; as also 'fancy canvas' such as ringtail, bull-driver and mizen royal staysail. And the custom of shortening sail at nightfall must slowly have fallen into disuse—if indeed it was not done away with at one blow during the years 1814–17.

The building traditions of the Indiamen were carried on in the later Blackwall frigates, and it is said that in 1857, when all the fastest ships procurable were racing out with troops to quell the Mutiny, the American clippers made much slower passages than the frigate-built and cumbersome Blackwallers. This was admittedly a case of knowledge against ignorance, but it serves to illustrate the contention that the increase of speed in the early nineteenth century was only partly the result of changes in naval architecture. The vital factor lay not in the ships but in the men on board them.

Chapter VI

THE SHIPPING INTEREST

THROUGHOUT the greater part of the eighteenth century, the ships of the East India Company, although large for their day, were very small when compared with contemporary ships-of-war. There had been some very large Indiamen in the late seventeenth century. Sixteen of them, built during the period 1675–80, had measured anything up to 1300 tons and could mount as many as sixty guns. But after the amalgamation of the Old and New Companies, the ships became smaller. This change was mainly due to naval jealousy with regard to the supply of large timber. As a result of the change the Indiamen of the early eighteenth century measured from 350 to 400 tons. They tended to increase slightly in size as the years went on, so that ships of 480 and 490 tons burthen became common; and from about 1735 onwards the latter tonnage became the most usual.

After 1750 an era of standardisation dawned in which all Indiamen were registered at 499 tons. This was more in the nature of a convenient fiction than a mathematical fact. It was somehow connected in men's minds with a law then in force by which vessels of 500 tons' burthen and upwards were compelled to carry a chaplain. Most of the ships had, in fact, a real tonnage greater than that assigned them on paper. They were all, nevertheless, of approximately the same size. So they remained until about 1773, when Indiamen of 676, 700 and even 800 tons began to multiply. By the end of the War of American Independence the normal tonnage of the East India ships was 758, while there were a few ships of 800 tons, and more of 500 and 600 tons.

One lesson learnt during the War of Independence was that ships of this size were by no means equal to the French and Dutch Indiamen of the period, which were as large as the English ships had been in the reign of Charles II. It was evident that, on the outbreak of another war, enormous damage might be done before an English squadron could round the Cape. To prevent disaster of this kind, it would be necessary either to build larger Indiamen or else keep a permanent squadron in the East Indies. As the Government of the day did not hail this latter solution with much enthusiasm, there was only one thing to do. Whatever the effect on the timber supply, larger ships had to be built. Those who advocated this policy of building 'a number of ships of force fit to serve either for commerce or war, in the manner other great Companies do, more particularly the French', were able to show that such vessels would be not only easier to defend but also, in proportion to their size, cheaper to navigate. One of the advocates for building larger Indiamen, Mr Thomas Newte, wrote that 'the adoption of such a plan will be productive of a two-fold advantage, the goods may be brought home cheaper, and the ships will not only be capable of defending themselves and the property on board, but the settlements of the Company in India'. He adds that 'Such ships may with ease, and at a small expence, be converted into men of war'.

To this argument that the same ship might be both a merchantman and a potential man-of-war, the objection was made that such a ship would fail in both capacities. The principal upholder of this belief was Mr Nathaniel Smith, chairman of the Court of Directors in 1784 and again in 1788. He admitted that larger ships might save considerable expense, but he doubted whether the saving would be as great as was expected, supposing the ships were neither overloaded nor undermanned. He contended that a ship of 1160 tons' burthen was capable of defence only 'if properly manned, her guns all mounted, and the middle deck sufficiently cleared either from goods or stores'. He did not think that such a ship was properly manned with less than 160 or 170 men. The proposed crew of 130 was, in his opinion, utterly inadequate. Such big ships would use up the timber needed for the Navy, and they would cause unemployment in the shipping and allied industries.

> ...However able they may be for defence or attack, if properly prepared, when called forth upon great emergency, they cannot be considered as proper ships to be ranged among those of the line in a regular fleet, as their general construction, adapted to mercantile purposes, the situation of their gun-decks, and the inferior weight of metal they are designed to carry, must alike tend to render them unfit for that station; for if they shall be properly moulded within, and filled within board for men of war, they will become unprofitable merchantmen; as in that case they ought not to be flat floored, and should have orlop beams and ports upon the lower decks, to enable them to carry heavy metal, circumstances absolutely necessary, if the ships were intended at any time to be ranged in the line.
>
> On the other hand, if they are to be considered as merchant ships, and at the same time to be framed from those sharper moulds used for the navy, and to have orlop beams, and lower deck ports cut out, such construction and arrangement would be very disadvantageous for stowing away goods, and render them incapable of taking in their proportionate tonnage, whilst ports along the lower deck would be liable to expose the cargo to damage, stowed either above or below that deck....
>
> (Memorandum dated 20th March 1789.)

There is much weight in this contention that a ship designed both for trade and war might be found unfit for either. And Nathaniel Smith proved to be right to this extent, that the larger Indiamen were never to be very effective as fighting ships. Their warlike equipment was never allowed to interfere much with commercial requirements; and they were not particularly satisfactory even when specially armed for war. Thomas Newte had supposed that 'a fleet of eight or ten of of such ships as are here recommended may go to sea with perfect security, without the protection of any of his Majesty's ships...'. It is sufficient to say that, during the French wars, no such risk was ever taken while any possibility remained of avoiding it.

This question as to whether it was desirable to build larger ships was decided, in the end, less by argument than by experiment. The first Indiaman to show a marked increase in size was the *Hartwell*, of 938 tons, built at Itchenor, near Chichester, in 1786. The *Belvedere*, of 987 tons, was launched shortly afterwards at the same place. Both, however, were almost instantly eclipsed by the launch, in the same year, of the *Nottingham*, of 1152 tons. The *Nottingham* was the first of the new class of Indiamen, and it was by her performance that the project of building bigger ships was tried. She was copied, to some extent, from some of the Swedish ships which traded to China. Her tonnage was almost the same as that of the *Gustavus III*; which ship, according to Nathaniel Smith, required a crew of between 160 and 170 and carried only 1273 tons of tea. The *Nottingham*, however, returned from her first voyage with 1570 tons of tea and a crew of 104. Sixteen of her guns, it was found, had been dismounted. Her gun deck was improperly stowed with cargo, her upper deck improperly encumbered with stores and waterbutts. And yet, however reprehensible this overloading, the result was undeniably impressive. With a crew scarcely larger than that of an 800-ton ship, the *Nottingham* had brought home almost twice as much cargo as such a ship could load. Such overloading, such undermanning, could not, of course, be allowed to happen again. Nevertheless, the upholders of the proposed building programme were as jubilant as their opponents were downcast. Henceforth there could be no question as to which class of ship should prevail in the China trade. Costing originally perhaps a third as much again as an 800-ton ship, the new type of vessel needed little more canvas and cordage than was required for the smaller ship. There was small chance of bringing an 1100-ton vessel into the Hooghly, but the Swedish example had proved repeatedly that Canton River was navigable for vessels of that burthen. Indiamen of the new type began soon to multiply. Three more had, in fact, been put in hand even before the *Nottingham* reappeared in London River.

The three Indiamen mentioned above, built in 1787, were the *Carnatic*, *Ceres* and *Boddam*. The *Ceres*, of 1180 tons, was the largest. Three more big ships were built in 1788, the *Ocean*, *Duke of Buccleugh*, and *Warley*. The *Ocean* and the *Duke of Buccleugh* were both slightly larger than the *Ceres*. Then, in 1789, came the *Royal Charlotte*, of 1252 tons, and the *Hindostan*, of 1248. The *Earl of Abergavenny*, built in the same year, of 1182 tons, soon became out of date, for five ships of over 1200 tons were launched in 1790. Meanwhile the smaller type of Indiaman was still being built with a standardised tonnage of 770–800. These, with the numerous smaller ships, still formed the bulk of the Company's fleet.

The first experiments in large ships having succeeded, a regular shipbuilding programme was drawn up in 1793. The effect of this was to perpetuate the existing strata into which the East Indies fleet had come to be divided. Henceforth, the Indiamen of 1740, of 1775 and of 1793 were to exist side by side as distinct types, employed for different purposes. The existing differentiation had been found useful, with the result that a state of affairs arrived at by accident was made permanent by intention. Thirty-six ships of the largest type would be required, it was decided, and some forty of the smaller kinds.

The 1200-ton ship came in with the completion of the *Brunswick* in 1795, and this became the standard, or at least the nominal tonnage of the China ships. The 1100-ton class was very largely superseded by the end of the century, both in numbers and in favour. There were still nine ships of this tonnage, however, in the last years of the century; at which period the 1200-ton Indiamen numbered sixteen. Some, perhaps most, of these China ships had a real burthen considerably in excess of the nominal tonnage; which, in its turn, exceeded the contract tonnage. The *Hope*, *Neptune* and *Hindostan* had each, it was believed, an actual burthen of between 1400 and 1500 tons; while the *Ganges* measured, it was said, a trifle over 1500. Eventually, the largest ships were found less satisfactory than those of 1200 tons. By 1810 there were thirty-four ships of 1200 tons and upwards, and only three of over 1000 but less than 1200 tons. The figures available as to tonnage are accurate enough to convey a general idea of the three types into which the Company's shipping was divided. In detail, however, they are somewhat contradictory, owing to the different methods of measurement in use.

The total number of ships in the Company's regular service, during the first decade of the nineteenth century, was between seventy and eighty. There was a decided increase, as we have seen, in the 1200-ton class. The 800-ton class numbered about twenty-five at the beginning of the century, had increased to thirty-three in 1806, and sank to twenty-eight in 1810. This slight rise in numbers was balanced by the disappearance of some of the ships of 500 tons. These were replaced by 'extra ships' of a similar size. In 1810 the ships of 500–600 tons' burthen, both regular and 'extra,' numbered thirty-nine altogether. The proportion between the numbers of ships in 1807 was as follows: twenty-eight 1200-ton ships, thirty-three 800-ton ships, and thirty-one ships of 500–600 tons. Perhaps as many as twenty of the last group would be 'extra ships'.

In 1811 there was, for some reason, a sudden reaction in favour of the old 1000-ton class of ship. Several were launched at about the same time. These took the place of some of the 1200-ton class, the numbers of which accordingly fell to twenty-nine. There were, by that time, seven ships of between 1000 and 1100 tons, and three of less than 1000 but more than 900 tons. These last, however, belonged rather to the 800-ton class and represented an effort to attain greater seaworthiness—an effort resulting from Mr George Millett's Memorandum of 1809. At the same time there was an increase in the numbers of the 500-ton class and the 'extra ships'; so that the total number of East India ships for that year, including several on the stocks, was a hundred and seventeen.

The total number of Indiamen in existence was always greater than the total number employed in any given year. Including the 'extra ships', the latter figure may be said to have varied in the region of a hundred. A hundred and two ships sailed or arrived home in 1800, a hundred and five in 1804, ninety-nine in 1805, ninety-three in 1808, and a hundred and one in 1810. A rough average for the period might make the number of ships a hundred, the aggregate burthen ninety thousand tons, and the number of seamen seven thousand.

To appreciate the size of the East Indiamen, it is only necessary to realise how small the average merchantman was. Two or three hundred tons was the burthen of the ordinary trading ship, and a great deal of merchandise was carried in brigs of half that size. A ship of 350 tons was thought respectable, a 400-ton ship was considered large. In 1809 the whole of the shipping registered in England, apart from the East Indies fleet, included but twenty vessels of over 600 tons. And of these not one measured as much as 1000 tons.

Surrounding the subject of shipbuilding for the East India Company there is a certain mystery. From at least as early as 1709 it had been the custom for the Company to hire, and not to own, its shipping. Why this custom should have grown up is by no means clear. For want, however, of better information, it may be said that the Company followed tradition.

From the earliest times the ship and the cargo have seldom been the property of the same man. The East India Company, after an early experiment in shipowning, reverted to this normal system by which the merchant hires but does not own the ship. The result was that there came into existence a body of men who made it their business to provide ships for the Company to hire. These men were not shipbuilders. All they did was to obtain the contract, provide the capital and order the builder to proceed. The ships were built with their money, officered in the first instance by their nominees and partly provisioned at their expense. In return, they received a freight of £42 a ton for the voyage in time of war and £10 less in time of peace. These shipowners were a kind of middlemen, and as such they flourished considerably; sometimes making fortunes and usually profiting from a good investment.

This system of shipowning cannot but seem very extraordinary. The man who obtains a contract of any kind normally at least professes to be the actual builder or manufacturer. Here, however, we have the interposition of a totally needless class of middlemen; and there was never, apparently, any attempt made to explain what advantage could result from the system. The Company was, it is true, in the position of the merchant who pays the freight. But the ships were built specially for the service and were most of them useless for any other purpose. It would obviously have been better for the Company to own the ship as well as the cargo. A modern Railway Company does not hire the same vessels repeatedly to make the same voyage. It finds it more convenient to buy them. But the East India Company was never much alive to its own interests. The waste involved in its shipping concerns is but one aspect of a tendency perceptible in all the Company's affairs.

Considering the size of the vessels, it was inevitable that the shipowners should obtain something in the nature of a guarantee that their ships would be employed. To finance the building of an Indiaman was a formidable undertaking, and one which no capitalist would consider as a speculation so long as any doubt remained as to whether the ship would be wanted. The Company could not expect to hire its shipping in the open market, for no ships of an adequate size were, or could be, in existence outside the East Indies fleet. Indiamen had therefore to be hired before they were built. And it also became an unwritten law that an Indiaman, once hired, had to be hired again repeatedly until worn out. By a by-law of 1773, a ship was considered worn out after four voyages, but the introduction of copper sheathing during the period 1780–90 shortened the average passage to India by at least a month while at the same time lengthening the life of the ship. It was resolved, therefore, in 1790, that an Indiaman might make six voyages in all if properly examined and repaired after the third voyage. Although, however, the shipowner was obliged, if only by necessity, to hold his ship at the Company's disposal for six voyages, the Company had only a moral obligation to retain the ship for as long. And moral, as opposed to written, obligations are apt to be too elastic. In this instance, the elasticity of the agreement worked ultimately in the shipowners' favour. How this should be so requires some explanation.

The governing factor in the situation was the exceptional size of the Indiamen; a size which, always great, tended latterly to increase. In other branches of overseas trade there was competition between merchants as well as between shipowners. But, in the East-India trade there was but one merchant. If an argosy designed for the trade was not freighted by the Company it would not be freighted at all. This put the Company in what should have been a strong position. It was a position, however, which the Company could not abuse. Only by enormous injury to itself could it ruin the shipowners. Those, therefore, who managed the Company felt bound to treat the owners with fairness. If too high a freight was demanded, they argued and persuaded and sought arbitration. They never dictated terms under threat of seeking other ships to freight; for they knew very well that no other suitable ships existed. The shipowners, on the other hand, found means to undermine the Company's position in two ways. Their first and most obvious move was to enter into strict alliance with each other. The Company had henceforth to deal with a society or trade union, and could make no bargain with individuals. This deprived it of all advantage which might result from competition among the shipowners. Their second move was to buy up India stock and so acquire votes as proprietors. As early as 1710 a by-law had been introduced to prevent directors from being concerned in the Company's freighted ships; but there was no regulation to prevent proprietors being so concerned. Thus there grew up what was known as the 'Shipping Interest' in the Court of Proprietors. Including all connected with it, the Shipping Interest seems to have been able to muster as many as three hundred and fifty votes. This was not a number sufficient to carry the day when a question arose directly concerned with freights or demorage; not, at any rate, when the interest of the proprietors as a whole had been aroused. But such a block of votes was bound to be important, perhaps decisive, at elections. By supporting or opposing particular directors and candidates, according to their known views, the followers of the Shipping Interest acquired considerable influence in the Court of Directors. The more disinterested proprietors, who might outvote the shipping people on a question of policy, were not in any sense united nor yet as constantly present when elections took place. Hence there might even be a majority of directors pledged to support the Shipping Interest as against the interest of the Company.

The results of this successful invasion of the General Court were very much what might be expected. It appeared from the House of Commons Report of 1773 that the

Company's expenses in freight and in demorage during the ten preceding years had amounted to five millions sterling; and that this was a third more than need have been paid. In 1781 the Company tamely submitted to the shipowners' exorbitant demands on the occasion of the war with Holland. In 1783 the Court of Directors reached a compromise with the owners, ultimately agreeing to pay freight at the rate of £33 per ton, despite the fact that other owners, unconnected with the Shipping Interest, were offering ships at £30 per ton. Then, in 1785, a certain Mr Anthony Brough offered to build eighty ships for the Company's service at from £22 to £24 per ton, according to destination. As the Society of Old Owners was then tendering ships at between £26 and £29 per ton, Mr Brough calculated that the Company would save £150,000 a year by accepting his tender. Nevertheless, his offer was refused; and perhaps not wholly from the corrupt motives which he attributed to the directors. Writing in 1786, he contended that the Old Owners

> ...have intimately blended their own interests with the interests of some individuals of the Company, by whom, and from whom, they give and receive such powerful support, that the most vigorous efforts made by others to be admitted to a small share of their trade, have hitherto proved ineffectual. They build ships on what terms they please, and exact the most exorbitant freightage, to the incredible loss of the East India Company.

Although unanimous in rejecting Mr Brough's tender, on the grounds that he would be unable to fulfil his undertaking, the directors were heartened by it to the extent of resisting the shipowners' demands. As the result of conferences with the directors, the owners offered to accept as little as £24–£27 per ton. This offer was refused. The Court, meanwhile, had accepted tenders of ships at £22 per ton from several gentlemen who, like Mr Brough, were outside the trade union of owners. For a moment it looked as if the shipping monopoly would be broken. The Old Owners, however, in conclave,

> ...perceiving that tenders flowed in apace, and the Company would be able to do without them, set about procuring the ship-builders in the river (who have docks capable of building Indiamen) to join in the league with them, and to agree not to build a ship for any person who would tender her to the Company at the reduced freight....

The effects of this alliance between owners and builders were soon apparent. Mr Fiott, one of those whose tenders at a lower freight had been accepted, found it impossible to have his ship built in the river:

> It will appear extraordinary that, after having obtained leave to build a new ship, I should meet with any difficulty in getting it built; yet, on my application to some of the chief builders in the river, I was astonished to hear the excuses made for declining to undertake it, by those who were fully able, and who have since expressed their wishes that they had not refused it. I confess that I could not avoid attributing this circumstance to the same spirit of opposition to any new Owners or new shipping interest, which had before operated against me.—Finding that there was not one of those who usually build Indiamen in the river likely to undertake mine at any price, though I was willing to have given the then high price of thirteen guineas per ton, I was compelled to seek out a place for building in the country....

Mr Fiott found no difficulty in building his ship. There were half a dozen yards in Sussex and Hampshire at which a large ship might be built, and he soon contracted for the vessel to be built at one of them. A certain Captain Tanner, however, was less fortunate. He entered into a verbal agreement with Messrs Randall and Brent, the builders in Lower Queen Street, Rotherhithe, opposite Limehouse Hole. Presently he found that no progress was being made with his ship. When he asked why nothing had been done, Mr Randall confessed that he had changed his mind. He could not undertake to build her after all. He explained 'that he and Mr Brent had pledged themselves, jointly with others, not to build for those who would tender at the reduced freight'. Probably because it was too late to have the ship built in the provinces, Captain Tanner wrote to the Company that he could not fulfil his contract.

It is exceedingly difficult to understand what can have induced the Thames shipbuilders to make common cause with the Old Owners. It was not especially to their interest to do so. One can only suppose that long-standing business connections had ripened into personal friendships, family connections and financial dependencies. Whatever the basis, however, of this alliance, the fact of its existence brought the Company to a standstill. The directors then played their last card. Seizing on Captain Tanner's statement, they asked counsel's opinion as to whether the action of the owners and builders constituted a conspiracy in restraint of trade, punishable as such under the common law. Counsel gave opinion that further evidence would be required before proceedings could be taken against Randall and Brent.

Whether sufficient evidence could have been obtained to convince the Court of King's Bench may be doubted. It is not always easy to prove what everyone in London knows to be a fact. The threat, however, had its effect. It produced, that is to say, a deadly counter-attack from the Shipping Interest. The constitution of the East India Company made it compulsory for the Court of Directors to summon a General Court four times a year; but it also provided for the summoning of a General Court whenever as many as nine proprietors should require it. Now, at this juncture in 1786, such a requisition was made. When the Court met a motion was made, urging the Court of Directors to accept the Old Owners' terms. The Shipping Interest having attended in force, the motion was carried by 362 votes to 94. As a result, the Company surrendered and once more submitted to the Committee of Managing Owners. Mr Fiott, admittedly prejudiced, referred to this committee and the Club of Old Shipping Owners, which it represented, as an 'enormous fungus' which had 'robbed the parent tree of its vital juices'.

He returned to the charge in 1791 with a motion, which he carried, for the printing of all papers relating to shipping for the last ten years. During the debate on this motion,

> ...He charged the Directors with having, during the last ten years, squandered away thousands and tens of thousands of the Company's money, by their improvident Contracts for Shipping; the cause, he said, was notorious; there existed a combination of powerful and monied men, who had long given law to both Director and Proprietor; they were the political creators of the former, whose obedience to their wishes was the natural result; the independent interest seldom exerted itself but upon great popular questions; hence these Gentlemen had not only been constantly enabled to secure a preference to their own ships, but absolutely to fix their own freight, and insist, that none should be employed that did not belong to some one of their association; an association carrying with it all the forms of a regular institution, speaking through the organs of its president, and sanctifying its high resolves with the signature of its Secretary....

Later, he wrote as follows on the same subject:

> The sway which the several branches of the shipping-interest possess in the Company's elections, is a fact too notorious to be disputed; and is another evidence of their wealth, and of the purposes to which they apply it. As they influence a sufficient number of votes to turn the scale in every contested election, it is not to be wondered that a majority of the Court of Directors are always favourable to them, and that the conduct of the Court is, in many instances, such as it is found to be.

Although Fiott was possibly wrong in crediting the Shipping Interest with a permanent majority in the Court of Directors, the voting on a number of motions in the General Court shows plainly that there was a great deal of truth in his main contention. It is only by grasping this fact that any attempt can be made to understand an essential feature of the Company's shipping concerns; namely, the system of 'hereditary bottoms'. It was a system which had grown up, in all probability, during the period 1750–70, if not earlier, and it was the result of a continual yielding on the Company's part, a continual giving ground before the encroachments of the Shipping Interest. That there was a connection and an understanding between the owners and many of the directors is hardly in doubt. The connection may have been one of blood or of marriage, of business partnership, neighbourhood or friendship; indeed, it was probably all these things. We have seen that there were occasional conflicts between the Company and the owners, but between bodies of men so closely connected there could be no mortal combat. The Company always showed itself reluctant to proceed to extremities, and the result was the system about to be described.

An 'hereditary bottom' was the claim of a shipowner to be allowed to replace his ship when worn out. We have seen how the Company had, of necessity, to hire its ships before they were built; as otherwise, no one would have built them. It followed that the Company was morally bound to employ them for at least a reasonable number of voyages. This obligation was, as we have seen, unwritten. It followed again, and reasonably, that the owner of a ship which was lost before completing the usual number of voyages should be allowed to build another vessel in her place. It followed also, naturally, that a damaged ship might be repaired by her owner and thereafter employed; even if the repair was so extensive as to amount to rebuilding; even if the rebuilt vessel was practically a new ship. From some such origin as this, perhaps, came the practice of 'building a new ship *on the bottom* of the old'. It may originally have meant the actual incorporation of the old ship's timbers, or such of them as were still sound. From this custom—if it indeed existed—it was but a step to allowing the owner to replace his old ship by one avowedly new. And, in such a family concern as the East India Company, it was natural enough to extend the privilege to a son or widow. Thus, by slow degrees, must have grown up a hereditary monopoly among the shipowners. At any rate, whether by this or by some other process, such a monopoly certainly came to exist and was, by 1780, firmly established and already rooted in the past. The right of providing a ship and replacing it by another when lost or worn out had come to be regarded as property, heritable and even saleable as such. By a mixture of fair dealing, carelessness and corruption, the 'enormous fungus' had been allowed to take root and flourish.

The Company's own description of the system of 'hereditary bottoms'—as stated in a Case drawn up for counsel's opinion in 1800—was as follows:

> Previous to May 1796, the East-India Company employed ships built specially for their service, and used in none other, during so long as they were considered fit for the Company's use, which was four voyages. They were officered by men devoted wholly to that service, and regulated by old custom and standing rules; there was no written engagement on the part of the owners, that they would continue their ships in the Company's service, nor on the part of the Company, that they should be employed; however, the custom was so well established, that the parties mutually relied upon it, each considering the other bound by ties of honor, and by their mutual interest, to observe their implied customary engagements. In point of form, when it came to a ship's turn to be employed, a regular tender, on the part of the owners, was sent in writing, offering the ship in question for the Company's service for one voyage, and proposing a particular person as captain; and upon this tender, a charter-party was entered into for one voyage, without any reference to any previous or subsequent service of the same ship; but although the ships were tendered from voyage to voyage, and a captain proposed for each voyage, yet the owners were not at liberty, without the consent of the Company, to displace any person, having been regularly put into the command of a ship according to the usage of the service.

A feature which must be noted in the system here described is the permanence of the captains, their being 'devoted wholly' to the service of the Company, their not being dismissible by the owners. It was a typically eighteenth-century arrangement and might be compared to the custom regarding benefices in the Church of England. Just as it was for the patron to select from among those qualified, for the Bishop to approve and then induct, so it was for the owner to propose and for the Company to appoint. Again, as in the Church, the owner of the office could not remove his own nominee without a regular process following proof of a specific offence. The result of this system was that the command of an Indiaman, like most eighteenth-century offices, was a thing to be bought. Why such a command should be an object of ambition will appear from the facts given on a later page. For the present purpose it is enough to note that the office was a valuable one. It was sold, in the first instance, by the owner to the captain. The captain then sold it to his successor, who sold it in turn to *his* successor—and so on until some captain should be dismissed or die without heirs, when the command would fall once more into the owner's hands. It will be observed that the office thus bought and sold was not the command of a particular ship, but of an 'hereditary bottom'. The captain of a ship on her last voyage had the right to the command of the ship built to replace her; a right which he could assume or dispose of as he thought best. His widow, moreover, were he to die whilst in command, had an equal right to sell the office. So far from being legal, the sale of commands was, and had always been, contrary to the Company's by-laws. But the custom was so well established that the Company had ultimately to take official notice of it, lending to it a kind of sanction by the very act which put an end to the practice.

The prices paid for commands during the period 1787–92 seem to have varied between £6000 and as much as £11,000. Occasionally, commands were sold for £5000, £4000 or even £2500. They may sometimes have been sold cheaply, or even given away, to relatives of the owner. Mr David Scott informed Mr Henry Dundas in 1791 that the average price would be about £8000; an estimate which would seem to be rather too high. The price would vary, of course, according to the destination of the ship. The value of these purchases depended very largely on the honesty of the owners and captains concerned; the transaction being, in any case, illegal, exposed the buyer to a certain risk, and cases of cheating were not altogether unknown.

On this subject, Fiott's remarks are interesting:

> The captain's good-will, in regard to his resale, however, depends greatly on the honesty of the husband, who has leave from the Company to put in whom he pleases, though not to turn out. Several instances have appeared where the husband has negotiated the purchase for a captain and refused him liberty to sell at the same price. A captain, for instance, has got his command at £8000, the ship's husband being the agent; afterwards the captain, on wishing to resign the ship, has been refused leave, unless he gave up the good-will at half its cost, and in some instances for nothing...as the whole negociation is contrary to the By-Laws, no redress can be obtained by the captain.

A case such as this explains, to some extent, how the system grew up by which it was normally the captain, not the owner, who sold the command of the ship. Fiott remarks that the captain, in the instance he gives, had no legal redress. Supposing, however, that his health was not permanently impaired, he could at least retain command of the ship. One or two more voyages, conducted without much regard to the owner's interests, might be expected to put the captain in a stronger position. Owners could not, in general, expect to sell their commands, as they had no means of compelling the existing captain to retire. For this reason it was the captain, rather than the owner, whom the aspiring officer had to conciliate. It always lay in a captain's power to refuse to resign.

It may be supposed that so powerful a body as the Shipping Interest, so involved and deeply rooted a system as that of 'hereditary bottoms', was not easily to be destroyed. Indeed, without intervention from a higher power, the Company would never, probably, have been induced to free itself from this entanglement. That such intervention came was largely due to the persistence of Fiott and other not wholly disinterested individuals, whose grievance lay chiefly in their own exclusion from the select circles of the Shipping Interest. Disappointed as he must have been by the Company's surrender in 1786, Fiott had persisted in his campaign. In carrying his motion in 1791 for the printing of papers relating to shipping, he had at least managed to draw attention to the subject. And such attention was important in view of the fact that Parliament was soon to consider the question of renewing the Company's charter; a question which would have to be settled in 1793. There was a debate in 1792 on a motion to the effect that too high a price was being paid for freights. The motion was defeated by 561 votes to 353, but the numbers voting showed a growing interest in the subject. Interest was not confined to the India House, and the Court of Directors presently received a letter from Mr Dundas, President of the Board of Control, suggesting that the matter required attention. This was early in 1793, after negotiations had begun for the renewal of the charter, so that the hint could not be ignored. The result was the shipping programme of that year, which fixed the number and size of the ships without touching on the main problem. A party, meanwhile, had been formed to oppose the Shipping Interest, led by Mr Thomas Henchman, Mr Randle Jackson and Mr J. Fiott. A manifesto was issued in 1794, and it became clear during that year that Mr Dundas was dissatisfied with the Court of Directors and more than inclined to support this opposition party. Mr Charles Grant, elected now for the first time as a director, had the open support of Mr Dundas and the Prime Minister. This was the more significant in that his views were known and his candidature hotly opposed by the Shipping Interest.

Events moved slowly in this campaign, months separating

each move of the contending parties. The next significant event, after the appearance of the manifesto of 7 November 1794, was the meeting held on 16 April 1795. This was the occasion when the Independent Proprietors of East India Stock, gathered at the Crown and Anchor Tavern in the Strand, resolved to support the Court of Directors in any measures which should be taken to regulate the Company's shipping with a view to greater economy. Heartened or intimidated by the numbers present at that meeting, the directors pondered the matter for nearly a year and finally produced, in February 1796, a plan for reforming the shipping system. The main points of the plan were as follows: A reduction in freight was agreed upon, which would mean a saving of over £183,000 for that year alone. All regular ships were to continue in the service, freighted on a regular scale. 'Hereditary bottoms' were to be abolished and the captains to be compensated according to what they had paid for their commands.

The directors were evidently not unanimous in recommending this scheme to the General Court. Nineteen, however, signed a declaration on 18 February, calling upon the proprietors to support the executive body by rejecting the proposals made to delay the decision. The appeal had its effect and, on the 24th, these proposals were rejected by 762 votes to 366. The battle was virtually won, and there was much less excitement when the General Court finally passed a resolution on 10 March agreeing with the report and so bringing the conflict to an end. Three years later, the by-laws framed in accordance with the principles of the report were embodied in an Act of Parliament (39 Geo. III, c. 89) and received the royal assent on 12 July 1799.

The reforms of 1796 had two important results, apart from the immediate saving of money. One was the abolition of 'hereditary bottoms', the other was the introduction of open competition into the Company's shipping concerns. Although allied, these two results are distinct. The one chiefly concerned the captains, the other the owners. The hereditary claims to be bought out by the Company were found to number eighty-seven, and the total cost of the transaction came to £376,505. The captains' claims varied according to the price each had paid for his command and also according to the number of voyages made since the command had been purchased. A captain who had made four or five voyages was held to have had at least partial value for his purchase money. Thirty-nine of the captains received the maximum payment, £5000, others were given between £3000 and £4000 in compensation, a few £1500 or less; the payments averaged £4327. Considerable as this outlay was, the cost was not ultimately borne by the Company itself. All the captains in the service had henceforth to contribute £500 a voyage until the whole amount was repaid. As none had any legal claim to compensation, and as the new captains to be appointed would not have to buy their commands, these terms were generous.

The question arises as to whether the buying out of all hereditary claims actually put an end to the sale of commands. The practice had always been illegal. What was there now to prevent it which did not exist before? How could the by-laws be enforced with respect to an offence so difficult to detect? One fact is suggestive, namely, that in January 1800, so soon after the Act had been passed, the Company filed a suit in Chancery against Sir Richard Neave for selling the command of the *Glatton*, and would not stay proceedings until the offender compounded by a payment of £3000. This may be taken as evidence that the traffic began again immediately; or it may, on the other hand, be taken to prove that the Company was vigilant to prevent it. The probability would seem to be, however, that the directors, having made an example, were content with what they had done. One may suppose that the sale of commands continued, furtively, on a smaller scale, and for smaller sums of money.

As regards the open competition, it was to be secured by a public advertisement for tenders. It was laid down in the Act of 1799 that

> ...whenever the said United Company shall have occasion to cause any ship or ships to be built for their service, the Court of Directors of the said United Company shall give notice thereof by public advertisement, and therein state the burden of the ship or ships wanted, the dimensions or scantlings of timbers and planks, number of guns, manner of building, providing, furnishing, and storing such ships...and the said advertisement shall fix a time (not less than four weeks from the publication thereof) for receiving proposals in writing, sealed up, for building and freighting the same to the Company, such proposals to specify the lowest rates of freight...required for such ships for six voyages to and from India or China, or elsewhere within the limits of the Company's exclusive trade....

The tenders offered had to be placed in a box, locked and sealed, which was not to be opened except publicly in a Court of Directors. The lowest tender had then to be accepted 'without favour or partiality'—unless, that is to say, even the lowest tender was not low enough. If several tenders stipulated for the same freight, the Court was to decide which offers were the more eligible.

These rules are admirable, but they suppose a degree of competition which never, probably, existed for long. Undoubtedly a few new men like Fiott were thus enabled to force their way into the shipping circle. But a clique does not cease to be a clique merely through a slight addition to its membership. Once the new members had been absorbed, there was nothing to prevent the owners from settling the freight among themselves beforehand, and, supposing they did so, all the tenders would be the same. Certain it is that the owners retained some organisation among themselves. Moreover, the number of new owners was necessarily limited; to raise the fifty or sixty thousand pounds needed to build an Indiaman was not within the power of many, and there were not very many shipyards capable of building vessels of the requisite size. Further, there had been public advertisements before 1796, and Mr David Scott had referred to them as a 'farcical annual notice' inconsistent 'with the dignity of the Court, or with common candour'. Altogether, the probable results of the reforms of 1796 must not be exaggerated. The threat of outside competition may have kept the owners within bounds, but it is to be doubted whether they ever competed much with each other.

Before quitting this subject, some account must be given of these shipowners, as apart from their corrupt practices and their undue influence in the Court of Proprietors. So far, frequent reference has been made to the owners of ships and no notice has been taken of part-ownership. It is now necessary to state that it was unusual for any one individual to own an East Indiaman. Originally, when the ships were very much smaller—until about 1770—it may well have been the normal thing for a ship to have a single owner, but the advent of the 800-ton ship, followed by the 1200-ton ship, had made such ownership a far more formidable undertaking. Latterly, 'extra ships'—a class of vessel which seldom exceeded 600 tons burthen—might often be owned by individuals, but the regular Indiaman would, as a rule, be the property of a syndicate. To have the sole ownership of a ship of that size was not very convenient for the average capitalist, for it meant sinking an entire fortune in a single venture. It was obviously safer to own a share in several ships; and this was what was usually done. This was the type of communication the East India Company would receive:

We, the underwritten part-owners of the ship Earl of Abergavenny, John Wordsworth, jun., Esq. deceased, late commander, do hereby authorize John Wordsworth, of Brougham Hall, Westmoreland, Esq. to apply to the Court of Directors of the East-India Company, for leave to build a new ship for their service, in the room of the said ship, reserving to ourselves the option of holding our respective shares in such new ship, or not, as we shall think proper.

Witness our hands

Wm. Dent	1/8th
Rd. Crawshay	1/16th
Michael Colling	1/32nd
M. Colling for Rt. Collins	1/16th
Hugh Parkin	1/16th
John Maddison	1/32nd
Willis, Wood, Perceval & Co.	1/16th
T. Long	1/16th
John Atkins	1/16th
J. Farrer	1/32nd
John Wordsworth	1/16th
T. Newte	1/16th

Now, there is here no mention of who was to be managing owner; nor have all the part-owners signed the document. Supposing, however, that the request was granted, it would be necessary to inform the Company as to who the other part-owners were. It would then be necessary for a majority of the part-owners to appoint the managing owner or ship's husband. In the above instance, it seems probable that the Wordsworth family had owned the 'hereditary bottom'. But, supposing Mr John Wordsworth lived most of the year in Westmoreland, the managing owner would have to be one of the part-owners who lived in London; John Atkins, say, or Thomas Newte, both already managing owners of other ships. The function of a managing owner was to represent the syndicate in all dealings with the Company, and to act, in general, much as if he were the sole owner of the vessel. He had to transact all business connected with the construction, fitting out and provisioning of the ship. It was to him, the ship's husband, that the captain looked for instructions. It was therefore all but essential that he should live in London, within easy reach of the river and the builders' yards. A capable managing owner could do much towards making the voyage a financial success, and his ability, together with his profits on his last venture, would often lead to his becoming managing owner of a second ship and a third, obviously a convenient arrangement. To a man who had to make constant journeys down to Rotherhithe or Blackwall, it was almost as easy to supervise two ships as one. Thus there grew up a group of men who made it their profession to manage East India ships. There were a hundred and nine Indiamen in 1802, but only fifty-two managing owners. Of these managing owners all but one had a London address—the exception being a Bristol man—and all the addresses were those of offices in the City or else of places still farther east.

At the beginning of the nineteenth century the chief managing owners were Robert Charnock, William Fraser, Robert Wigram and J. Woolmore. Of these the first managed nine ships, including extra ships, and the others each managed six. Other managers of four or five ships were Agar Moses, John Locke, Sir R. Preston, Wm. Moffat and Matthew White. All these were City men, with offices in Cornhill, in Bishopsgate or the Old Jewry. It was with men of this type that the Company had to reckon in any conflict with the Shipping Interest. By 1812 fresh magnates had arisen, Henry Bonham, with nine ships, W. and R. Borradaile and John Pascall Larkins. The only survivor in eminence of the former group was Robert Wigram, who was by that time a baronet and the managing owner of no less than ten ships.

Wigram was not altogether typical of the managing owners if only because he was more successful than most of them. He was a drug merchant who had begun life as surgeon in an Indiaman in 1764. He came ashore in 1772, prospered in business, and bought shares in his first ship in about 1788. He founded his fortune with another ship, the *True Briton*, which performed a series of successful voyages between 1790 and 1809, the profits from which enabled him to acquire an interest in ships previously managed by Sir Robert Preston,

Sir William Fraser and others. He bought half the shares in the Blackwall Yard in 1810, became chairman of the East India Dock Company and a partner in Reid's (now known as Watney's) Brewery. Two of his sons became East India directors, another a Bishop, a fourth a Member of Parliament, which still left two more to carry on the business at Blackwall.

In a career of this sort lies the clue to the East India Company's reluctance to extinguish the Shipping Interest; as, for example, by owning its own vessels—a possibility never mentioned even during the height of the struggle over freights. The conflict may have been real enough at the time, but the opposing interests were not distinct. The shipowners sat in the General Court and had their representatives in the Direction. For a managing owner to have two sons among the directors was perhaps exceptional. Neither, for that matter, can many shipowners have had their representative in both the House of Lords and the House of Commons. On the other hand, Wigram's career shows the connection between the various groups interested in the East India Company; the sea officers, the shipowners, the builders, the proprietors and directors. There were families with a representative in each of these groups. And, although there was a by-law to prevent directors having an interest in shipping, a man might be successively what he could not be simultaneously. Numerous themselves in the first place, each group had its ramifications and alliances, spreading throughout London. The shipbuilders, to take one instance, had connections with a host of lawyers, purveyors, timber-merchants, underwriters, ropemakers, twine-spinners and manufacturers of sailcloth. The shipowners, again, would appoint their sons and their nephews to command their ships. Retired East India captains would have shares in shipping as well as relatives in the Company's civil service and votes in the Court of Proprietors. Outside these privileged circles were crowds of semi-dependent manufacturers: gunsmiths, oilmen, ironmongers, gunpowder-makers, boatbuilders, ship-chandlers, brewers, distillers, butchers and block-makers. It is only by understanding the complex intertwining of all these interests that one can grasp the importance of the Shipping Interest as a power in the Company's affairs.

Chapter VII

THE MARITIME SERVICE

THE commander of an Indiaman was appointed, we know, even before the vessel's keel was laid, and almost invariably before she was launched. It has been described how, before 1796, the retiring captains sold their commands to those who succeeded them. Even in those days, however, the appointment lay ostensibly in the owner's gift; and, after the abolition of 'hereditary bottoms', it lay with him to select whom he would from among those duly qualified. That owners sometimes sold their commands is probable; often, however, they appointed relatives or friends. There were some owners who held that to sell a command might be a financial blunder, as a really efficient captain was worth more to his owners than an incompetent captain would pay. Others, again, were too high-minded to engage in any such transaction. The captain, having been nominated by the owner, as a result of purchase, interest, friendship or through being his nephew or son-in-law, had to gain the consent of the Court of Directors.

This last step in the process of obtaining a command was the easiest. The candidate, to satisfy the Court, had only to comply with certain regulations. The Court, that is to say, confined itself to ascertaining whether the candidate was eligible. To fulfil this condition, he had to be at least twenty-five years old, and either have commanded a regular or extra ship before, or else made at least one voyage in a regular ship as chief or second mate. As all officers had to produce a birth certificate before appointment as fourth mate, a reference to the Company's books was sufficient to satisfy the Court on these points. It may be added that few men could hope to attain a command at anything like so early an age as twenty-five. In 1795 there were found to be a hundred and fifty-six chief and second mates who had served in those capacities for upwards of ten years. Six had served for thirty years or more, thirty-seven had served for between twenty and twenty-seven years, forty-one for from fifteen to nineteen years, and seventy-two for from ten to fifteen years. Fiott pointed out that some of these 'were in the service of the Company before some of the present captains in it were born'.

Every officer, on becoming fourth mate, took an oath of fidelity to the Company. Henceforth, after being sworn in before the Court, he had a dual allegiance. He was the sworn servant of the Company, enjoying a definite place in its hierarchy; and yet he was employed, and even paid, by the owner who appointed him. Except for the few who rose by seniority in the Company's own ships, all captains were in this anomalous position.

The Court sanctioned appointments in the following terms:

To Captain ——, Commander
of the Ship ——————

Sir

The Court of Directors having approved of your appointment to the command of the ship ——, I am directed to furnish you with the accompanying papers, containing what is immediately necessary for your information and observance, and to require of you the most punctual attention to all they contain. In the providing officers and ship's company, and in every necessary equipment, your utmost diligence is to be exerted; and by a constant and unremitting attention thereto, and frequent inspection of your ship, you are to hasten and expedite her departure, so as to comply with the times in your charter-party.

The stowage having been subject of great complaint, and the little attention to this branch of duty making the most pointed orders thereon necessary....

The missive goes on to threaten the recipient with punishment, should he neglect to keep a hold book. A similar letter was sent to all the officers, as soon as they were appointed, threatening them with every penalty should they be found carrying on an illicit trade.

It will be observed from the above letter that the appointment of officers and crew lay ostensibly in the captain's gift. It was for him to present the four principal officers to the Court, for them to take the oath. Actually, most of the officers were selected by the owner and captain in consultation, or else by the owner alone, the captain probably retaining a right of rejection. And, through the owner, the patronage was spread among a wide circle of people. The owner's friends and relations, his partners in business, his acquaintances in the City, his lawyer, his banker, his patron in the Court of Directors—all these might mention names to him in varying tones of entreaty and command.

1801.——A friend of Mr John Holley's (Mr Edmund Antrobus, teaman and banker, 480 Strand, London) procured me a midshipman's berth in the Honourable East India Company's maritime service. In the month of December 1801 I left home for the first time for the grand metropolis, and the above gentleman gave me a most friendly reception at his house. In a few days Mr Antrobus took me to Mr White, of Finsbury Square, the managing owner of the ship Marquis Wellesley, who had granted him the midshipman's appointment to that ship for me. This gentleman confirmed the grant with the greatest civility, and gave me an introductory letter to Mr Le Blanc, the chief officer of the ship....

So begins the journal of Thomas Addison. Of course there was this difference between the appointment of a mate and that of a midshipman, that with the latter no qualifications whatever were necessary except youth, whereas with the former the choice was limited. For a chief mate had to be twenty-three years old and have made at least one voyage as second or third mate. A second mate had to be twenty-two years of age, with two voyages to his credit as third or fourth mate; a third mate, twenty-one with one voyage; a fourth mate, nineteen, with one voyage. These last two officers might have made their previous voyage either as fifth or sixth mates or midshipmen. These rules prevented the owner from appointing children to navigate ships—an abuse not unknown before these regulations were issued, in a slightly different form, in 1791. The owner's patronage was also limited somewhat by the fact that a captain might wish to bring officers with him from his last ship. This still left, however, considerable room for 'wire-pulling'; and it is evident that both commands and berths were given away, exchanged or bartered across London dinner-tables or on the steps of the Exchange.

The officers who, by devious means, rose through the successive grades of the service, came from that middle class which was gradually gaining a secondary gentility towards the end of the eighteenth century, and which was to form the backbone of nineteenth-century England, declining in importance again in our own time. They came from the same class as that from which the Navy drew its officers, and the Company's service, like the King's, was open to talent. At least, it was open to such talent as could raise, borrow or beg the sum of about six hundred pounds. Those without this sum were debarred by the fact that the junior officers could not live on their pay. No rank, it was thought, below that of second mate, afforded a maintenance. The excess of expenditure over pay in the lower grades came to about five hundred pounds over and above the initial cost of fitting-out.

The comparison is interesting between the cost of entering the East India Company's service and that of entering the Navy. Captain Watkins, in his *Advice to parents*, stated the cost of outfit for the Navy as £50; but A Master's Mate of Six Years wrote an open letter to Lord Melville in 1812, in which he stated the cost as about £150, owing to the rise in prices during the war. The average time it took to reach the rank of lieutenant was seven years and a half, during which period a boy required at first £70 and at the end £50 a year in addition to his pay. So that the average cost of a lieutenant's commission came to about £585—not much less than the price of a captaincy in the Army. As the midshipman in the Company's service had equally to provide himself with uniform, bedding and navigational instruments, it is evident that he paid rather more than his contemporary in the Navy. And, by one account, he paid twice as much.

Some writers have conveyed the impression that berths in the Company's maritime service were sought by the younger sons of even noble families. This is incorrect. About 1800 there were two 'Honourables' in the service, and one Scotch Baronet—a second officer, who went down when the *Earl Talbot* foundered in the China Seas. And, of the 'Honourables', one—who was also Scotch—had been dismissed from the Navy. It would seem rash, on so slender a basis, to credit the Company's service with having had an exclusive atmosphere.

On the other hand, there is strong evidence for there having been something like social equality between officers of Indiamen and officers of the Navy. Their social origin, at least, was the same. The Naval officers, however, contended that the Company's officers had lost caste through trading; while the latter could console themselves by reflecting that the advantage in wealth undoubtedly lay with them. There was, as a matter of fact, a close connection between the two services in that not a few officers had served in both. Lord Keith had once been mate in an Indiaman. Captain Grant, of the H.C.S. *Brunswick*, used to tell 'long yarns about his having served midshipman in the navy with the Duke of Clarence'—an intimacy which had 'filled his mind with aristocratic notions'. Yet another close connection was that of relationship. Lord Duncan had a brother who was an East India captain, and so apparently had Lord Keith.

Many contemporaries vouch for the social standing of the Company's officers. Eastwick writes of the *Barwell* Indiaman in 1792: 'There were seven officers on board, and they were one and all gentlemen by education and family....' Captain Grant, according to Addison, always treated his midshipmen 'as officers and gentlemen'. Captain Hall gave his testimony that 'The East India Company's officers are bred up in many respects like naval men.... Being sprung from as good a stock as the officers of the brother-service of the Navy, they possess a kindred gentlemanlike spirit....' Beginning with a handsome admission, he nevertheless feels compelled to finish on a regretful note. Trade was not really compatible with gentility. 'Unfortunately, manage it as we will, the habit of buying and selling goods must have a tendency, in spite of his best exertions, to detach an officer's thought from those high and delicate refinements which constitute the characteristic distinction between the art of war and the art of gain.' Not all Naval officers were as generous. Admiral Drury wrote of the Company's officers as 'Men bred to every species of traffic'; and he ended his remarks with the outburst: 'The Captain of an Indiaman is but a mongrel kind of Gentleman or officer, turbulent, insolent and overbearing....' This contempt for the Merchant Service was a novelty in those days. Of Admiral Drury's two immediate predecessors in command, one was the son of a packet-captain, the other had himself commanded a merchant ship. Yet even Drury admits that an India captain was a *kind* of gentleman.

The status of its officers was a subject to which the Company gave some attention. In official correspondence a style was used akin to that used by the Admiralty. A captain was addressed as —— Esq., Commander of the Hon. Company's Ship ——; and 'Esquire' was in those days a word of some significance. 'Captain' was already a title given in conversation to the Master of a Merchantman, or at any rate of a large Merchantman. And it was perhaps for this reason that the Court of Directors usually, though not always, showed a preference for the title 'Commander'. It drew a kind of distinction. Nevertheless, the commander was always called 'Captain' in private life, and also among his officers. The latter retained the ordinary mercantile title of 'Mate', but the apprentices usurped the rank of 'Midshipman' when old enough to escape the epithet 'guinea-pig'.

An important factor in the officers' status was the wearing of uniform. The full uniform of the commander of a regular ship was of blue cloth, with black Genoa velvet cuffs and lapels and gold embroidered buttonholes. The skirt of the coat folded back, showing a buff silk lining, and the buttons were gilt, with the Company's crest. Buff waistcoat and breeches, black stock, white stockings, black velvet cape, cocked hat and sword completed the costume. This full uniform was worn only on state occasions, as when waiting on the Court of Directors or a Governor in Council in India. A modified version of it served as an undress uniform, worn probably on Sundays or when going ashore. Chief, second, third and fourth mates all wore a rather similar dress, their exact rank being indicated by the arrangement of the buttons on the cuff. The commanders and mates of extra ships wore much the same type of uniform, with some slight variation to denote their humble station. Fifth and sixth mates, not being sworn officers, were scarcely deemed to exist, and therefore had no official uniform. They wore uniform, nevertheless; as did also the midshipmen, who were distinguished by a dirk and a round hat with a cockade. The surgeon and purser, though free to wear what they liked, probably wore garments of a more or less congruous pattern. Throughout the regulations regarding uniform there runs that mystical English passion for rendering imperceptible all the outward indications of rank. Characteristically again, the officers almost certainly refused to wear uniform at all except on the most solemn occasions. We know, at any rate, that when the *Brunswick* was taken, the first thing the captain did on hauling down his colours was to send his officers to put on their uniforms. They could not give up their sidearms until those weapons had, perhaps with difficulty, been found. This seems to throw some light on their normal habits, even under a captain with 'aristocratic notions'.

With the Company's support, the commander of an Indiaman maintained in England the status of a gentleman; but in India, where the Company ruled, he was treated as a personage. His ship was saluted as it came into harbour, and the commander himself landed under a salute of thirteen guns. They turned the guard out as he entered or left the fort. And in that Indian society, still so oddly obsessed with precedence, he ranked as a colonel, superior to a captain in the Bombay Marine and but little inferior to a Member of Council.

To some this question of status may seem merely trivial. It was not thought so at the time. For the status—and in consequence the education, ability, courage and integrity—of the nineteenth-century sea captain was obviously inherited from the East India Company. The tradition, for instance, of calling reefers 'young gentlemen' could almost certainly be traced back through the Blackwall frigates to the Company's service. The effect of this tradition was to produce two or three generations of captains who—if only to judge by their portraits—must have represented the finest type England has yet produced. Through them was opened up a whole world of astronomical, meteorological and hydrographical science, a whole field of knowledge they alone could explore, a body of information based almost entirely on the accuracy of their observation. These were men fit to ennoble their calling, Christians, gentlemen and scholars. And if the tradition which formed them owed anything to the East India Company—as surely it must have done—no ceremonial was wasted which could uphold it. The guns, then, which saluted the

Indiamen were fired with good effect. Never was gunpowder so well expended.

The captain, officers and crew of an Indiaman were paid by the owner of the ship, through the agency of an office established by the Company. But how much were they paid? The captain received £10 a month, the chief mate £5 a month, the second mate £4, and so down to the sixth mate, who received £2. 5*s.*—twenty-five shillings less than the boatswain and a pound less than the captain's cook. A study of the list reveals an apparently crazy world in which the carpenter's mate is paid as much as the surgeon, and the purser less than the cook. Considering, moreover, that the captain had at one time to pay the Company £500 on his appointment, it is clear that he was not, in effect, paid anything at all. Indeed a single voyage would seem to leave him about £300 in debt.

The fact was, of course, that the officers were not remunerated in the form of salary but by permission to trade on their own. They were allowed to own a certain proportion of the cargo. Although this system may seem strange to modern minds, its origin is sufficiently obvious. The captain was allowed to trade simply because there was no possible way of stopping him. The regulations which gracefully ceded the point were merely a not very successful attempt to keep him within bounds. The Company's Indulgence of Private Trade and the Privileges of import and export have an air of generosity which the circumstances hardly warranted. It was, as a fact, the custom of the time. Those in power confined their efforts to checking the practice in the packet-service and the Navy; and even here they were not altogether successful.

The right of trading privately was more especially valuable in the East India trade in that the officers thereby shared not only in a trade but in a monopoly. Their lawful gains were very large, and not all their gains were lawful. The Company's efforts to prevent abuses, moreover, were half-hearted and ineffectual. Discovery of the offence was unlikely, and even when it took place some of the penalties were so light as scarcely to merit the name. Here, in short, we have another instance of the Company's prevailing weakness. The directors would not be severe on a body of men so closely connected with them. Among the captains of Indiamen they numbered their friends and relations and schoolfellows. And there were retired captains among the directors; not many, perhaps, but still they were to be reckoned with. In our period some four or five retired seamen were or had been directors—Joseph Cotton, George Millett, Robert Williams and two or three more. With their influence added to that of the directors who had nephews at sea, the officers as a body may be said to have been amply represented. Of course, decency had to be preserved; there was a limit to the Court's connivance. A line was drawn at smuggling—and yet even this line was occasionally overstepped.

On the outward voyage the commander of any ship of over 755 tons was allowed a space of over fifty-six tons for his private venture. The chief mate was allowed eight tons, the second mate six, the third mate three and the surgeon and purser the same. The fourth mate and the surgeon's mate might occupy two tons each, the fifth mate, boatswain, carpenter and gunner had one ton each. Then about twenty petty officers were allowed ten feet each. Captain and crew occupied altogether some ninety-two tons, the captain having the lion's share. The captain may, indeed, have had more than his share, for it is hardly to be supposed that midshipmen, for example, would wish to trade, and there can be little doubt as to who would occupy any space left over. Eastwick is positive that junior officers made no profit from their voyages. So is Milburn—who, incidentally estimates their total expenses as over a thousand pounds. The passage is worth quoting in full:

> The junior officers derive very little advantage from the privilege granted them to trade; and a young man entered into the service will, notwithstanding the greatest economy, expend up-

wards of £1000 before he can, with the best interest, and most fortunate circumstances, arrive to be a second officer, which is the first station wherein his pay and allowances afford him a maintenance. From that station he occasionally becomes a Commander; but most frequently has to perform one or more voyages as chief officer.

The chief profits, then, on trading, were made by the captain and the chief and second officers. They might export what they liked, except woollens and warlike stores. Those bound for India invested in goods likely to be required by the English residing there. This was a trade which the Company resigned wholly to the officers of Indiamen, who had therefore almost a monopoly in it. The type of goods sent out has been indicated on an earlier page. Food and clothes and wine were included, glass-ware, watches and clocks, snuff and tobacco, carriages and toys, garden seeds and duelling pistols; the necessaries, in short, of a civilised life. Those bound for China by the direct route had more difficulty in finding goods to export. If the captain's investment in goods fell short of £3000 in value, he was accordingly allowed to take out enough silver bullion to make up the amount; and the other officers had the same privilege on a more modest scale. Over and above this amount, a captain of a China ship might take out the value of £3000 in silver, provided that it was expressly intended for the purchase of gold. He could also invest as much as £2000 in precious stones. His bullion had to be included in his allowance of tonnage, but he was sometimes allowed to export flints, as ballast, in addition. And if the provisions needed for the voyage could be reduced, so as not to take up the space allotted for them, the captain had the option of filling the vacuity. If bound for India, and calling at Madeira, he had also the privilege of collecting two pipes of wine there.

It is to be doubted whether officers ever exceeded their privilege on the outward voyage. For one thing, they were allowed to do so on occasion, having only to ask permission of the Court of Directors. The favour was a cheap one, considering that the ship was often half empty. And for another thing, the market was limited, especially in India. The English who lived there certainly lived at an extravagant rate, but then there were very few of them. With the best will in the world they could not consume or waste beyond a certain point; there are physical limitations.

On the homeward voyage, the officers' privilege of private trade was more restricted. The captain was allowed only thirty-eight tons, the chief mate eight tons, the second mate six, and the rest as on the outward voyage, except that the petty officers are not mentioned as having any space allotted them. This was the scale of privilege in China ships. The vessels returning from India had a smaller scale—probably because they were smaller ships. In them the captain had only thirty tons and a half allowed him, and the other officers were privileged on a similarly reduced scale. There were restrictions as to quantity with regard to some goods, and there were rules forbidding India ships to import the produce of China or China ships the produce of India. Tea, of course, was the chief investment of the captains of China ships. They were allowed to import over nine thousand pounds of it, on paying a certain percentage to the Company; and the chief mate was permitted over twelve hundred pounds, the others in proportion. Tea was reckoned as part of their allowance of tonnage.

With the tea came the china-ware to drink it out of. The Company did not itself import china-ware, so that this was a monopoly enjoyed by the officers, and not reckoned as part of their allowance of space in the ship. China-ware came in boxes, not to exceed thirteen inches in height, which were disposed so as to form a flooring for the tea. At first sight, one might be disposed to question the wisdom of using crockery as a foundation on which to pile the rest of the cargo; but there was method in it. All wooden ships leak a little, and the bilge water consequently washing about in the hold had to be reckoned with. Tea, once wetted, is ruined. Once soaked in bilge water, it is never the same again. Crockery on the other hand is not harmed by damp.

There was a further conditional privilege in addition to the above allowances:

> ...as an encouragement to the Commanders and Officers to do their utmost to lade all Goods tendered by the Company's Agents, and to bring home as much surplus Tonnage as their Ships will safely and conveniently stow, the Court, on their Part, permit the further Importation of Goods on account of the Commanders and Officers according to their respective Privileges, not exceeding in the whole 30 Tons for each Ship, provided such Goods are stowed in Places not allotted to the Company's Cargo, or that they have not Goods tendered to them by the Company's Agents in India or China, or in the event of the Ship not bringing home her expected Quantity of Goods, they produce satisfactory proof to the Committee of Private Trade, that such Deficiency was not occasioned through any Default of the Commander or Officers.

This seems a strange method of encouraging the officers to lade the maximum quantity of goods for the Company. One would suppose that an exactly opposite effect would be produced. There was here, in fact, an almost irresistible opportunity for collusion between the officers and the Company's agents abroad. But this was not the end of the officers' import trade. Besides the captain's two pipes of Madeira, which he might take to England if he liked, besides his thirty tons or more of china-ware and his original allowance, there was the dunnage.

Dunnage was the packing put in to protect the cargo from injury; the straw and tissue-paper, as it were. The crockery was used, in fact, as dunnage, although it was not given that name. Now, dunnage was the property of the captain. He bought it, or was given it as a bribe, in India or China, and sold it when the voyage was over. It consisted of rattans, wanghees, canes, bamboos, sapan, or anything else that would serve the purpose. It was stuffed into crevices to prevent the cargo shifting. As the sale of dunnage was highly profitable, it sometimes happened that the crevices to be filled.were rather large. In some ships the cargo threatened to become merely incidental, and the Court of Directors issued appropriate warnings on the subject, probably without a great deal of effect. The quantity of dunnage, however, was necessarily limited by the demand in England. The desire for malacca canes and bamboo furniture was not, presumably, infinite.

Whereas there was not much temptation for the officers to export more than they were supposed to do, there was the strongest temptation to import goods in excess of their allowance. One exasperated owner, in 1803, complained of his captain 'having smuggled on board so great an investment, which almost exceeds belief' as to exclude the Company's bales from the after-hold. This was 'through bribery of the Company's officers'. The profits to be made were immense. As for the risk it was slight. If, for example, any captain was convicted of carrying dunnage to the exclusion of cargo; what was the penalty? He was made to pay the freight. There were worse abuses than that, of course, some of which led to dismissal or suspension for three years. But captains were sometimes fined for smuggling in a court of law without the Company ever learning of their offence. Indiamen, the Court of Directors would complain, were apt to 'loiter' in the Channel, clearly in order to transfer illicit imports to the smuggling craft and interloping merchantmen from Liverpool and Glasgow.

The value of goods exported from London by the officers, in private venture, seems to have varied between £100,000 and £150,000 a year. £120,000 was about the normal between 1784 and 1790. The rate of profit fluctuated but was nearly always high. In 1789 a total investment of £118,310 brought in goods of which the admitted sale price was

Plate IV. An East Indiaman off Dover.

From the watercolour by Atkins

£930,930. An outlay of £113,840 in 1791 brought in £703,578 in the following year. This was the normal state of affairs. The trade nearly collapsed about 1800, but afterwards recovered, so that the profits made during most of the later period were probably much the same as formerly.

Not all the above-mentioned profits arose directly from the outlay in London, for the captains had two other sources of wealth and the profits from each might come home in the form of goods—and indeed would normally do so. What little did not return in the shape of tea or piece goods was put out to high interest among Indian bankers. The rest went to swell the apparent profit on the investment. These two sources of wealth were, first, the trade from port to port in the East; and, second, the profit made out of the passengers.

With regard to the trade between port and port, it must be grasped that many Indiamen made round voyages, calling at several different ports and then returning to the Thames. Some went direct to China and back, but more made voyages such as: Madras, Bengal and Bencoolen; Ceylon and Bombay; Bencoolen and China; Bombay, Madras and China; Bombay, Bengal and Madras. On such voyages as these a commander could invest and reinvest; but more especially was this the case with the voyage to Bombay and from thence to China. Here a double profit was made. The beer and pomatum, the boots and shoes and fowling-pieces were sold to the garrison at Bombay, and the profit therefrom was all invested in raw cotton. The cotton was sold at Canton and the profit invested in tea and china-ware. The tea and china-ware, after paying duty and a percentage to the Company for warehousing, was sold at the Company's sales in London. Only three or four ships each year made this particular voyage, so that a captain could hardly hope to have the chance more than once in his life, if indeed he had it at all. But a single voyage of this kind might enable him to retire in comfort. The voyage to Madras and China offered a similar opportunity, though on a much smaller scale. On these voyages, if the Company did not require any portion of the hold, the officers were allowed to fill it, provided they paid the freight.

Even the ships sailing direct to China were able to do a little business by calling at Penang or elsewhere in the Malay Archipelago. There was, besides, a practice which Elmore unblushingly described in print in 1802. Country ships would waylay the Indiamen as they went through the Straits of Banca, put on board them their cargoes of tin, pepper, birds' nests and so forth, paying freight to the captain and taking in exchange a deposit of Spanish dollars—China ships always carried a proportion of specie. The country ships would then fill up with a second cargo of Malay produce and follow to Canton, where they would sell both cargoes and repay the loan. Taking interest on the specie, together with freight, the captain of the Indiaman would clear about 12 per cent. on the value of the country ship's first cargo—say, about three thousand sterling at one blow 'without trouble, risk, or delay'. The mysterious feature of this operation would seem to be the Indiaman's carrying capacity. As she was already laden with woollens, it is not very obvious where the pepper and tin was stowed. But here it must be remembered that the Indiaman was nearing her destination. A large proportion of her provisions and water would have been expended; and this, with a crew of over a hundred, was no small item; ships used to ride perceptibly higher in the water as the voyage went on. Part of the hold would therefore be empty. Again, China ships rarely carried any passengers, so that there was no objection to lumbering up the after part of the gun deck. And, lastly, as a little discomfort for all hands did not signify when within two or three weeks of Canton, pepper could be stowed between the guns.

Then the India ships had their passengers, both outward and homeward; yet another source of profit to the captain. Passengers were of two species; those in the

Company's service, and those not in the Company's service. The captain received the fares of both types, but whereas the fare paid by the Company's servants was fixed, that paid by other people was a matter of arrangement. The highest officials of all, Governors and Governors-General, did not travel in Indiamen at all, but had men-of-war allotted them. General officers were therefore the most important passengers in the Company's ships. They paid £250 for their passage to India, of which sum £15 came from the Company—the charter-party allowance to the owner. Including that allowance in each case, Gentlemen of Council and Colonels paid £200. Lieut.-Colonels, Majors, Senior and Junior Merchants paid £150. Captains paid £125, writers and subalterns £110, assistant surgeons and cadets £95. The voyage from India to England was more expensive. Lieut.-Colonels, for instance, had to pay Rs. 2500, or rather over £300; and even writers paid nearly £190. The difference between the passage money out and home was due, possibly, to the higher price of provisions in India.

Commanders were restrained under heavy penalties from demanding more than the proper sum. They were obliged, moreover, to receive the Company's servants as passengers, and so had no power of bargaining. To protect cadets from extortion, it was made a rule that they should pay—or that their parents should pay—their passage money to the Company's paymaster. An order for their being received on board was then made out, on production of the pay office receipt. The only way a commander could obtain an additional sum from an official passenger was by allowing him additional cabin space—at the expense of his own.

Passengers not in the Company's service—women, for instance, going out to join their relatives—had to drive their bargain as best they could. How much they paid is not easily ascertained. In 1810 ladies were said to pay £500 for their passage. William Hickey, a successful attorney, paid Rs. 8000 for his cabin and passage money when returning to England in 1808. This sum, equal to £1000, was a small fortune in those days; but then he seems to have insisted upon having rather princely accommodation. The passage money, in fact, is more readily explicable than the 20,800 rupees he claims to have spent in clothes and cabin furniture. Bosanquet, whose habits were less luxurious, paid only Rs. 3500 in passage money, and did not think the cost of furniture worth mentioning. On the other hand, a family might have to pay as much as £2500 for a passage to England.

As to the numbers of passengers, it is difficult to find what the average number was. Here are the statistics for half a dozen ships arriving in India in 1805: *Indus*: 4 ladies, 6 gentlemen, and 9 cadets. *Lord Keith*: 1 lady and child, 12 gentlemen and 13 cadets. *Ocean*: 3 ladies, 4 gentlemen (all army officers) and 9 cadets. *Huddart*: 8 gentlemen. *Harriet*: 4 gentlemen (officers), 3 cadets for Bengal, 14 cadets for Madras. *Euphrates*: 2 gentlemen, 1 lady and child. Taking these ships to be typical, we may suppose that a dozen passengers would be thought neither few nor many. The outward flow of boys is evident in the above figures. The numbers of passengers homeward bound were, of course, very much smaller; but then they paid a great deal more. When the East India Company lost its monopoly, the captains, in asking for compensation, estimated the average profit per voyage on passage money, after deducting the cost of provisions and stores, as £1500.

The whole question of the commanders' profits is best summed up in Milburn's words:

> It is impossible to form an average estimate of the profits arising from the command of an East Indiaman, so much depends upon the skill and good management of the Commander and the persons employed by him, the risk of the markets, his connections and interest, which enable him to select his passengers from among opulent persons returning to Europe, and many other

circumstances depending on chance. Although upon a voyage out and home, the Commander's investment has sometimes produced a small, and at other times a large profit, instances have occurred, and those not unfrequently, wherein a considerable loss has been sustained. The least productive of the voyages may be generally estimated at £2000 per voyage; while upon some others, such as the circuitous voyages to Bombay and China, of which there are not above four in a season, the gain may be from £8000 to £12,000; the major part of the voyages may be averaged from £4000 to £5000. The time occupied in performing a voyage, from the period of the ship commencing to receive her outward cargo, to her being finally cleared of her homeward one, varies according to the ship's destination, from 14 to 18 months.

Milburn's estimate, which dates from about 1812, is cautious and sound. There seem, however, to have been instances of larger sums being made. He does not take into consideration the kind of transaction which Elmore describes as taking place in the Straits of Banca, nor does he discuss the profits which may have arisen from smuggling. To obtain any information on these topics would of course be difficult, and it is to be supposed that the commanders who made the largest profit were those who said least about it. On the other hand, it is clear that captains sometimes lost rather than gained by their investments. In 1800 the Court of Directors received petitions from Captains John Skottowe, F. W. Leigh, John Price, Robert Reay and Nathaniel Dance, each petitioner 'stating his services and losses, and his present distressed circumstances, and praying relief'. In some instances, the abolition of the system of 'hereditary bottoms' proved a heavy misfortune. More commonly, it was the taking of Indiamen into Government service which ruined the unfortunate commanders. The following petition is typical and not uninteresting from other points of view:

> Memorandum of the Case of Captain Sampson Hall, of the Honorable Company's late ship Sulivan.

Captain Hall begs leave to represent, that he was chief mate of different ships in the Honorable Company's service, from the year 1781 to 1793, during which period, (having a wife and family to provide for) he sunk upwards of £2000. In February, 1794 (on the death of Captain Pouncy of the Sulivan) Captain Hall was appointed to the command of that ship, and for which command he paid £6000, and has since received £5000 in remuneration bonds [i.e. by compensation in 1796]. He further begs to represent, that upon his return to England, at the expiration of his first voyage as commander, in the year 1795, the Sulivan was immediately ordered into Government service, to carry troops to the West Indies, with Admiral Christian's fleet; which service, he trusts, was performed to the satisfaction of Government, but wherein, he is sorry to say, that he sustained a very considerable loss. Captain Hall, on his return from that service, proceeded upon his second voyage to India, as commander of the Sulivan. On his return from thence, in 1798, he found, by the change of the shipping system (the Sulivan having made six voyages) that he had no chance of building another ship on her bottom, in consequence of which he had the mortification to find, that he was compelled to submit to a statute of bankruptcy, to satisfy the demands of his creditors. Had the former system continued, he should have commanded the new ship that would have been built in the room of the Sulivan; and he is confident, that his creditors would not have taken such measures against him, as by his industry he might have been able to retrieve his losses. He is, therefore, left destitute of employ, with a wife and three children, and no means of support, except from the assistance of his friends.

That the above statement is strictly true, I am ready to verify on oath.

SAMPSON HALL

London, 2d June, 1800.

There existed a fund, on a contributory basis, known from its connection with the Company's hospital or almshouses at Poplar as the Contingent Poplar Fund, and it was to this source that impoverished captains looked for relief. Captain Skottowe, for example, one of the above-mentioned petitioners, was given a pension of £300 a year. This was calculated in the following manner: £120 for himself, £80 for his wife and £25 each for his four children. Other officers were pensioned on a similar scale. In most of these cases, the relief was temporary and came to an end as the recipients found fresh employment. Pensions were also paid, however, to retired officers who had failed to earn a competence and who were unable, from age or sickness, to go to sea again. That many such pensions were paid is an indication of how frequently officers lost rather than gained by their trading. Captain Basil Hall, R.N., writing on this subject, held that the East India captains' blend of trade and war made 'rather an agreeable than a profitable mixture'. He added that 'their mercantile bargains, both in respect to sales and to purchases, are, I fear, none of the best for themselves, poor fellows!' He may, perhaps, have had to listen to tales of losses, without realising that a mercantile loss is often but an unexpectedly small gain. Some of those, moreover, who were bewailing their poverty in 1800–2 lived to retrieve their losses and even make their fortunes at a later period. Nathaniel Dance had the most persistent ill-luck for many years and yet ultimately attained both fame and fortune.

No estimate seems to exist of the profits made by officers below the rank of commander. The mates, it is clear, lived only in the hope of becoming captains. Those who failed to rise so high, like Addison, were finally given a pension of about £100 a year, with £128 as the maximum. But most of those who survived must eventually have become captains, which was sufficient reward for their former services. Many, from lack of interest, failed to achieve promotion, but most of these must have died before reaching a retiring age. Pursers had their perquisites, the amount of which cannot be guessed. Eastwick, however, tells of a purser of an Indiaman who profited so largely that he was able to settle down as a shipowner in India. Surgeons also had their perquisites and allowances, notably for attendance on the troops carried. Some of them, like the founder of the Wigram fortunes, may have traded profitably in drugs.

Nothing has so far been said concerning the numbers of

men carried by the various classes of ships in the Company's service. The smallest of the East Indiamen, extra ships of about 500 tons, carried a crew of fifty. In the regular ships the principle was to carry about a dozen men to every hundred tons; that is, in the 500-ton class. Sixty was thus the minimum complement. Larger ships carried 101, 110, 120, 125 or 130 men. A ship of 750 tons and upwards carried, besides the six mates, surgeon and purser, a boatswain, gunner, carpenter, five midshipmen, a surgeon's mate, caulker, cooper, captain's cook, ship's cook, captain's steward, ship's steward, sailmaker, armourer, butcher, baker, poulterer, barber, and six quartermasters. These, with their respective mates and servants, together with fifty seamen, made up a total of about a hundred. In the 1200-ton ships the crew was larger by the addition of another twenty or thirty seamen.

The organisation of an Indiaman's crew differed little from that of a ship-of-war, except that the offices of captain and master were amalgamated and that there were no marines. The inferior officers, although allowed some small privilege of trading, were dependent on their wages, which were for that reason a reality. There were two scales of wages, one for peace and one for war. We are concerned only with the latter scale, which was not unlike that of a frigate in the Navy; the chief difference being that, while the petty officers were paid a little less than those in the Navy, the seamen were paid a great deal more. A boatswain in the King's service received from £3 to £4. 16*s.* a month. The boatswain of an Indiaman received £3. 10*s.* a month. The carpenter of a third-rate was paid £4. 16*s.*; that of an Indiaman, £4. 10*s.* On the other hand, a quartermaster in the Navy drew only £2. 5*s.* 6*d.* as compared with the £2. 10*s.* drawn by his equivalent in an Indiaman. The divergence becomes more marked among the foremast men—a difference between £1. 13*s.* and £2. 5*s.* for able seamen, between £1. 5*s.* 6*d.* and £2 for ordinary seamen.

In time of war the operations of the press-gang robbed the

Indiamen of all their best seamen, leaving gaps which had to be filled up with foreigners, lascars, boys and landsmen. Even so, the ships were too often without more than skeleton crews, as deficient in numbers as in quality. This was more especially the case on the homeward voyage, after the original complement had been reduced by disease, desertion, accident, and above all by impressment. The East Indies squadron was eternally in need of men and could get them in no other way than by impressing the crews of Indiamen. The Company strove manfully to send out its ships properly equipped and fully manned, but they always came home stripped of their original complement. The disease-ridden frigates were insatiable. At first the rule was that the lascars who manned the home-coming ships should be sent back to India as passengers, either in extra ships or licensed country vessels. This was always to some extent done. The *Elizabeth* country ship, wrecked off Dunkirk in 1810, was taking no less than 347 lascars back to the East. It was thus hoped that Indiamen might at least sail with a European crew. A process of this kind could not continue indefinitely, however, for two reasons. In the first place, the supply of European seamen was unequal to this eastward drain; in the second place, the probability of being impressed in India discouraged even landsmen from joining an eastward-bound ship. The result was that Indiamen began occasionally to sail from England with almost as large a proportion of lascars and Chinese as they had on arriving there.

The ratio between the European and native parts of an Indiaman's complement is best illustrated by a few examples. One commander of an Indiaman sailing from India in 1809 had a crew of 42 Europeans and 27 lascars. This ship, the commander said, was 'considerably better manned than on his former voyages'; this was because he had enlisted a number of Danish prisoners of war. Another, in the same year, thought himself fortunate in having 65 Europeans and

44 lascars. Other ships were stated to have had a smaller proportion of Europeans. The *Streatham*, taken in 1809, was manned by 44 British, 16 foreigners, 33 Chinese and 40 lascars. The *Europe*, taken at the same time, had a crew of 41 British, 31 foreigners and 56 lascars. Hickey, returning to England in 1808, wrote that the Indiaman he voyaged in was manned by 'a strange motley crew, consisting of natives of almost every nation of Europe, besides nine Americans and eighteen Chinese. Certainly we had not more than ten English seamen on board.' It is clear that, from ships like these all the British had been impressed that were subject to impressment, the remainder being the officers, leading petty officers and boys. Addison relates that by the time the various press-gangs had finished with the *Brunswick* China ship, there were left 'about thirty of the lame and awkward'.

As regards the manning of the outward-bound Indiamen, the efforts of the Company to maintain the quality of their crews is shown in the composition of the ship's company of the H.C.S. *Hope*, when about to sail from the Thames in 1811: officers and seamen, 139; passengers, 12; recruits, 100; women attached to them, 6; Chinese seamen, 40; Portuguese and lascars, 87; Total, 384. The Chinese, Portuguese and lascars were evidently being sent home as supernumeraries. Wathen, who gives these facts, does not state how many of the Europeans were British. He makes it sufficiently clear, however, that many of them were not. 'The aggregate', he writes, 'of this microcosm was composed of English, Scots, Irish, Welsh, Americans, Portuguese, Spanish, French, Swiss, Germans, Chinese, and other natives of India.' It will be observed that Wathen classes the Portuguese and lascars together, without attempting to settle the proportion between them. This was because the Portuguese here referred to were not Europeans but 'the degenerate posterity' of the original Portuguese invaders of India. They were distinguishable from the natives only by their religion.

Neither lascars nor Chinese made bad seamen, both being useful in fine weather and the Chinese especially so. But the Chinese were not so easily obtainable, and it was chiefly with Portuguese and lascars that ships had to be manned. Those sailing from India, in particular, had often no choice in the matter. Like the Chinese, the Moslem natives of India called lascars had their virtues; their morals were, in general, better than those of European seamen, they were sober, hard-working and obedient; and some of them knew a few words of English. They were content with Rs. 10 a month. Food for them was easily procurable and cheap, so that they cost only 8*d.* or 1*s.* a day to feed when a European cost from 1*s.* 3*d.* to 2*s.* The objections to them were that they were physically weak, cowardly, and unaccustomed to cold.

David Macpherson wrote that lascars 'from their feeble habit of body, and being accustomed only to short voyages during the fine-weather season upon the tranquill seas of India, are unable to bear the cold, and utterly incapable of the vigorous exertion and rapid movements necessary in the boisterous seas of Europe...'. Eighty or ninety of them, it was thought, were hardly equal to fifty British seamen; and, in a gale, when it came to clearing away the wreckage of a fallen topmast, they were more or less useless.

Then, as regards their courage or lack of it, most evidence points to the conclusion that they would not fight. Neither, for that matter, would the Chinese—whether from cowardice or indifference is not clear. Here is the captain's account of the defence of the *Streatham*:

...I sent Mr Maxwell, the chief officer, below to encourage the people at the guns, he returned shortly after to inform me that the Chinese and Portuguese, who were stationed on the gun-deck, could not by any exertion of the officers be kept to their quarters, deserting as fast as they were brought back, and that our firing was almost exclusively maintained by the Europeans....

The captain of the *Europe*, on the same occasion, reported that his lascars were equally useless:

> I have the pleasure to inform you, that Mr Hardyman, chief officer, as well as Messrs Jackson, Hall, Charetir, and Mills, did their duty in a most handsome manner. The petty officers and the Europeans did also behave with great courage; but as for the Lascars, they were only in the way.

The general testimony is strong as regards the lascar's insufficiency in the hour of danger, whether in a battle or a hurricane, but it is only fair to add that there were examples to the contrary. After coming through the great gales of 1809, the commander of the ship *Sir William Bensley* reported that 'the Lascars, although they deserted their posts two or three times, did better in the end than could have been expected. We have few European sailors on board.' The country ship *Eliza Ann* was manned by lascars when she beat off the *Confiance*, privateer. It is possible that there were ships in which the native seamen had come to fear their officers more than they feared the elements or the enemy.

The last objection to the lascar was that he died. He was killed by the cold, perhaps in rounding the Cape, perhaps in the Channel. In the H.C.S. *Hope*, according to Wathen, ten Portuguese and lascars died on the voyage between England and the Cape; this, even when probably doing little duty and standing no watch. Only one European sailor died during the same period. But this was a mild case. The *Lucy Maria*, country ship, which sailed for England in 1801, shipped eighty-six lascars for crew. Twenty-two died on the voyage, and twenty were ill when the ship arrived in England. The *Surat Castle* sailed at about the same time, shipping a hundred and twenty-three lascars. Thirty-six died during the passage, forty-five were ill by the end of the voyage. How many of these sick lascars would recover in England? Few, in all probability. The Company tried to collect them into an official kind of lodging-house or barracks, with a view to shipping them back to India at the earliest opportunity. 'But many of them are so much vitiated by intercourse with worthless women, as to prefer a state of beggary....' These 'miserable creatures' were a familiar sight in London streets, where numbers of them perished from want and disease.

Discipline on board an Indiaman was maintained by the same methods as used in the Navy. Deprivation of grog, 'starting', confinement in irons, and flogging were the standard punishments. They were inflicted frequently or seldom, severely or otherwise, according to the ideas of the individual commander. Grog was stopped as a penalty for trivial offences such as having a slovenly appearance on Sunday. Confinement in irons was the standard method of bringing the drunkard to his senses. 'Starting' was the punishment meted out to those suspected of scamping their work or failing to pull their weight. A boatswain's mate was called, who beat the offender on the spot with a rope's end. It was a cruel punishment, falling chiefly on a man's arms and shoulders, and it was already going out of use in the Navy, being finally forbidden in 1811. The worst feature of it was that it was often ordered in a fit of anger or impatience, when a little reflection might have shown the injustice or needlessness of it. The officer of the watch might inflict it without reference to the captain. There was a case in one Indiaman of a mate having an old seaman 'started' until he dropped unconscious—all this quite unjustly, as it afterwards appeared. Lascars seem to have been punished in the same way, but by their own 'serang' or native boatswain.

In most Indiamen a flogging was a rare event, inflicted for mutinous behaviour or attempted desertion. A dozen lashes at the gangway might be the maximum punishment with men like Captain Larkins or Captain Grant in command. A certain Captain Rawes, however, was said to give two dozen as a minimum.

In another Indiaman, the Captain had a greater aversion to

hear a sailor cry out under punishment than to inflict it; and when any one *squeaked*, as he called it, he used to *double his punishment*, saying, I gave you *one dozen* for drunkenness—I now give you *two dozen* more for crying out whilst receiving the first!

(*Naval Chronicle*, 1814.)

This kind of severity was unusual, and was recounted as being so. Sailors were 'hazed' as a rule far less in an Indiaman than in a ship-of-war. And this makes it less easy to understand why men sometimes deserted from them. That they should have been tempted into American ships at Canton, as Archibald Campbell was in 1807, is sufficiently comprehensible. By his account, they were offered higher wages and a bounty of twenty dollars on joining—together, probably, with papers proving their American citizenship. But why should they have deserted to the Navy? Why did they volunteer? Addison gives several instances of their doing so, as that the men 'were very plaguy in giving themselves up to ships of war', but he volunteers no explanation.

Private grievances may have had something to do with these sudden fits of patriotism to which seamen were apparently liable. Captain Grant we know to have been 'a martinet and great disciplinarian'. And together with the particular grumbles against individuals, we must allow for the permanent inability of the sailorman to know when he is well off. But there were general causes besides these. A sailor could avoid impressment into one of those legendary vessels such as H.M.S. *Disreputable* (Captain Tauthand), or the *Red Rover*, gun-brig—'but quite a yacht'—(Captain the Right Honourable Viscount Scorethem), by being safely entered in some other man-of-war. Men were hardly ever transferred from one ship to another. Once under a popular captain, a man was tolerably safe from the sadism of the notorious tyrant; there was no such security in an Indiaman. And it must be remembered that the most active press-gangs were those from the worst ships. It was in some hell afloat, commanded by an

'Easy Dick' type of captain, that most recruits were needed. For it was because of inhuman treatment that men deserted, because of callousness and stupidity—often—that they died of disease, because of terror that they were killed in working aloft. Another factor to be reckoned with was this: when the greater part of an Indiaman's crew had been taken by the press-gang, the remainder tended to follow of their own accord, knowing that their work would necessarily be doubled if they remained. 'Tween decks that were half empty would always tend to become wholly empty. Some men might volunteer, again, in order to join their friends. A few, such as midshipmen and surgeon's mates, would transfer to the Navy in the hope of bettering themselves socially if not financially. Lastly, there was the magic word 'Prize-Money' which must have decided many a waverer. The captain of an Indiaman had much to put up with in time of war.

A final aspect of the East India trade to be considered is its function as a school of seamanship. Although the East India Company's ships were, in a sense, the aristocrats of the Mercantile Navy, they did not rank very high as training ships. The Company claimed that its captains were the finest navigators in the world. They were quite clearly nothing of the kind. They kept to a beaten track in which there was no scope or need for brilliance. Apart from the solitary adventure of Captain Butler, who sailed round Australia in 1794, all the navigational feats of the generation with which we are dealing stand to the credit of naval men—and not the least of them to a Frenchman. In knowledge of the Indian Ocean and the East generally, they were of necessity inferior to the captains of country ships, from among whom the East India Company drew its most famous hydrographer. They had, certainly, a reputation for a knowledge of the winds, and yet, when questioned as to the climatic causes of the catastrophe of 1809, they all flatly contradicted each other. Their skill, one is inclined to suppose, consisted in a mass of traditional and accumulated experience, gained in conversation with each other at the Jerusalem Coffee House and based on the table-talk of the commanders under whom they had been trained. Such empirical knowledge is not science, it is only useful while on a beaten track. The East India captains never discovered the Degree-and-a-half Channel for themselves.

The foremast men in an Indiaman were, on the whole, less skilled than those in several other trades. The more adroit their commander was in securing a following wind, the less variety of weather had they to encounter. It was part of an India captain's religion to sail always at the proper season, and so voyage for weeks almost without touching the canvas; but this did not make for good seamanship. The crews improved more in ships that sailed out of season. As expert seamen, an Indiaman's crew, in so far as the men were bred to the trade, were probably inferior to the men trained in West Indiamen, Newfoundland craft, South Sea whalers or collier brigs. Their excellence was less in seamanship than in making a smart appearance, and perhaps in handling the great guns.

How able and willing an Indiaman's crew might be to prepare for action may be gathered from Bosanquet's account of his voyage in 1810:

Our Captain had been in the King's service. He was the shortest man I ever remember to have seen; and whilst walking the deck with our lady passengers (a thing, by-the-by, which he seldom did)—one of whom, by accurate measurement, was six feet two—the contrast was one scarcely ever seen, even at a show. He was a little touchy in his temper, and the captain of the man-of-war, [the convoying ship which had just parted company] much his junior in age, seemed to elicit many sparks, which the flint-and-steel rivalry of their peculiar positions alone kept up. Captain Colnett was now commodore.... I forget the exact latitude we were in; but, whilst conversing with the little captain, the word was passed that two strange sail were in sight. Up *came* the Captain—up *went* the glass. 'Frenchmen! and frigates, too! Master-at-Arms, ahoy! Signalise the Amelia and the Rose.' 'Ay, ay, sir!' And in a moment the pendants floated from the mizen. Then followed orders I understood not; but in a moment the two ships, with all their canvas spread, might be seen gradually separating themselves from their companions, and following hard in the wake of the Frenchmen, who, being to windward, had no difficulty in supporting their distance and remaining in security, though the fleet, large as it was, would have proved [no?] more than a match for them in a fair and close fight.

'Make ready there! clear away for action!' said the little Captain; and the bulkheads began to move, the tompions were taken from the guns, the men began to collect to their posts, and the little Captain, for the first time I had seen him quite happy, took me below decks, and entered into an argument of his advantages arising from his diminutive stature. For myself I could scarcely analyse my feelings. The whole preparation showed the nature of our employment in prospect—the ideas of broken limbs and shattered hulls were not tempting; and though I had not much doubt of fulfilling the duties that would devolve upon me, and standing to my gun, yet I cannot say that my feelings were divested of that anxiety which accompanies the doing of a thing of moment, or that the scene was to me, as to the little Captain, one of entire and unalloyed zest. With what anxiety did we witness the chase! But our own course was not the same; and as the evening drew near it was evident that our heavy companions were quite unable to bring their unknown fugitives to bay; and the little Captain—who probably, from the commencement, had a shrewd guess how the affair would terminate—hoisted his signal of recall, observing that, if the Indiamen were separated a little more from the fleet, the frigates might capture them before the rest could come up, and bear away the prize during the night. When the course of the pursuing vessels changed, it became evident how changeable is the heart of man—the preparation for combat (though we, excepting the ship's officers, could gain nothing by it), a considerable item in excitement, was stirring in the mind, and a vacant feeling of disappointment followed the announcement that the enemy was safe.

In thus seeming to seek an engagement, Captain Colnett, as commodore of the convoy, was not obeying the letter of the Company's instructions. He was, however, following a tradition of the service; a tradition which, strengthened by the capture of the *Médée* in 1800 and by the result of Dance's action at Pulo Aor in 1804, was rooted in a more remote past. The theory behind this tradition was that a merchant ship could often best escape by steering directly towards the enemy. Such an action, disconcerting in itself, had the effect of preventing him seeing one's broadside. Such boldness might end in disaster; but then, so might the alternative policy of running away. On the whole, and especially was this true for Indiamen, safety lay rather in bluff than in flight.

Wathen, in his journal, comments on the willingness to fight shown by the crew of the H.C.S. *Hope*. That Indiaman, with the *Taunton Castle* and *Amelia*, sailed from Madras for China in September 1811, and sighted three strange sail a week later.

> ...It was supposed they were French frigates cruizing to intercept us. Preparations were instantly made for a vigorous defence—bulk-heads and cabins all laid down, and the decks cleared for action.—We were on the alert all night; communicating with the commodore by signals; all hands on deck, and all busy. I could not help admiring the alacrity of the seamen—one would have thought by their looks, and the cheerful bustle they were in, that they were preparing for some jovial entertainment or some grand festival; but the brave fellows were disappointed;—for, at five o'clock the next morning, the strange ships had disappeared, and we saw no more of them.

The *Hope*, it may be remarked, was exceptionally well manned, having about a hundred and thirty English seamen and officers on board. Not all Indiamen were as ready for battle. Lady West, describing the *Milford* in 1822, wrote that the crew included 'only 40 English Sailors, the other 86, Malays, Arabs, Portuguese, Africans, of every Nation almost under the Sun; all looking savage, dirty and miserable'. She was reassured by the information that they were really 'all that is gentle and timid'. This reassurance was very well for a time of peace, but it lost some of its force during a time of war.

Far too little is known at present of the lives of individuals in the Company's maritime service. It is difficult to believe that there are no biographies in existence, in print or in manuscript, of East India captains. Without some knowledge of the lives of such men as Sir Nathaniel Dance, Sir Charles Mitchell, Captain Grant, Captain Colnett, Captain Hall, Captain Joseph Cotton and Captain Templar, together with a dozen more, it is exceedingly difficult to form an impression of the type of sea officer the Company employed. The stray references available are, many of them, suggestive; but the picture, for lack of private journals and biographies, is necessarily incomplete. What would one give to know more of that brother of Lord Duncan who commanded an Indiaman and who, according to Rear-Admiral Monkton, 'turned field preacher; and annoyed his Lordship very much in Scotland by his notoriety'? Oddly enough, of the very few descriptions of life in an Indiaman, other than as a passenger, two are by foremast men and a third by a midshipman. The Journals of Thomas Addison, covering the period 1801–30, and partly printed by the Navy Records Society, are written, indeed, by a mate; but the more personal and interesting parts relate to the period when the writer was a midshipman. His narrative of his second voyage begins with an account of his reception by Captain Grant:

1803.—On preparing for a second voyage I expressed to my friend Mr Antrobus a desire to go to China. He kindly met my wishes and soon obtained for me a midshipman's berth on board of the Brunswick, Captain Grant, a regular China ship of 1200 tons. I was introduced to the captain, who was very civil and gentlemanly; was pleased to find I had been a voyage, as none of the other youngsters going had been at sea; therefore, as senior, of course he should make me his midshipman coxswain, allow us a cabin, servant, and every comfort etc., as long as we conducted ourselves like officers and gentlemen. What a different reception and treatment was this to what I met with on my last voyage, or rather first commencement! the contrast I soon experienced was most striking and delightful, especially to us mids. Captain Grant was a martinet and great disciplinarian, which latter was exacted in all its branches from both officers and men; always made a point of treating and supporting us mids as officers and gentlemen. There were five of us; two were stationed as signal midshipmen, as he was commodore; the other three in three watches, one in each. I was in the latter; never allowed to quit the lee side of the quarter deck, except on duty or on general occasions of reefing or furling. Two of us dined with him every day, and nothing could exceed his politeness and kindness at the table....

A very different account of a midshipman's life in an Indiaman is contained in the memoirs of Edouard de Warren, who went out to India in that capacity at some period after the termination of the wars. It is not by any means clear, however, that the *Aurora*, in which he sailed, was a regular Indiaman. He states that there were five midshipmen, who berthed in a cabin six feet long, four feet broad and five feet high. They were fed on mouldy cheese and worm-eaten biscuit and 'harassed, robbed, tormented on all sides, beaten by every one'. Warren remarks that they were worse treated than the sailors, as being less useful:

...That bell which recalls the cloister or the prison, sounding every hour and calling periodically the crew to the same duties—work, meals, sleep; that idleness, overwhelming, deadly, but nevertheless inevitable; for what study is possible amid that incessant movement; those abominable sounds that pursue you everywhere; the raucous voices of the officers issuing commands; the complaints of the passengers; the cries of the sailors; the creaking of the planks of the ship's sides; the wind in the rigging; the lapping of the water; it is cacophony, universal, ceaseless, without relaxation or respite. And then there are the appalling odours from which there is no escape, that detestable tar, the emanations from that odious galley; in the midst of these nauseating things it is impossible even to read; the day drags, is wasted in words....

Warren's experiences may have been peculiarly unfortunate, while he himself was probably peculiarly unsuited for life at sea. On the other hand, Addison expressly states that his treatment by Captain Grant was a striking contrast to the treatment he had received on his first voyage. The conclusion would seem to be that the *Brunswick* was at least as much above the average as the *Aurora* was below it. On the whole, it may be said that a midshipman's life, in an Indiaman, was a hard one. That it was better than that of the sailor is clear. Archibald Campbell's narrative contains little information about the seaman's life in an East Indiaman, and no criticism beyond what was perhaps implied by his own desertion. In the reminiscences of Silas James, on the other hand, the sufferings due to short rations and bad water are depicted in some detail. For such of the seamen who grew old in the Company's service or who were disabled in action there were pensions or accommodation in the hospital at Poplar. Few lived to receive either. In time of war, the seamen in the Company's ships were mostly impressed, sooner or later, into the Navy. Of those impressed, the majority had to serve in the ships of the East Indies squadron. Many died in that unhealthy service, and many more were invalided home; not half of them can have lived to be paid off in an English port. Only at the end of the war did this dreadful mortality cease.

Chapter VIII

THE VOYAGE

In the early nineteenth century the Port of London extended from London Bridge to Deptford. It comprised the Upper Pool, stretching from the Bridge down to Union Hole; the Middle Pool, the part from Union Hole down to Wapping New Stairs; and the Lower Pool, from there down to Horseferry-tier, near Limehouse. These three stretches, the medieval port, were for ships of from 250 to 400 tons. Below them were two further stretches, also part of the Port of London, but more lately come into use; the first from Horseferry to the mooring chains at Deptford, the second being opposite Deptford itself. Of these, the one was fit for ships of 450–500 tons, drawing seventeen or eighteen feet of water, the other was deep enough for the biggest ships in the Merchant Navy. Including colliers, of which there were about three hundred, and coasting vessels, some of which might lie between London Bridge and Blackfriars, the whole Port could contain as many as fourteen hundred vessels at once.

The only part of the Port of London used by the East India Company's ships was the lowest stretch of all, that opposite Deptford. A great many Indiamen had their moorings there. Those that did not moor there, moored at either Blackwall or Northfleet. These three anchorages were opposite the yards where the ships were built and repaired. A ship's arrival at Deptford, Blackwall or Northfleet, after fitting or refitting in dock, in the Brunswick basin or elsewhere, was known as 'coming afloat', and it was the first stage in the process of commencing a voyage. A ship, on coming afloat, would still be in the hands of carpenters and riggers and watchmen. It would be towed or warped to its moorings by a gang from the yard where it had been repaired. A new ship would come there from the dock where they had finished coppering her after the launch. Coming afloat was a landmark in a ship's career, comparable with being taken up or launched.

Once at her moorings in the river, she would probably be joined, first of all, by the chief mate and boatswain, then by the other officers and the nucleus of the crew. No officer was allowed to proceed to his duty on board the ship until he had signed a contract for performing the voyage, together with a petition for his private trade. Nor was any of the Company's cargo delivered on board until the four chief officers had been presented by the commander to the Court of Directors, and the fourth sworn in if he had not taken the oath previously. Then, as soon as the first of the cargo began to arrive in lighters or hoys, sent from up the river, the third and fourth mates, and either the chief or second mate, had to be on board the whole time until the ship sailed. This was the more essential in that stowage, in those days, was something of an art. It is still, for that matter, a subject on which books are written. The trim of a sailing ship, and its centre of gravity, depend on how the cargo is stowed; and it was not enough to see that the iron was put at the bottom and the woollens on top.

So far, the commander would only have paid a few fleeting visits to the ship. Only when the cargo was all shipped did he take command. He and all his officers had to be on board while the ship dropped down to Gravesend, the second stage in commencing a voyage. When the ship was at anchor in her new berth, the commander probably disappeared again, leaving the chief mate in charge. During the ship's stay there, in Long Reach, which might last a month, he had only to visit her once a week, and it was very likely beneath a captain's dignity to appear more often.

At Gravesend there was sent on board the most valuable part of the Company's export; namely, boys. The boys were of two kinds. Some were of more or less gentle extraction and were called cadets. The rest were from the lower classes and were called recruits. The cadets, if intended for the Civil Service, were from fourteen to eighteen years of age; if for the Army, from sixteen to twenty-two. The recruits, enlisted for twelve years, or else for life, might vary in age from sixteen to twenty. The word used here—recruits—is used advisedly; and it must not be taken as meaning young soldier. The recruits were the raw material from which soldiers are made. During the eighteenth century the Company had no training establishment in England; its troops were sent out as mere children, without arms, without training, and sometimes even without uniform. They had no officers with them, or even non-commissioned officers. In 1801 a depot was established in the Isle of Wight; but, even then, not all recruits seem to have been sent there. When Lord Minto was sailing to join the Java expedition in 1811, the *Modeste* frigate in which he was accommodated had thirty men of the Company's Bengal European Regiment serving on board as marines. In the Governor-General's words: 'They are all recruits just come out, and all boys of about sixteen or seventeen years of age,—fine-looking lads, but never having seen a firelock, without clothing...or so much as a corporal....' In this case, they learnt their platoon drill from the Governor-General's younger son, then acting as his secretary. They had clearly known nothing when they sailed from England and as little when they arrived in India.

There seems to be no readily accessible information as to how these recruits were obtained. That a fair proportion of them were Irish is shown by their willingness, in some instances, to fight on the other side when taken prisoner.

There were whole units of Irish in the French service before the end of the wars; as indeed there were in the Spanish Army before the wars began. But by what process of famine, kidnapping, crimping or persuasion, these boys arrived at Gravesend is not clear. They were probably tumbled on board either unconscious or, more likely, drunk. At any rate, their first impulse, on grasping the situation, was to escape; their second impulse—when thwarted in the first—was to get drunk again. To achieve this latter aim, when destitute, their only means was to sell the clothing which the Company had provided. Care, however, was taken to prevent them. Taught by long experience of this tendency, the Company issued full instructions on the subject. The ship's officers had to see to it that the recruits 'do always appear in the several articles of clothing provided for them by the Company'. They were to be extremely careful that 'they do not dispose of their clothes for liquor or otherwise'. And, lastly, they were 'to exert their best endeavours to keep the men quiet, and prevent their making their escape...'. An Indiaman with recruits on board had to be turned into something of a prison. A quarter watch was kept, night and day; the boats alongside were chained and locked, and no boat was allowed to leave the ship before being examined.

As regards the numbers of the cadets and recruits, there might be six or eight of the former and perhaps twenty or thirty of the latter. The *Hope*, in 1811, had a hundred recruits on board and, probably, three or four cadets. Many ships, however, carried neither, and a captain must have thought himself peculiarly unlucky to have both. As he had a sort of parental control over these juvenile passengers—both classes of whom could give him a great deal of trouble—his responsibility was heavy. It is to be doubted whether any number of these boys can have added much to the strength of the ship. An Indiaman that carried real soldiers, on the other hand, was rendered more formidable thereby. The troops, if there were any, were not shipped at Gravesend but at a later stage in the ship's progress.

Supposing a vessel had its full complement of seamen, a hundred or two hundred soldiers and ten or twelve passengers and cadets, or even if it had only twenty or thirty recruits and a crowd of lascars being sent home as supernumeraries, a large proportion of the hold would have to be devoted to them. Stores, that is to say, would have to be carried in considerable quantity. Six months' provisions for anything from a hundred and fifty to four hundred people—here was, in some cases, the answer to the problem of what the Company could find to export.

The East India Company's affairs had always a tendency to become entangled in the intricacies of rights and customs, privileges and monopolies. Even the watermen on the Thames had formed themselves into old-established firms, attached by immemorial right to particular ships. And the victualling bill of an Indiaman looks very much as if it had come into being in this general atmosphere of haphazard growth and deep-rooted conservatism. But perhaps there was more method in it than there at first appears to be. Some articles had to be provided by the owner, some by the Company; but there seems to have been no general principle governing the system.

The managing owner of a ship was also known, for particular purposes, as the 'Ship's husband'. In the preparing of the ship for sea, he or his agent had to deal with an official called the 'Company's husband' who acted presumably as a check on the owner and commander. Then there were other officials known as 'The Sealers at the India Wharf', who had a separate function to perform. All stores were received on board by order of either the Ship's husband, the Company's husband or the Sealers at the India Wharf. The Ship's husband had to provide spare canvas and cordage, pitch, rosin, tar, iron shot and gunpowder. Then he was to supply billet wood, brimstone, coal, turpentine, candles and vinegar. So far, the list is what one would expect—the owner supplying non-edible stores, vinegar being included as a disinfectant. But then a series of less comprehensible items is added to these: limejuice, brandy, fish, butter, cheese, red and white herrings and salt. He had lastly to provide the water. The Sealers at the India Wharf were responsible for sending on board the beef, pork, bacon, suet, tongues, beer, bread, flour, grocery, mustard, oatmeal, oil, oats, barley, bran, oranges, lemons and pease. They also supplied the surgeon's stores, lead shot for the small-arms, sheet-lead, slops, tobacco and tobacco pipes. The Company's husband or his assistant provided four tons of iron for store, together with the ale, beer, wine and other liquor for the commander's table—eleven tons, allowing two hundred and fifty-two gallons to the ton.

From the point of view of stowage, water was the biggest item in the victualling bill. There had to be a minimum of forty tons, and a large ship with troops on board needed a hundred tons or more. The beer casks—twenty-eight tons—were the item second in importance; the beef and pork and biscuit coming third. Not included in the victualling bill are the stores allowed—apparently by the Company—to the mates, surgeon, and purser. The chief mate was allowed twenty-four dozen of wine, beer, or other liquor, two firkins of butter, one hundredweight of cheese, a hundredweight of grocery, four quarter-cases of pickles and—usually—a puncheon of rum. The others were supplied with much the same articles on a scale reduced in proportion to their rank, all except the sixth mate, who was not included.

During the last few days at Gravesend the livestock was brought on board, together with the vegetables for immediate use. Later in the nineteenth century ships were content to boast of 'a good milch cow and an able surgeon' or words to that effect. But an Indiaman of our period, provided there were passengers on board, carried a small farm-yard. In *Newton Forster* Marryat describes how the poop of an Indiaman was crowded with coops and noisy with the sounds made by chickens and geese and turkeys; while the waist of the ship was tenanted by other livestock:

> The booms before the mainmast were occupied by the large boats, which had been hoisted in preparatory to the voyage.... The launch contained about fifty sheep, wedged together so closely that it was with difficulty they could find room to twist their jaws round, as they chewed the cud.
>
> The sternsheets of the barge and yawl were filled with goats and two calves, who were the first destined victims of the butcher's knife; whilst the remainder of their space was occupied by hay and other provender, pressed down by powerful machinery into the smallest compass.
>
> The occasional baaing and bleating on the booms was answered by the lowing of the three milch cows between the hatchways of the deck below; where also were to be descried a few more coops, containing fowls and rabbits. The manger forward had been dedicated to the pigs....
>
> The boats, hoisted up on the quarters, and the guys of the davits, to which they were suspended, formed the kitchen gardens, from which the passengers were to be supplied, and were loaded with bags containing onions, potatoes, turnips, carrots, beets and cabbages....

This picture is not exaggerated. According to Wathen, the H.C.S. *Hope* sailed from Northfleet with one cow, fifty sheep, seventy-one pigs and over six hundred geese, ducks and fowls. The cow and sheep consumed two hundredweight of hay a week and fifteen gallons of water a day. It may be imagined that the shipping of all this livestock and forage, together with passengers' luggage, kept an Indiaman in a state of confusion during her stay at Gravesend.

Another source of confusion was the shipping of the commander's and officers' goods in Private Trade. Sometimes a part of these goods was taken on board while the ship was still at Blackwall or Deptford. When this was done, the commander had to petition the Committee of Shipping seven days before the ship came afloat. More often, however, the bulk or the whole of the goods was shipped at Gravesend, the commander and officers signing their petitions within four days of the ship's arrival there, or else within four days after their appointment.

The Private Trade Indulgence is not very easy to understand. The theory seems to have been that the Company was entitled only to the tonnage it paid for, so that when a ship was freighted with a chartered tonnage of twelve hundred tons and an actual burthen of fourteen hundred or more, the odd two hundred tons, on which no freight had been paid, were at the disposal of the managing owner. He could, if he liked, have left the space vacant. What he could not do was to ship goods on his own account, for this would have been to infringe the Company's monopoly. Now, what in theory happened was that the Company allowed the owner to allot a proportion of this tonnage to the ship's officers. This was to encourage them to refrain from defrauding the Company in other ways; and also perhaps to induce them to defend the ship, which they would be more likely to do if they owned a part of the cargo. The officers, for their part, were therefore beholden for their Private Trade Indulgence both to the owner and the Company. The space they might occupy was given them by the owner, but it was only through the Company's permission that they were allowed to put anything in it. That is why their petition was addressed to a committee of the Court of Directors. What they shipped had to be passed by the officer in the Private Trade Branch, measured for tonnage by the Elders at the East India Wharf, and shipped within three days.

There was a final ceremony before an Indiaman quitted Gravesend, and that was the farewell visit of the managing owner or Ship's husband. He would appear on the day before the ship was due to sail, attended by his agents and perhaps a few friends as well. The business of the agents was to pay the crew a part of their wages in advance. To procure seamen in time of war was exceedingly difficult, and wages were correspondingly high. In peace-time an able seaman was paid only twenty-six shillings a month, but thirty-two and even forty-five shillings had to be paid him after the outbreak of war. In May and June 1803, there was trouble with the seamen who had been engaged at a fairly low rate before the war began. On 11 May the managing owner of the *Woodford* informed the Committee of Shipping that the press-gang had taken six of his men and that the remainder refused to sail unless their wages were raised to forty-five shillings a month. On 9 June came a similar complaint from Mr Bonham. He reported that, while refusing to pay more than thirty-five shillings a month, he had distributed £342 among the crew of the *Essex* and £264 among the crew of the *Lord Melville*, as a bribe to induce the men to weigh anchor. 'On these terms', he wrote, 'the people have been induced to go, notwithstanding other ships at Gravesend, in the service of the Company, were the same day giving the full war wages of 45*s*. per month.' Labour troubles would sometimes delay a ship's sailing for weeks. Seamen were also troublesome in deserting from one ship to another. The China ships were far more popular than those bound for India, and it was often almost impossible to man the latter so long as the former were in the river. The men would desert as fast as they could be procured. Altogether, and especially in time of war, the owners were relieved when the day came to pay their crews, for it meant that these disputes about wages were at last at an end.

Seamen were procured by means of crimps, who were often Jews and always 'furnished by that class from which we derive informers, thief-takers, sheriffs' officers, executioners, and other odious, though necessary, appendages to civil authority'. The crimps were paid at the same time as the seamen, on the day before the ship sailed. There were often comic and occasionally violent scenes between these men and the sailors they had supplied. In war-time the crimp had sometimes to be paid not only for finding the men but also for hiding them ashore until the last moment so as to save them from the press-gang. The Company often succeeded in obtaining 'protections' for its ships, but during a 'hot press' all such legalities were ignored.

After the owner had gone and the last crimp been bundled over the side, the ship was ready for sea. The anchor would be weighed with the first of the ebb, and, in two or three tides, the ship would come to anchor again in the Downs. There a cluster of other Indiamen would join her in the course of a few days. In peace-time, and sometimes in time of war when there was a frigate there to give them convoy, the East India ships might sail from the Downs—the last and richest passengers embarking at Deal and being brought on board by extortionate Deal boatmen. More often, however, in war-time, the Indiamen had to assemble at Spithead. When they did so, perhaps in two or three days or possibly after being kept windbound for three weeks, it was from Portsmouth that the most belated passengers came. There also were embarked the troops.

When a whole regiment was being sent out to India, each ship might have to embark a considerable number of men, not to mention women and children. When a convoy of Indiamen sailed from Spithead in 1804, with Rear-Admiral Sir Edward Pellew to protect them, the whole of the 17th Regiment was embarked in eight ships. Altogether there were 1336 soldiers, 75 women and 44 children. One ship, the H.C.S. *Hawksbury*, had no less than 292 men, 15 women and 12 children on board, making the ship's company number 412. The *Airly Castle*, *Worcester*, and *Duke of Montrose* were similarly crowded, the first two having in the region of 400 souls on board. With vessels so packed, the acute problem was how to carry sufficient water. In this instance, the largest ships took in nearly two hundred tons; in other cases, the problem proving too difficult, ships would be on short allowance from the day they sailed.

At Portsmouth Indiamen received the mails for India, which were not sent from London until the last moment, so that the official dispatches might contain the latest possible news. After the commander had taken his official leave of the Court of Directors, attending in full uniform at the India House for the purpose—a ceremony which happened while his ship was at Gravesend—he was not allowed to sleep on shore again. He was given his sailing orders, and none of his officers might from that time remain more than twelve hours absent from the ship; none, that is to say, except the purser, to whom the dispatches were entrusted. The system probably was that the purser went with the ship to the Downs, and then posted back to London as soon as the ship was under way with a fair wind for Portsmouth. Collecting the mails at the India House, he might then take the next coach for Portsmouth, where he might easily arrive as soon as his ship did. Travel by road was fast enough for that. The day had already come when a stockbroker could live in Brighton.

In time of war Indiamen scarcely ever sailed singly, but usually in divisions of eight or ten, escorted by a man-of-war whose captain took command of the convoy as soon as the Indiamen reached Spithead. Their stay there was not long, but its length was determined by Naval officers. Henceforth, the Indiamen had to obey signals from the escorting ship, and it was at a signal from her that the convoy sailed. As a general rule, the Company's ships were painted after the same style as the King's ships, so that a convoy of them had a formidable appearance, as Captain Hall testifies:

> There sailed along with us in the Volage, from Spithead, the Princess Caroline 74, and the Theban frigate, to aid in protecting a fleet of the following ships of the East India Company:—the

Elphinstone, Wexford, Cirencester, Marquess of Huntly, Bombay Castle, and Alnwick Castle, all for China direct. As these ships were of the largest class, well manned, well commanded, and were likewise pretty well armed, and got up to look like men-of-war, our force had not only an imposing aspect, but, in the event of coming in contact with an enemy, even in considerable strength, we should either have beaten him outright, or baffled him by crippling his spars in such a way as to prevent his interrupting our voyage....

The phrase 'got up to look like men-of-war' had, probably, a more definite significance in 1812, when the above convoy sailed, than it had throughout the earlier part of our period. Only after 1805, and in slow degrees, did the Navy adopt a uniform style in paintwork. But the 'Nelson Chequer' may have become fairly universal by 1810; and it may have been about that period that the East India Company followed suit, introducing a camouflage which the whole Merchant Navy promptly copied and retained throughout the rest of the sailing-ship era. The ships-of-war in the East Indies were probably slower to follow the fashion than the rest of the Navy; for there, while it was the object of an Indiaman to look like a man-of-war, it was as often the object of a man-of-war to look like an Indiaman. Except, however, when a ship-of-war was purposely disguised, there were probably a hundred ways in which an English seaman could distinguish her. There must have been little differences in the rigging and in the handling of the sails. The saying 'I don't like the cut of her jib' has become embedded in the language along with a score of similar nauticalities. It dates from a time when the art of telling friend from foe at sea was a matter of vital importance. Just as Indiamen were sometimes taken through failing to recognise an enemy in time, so they sometimes escaped through not being recognised themselves.

Once an Indiaman was fairly at sea, one of the first things the captain did was to make out a 'Quarter Bill', in which every person in the ship, passengers included, was assigned an action station. The much more difficult business of settling the order of precedence at the cuddy table had probably to be faced at about the same time. There was a host of regulations on every topic, some issuing from the East India Company, some from the captain of the ship. Once all these had been made known, a settled routine was observed for the rest of the voyage.

The crew of an Indiaman was normally divided into two watches, starboard and larboard, the one commanded by the chief mate, the other by the second mate. When the crew was exceptionally large—and there were instances of a hundred and ninety or even two hundred men being carried—and again when the ship was in harbour, there might be three watches. The third, or mid-watch, would in that case be commanded by the third mate. The officers were, in any case, divided into three watches; a convenient arrangement when there were six of them. There were thus two officers in each watch, the senior being on the quarter-deck and the junior taking charge forward. Of the five midshipmen an Indiaman might carry, one would act as signal officer and one, perhaps, as captain's clerk. The remaining three, including the senior midshipman who was also coxswain, would stand watch with the mates. A midshipman's principal duty during his watch was to heave the log every hour. Presumably the arrangement was for the sixth mate and junior midshipman to be in the chief mate's watch, the fourth mate and senior midshipman in the third mate's watch.

As regards the berthing of the officers and men, much depended upon the number and quality of the passengers. If there were none, the mates would usually have cabins in the round-house or poop where the captain's state-room was always situated. If there were many, the mates had to have their cabins in the steerage, the after part of the gun deck. The chief mate had a cabin on the starboard side, just forward of the 'great cabin'. This berth might measure twelve or fourteen feet long by ten or twelve feet broad. It would include a port and might well merit Twining's description, 'a neat well-furnished little room'. The second mate had a corresponding, but smaller, cabin on the opposite side of the ship; the third mate's cabin was on the starboard side, next to that of the chief mate; the fourth mate's cabin was forward again of this, on the same side. The corresponding cabins on the larboard side were occupied by the surgeon and purser. Of these six cabins, perhaps four would include ports. The aftermost ports on each side normally had no guns. The guns from the next pair of ports would normally be run forward and lashed to the ship's side, muzzle pointing towards the bows. But, in war-time at any rate, the remaining cabins on the gun deck, forward of those just described, would many of them be encumbered with cannon. In the absence of passengers, these would be occupied by the fifth and sixth mates, boatswain and carpenter. Another cabin, of rather larger size, might be shared by the midshipmen. When passengers were numerous, however, all but the six sternmost cabins were resigned to them. What happened then to the inferior officers is not apparent. Presumably, they retreated into the gloomy recesses of the lower deck.

The petty officers and crew of an Indiaman slung their hammocks forward on the middle or gun deck. There also they had their meals, divided into messes of five or eight men, according to the size of the ship. Each mess had its appointed space between the guns, where the mess utensils were kept. When recruits were carried, or any small number of troops, these also slung their hammocks on the forward part of the gun deck. They were grouped into messes on their own, space being found for them between the guns. With a crew of normal numbers, there was plenty of room for troops. When, however, the soldiers were numerous, they had to be consigned to the lower deck. Only very rarely was the lower deck required for cargo on the outward voyage, and only very rarely were troops carried in any number on the homeward voyage; so that there was normally no difficulty on the score of space. The lower deck was, however, a dark and airless place in which to lodge a considerable body of men.

The day's work in an Indiaman began at 5 a.m., when the fresh water was served out. At 6.30 the watch on deck began to wash and swab the upper deck. The hammocks were piped up at 7.30, and stowed in the nettings as in a man-of-war. All hands breakfasted at 8.0. For the crew, breakfast was probably worse than it was in a King's ship. There may have been burgoo or 'Scotch coffee' but there is no mention of cocoa in the list of provisions. In some ships the crew may have had tea, on the homeward voyage at any rate. During the earlier part of the voyage, some crews may have had beer. To eat, there was 'bread'; that is to say, biscuit. The troops, if there were any, fared the same. The officers' breakfast was on a more generous scale and might consist of tea, biscuit, corned-beef and boiled rice. After this meal, those who had the morning watch came on deck. Dinner, for the crew, took place shortly after noon, the grog being served out exactly at midday and the messes being served with their rations soon afterwards. What their meal was can be gathered from the details already given of the stores which an Indiaman carried. Salt beef, salt pork, pease soup, biscuit and grog formed the basis of the seamen's diet, with beer during the first few weeks outward bound. Although unappetising, monotonous, and unhealthy, this was the food to which the men had become accustomed. In the East and on the homeward passage, rice tended to take the place of biscuit and arrack sometimes took the place of rum.

As in the Navy, each watch was on duty for four hours, except that the period from 4.0 to 8.0 p.m. was split into two periods of two hours each. During the first dog-watch, at 5.0, the decks were cleared, sail trimmed for the night, and the hands allowed to knock off until 8.0. On fine evenings the sailors were allowed to 'skylark'; that is, do gymnastic feats, 'such as leaping, tumbling, balancing, etc.' They sometimes danced the hornpipe or organised concerts among themselves. The lascars took part in this 'mirth and frolic' but the Chinese, if there were any, only looked on or played chess among themselves. The Portuguese also remained apart and inactive. When troops were carried, a certain amount of the sailors' spare time was spent in quarrelling with them. At 8.0 p.m. the watch was set, and all lights had to be out on the middle deck by 9.0, and in the cabins by 10.0. The watch was relieved at midnight, and again at 4.0 a.m., and so another day's work began.

On Wednesdays and Saturdays they cleaned and holystoned the middle or gun deck, and on Saturday an inspection was held afterwards. On that day the procedure was as follows: All the seamen's chests having been sent below (they were normally kept on the gun deck) and all hammocks brought on deck to be aired, the middle deck was swilled down by means of the fire-engine and afterwards cleaned thoroughly. All the officers, passengers and soldiers, with most of the crew, were assembled meanwhile on the upper deck, and the occasion was seized to inspect the sailors' clothing. Most seamen were cleanly in their habits, but many recruits were so much the reverse as to be verminous. Afterwards, the captain and officers made their rounds and inspected the ship, examining the mess kids, tin pannikins, brass pots and kettles to see that all were properly scoured and polished. The surgeon accompanied the captain on these occasions in the interests of hygiene. The inspection over, the drum beat to quarters and every soul on board hurried to his station as for action. The seamen manned the guns and went through the drill of loading and training them. Soldiers, recruits and passengers were formed into parties of marines, falling in with small-arms on poop and forecastle, under the command of such military officers as there were on board.

The surgeon, with the women and the sick, went down to the cockpit. Thus, the routine of preparing for action was perfected week by week. It does not appear, however, that any ammunition was allowed for practice.

One day every week was set aside for the washing of clothes, and once every month the hammocks were scrubbed. Both these operations being to preserve health and prevent infection, they took place 'in the ship's time'. On Sundays, if weather permitted, a service was held, the captain being liable to a fine of two guineas for every occasion the service was omitted without sufficient cause being entered in the log-book.

> On every recurrence of the Sunday (weather permitting) the ship's company were expected to be dressed in the neatest manner, and to be perfectly clean. The main-deck was converted into a commodious chapel. On each side of the main-mast, seats were placed for the sailors and soldiers; a table stood in the centre; the officers, passengers, and cadets, had appropriate places; and Bibles and Prayer-books were distributed. An Awning was thrown over the deck, and the sides were hung round with the ship's colours. A bell tolled in the forecastle for a few minutes; silence was ordered; and the Service was read by the Captain (his purser, or first officer, assisting) in a manner equally serious and impressive; while the utmost decorum was observed by every person on board....

The crew was mustered and called over after the Morning Service, each man in turn making his bow and scrape to the captain, who reprimanded any who were not sufficiently neat and clean in their appearance. The lascars and Chinese paraded separately in their own peculiar garb, the only people for whom the service was not compulsory. These came nearer to wearing a uniform than did the white seaman, who wore what they liked. The Europeans, in foul weather, usually tended to wear coarse wide trousers with a long pea-jacket and a 'sort of coal-heaver's hat...the flap stretching half-way down the back'. Others preferred a red nightcap. For this

Sunday parade they probably dressed very much as sailors did in the Navy, with white or blue trousers, striped shirts and blue jackets. There is an account of Sunday on board an Indiaman in Bishop Heber's Journal. He describes how he failed to make the crew attend Communion but succeeded in persuading them not to fish on the Sabbath.

When troops were carried, they had seldom any duty beyond a daily parade and the care of their arms and equipment. But the future Duke of Wellington, when a colonel, contrived to keep the men of the 33rd Regiment occupied while on board ship in 1797, and perhaps his methods were occasionally copied by other officers. He insisted that the soldiers should lash and stow their hammocks as the sailors did, and scrub them at least once a fortnight. He ordered that they should remain on deck all day except in bad weather. They were to be divided, moreover, into three watches, standing watch at night and not going below until relieved. A guard was to be mounted, and sentries posted in different parts of the ship. All subalterns had to stand watch, and an orderly officer of the day had to see that the decks were swept every morning and evening. The troops 'should all be exercised both morning and evening with dumb-bells, in order that they may preserve their air and appearance, particularly those whom the commanding officer may observe gaining a stoop in the shoulders'. The soldiers were also to be trained to handle the great guns and assist in the defence of the ship.

It is interesting to note in this connection that the soldiers of the 33rd Regiment were largely instrumental in saving the *Fitzwilliam* Indiaman in 1798. She went ashore in the mouth of the Hooghly, on the Saugor Reef, and it was the troops on board who heaved her off, afterwards taking their turn at the pumps until the ship reached Madras. Colonel Wellesley was himself on board at the time, and it was he who advised the commander to jettison part of the ship's cargo of saltpetre.

That Wellesley's plan of keeping the soldiers occupied was followed by others is clear from Lady Nugent's Journal. Sailing in the H.C.S. *Baring* in 1811, she found that her husband's two aides-de-camp, Fortescue and Fraser, were made to stand their watch just like the mates of the ship. She accordingly saw to it that they had some chocolate to drink every night after their watch 'which is not only a treat, but nourishment to them as growing boys'. The children in question, it may be observed, had been sitting on a court martial a few days before that remark was made in her diary. The point to notice, however, is that Sir George Nugent evidently found something for his subalterns to do. And it seems very probable that he and other commanding officers were often as careful to find employment for the men. The dangers of enforced idleness were fully recognised at the time, and it was often remarked that soldiers succumbed to disease on board ship far more readily than sailors. The nautical proverb 'Work and keep the scurvy out of your bones' was one which appeared to fit the case.

One of the first people to give serious attention to the question of preserving the health of troops on board ship was Sir John Burgoyne, who fully deserved his reputation as the soldier's friend. The following letter to Lord Amherst dates, apparently, from October, 1781:

My Lord

I beg to offer to your Lordship's consideration some circumstances relative to the troops going out to India, which I hope your Lordship will think not unworthy of it.

I find that the number of soldiers proposed to be sent on board each India ship, is from 200 to 250, a number in my opinion much too great, and I am induced to think so, first, from the situation soldiers must be in on board them, and secondly, from a knowledge that less than one half of that number has been found too many in the expedition under Colonel Meadows. The soldiers lie on the orlop deck, where it must be exceedingly close, as there are no port-holes to give air, and whatever comes in must be by wind sails. It may be said, you must keep the men chiefly on deck, but in blowing weather one-third of the number will be found to impede the management of the ship; 18 Indiamen are all that now are taken up for the men who are to go; your Lordship will therefore easily know what number each ship will have; the crews, one with another, are 125, this being the case, my Lord, I humbly conceive it will be absolutely necessary for the preservation of his Majesty's troops, first, that they should have more room; secondly, that an hospital ship is absolutely necessary; and thirdly, that a large quantity of anti-scorbutics should be provided for the troops, viz. sour krout, essence of spruce and essence of malt: I need only refer your Lordship to the Journal of the late Captain Cook, to prove the efficacy of these salubrious ingredients. The Company, I find, have only ordered a small quantity of lemon juice. I wish, my Lord, to exert my utmost abilities for the preservation of the troops under my command, and I am confident their wants need only be made known to your Lordship to be relieved; if some steps are not immediately taken it will be too late, and the matter not to be remedied. Relying therefore on your Lordship's humanity and zeal for his Majesty's service, I look up with a thorough conviction to your Lordship that such steps may be taken as will insure the troops, going out, that ease and preservation which men serving their country are entitled to.

I have the honor to be

Your Lordship's. . .etc.

J. Burgoyne

In another letter, to the Earl of Hillsborough, Burgoyne is emphatic on the need for a hospital ship:

My Lord

I think the subject on which I now address you of so much consequence, that I hope any apology on the occasion is unnecessary. I mean, my Lord, the absolute necessity there is of an hospital ship being sent with the armament now fitting out for the East Indies. The Indiamen destined to carry out the troops, are obliged to take a much greater than usual proportion, and the manner in which soldiers on board the Indiamen are obliged to swing their hammocks, makes every precaution against any epidemical sickness more than ordinary necessary. I should therefore advise, in the strongest manner, that an hospital ship should be sent with us, that in case of fever, or any other disorder that is catching, the sick may be removed. If this is not complied with, I can venture to foretel, the consequences will and must be fatal. So many men crowded on the lower deck of an Indiaman, where there is no air but what comes down the hatchways by a windsail, in a very hot climate, must, before the voyage is over, fall sickly; and, if the sick remain among those who are well, the sickness must spread, and the loss of men will very soon much overbalance the expence of the requisition I make of an hospital ship. I have, therefore, my Lord, in the strongest manner, to urge my request, and to hope for every assistance from your Lordship, which your known attention to the King's service can afford.

I am etc.

J. Burgoyne

Hertford St., 21st Nov., 1781.

On the voyage to India, scurvy was a very real danger both to troops and seamen. If the soldiers were especially liable, owing to their comparative idleness and through their being, often enough, berthed on the ill-ventilated lower deck, the seamen were by no means exempt. Captain Bartlett told of a homeward voyage in 1789 during which his crew was so devastated by scurvy that there were only four men on deck when the ship reached St Helena—the captain himself being at the wheel. James Forbes, who sailed for India in 1765, left the following account of this scorbutic disease:

On our second approach to the equator, we met with calms and contrary currents, which drove us quite out of our reckoning; fresh provisions and water became scarce, and the men were attacked by the scurvy: a distemper which was then very incidental to mariners in long voyages. It is various in its symptoms and progress; but is generally attended with heaviness, restlessness, swelled limbs, livid spots, and ulcerated gums: the last stage seems to be a total putrefaction; which soon carries off the unhappy sufferer. The scurvy baffles all the art of medicine; but if the patient is taken on shore, to breathe a pure air, and enjoy the refreshment of fruit and vegetables, he generally recovers. Before we experienced this happy change, many of the seamen, and more of the recruits for the army in India, fell a sacrifice to the malady;

and we were often called upon to attend the awful ceremony of committing their remains to the deep.

The ravages of scurvy were greatly reduced even before the beginning of the period with which we are dealing; and still more had been done to combat it before the wars ended. Nothing, however, seems to have been done towards abolishing the chief cause; that is, the unhealthy diet. In 1801, the East India Company computed the cost of victualling seamen and soldiers alike on the following basis; for each man, one pound of meat (sevenpence), one pound of biscuit (sixpence), and two quarts of beer (threepence); total cost per day, exclusive of vegetables, one shilling and fourpence. Now, as vegetables were not obtainable after the first few days out of port, it is very easy to imagine what the effect of such a diet, over a period of months, might be. Variety, apart from the occasional substitution of cheese or pease soup for meat, there was none. And the superseding of beer by grog as the voyage progressed was not by any means an improvement. One article of diet which can hardly have improved the general level of health was the water. The following lines, taken from Silas James' narrative of a voyage to India in 1781, may serve to illustrate this point:

> ...The weather now fell calm, and we all felt great anxiety and distress; the poor soldiers still dying in as great numbers as at the commencement of the disease. The allowance for each private, for twenty four hours, was a purser's quart, or a Winchester pint, and that was so strong, and stank so much, that when the steward broached a cask, and applied the lighted candle to the bunghole, it burnt blue like spirits: this was the Thames water....

The difficulty of preserving water was scarcely tackled until after 1815. During our period, and for some years afterwards, Indiamen relied for the most part on Thames water in wooden casks. The results of this rash custom were often discouraging and never wholly satisfactory. How discouraging the results might prove depended mainly on the use to which the casks had previously been put. The Navy also used wooden casks of dubious origin, but usually succeeded in filling them with something better than London sewage. An Indiaman's casks would vary a great deal from each other, some being worse than others. The water in them was said to foul and sweeten again several times during the voyage. At its worst, it was 'thick as treacle, blue as indigo, with a smell you could not stand up against'. At its best, it was dirty, smelly, and remarkable for overgrown animalculae. Tea made from it was 'frequently nothing better than thin mud, bearing an odour very different from that of hyson or pekoe'. It was the custom in some ships to filter the water used in the cuddy, and epicurean passengers would filter their own allowance with a private apparatus. But to have filtered the whole daily supply for the ship would have been an impossible undertaking. The iron tank was not yet thought of, and other devices, such as putting lime in the casks, do not seem to have been widely practised.

The allowance of water was six pints a day for each person, served out with religious care by means of a hand-pump through the bunghole of the cask. People did not drink much of it, except in the form of tea or cocoa or grog, nor perhaps any while the beer lasted. But the six pints, reduced when there was a shortage to two quarts or less, had to serve for washing as well as for drink. One cannot wash in salt water, not, at any rate, with soap. Still less does salt water suffice for washing clothes. Canvas garments can be scrubbed initially in sea water, but, unless at least rinsed in fresh water, they seem never to become completely dry. The period of the French wars was incidentally a period of clean-shaving, which meant that there was yet another use for such water as there was available. The allowance was therefore far from lavish, even when it was not reduced. And, when the ship's company was large, it usually was reduced. There was, moreover, a certain temptation—more especially on the homeward voyage—for the captains to ship an insufficient quantity, in order to make room for cargo in private trade. Admiral Drury remarked on this tendency in a letter to the Admiralty in 1808:

> I beg permission to mention another circumstance as likely not only to affect the health of the Crews, but every description of person sent out by the East India Company to serve in this Country. It is the want of water, some of the Ships in question having been already supplied from the Monmouth and others are reduced to a proportion for a few days, notwithstanding their people have continued for some time past at the scanty allowance of three pints a day, including every expense for their support during the twenty-four hours, which is by far too small a quantity to counteract the pernicious consequences attending so long a Voyage, and more particularly in a Warm Climate.
>
> (P.R.O. Ad. 1/180. 17 Feb. 1808.)

Drury attributed this lack of water, on the outward voyage, to a defect in the contract, or else to the wilful neglect of the captains. The second suggestion is not very convincing, owing to the absence of motive. But there can be no doubt that the contract with the owners was defective. It merely stipulated for forty tons and as much more as was desirable. Owners may sometimes have taken the opportunity to save on the number of casks supplied.

Little or no improvement was made during our period either in diet or in the quantity or quality of the water supply. Scurvy was, instead, very largely checked by the use of anti-scorbutics; and particularly by putting lime-juice in the grog. It was the East Indian lime that was used, which has properties lacked by the West Indian variety, and it was from India that this medical discovery came. The introduction of lime-juice was, however, a slow process. It was known for a generation before it came into general use. As late as 1804 the Calcutta *Gazette* could have such a notice as this:

> Capt. Marshall of the H.C. freighted ship "Sir William Pulteney", 1st July 1804, reports reaching England 'without one on the sick

list.' Thirty or forty lascars were affected with scurvy—mouths affected and legs swelled—when off the Cape. But two limes apiece to the sick and one each to the others cured the outbreak in three weeks.

In September 1805 the Medical Board at Fort William published in the *Gazette* 'Mr Palmer's tried and approved processes for preserving lime-juice, limes, sourkrout etc.'. The method recommended for preserving lime-juice was to pour it into large casks or pipes 'from which rum, brandy, or madeira has been lately taken out' after first quenching a hot iron in it twice. To each cask was then to be added half a gallon of rum for every ten gallons of juice. After the cask had stood for a fortnight or three weeks, to settle and clarify, the liquid might be drawn off for use into small casks or bottles. To preserve the limes themselves the plan was to fill a fifteen-gallon keg half full of the fruit and then fill it up with the juice, as prepared by the former process. Limes thus preserved would keep for a year or more. Sourkrout was to be made by the following process: sliced-up cabbages were to be, first, rubbed with salt, and second, soaked in brine. After soaking for three days the next thing was to put the cabbage into small casks, press it well down, and fill up each cask with 'one gallon of vinegar, and an equal quantity of lime-juice with two ounces of caraway seeds, four of cassia or cinnamon, and four of allspice', together with as much pickle as necessary from the pickling tub. Finally, should it be necessary to fill up the ullage, a further quantity of pickle, that is to say brine, was to be added.

By the aid of such remedies as lime-juice and sourkrout, scurvy was to some extent curable and indeed very largely preventable. Henceforth, the number of soldiers and seamen to die on the outward voyage was very greatly reduced. In India itself the sailors were apt to die of other complaints, such as dysentery and fever. In the Hooghly especially, at and below Diamond Harbour, some three hundred European sailors died each year, according to the East India *Vade-Mecum*. The surrounding forests and swamps were responsible. They could not be cleared if only because they formed the natural defence of the country. Eastwick tells of how the H.C.S. *Lord Eldon* lost her captain, all the officers but one, and half the crew while loading at Poulo Bay. It was thus in India that the greatest mortality occurred; and deaths which occurred on the homeward voyage were often the result of diseases contracted in Indian harbours. The present writer has been enabled to discover only one memoir written by the surgeon of an Indiaman, and that is one dating from as late a period as 1821. James Wallace, the author, gives a list of his books on tropical disease: 'Lind on Climate', 'Mosely on Tropical Diseases', 'Clark on long Voyages', and 'Johnson on Tropical Influence'. It was on the last-named book that he relied:

> ...Possessing Johnson's work, I could very well have done without the others....It is in it that we find perhaps the best view of tropical disease that has yet been taken; that so intimate a connection is traced between fever, and hepatitis, and dysentery, as almost to shew them to be modifications of the same disease; that the same remedies, modified a little, are applicable to all.... In it the surgeon is taught, that if he has the lancet, and calomel, and opium, and purgatives, he requires little else....

Unfortunately, the first edition of *The influence of tropical climates on European Constitutions* by Dr James Johnson did not appear until 1813. And, during a part of our period (1803–6), Johnson was still painfully gaining his experience as surgeon of the *Caroline* frigate. Until his book appeared, perhaps the best-known medical authority in India was Dr J. Anderson, the botanist, of Madras. It was he who introduced the Nopal plant as a cure for scurvy, failing, however, to bring it into very widespread use.

Apart from occasional outbreaks of disease and occasional burials at sea, the voyage to India was apt to be almost entirely devoid of incident. There might be rough weather and there might be a cry of 'Man overboard' from time to time. Such excitements were rare, though, and rarer still the occasional encounters with the French. The normal voyage was so tedious that a distant sail was a source of excitement and a topic of conversation for the rest of the day. Those on board an Indiaman were always greedy for news, of which they were often deprived for months at a time. So that it was a great event when a ship came within hail. The stranger might be more recently out from Europe, armed with echoes of the latest battle. To the hail 'What news?' there might come the reply 'Badajoz has fallen after a terrible siege'. This was enough to banish boredom for days to come.

A pleasant incident in the voyage to the East was the call at Madeira which many ships made. Water was taken in there, as also a fresh stock of fruit and vegetables; but the chief object was the wine. Madeira was then fashionable and expensive, costing £88 the pipe in 1807. It had come into prominence as the drink of the 'Nabob'—the man who returned to England after shaking the pagoda tree. Both in a literal and metaphorical sense, it had reached England via India, for it was the taste of the Anglo-Indian which made it known and it was in the Company's ships that most of it came. As the Indiamen did not call at the island on the homeward voyage, the wine often came to England by way of Bengal or China. This route, if not the shortest possible, had the merit of guaranteeing a certain minimum age, an essential virtue in the Anglo-Indian's eyes. He was never in India long enough to have a wine-cellar there, and yet returned home too late in life to fare any better at Bath or Cheltenham.

Madeira was the ideal wine for upstarts; hence, perhaps, its vogue under the Regency. Constantia was another wine which England owed to the East India Company, but there was never enough of it. Madeira, on the contrary, was plentiful; rather suspiciously so, in fact, as a part of the supply came latterly from Teneriffe. In our period, it stood at the height of fashion; and indeed might cost about 70*s.* a dozen—as compared with port at 45*s.*—as late as 1818. Some time after that, but before 1830, it was suddenly ousted by a fashion for sherry. Such fluctuations in taste must always override mere physical facts. Inferior bottles of Madeira had henceforth to be labelled 'Sherry'; the slight alteration in colour presenting no difficulty to the wine merchant. All this, however, lay in the future. During the Napoleonic wars there was loud grumbling if a convoy of Indiamen failed to call at the island; especially from passengers, who were always 'the most dissatisfied, growling, and troublesome, because the most idle, of mortals' and whose sole pleasure was in tormenting 'their wretched victim, the captain'.

The longest voyage will end at last, and the slowest Indiaman would eventually reach its destination, whether it were Bengal, Madras, Bombay or Canton. Once arrived at any of these ports, cargo was discharged and a fresh cargo shipped. The ships bound for Bengal would have little to land except recruits, passengers, military stores and goods for European use. The articles under this last head were imported by the captains of Indiamen, and the profit made depended on the time of year at which the ship arrived. During the hot season, from the beginning of March to the beginning of August, there was little trade to be done. The best time to arrive was either in August or at the beginning of the cool season, in November. This was because the chief requirements of Fort William were pale ale, porter, wine, cider, perry, cordials, spirits, hams, cheese, pickles, groceries and confectionery. These were needed in considerable quantities, but only during the cold season, the time for entertaining. Fortunately for the importer, however, he had not to compete with the goods left over from the last season, for such of these as were perishable had perished, and the rest had gone out of fashion.

Thus the fluctuating, precarious, and perishable state of the Bengal markets, and those of India in general, is certainly eventually favourable to the consumption of the investments of the commanders, officers, and private traders, whether sold or not; for if the inhabitants do not consume, the climate soon does: hence it must constantly want a fresh supply; but care must be taken not to overstock the market at once.

(Milburn, *Oriental Commerce.*)

Ships bound for Madras were very few in number. Most of the ships calling at Madras were 'Coast and Bay' vessels, on their way to Calcutta. They could land there much the same type of goods as was in demand at Calcutta, with the addition of naval stores, pitch, tar and deals. The piece goods taken on board were added to the cargo, of which the bulk would come from Bengal. Occasionally, ships would call at Madras on their way back from Bengal in order to add some piece goods to a cargo of saltpetre or sugar. The China ships which called at Madras on their outward passage would ship piece goods for the Chinese market, mainly on account of the commanders and officers. It was seldom that any China ships visited India on their homeward passage; that trade was left in the hands of private merchants.

Comparatively few ships sailed to Bombay, and those that did so were of the smallest class, excepting three or four favoured ships on their way to China. The Indiamen bound for Bombay and China rather resembled the Civil Service at Canton. The commands of these ships were obviously reserved for the well connected, for the officers who had friends or relatives among the directors. After discharging the Company's cargo—military and naval stores, recruits and cadets—and after landing the commander's investment of European goods, the loading of the cotton began. By a resolution of the Court of Directors in 1805 the commander and officers of a ship were allowed nearly two-fifths of the vessel's carrying capacity, free of charge. If the Company did not require the remaining space, it was sold to the highest bidder, preference being given to the commander and officers. This privilege of carrying cotton brought the commanders a princely income. The favour lay entirely in the gift of the Court of Directors, for the owners had no voice whatever in the stationing of their ships.

Before being shipped, the bales of raw cotton were 'screwed'. This process meant the reduction of their bulk by powerful compression. The engine was primitive but effective. It worked on the principle of an early printing-press and looked like a gigantic capstan, manned by over two hundred native labourers. The town was immensely proud of this piece of mechanism, which was even more impressive to watch than the new steam-engine used for pumping out the repairing docks. The Company issued stringent regulations to prevent the commanders having their own cotton screwed at the Company's expense. There was, it seems, a tendency for their cotton to get mixed up with the Company's when the screwing process was going forward—a piece of inadvertence which was rectified, of course, before the cargo was shipped.

The proportion between the number of vessels sent to the three Indian Presidencies may best be judged from the actual figures for the year 1807. The ships calling at Madras and Bengal numbered eighteen; those at Madras alone, two; those at Calcutta alone, four. The ships for Bombay alone numbered five. One ship called at Madras, Ceylon and Bombay. Of the China ships, four called at Bombay, three at Madras.

While an Indiaman lay in an Indian harbour there was always the dreadful risk, from the commander's point of view, that she would be chosen for duty as an armed ship or transport. At regular intervals the Supreme Government felt called upon to supplement the efforts of the Navy by fitting out ships for the protection of Balasore Roads and the Sand-heads, a station which all Naval officers dreaded on account of its unhealthiness. Again, there were expeditions, from time to time, against French or Dutch possessions; expeditions involving the carrying of native troops to the Red Sea or to Java, or to somewhere equally distant. To be compelled to serve in either of these capacities was a serious misfortune, the commander being thereby deprived of his usual emoluments for the period of his service. A temporary commission in the Navy was a poor consolation for losing a few thousand pounds. The only officer who may be said to have gained by his naval exertions was Commodore Mitchell, who was knighted for his services after cruising with three armed Indiamen in 1794. And yet Sir C. Mitchell paid dearly for the honour. He was so impoverished by 1800 that he was glad of a pension of £250 from the Poplar Fund. Perhaps the commanders of the seven Indiamen which lay in wait for the Dutch East India ships off St Helena in 1795, capturing all nine of them and ruining the Dutch Company at a blow, may not have been losers on the transaction. But the commanders of the three Indiamen at the blockade of Pondicherry in 1793, of the three others at the first taking of the Cape, and of those which served occasionally in 1799, 1804 and 1805, must all have been left the poorer for their services.

If police work was unpopular among the commanders, the transporting of troops was more so, being equally unprofitable and not in the least likely to result in a knighthood. The captain of a transport had to provide a table for the officers commanding the troops, but was given an allowance hardly equal to the expense of catering. He was, moreover, fairly certain to have trouble with his guests sooner or later. This was rendered all the more probable by the bad mood in which he himself would receive them. When an expedition was being fitted out in 1797 for an attack on Manilla, General St Leger ordered that the troops should be under the command of the captains of ships in the event of meeting the enemy at sea. Colonel Wesley protested strongly at being put under the orders 'of persons who have thrown so many difficulties in the way of the Service, and who are now throwing so many, that I shall probably be obliged to write an official complaint of some of them before the fleet sails'. The protest was successful, but the point to notice is that the commanders, being dragged unwillingly into service, raised every possible difficulty in the hope of escape. They did not escape, but merely succeeded in annoying the military.

An Indiaman acting as a transport had usually to carry native troops, as the European troops could be carried in ships-of-war with greater convenience. Occasionally a ship might carry both, in which case she had to be filled with two separate cargoes of provisions. Such a ship would have to carry beef, pork, suet, biscuit, flour, rice, peas, tea, raisins, mustard, sugar and rice for the Europeans; dhol, churah, ghee, boot gram, turmeric, chillies, garlic, oil and sweetmeats for the Indian troops; as also enormous quantities of water, arrack, rum and vinegar. An expedition preparing in 1800, in which two battalions were to embark, had to allow for eight pipes of Madeira and a hundred and forty-four dozens of port for the officers. With them, such expeditions were not unpopular; indeed, it was only when afloat that the subaltern could live on his pay. But they were the nightmare of East India captains, who hated these unprofitable cargoes of sepoys, rice and garlic, arrack and ammunition.

Canton was the port where the Company's ships appeared their best. When the whole China fleet was collected there, twelve or sixteen of the largest merchantmen in the world, together with the country ships, the spectacle must have been magnificent. They began to arrive in October and did not leave Whampoa until January at the earliest. On arrival, they first received permission to pass from the Mandarins of the fort at Bocca Tigris and were furnished with (often useless) pilots. Then they went up to Whampoa Reach, anchoring in a long line, which lengthened as the later divisions came in. Here, as at Calcutta, the captains lived ashore. The senior captain, or commodore, was allowed £500 by the Company to cover the cost of his entertaining; the next in seniority being allowed £300 for his share in it. The ships took it in turn to provide a boat to row guard up and down the fleet. Sometimes the Viceroy would come down to visit the fleet, attended by a retinue of other nobles and officials. On such occasions, the third mates had the ships in review order, with polished brass-work, the guns run out level and clean painted, and the decks 'such as one might eat off'. The ships were decked to receive the great man, with yards manned and officers in full dress, and the affair ended with the captains dining together.

The return voyage, whether from India or China, differed only from the outward in that the ships were fully laden, undermanned, and without many passengers. Convoys often called to water and obtain refreshments at St Helena, which corresponded to Madeira on the outward passage. On arrival in the Thames, during the early part of our period, cargoes were discharged into decked hoys at the ships' moorings at Deptford, Blackwall and Northfleet. There was a certain amount of pilfering in connection with the unloading of ships, which was done, of course, by gangs of 'lumpers' or stevedores. But the Company's ships had never been robbed to the same extent as the West India ships, and the establishment of the Thames Police Office in 1798 did much to check what pilfering there may have been. The hoys took the goods up to the Company's wharves, from whence they were carted to the bonded warehouses, which were said to be 'splendid and commodious in the highest degree'. Saltpetre was taken to a special warehouse on Cock Hill. Muslins, calicoes and silks were housed in Bishopsgate, spices in Leadenhall Street, the Bengal warehouse was in New Street, bale goods went to Cutlers Street or Houndsditch, tea to Fenchurch Street, Haydon Square, Cooper's Row, Jewry Street and Crutched Friars. For goods in private trade there was a separate warehouse in Billiter Lane.

Certain of the officers had probably to remain on board until all the cargo was discharged, but the captain would go ashore on arrival to report at the India House and give in the ship's log. These journals were at first handed over to the hydrographer (Mr Dalrymple until 1810, and afterwards Mr Horsburgh). After inspection, they were consigned to the gloomy archives under the building. The ship's surgeon had likewise to send his journal to Dr Hunter, of Charles Street, St James's Square. To save the journey westward, he might leave it to be forwarded by Mr Pepys, a cutler living in the Poultry.

The procedure on arrival in the Thames was entirely altered when the East India Docks were opened in 1806. The agitation which resulted in these docks being constructed began among the managing owners. In a case prepared for legal opinion in 1808–9 the Company showed that its own part in the matter had been mainly passive:

> In 1803 an act of Parliament passed, for making docks at Blackwall, for loading and unloading East-India ships. The Company, in giving their consent to the construction of these docks, stated in their report, as one of the grounds of their acquiescence, that the short detention the ships would experience in the river would considerably reduce the expences of delivery, and consequently lessen the sum which the Company paid for the extra charge arising from a state of war. The Company were not the projectors of the docks; the owners were the original proprietors, and applied to Parliament for the Act....

The owners, then, had their own motives for proposing the construction of wet-docks, and the Company had its own motives for agreeing to the scheme. Both owners and directors, however, were at one in a desire to prevent pillage; and Parliament, in passing the Act, was influenced not only by considerations of revenue but also by a desire to make more room in the river for other shipping. According to the preamble of the Act of 1803 (43 Geo. III, c. 126) the need for wet-docks for unloading purposes, properly surrounded with walls and ditches, was urgent because,

> ...by the present system of loading and discharging the cargoes of such ships, the navigation of the River Thames is frequently impeded, and delays, losses and inconveniences experienced, and the cargoes of such ships are subject to plunder, and the East India Company and owners thereof injured, and the public revenue defrauded to a considerable amount....

The revenue suffered because the duties were not paid on imports but on goods sold from the bonded warehouses. Once the docks were opened, the revenue suffered no longer. The hatches of all East Indiamen were locked down, henceforward, on the ships' arrival at Gravesend; nor were they opened until the ships were safely within the dock walls.

As a result of the Act, a joint-stock company was formed, called the East India Dock Company, with power to raise a capital of £200,000 in the first instance, to be increased to £300,000 if found necessary. The stock was to pay 5 per cent. at first and, by a later period, not more than 10 per cent. Most of the capital must have been raised by the owners themselves, and it will be seen that they were strongly represented on the board of directors. By the provisions of the Act, four directors of the East India Company were to be included among the directors of the East India Dock Company. The original four, named in the Act, were John Roberts, Stephen Williams, Joseph Cotton and William Thornton. The most prominent of the owners who were also directors of the Dock Company were Sir William Curtis, Bart., John Atkins, Henry Bonham, Robert Wigram and John Woolmore. The builders appear to have been represented by William Wells, the younger. By 1806 it had been found necessary to increase the Company's capital to £400,000. And the capital had to be increased to £500,000 in 1814 when warehouses were built inside the dock walls.

The East India Dock Company had a sort of monopoly in

that all vessels arriving from India were compelled to discharge their cargoes within the Company's docks. And this applied not only to regular and extra Indiamen but also to such India-built vessels as the East India Company might allow to sail for England under licence. Outward-bound Indiamen were allowed to load in the docks but were not compelled to do so, provided that they did their loading below Limehouse Creek. On the other hand, the Dock Company was bound by certain regulations. The charge made to the owners for the use of the docks was fixed at fourteen shillings per ton for each Indiaman unloading and loading again there, four shillings per ton for each new ship loading for her first outward voyage. The charge for India-built ships, licensed by the Company, if navigated by lascars, was only twelve shillings per ton, to allow for the cost of maintaining the lascars until the ship sailed again. The East India Company also paid for the use of the docks, according, again, to a fixed scale. Two shillings per ton was paid on the goods landed and a further two shillings per ton for loading the goods into the waggons. Thus, the East India Dock Company might receive as much as £1048 altogether for unloading a China ship like the *Warley* or *Hope*. On smaller ships the charge would be proportionately less, according to the registered tonnage and the amount of cargo landed.

The expectation of the East India Company was that the construction of the docks would bring about a considerable saving in the cost of unloading ships. The actual saving was small, but the new system had the advantage of keeping the cost at the same level in time both of peace and war. To unload an 800-ton ship in the river, allowing for river pay and provisions for seamen, wages for lumpers, wet-dock dues when masting and unmasting, ship-keepers' wages and pilot's and watermen's wages, cost about £579. At fourteen shillings per ton, the East India Docks charge for the same vessel would be £560. The Company's gain was in the stability of this charge and the consequent reduction of war allowances; the owners' gain was mainly in the saving of ground tackle and of general wear and tear; both Company and owners gained from the prevention of plunder and damage.

The choice of a site for the new docks was almost inevitably dictated by the pre-existence of the Brunswick basin which had been built by John Perry at Blackwall between 1789 and 1790. The dock consisted of two basins, each with an entrance from the river. The one was large enough to contain thirty large Indiamen while the other could hold as many smaller vessels. Now, it was a much simpler proposition to purchase and extend the Brunswick basin than to begin excavating on some entirely new site. The most obvious situation was already taken up by the West India Docks, which had been in existence for some time, to satisfy a far more urgent need. Any site on the Surrey side of the river would be on the wrong bank, for the Company's warehouses were all in the City or the east end. The Company had, moreover, traditional associations with Poplar and Blackwall. Everything, then, pointed to the development of the Brunswick basin. The purchase was effected, and work was begun in August 1803.

The East India Docks were opened in August 1806. They consisted of two basins, connecting with each other and with the river by means of a small entrance basin. The old Brunswick Dock extending to eight acres was absorbed in the lesser or outer basin, the export dock, which measured 780 feet in length and 520 feet in breadth. The inner and more important basin, where the unloading was to take place, measured 1410 feet long and 560 feet broad. The area of water, including the entrance, was thirty acres and a half, and the depth throughout was twenty-six feet. The inner basin was surrounded by a high boundary wall. The outer, although shut in on one side by Perry's Yard and defended on the other by the entrance basin, had no particular defences of its own.

Plate V. A view of the East India Docks. Drawn, engraved and published 1 October 1808, by William Daniell.

It must be observed that the East India Dock Company did no repairs of any kind, and was actually forbidden to undertake any. Repairs at the end of a ship's third and sixth voyages continued to be done as before in the builders' yards. An Indiaman had to be stripped to the lower masts before entering the import or unloading dock, and had previously to have landed all her gunpowder. If repairs had to be executed, the ship would have to proceed to the builder's when her cargo had been discharged, returning to the East India Docks when the time came for loading again. Repairs and refitting might take as long as three months. A China ship, arriving in July, might 'come afloat' again in October or November, and sail again in the following February. A China ship which came in as late as September might be ready to sail again in April.

Chapter IX

PASSENGERS

In return for his passage money, a passenger was given accommodation which varied according to the amount paid. Official passengers, those in the Company's service, that is to say, together with officers going to serve with the King's troops in India, paid an amount fixed by the regulations and proportioned to their rank. The actual position and size of their cabins was in some cases laid down. Unofficial passengers had to settle with the captain, or more often the purser, both the sum they were to pay and the accommodation they were to have. In a ship carrying many passengers, the later arrivals had to purchase cabin space from such inferior officers as were willing to give up their own proper accommodation. It must here be emphasised that what the passenger bought was not so much a room as a portion of the deck. Cabins were not solid and permanent structures. As in ships-of-war, they were made so as to allow of being struck in a few minutes when the ship cleared for action. In peacetime they were made with light wooden frames and panels, each with a wooden door and lock 'very complete'. In time of war they were formed by canvas screens, fixed to the beams above and laced down to battens nailed to the deck. The corners were defined by uprights or stanchions, to one of which a canvas-panelled door was hung. To strike such a cabin as this, it was only necessary to unlace the canvas at the foot, roll it up and secure it to the beams overhead. Again, with such light structures, it was a simple matter to vary their size, adding to one and taking from another.

The sums paid for cabins entirely depend upon the demand, their size, the ship's destination, and the circumstances of the person selling his accommodation. The several portions of the round-house and great cabin, both of which are considered the captain's property, of course are paid for in proportion to their respective dimensions: it may, however, be taken as some guide, that, outward bound, a slip, including one window, may produce from £200 to £300; and that the several mates' cabins may be averaged at from £3 to £5 for each square foot of the enclosed area. Homeward bound, on account of the number of children and servants shipped with a family, the rates are yet higher: I have known, more than once, the whole of a great cabin let for £2500!

In the above extract from the East India *Vade-Mecum* it is apparent that what the passenger purchased was deck space. It is also clear that, apart from the round-house and great cabin, the space to be bought was that which otherwise belonged to the ship's officers. Those who chose thus to part with their cabins may perhaps have berthed where boatswain, carpenter and midshipmen would normally have been; the inferior officers so displaced moving elsewhere, either forward or below.

To reconstruct the exact cabin plan is no easy matter, if only because of the many variations to which it was subject. The general arrangement, however, is sufficiently clear from the descriptions available together with such scraps of information as can be gleaned from prints. First of all, it must be understood that an Indiaman had a poop, rising a little above the line of the bulwarks and extending forward so as to cover from thirty to forty feet of the upper deck. It might include four ports on each side, ports which scarcely ever contained guns. At the break of the poop, just forward of the mizen mast, ladders ascended to what might be called the poultry-farm. The poop was sometimes pierced for guns, but can never have mounted any. Beneath it, and opening on the quarter-deck (which in flush-decked ships was merely the after part of the upper deck, as far forward as the mainmast), was the round-house and cuddy.

The cuddy was under the fore part of the poop, the name applying to a portion of the deck from ten to fifteen feet wide and extending right across the ship from one side to the other. The starboard side of this was cut off, as a rule, to form the captain's state-room, which opened by a glass door on to the quarter-deck. The remainder, to which the word 'cuddy' was more particularly applicable, was usually used as the dining-room for all who were to sit at the captain's table. When the passengers were very numerous—and Mrs Sherwood gives an instance when they numbered forty-four—this space proved insufficient. The company had then to be divided into two parties, dining successively in rotation.

Abaft of the cuddy, and communicating with the quarter-deck either by a central corridor or else through the dining-saloon, was the round-house. This extended to the stern of the ship, where there were two doors opening on the stern-gallery and, between them, a row of glass windows. According to the size of the ship, the round-house might be divided into from three to six or even more cabins. Supposing there were six or eight, they would be ranged along either side of the ship and separated by a corridor opening at one end on the cuddy and terminated at the other by the stern cabin or cabins. The corridor would be lighted by a skylight and all or most of the cabins by ports. The cuddy had windows opening on the quarter-deck as well as a port on each side of the ship. At either side of the round-house were the quarter-galleries, projecting from the ship's side. These served a double purpose, each containing both a flight of steps and a latrine. The starboard quarter-gallery had a latrine on a level with the gun deck, the larboard on a level with the round-house. In the smaller ships there may have been but a single latrine, the other quarter-gallery serving solely as a means of communication between the two decks. The poop stern-cabins were thought to be the best in the ship. As late as 1843 from £200 to £300 would be paid for each person accommodated in one, as compared with £150 to £200 for each person accommodated in the stern-cabins on the gun deck. The round-house was, in general, the abode of the wealthy and distinguished. Ladies were usually berthed there when travelling alone, partly for privacy and partly because they were under the captain's protection.

There were several alternative arrangements of the round-house and cuddy. If there were no passengers or very few, the round-house might become the dining-saloon and the larboard half of the cuddy be given as a cabin to one of the ship's officers. Or, again, if the passengers were numerous, the whole of the cuddy might be used as the dining-saloon, the captain taking a cabin in the round-house. The temporary nature of the partitions allowed of considerable adjustment in the cabin plan and it would be difficult to say which arrangement was the rule and which the exception.

Immediately below the round-house was the great cabin, corresponding to the poop stern-cabin but broader, having perhaps eight stern-windows as compared with the six of the cabin overhead. There was a lower stern-gallery in some ships. On either side of the great cabin were the quarter-galleries, the functions of which have already been described. They were not continued below the level of the gun deck, but were finished off with a moulding. As seen from the outside, the quarter-galleries formed a handsome architectural feature of the ship, but they were an insecure excrescence and were frequently washed away in rough weather. There is an instance of one so disappearing just as a man had quitted it. The great cabin was usually divided by fore-and-aft partitions into two or three parts, leaving a corridor athwartships by which the quarter-galleries might be reached. From the stern to this corridor the distance might be about fourteen feet. If a ship carried army officers in any number, the whole of the great cabin would be assigned to the unmarried among them, to the number of eight or twelve. There might be standing bedplaces or bunks for them, built against the sides and the forward bulkhead, which was rather more permanent than the other partitions. If there were only two officers, it was laid down that they should have the larboard third part of the great cabin, exclusive of the passage to the quarter-gallery. In the absence of official passengers, this part of the ship was hired by such as preferred it and could afford it. 'I closed with Captain Colnett,' wrote Hickey, 'taking the starboard side of the great cabin, upon his recommendation of that situation in preference to the round-house....'

Forward of the great cabin and extending as far as the well was the steerage. This was a central space, separating the cabins on either side, and occasionally used, it seems, to accommodate passengers when the ship was overcrowded. It was here that the third mate had his table, so that the steerage was given over to subalterns, cadets, writers and bachelors generally. If there were ladies in any part of the great cabin they would gain the deck by the quarter-gallery, not by passing through the steerage. At the forward end of the steerage there might be a cabin fitted with a number of bedplaces or bunks, to be shared by the cadets and writers—possibly the accommodation assigned otherwise to the midshipmen. The cabins in the steerage corresponded roughly with the four aftermost ports on each side. The six sternmost cabins, three on each side, were normally occupied, as we have seen, by the chief, second, third and fourth mates, the surgeon and the purser. They may sometimes, however, have been let to passengers, for a consideration. Such cabins as there were forward of these, and which passengers might occasionally occupy, as Mrs Sherwood actually did, had the disadvantage of being near the ship's pumps, near the soldiers' berths on the middle deck; and also of being encumbered with cannon. In peace-time some of the guns may have been dismounted and carried as ballast; but in time of war this was an offence, both against the East India Company and the underwriters. Even a cabin, however, which had to be shared with a medium 18-pounder was better than no cabin at all; a point made clear in the East India *Vade-Mecum*:

> If the circumstances of a passenger should enable him to hire a cabin, his comfort will be increased inconceivably, even though he should have barely room enough to swing a cot, or to put up a standing bed. But, that he may not deceive himself in respect to the accommodation he is to derive from such a retirement, it would be proper for him to pay a visit to the vessel while lying in the river, probably at Gravesend, or the Hope....
>
> ...Some cabins include a port-hole, which, in large ships, is peculiarly comfortable; especially under the Line, when a current of air is invaluable; but, in bad weather, when the port is shut, those cabins that have only skuttles, about one-fourth the size of a port-hole, become preferable; especially when they are provided with glass shutters; which can be at any time made by the ship's carpenter, if not previously attached. The skuttles being higher up in the side of the vessel, and nearer to the deck above the cabin, are well calculated for allowing rarefied air, which would float above the level of a port-hole, to escape. They are usually placed at intervals between the ports. When a cabin is built so as to include a port, the gun appertaining thereto is commonly sent forward, and lashed up to the ship's side, the muzzle pointing forward; but, on emergency, the cabin is knocked down, and the gun is run into its place. Hence, each kind of cabin has its advantages, and disadvantages.

This process of moving the guns forward did not apply, of course, to the smaller cabins which were almost amidships. It must also be remembered that the pair of ports farthest aft were vacant in any case. The question as to whether it was better to have a port or a scuttle in one's cabin was to be answered, possibly, with reference to the date on which the vessel was due to sail. That the various cabins had advantages and disadvantages is sufficiently evident, though it was on the latter that writers of the time were more disposed to dwell. Although the East Indiamen provided the most luxurious accommodation known to that age, the choice of cabins was, even for the wealthy, a choice of evils. Ruling out the steerage as manifestly comfortless, the choice lay between the round-house and the great cabin. Those who had tried both generally decided that the round-house was preferable. Hickey, who chose the starboard side of the great cabin, lived to regret his choice; he wrote that he would never recommend anybody to take a berth between decks while there was a chance of accommodation in the round-house.

> ...The objections to the round-house are the frequent noises that must occur upon the poop from the seamen performing the necessary manoeuvres with the sails attached to the mizen-mast, especially that of working the spanker-boom, and the feeding of the poultry kept in coops there, with the consequent pecking twice a day, and both points undoubtedly are extremely unpleasant and great annoyances. But on the gun deck, if you avoid the noises above specified, they are more than counter-balanced by a variety of inconveniences, the grand one that of being completely debarred of all daylight in tempestuous weather by what is very expressively termed 'the dead lights' being then fixed in all the windows in order to prevent the sea breaking in, which nevertheless it does not effectually do, for I was often set afloat in my cabin by heavy seas breaking against those dead lights, and entering at the seams, especially so at the quarter gallery door and window, where it poured in in torrents, beating even over my bed....

He goes on to hint at other horrors, the noise of children crying—or, worse, playing—in the steerage; the being half-poisoned by 'a variety of stinks'; the 'perpetual creaking of bulk-heads, accompanied by the *music* of the rudder working'. A thousand pounds certainly seems a high price for a noisome and noisy 'dirty hole of a cabin' constantly deluged with water.

A lady, writing in the *Asiatic Journal* for 1835, is equally emphatic on the superiority of the round-house:

> Notwithstanding the noise which is the invariable accompaniment of a cabin on the poop, old sailors will always make choice of this situation, as more light and freer circulation of air can be obtained

there than in those below. But, as some of the party must inevitably take the second deck, they should endeavour to guard against the possibility of injury to things of value in the event of shipping a sea. In the most exposed parts of the cabin, the boxes should always be raised a little from the floor, in order that the water may run under them; or it is a good plan to dispense with boxes altogether, and dispose of their contents in canvas, or other bags, suspended from the ceiling.

This advice to those condemned to berth on the middle deck gives the impression that the cabins there made up in free circulation of water for what they lacked in free circulation of air.

Emma Roberts, in *The East India Voyager*, strongly recommends all ladies to secure a cabin in the round-house. It seems very probable that she was also the authoress of the article quoted above in the *Asiatic Journal*.

To ladies, whether married or single, the upper, or poop-cabins are certainly the most desirable, the disadvantages of the noise overhead being more than counterbalanced by the enjoyment of many favourable circumstances unattainable below. In the first place, these cabins are much more light and airy: it is seldom, even in the very roughest weather, that the ports are compelled to be shut; and it is almost inconceivable to those who have never been at sea, how great a difference it makes in the comforts or discomforts of a voyage, whether a delicate person can have the enjoyment of light and air in bad weather, or be deprived of both, condemned in illness to a dark, close cabin, without the possibility of diverting the mind by reading, or any other employment. There is also another great advantage above stairs, which is the comparative degree of seclusion attainable in these cabins. A few steps lead from them all to the cuddy, or general apartment: there is no necessity to go out upon deck, or to go up or down stairs to meals; thus avoiding much of the annoyance of a rolling vessel, and all the disagreeables attendant upon encountering persons engaged in the duties of the ship. It may seem fastidious to object to meeting sailors employed in getting up different stores from the hold, or to pass and repass other cabins, or the neighbourhood of the steward's pantry; nevertheless, if ladies have the opportunity of avoiding these things, they will do well to embrace it; for, however trivial they may be in a well-regulated ship, very offensive circumstances may arise from them. The two after-cabins on the lower [i.e. middle] deck are generally considered to be the best in the ship; and when, as is sometimes the case, there is a communication immediately from them to the cuddy, without the necessity of passing through the steerage, much of the inconvenience is removed. They are certainly more free from noise than any others in the vessel; but there is a greater difficulty in keeping them clean, and a much greater danger of their being infested with rats or other vermin. The upper cabins, on the other hand, may with a little care be always neat and comfortable; nor are they liable to have the sea wash into them, which may be the case in fine weather below, if by any awkwardness in the management, the ship should make a sudden dip: but they are certainly noisy. Neither during the night nor the day can the inmates of the poop-cabins expect peace: persons on duty are always stationed above their heads, and it is a favourite walk with the passengers; added to this, the hen-coops are usually placed upon the poop.... In bad weather, or during the working of the vessel, the noises made by trampling overhead, ropes dragging, blocks falling etc. etc. are very sensibly augmented by the cackling, chuckling, and screaming of the poultry, while throughout the day, whether fair or foul, they are scarcely ever silent. In those ships in which the comfort and convenience of the passengers are paramount considerations, the hen-coops do not occupy a place upon the poop, and it is probable that a general doom of banishment will shortly be pronounced against them....

Not every passenger, of course, had a cabin, whether on the upper or middle deck. Cadets and others, as we have seen, had to share a common dormitory in the great cabin or steerage. For those so travelling, the great cabin was in every way preferable.

...Those who have fixed bed-places in the larboard division of the great-cabin, are by far more privately, and more comfortably, situated than such as have them in the steerage, ranging along the bulk-head of the chief mate's cabin: in either case, there are always two tiers, or ranges, of bed-places, one above the other; the lower are certainly most convenient.

As priority of embarkation, or at least of adjustment, gives a right to selection, it is advisable to visit the ship so soon as an order for being taken on board is obtained; when a choice should be made as to the situation of a bed-place; those of the lower tier, nearest the stern windows in the great cabin, are to be preferred, they being both more airy, and more light: the latter will be found an object to those who are studious, or partial to reading in bed, which, on board ship, is held to be a most delectable recreation.

In adjusting with the captain, or his purser, it is proper to be very exact in stipulating for a berth in the great-cabin; and it would be as well to notice the conveniences to be afforded, in the body of the receipt given for the passage-money....

The author of the East India *Vade-Mecum*, Captain Williamson, hurriedly adds that no sort of insinuation is intended, but that mistakes are only too liable to occur in the hurry of business. Those who failed to secure berths in the great-cabin were fortunate if they were given a cabin to share in the steerage. The alternative was to be lodged in the steerage itself, against 'the bulk-head of the chief mate's cabin'. Those who were thus accommodated had to live in 'an open passage, totally devoid of privacy, exposed to violent currents of air, not always of the sweetest, and subject to many obvious inconveniences'.

Intending passengers usually began their negotiation for a passage by a personal call on the commander of the chosen ship. The wise among them normally followed this up by an invitation to dinner. Parents of cadets were careful to perform this civility on behalf of their offspring. Then the position and size of cabin, or the situation of the berth, was settled in argument with the purser, with or without a personal visit to the ship. The next thing was to purchase the necessary cabin furniture and send it on board, together with one's personal baggage.

Official passengers were allowed a quantity of baggage proportioned to their rank in the Company's service; a quantity varying from three-and-a-half to one-and-a-half tons, exclusive of bedding and cabin furniture. This would nearly all be carried in the hold, to which passengers had access at stated intervals during the voyage. Sometimes, on the very rare occasions when an outward-bound Indiaman was overladen, a room was built up amidships between the main and fore hatchway; and it was here, in such cases, that the baggage was stowed. The *Jane, Duchess of Gordon* had this arrangement in 1805, the baggage thus being on the gun deck and the lower deck being taken up by pigs of lead, jars of oil, odd packing-cases containing drums and bunting and stationery, and a coach consigned to a Member of Council in India. Baggage was supposed to consist only of 'wearing apparel' and articles for use on the voyage. Books might be carried, and 'musical instruments for ladies' but not furniture or crockery for use in India. A private stock of wine was allowed, provided that it was consumed during the voyage.

The baggage problem was more serious on the homeward than the outward passage. For one thing, the ship had a full cargo, so that space on board was more valuable; for another, the temptation for the passengers to smuggle goods under the guise of personal gear was then much stronger. They probably yielded to it as universally as they do to-day in the matter of Tauchnitz editions. Again, the returning Anglo-Indian might have trophies of war or the chase, not to mention children and a more or less extravagant wife. The breaking point was reached about 1801, when one passenger succeeded in bringing home sixty-three tons of baggage. This was too much even for the long-suffering East India Company. The above-mentioned regulations were put in force there and then, in order, it was said, to prevent 'the ultimate exclusion of the Company's cargo'. In 1808 the maximum amount of baggage was increased to five tons in the case of individuals of the highest rank. There had to be very strict rules about bringing black servants into England.

As regards cabin furniture, it must be understood that, in return for his passage money, a passenger was given a bare cabin or an empty berth. All conveniences other than deck space, partitions and a door, had to be supplied by himself. The nature of the furniture allowed was laid down in regulations, and the pattern was to some extent standardised by the fact that many passengers resorted to the same upholsterers in the vicinity of the East India Docks. Many also sold their furniture on their arrival home, probably to dealers intending to supply outward-bound passengers. The furniture used, then, normally consisted of a table, a sofa (or else two chairs), a wash-hand stand, and bedding. Most people bought a special kind of sofa, fitted with drawers underneath. Many, again, bought a wash-hand stand made to shut in and form a table. The place of the table could then be taken by an easy chair and perhaps another chair as well. This allowance of furniture was not included in the amount of baggage which might be carried; it was additional, over and above the stipulated quantity. Other articles of furniture were allowed but would count as baggage. These might consist of a couple more chairs, if there was room for them, some shelves for books, and perhaps a perforated shelf for crockery and glasses. Experienced travellers would include in their equipment a filtering machine, candlesticks, lamp, and an apparatus for making tea or coffee. Passengers normally slept on their sofas, but, for rough weather, they supplied themselves with cots. A cot was a sort of shallow wooden coffin suspended at each end from the deck-beams overhead. It was often made of canvas stretched on a frame. A cot was difficult to get into, and by no means hard to fall out of. It was, however, occasionally preferable to anywhere else, especially after a sea had been shipped. Among the little luxuries with which passengers could provide themselves were already such things as soda-water, 'portable soup' (a kind of beef extract), essence of coffee and a kind of condensed milk. They always brought tobacco, brandy and bars of soap with which to bribe sailors to do odd jobs for them.

Having sent his furniture, trunks and boxes on board, it

remained for the passenger to join the ship in person. He would normally do this at Gravesend a few days before the ship was due to sail. His first duty, on coming over the side, was to make his bow to the captain or chief mate, one or other of whom would be ready to receive him on the quarter-deck. He would then be shown down to his cabin, where he would find much to occupy him for the rest of the day—unless, indeed, a trustworthy servant had been sent to make the necessary arrangements beforehand. In the middle of the cabin he would find his furniture 'huddled together, after the fashion of a midshipman's chest, where every thing is at the top, and nothing to be found'. After arranging the various articles in some sort of order, the first anxiety of the wise traveller was to secure his belongings against the probable effects of blowing weather. Unless he did so at once, he ran the risk of seeing his trunks and boxes all 'coursing like so many race-horses along the decks'. He therefore spent his first few hours on hands and knees, hammering cleats and staples into the deck and securing his possessions with an elaborate system of cords and knots. The next thing was to 'swing' the cot. The overhead beams may sometimes have been fitted with permanent cleats for this purpose. Otherwise, there might be some left in position by the last tenant. In any case, the rule was to suspend the cot so as to hang fore and aft. If it were hung athwartships, the head and foot of the bed would have to change places whenever the ship went about in tacking. In all the arrangements the traveller had to make, he could expect no assistance from the ship's carpenter, who had employment enough for days and weeks to come. Ladies might, however, have the help of one of the two or three men or boys detailed to attend the passengers, fetch water for them and clean their boots. Experienced travellers seized the first opportunity to make the acquaintance of the captain's steward, 'no small man in his way' and one on whom their comfort would largely depend.

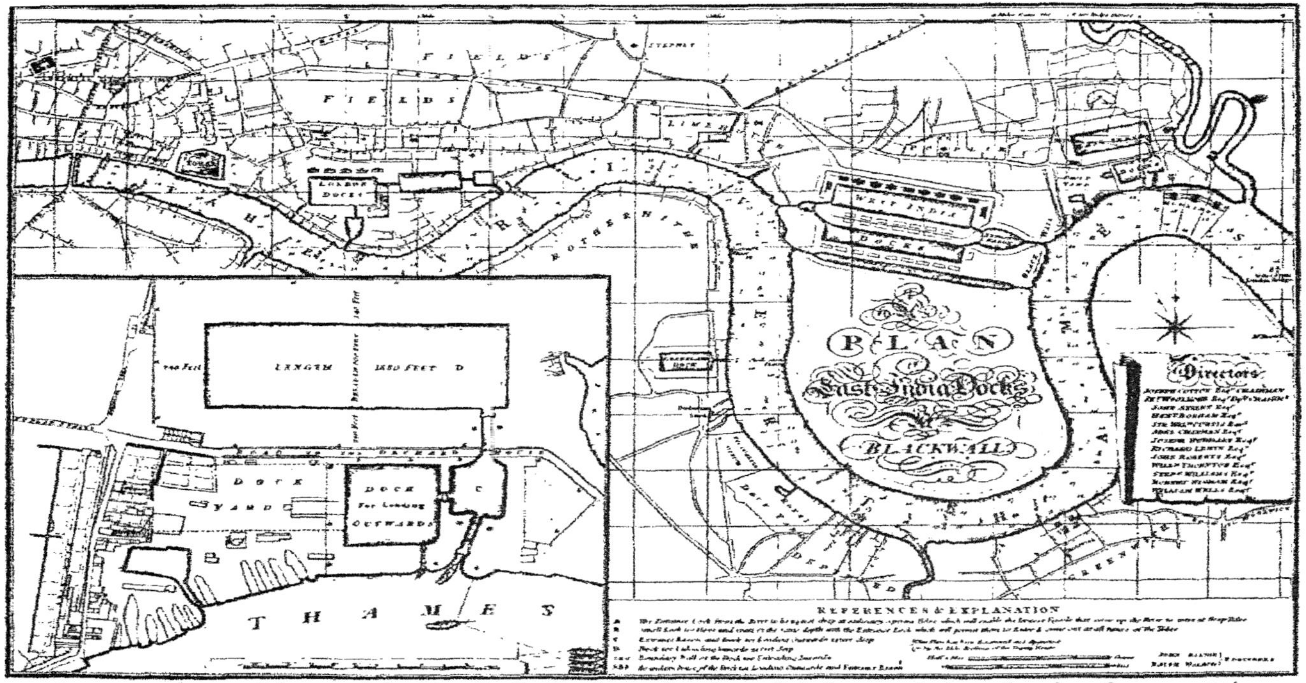

Plate VI. London River and the East India Docks at the time of their completion, showing the connection by road between Leadenhall Street, Poplar, and Blackwall.

Having set his cabin in order, the passenger might emerge cautiously from his abode and as cautiously find his way on deck. Having done so, he would find himself a passive nuisance in the midst of a scene of real or apparent chaos.

Nothing can exceed the bustle and confusion which prevail on board a ship upon the eve of sailing; even the strict discipline and formal regularity of a man-of-war must be relaxed upon such an occasion; and merchant-vessels, boasting little pretensions to either, present a scene of turmoil and hubbub, which it requires no small degree of fortitude to endure uncomplainingly. Those splendid argosies, the proud chartered vessels freighted by the East-India Company, in the period of their commercial prosperity, were not a whit less disorderly in their appearance than the humbler free-traders: the passengers of both had reason very heartily to wish they were fairly at sea, since, either from necessity or long custom, nothing like method could be achieved in the arrangements until they had cleared the land.

One source of confusion was the presence of the friends and relations of the owner, the captain and the passengers. These well-wishers crowded the ship, even sleeping on board on chairs and tables. After his reception by the captain or chief mate, the passenger had no sort of certainty as to who anyone was. A kind of 'open house' was kept on board, and there was no telling who were the passengers and who had come merely to see them off. Although the passenger would find 'the cuddy crammed full of people, usually employed in the agreeable office of eating and drinking', he and his fellow-travellers, 'amongst whom more or less stiffness at first will always prevail', would eye each other with that cold suspicion which was already becoming a national substitute for courtesy.

In the hospitality shown on board the East India Company's ships critics of the Company saw a proof of the officers' illicit gains. This hospitality had formerly been more famous than it was during our period. Writing in about 1795, Fiott spoke of it as, to some extent, a thing of the past. 'The term of floating taverns was scarcely sufficiently descriptive of their vessels, they were floating villas, with princely accommodations.' Mr Anthony Brough, however, in 1786, spoke of the practice of extravagant hospitality as a present evil:

> What is done in no other merchant-ships in the world, Captains will purchase their commissions for no less than seven or eight thousand pounds each. Will any man in his senses imagine that such a sum, and a proportionate interest, together with pay for the Captain's time and trouble, can be amassed, in two or three voyages, by legal means; or without detriment to the trade of the Company in general? Go on board of an Indiaman, count over the servants, the cooks, the musicians; behold the feasting and attendants! Listen to symphonies, and tell me sincerely, whether it would not rather impress you with an idea of Cleopatra sailing down the Cydnus to meet Mark Anthony, than a rough Captain venturing across immense oceans, and defying their storms and hidden rocks, to import the merchandise of India? Whence all this luxury? Can the Company be in want of parliamentary supplies, while it thus can squander, or shall I say prostitute, its riches?

Whatever the festivities may have been—and a suspicion is bound to dawn that Brough's account of the farewell banquets is exaggerated—they were finished by the time an Indiaman left Gravesend. It was from there, in a sense, that the voyage started. Nevertheless, a call was made in the Downs and also possibly at Portsmouth. Some captains did not allow their passengers to join until the hour came for sailing from the Downs. Some passengers, also, dreading sea-sickness, chose to join there at the last moment so as to avoid the days and even weeks which might be spent at anchor in the Downs, waiting for a favourable wind. One such passenger, who thus joined in the Downs from preference, was Thomas Twining. He sailed for India in April 1792, when just seventeen. In his reminiscences he says nothing of the expensive lodgings at Deal of which other people complained when kept involuntarily ashore. Nor does he mention the extortionate Deal boatmen, from whose cupidity others were apt to suffer.

After waiting three days, he hurried on board when he heard that 'the fatal blue peter' was seen from the beach.

Having made a bow to the Captain and officers, whom I found upon the quarterdeck, or part between the main and mizzen masts, and glanced my eye, for a moment, upon the ship from head to stern, I inquired where my cabin was, when I was conducted down a ladder to it, on the lower or gundeck, not far from the stern, on the larboard side. Here, the port being shut, there was scarcely light enough for me to survey my new apartment. I soon found, also, that the ship had considerably more motion than was apparent from the boat, and that the relief which I felt in coming on board was of very short duration. For I was scarcely able to stand without laying hold of some fixed object. I also became exceedingly oppressed by a close suffocating air, and by a sickening offensive smell, to which I know nothing comparable, and can only designate it by its usual appelation on board—*the smell of the ship*. My head and stomach soon began to yield to this irresistable combination. I could hardly help returning to the deck to breathe a little pure air. It was necessary, however, that I should go to work below, and place my things in order before the ship should get under weigh, when I should doubtless become more unwell and helpless. I therefore made an effort, and looked about me as well as I could, and inquiring what berths, or bedplaces, were already engaged, I chose the one which I thought the best of those not yet taken. I next had my principal trunk tied or *lashed down* to the deck, close to the side of the ship and directly opposite my sleeping place. I made such further distribution of my things as the pitching of the ship and my giddiness would permit. There being, in all, seven passengers in this small cabin, six of the berths were arranged in two lines against the bulkhead or partition which formed the side of the room, and ran parallel to the ship's side, at the distance of about six feet—this being the cabin's width. The seventh bed occupied the further end of the cabin towards the stern, and had a small window above it, for the sake of giving light to a passage; from which it received, in return, most offensive smells. It was, on this account, the worst berth of the whole set, though at first view it appeared to be the best, from being detached from the others and having no other above or below it.

After some consideration I fixed upon the first in the upper tier on entering the cabin, No. 1. I was rather doubtful whether to take this or the one under it, No. 2. But I considered that the occupier of the lower bedplace was subject to the inconvenience of having his neighbour in the upper story pass before him every night and morning, and perhaps of having a foot upon his bed or pillow in rolling weather. Besides, the upper range had the convenience of *lockers*, small recesses by the side of the bed between the beams of the deck. These were evidently of considerable advantage, being capable of holding many small things which it might be convenient to have at hand. I observed also that the port was nearly opposite my bed, as well as a smaller aperture, about nine inches square, called a scuttle. Its use was to admit air and light in bad weather, when the port might be shut. Being near the door also, I had the chance of a little fresh air down the *companion*, or opening in the upper deck, not far from the door. Upon the whole, notwithstanding my inexperience and the wretched sensations which oppressed me whilst I remained below, I flattered myself that I had chosen the best berth which this confined and crowded room afforded; for it appeared to me that the space allotted to seven persons was very limited, especially when the sum paid for it was considered....

The sum Twining paid was a hundred pounds, for first-class accommodation—that is, for having a place at the captain's table. From this account, one would conclude that, in comparing an Indiaman to Cleopatra's barge, Brough was taking a somewhat superficial view. Twining was a studious youth and suffered as much for want of privacy as from lack of comfort.

...I did not join in the loud and general complaint of the other passengers, as they, one after another, groped their way through the dark to make *their* survey and choice as I had done; and I have had less reason to complain since, for of the seven inmates thus crowded together, through the hot climate of the tropics and the rough seas of the Cape of Good Hope, when, the port and scuttle being both closed for many successive days and nights, we had no fresh air nor a ray of light,—of this number, as well as of many other passengers who occupied different parts of the ship, I, who was the youngest and considered the least robust of all, am the only one who lived to return to England; an instance, amongst many others contained in these pages, of the protection...etc. etc. ...The first part of the voyage was destitute of comfort in other respects of more importance [than sea-sickness and inability to drink the offensive water, or rather the tea made from it]. My companions kept the cabin in a constant state of noise and disorder. Their behaviour indeed was such that I thought it best to avoid, from the beginning, further communication than civility required.... I greatly regretted another circumstance; this was, having no room, however small, to myself, no place where I could read or write; for it was impossible to do either in the cabin which I shared with so many others, not only on account of the uproar which almost always prevailed there, but often from an insufficiency of light, and indeed a want of convenience of every kind....

Twining's plight was noticed by the chief officer, who allowed him the use of his own cabin. This enabled the young man to begin the study of Persian—the diplomatic language of the East which some, at least, of the writers were supposed to know.

On the subject of sea-sickness, Twining merely records that he did not appear at dinner until after the ship had passed the Bay of Biscay. James Wallace, however, the surgeon of the *Lonach*, sailing in 1821, seems to have experienced worse weather. The *Lonach* sailed from the Downs on 15 March in fine weather. After a day or two the wind freshened:

...On Thursday, the weather was still fine, and for that day also, I may say we were all well enough. Towards evening, indeed, some felt a little lightness of head, and rather a diminution of appetite.... At the call to breakfast, I went in, although I had little inclination for the meal, to take my seat at table along with the rest; but I found few others there; few, out of our number, had made their appearance, and even these few, as soon as the eating articles were produced, and the caterer had commenced sending them round, got up and made their exit rather hurriedly. I followed very soon, for I found things far from being right, and, like the others, took the way to my cot, into which I tumbled in a most pitiable condition.

All Friday it continued to blow, and all that day, I and many others, were, as we supposed, in a state of greater misery than ever mortal was in before. The moment we raised our head from the pillow, such horrible sensations ensued, that we were glad instantly to get it down again. Some who fought against their feelings, and got out of bed, had scarcely reached the floor, when a tumble of the vessel sent them tumbling to the other side of their cabin; and before they had time to recover themselves another roll would send them as quickly and roughly back again.... Others who got the length of beginning to dress, in the attempt to draw on a stocking, or in any other act which occupied both hands, and put the body on rather a ticklish balance, were thrown down with such violence, that for some days afterwards they had cause to remember it. And to increase the misfortune, the same lurch that upset the man, generally upset along with him, some of the cabin furniture....

The total time which might elapse between the day when an Indiaman left her moorings in London River and the day when she sailed from Portsmouth with convoy is well exemplified by Wathen's experience in 1811. He was one of that rare species, a passenger bound for China. The H.C.S. *Hope*, however, in which he sailed, was to call at Madras on the way and therefore carried a dozen passengers bound for that Presidency. Wathen went on board the *Hope* at Northfleet on 22 January 1811, accompanied by two friends. He went early to bed and was awakened at 6.0 a.m. by 'the crowing of cocks, and all the discordant noises of a farm-yard, proceeding from the fowls, geese, ducks, and animals on board'. On that day, the 23rd, the captain came on board 'and brought a company of ladies and gentlemen to dinner with him'. The captain disappeared after this, but returned next morning. That day was spent in stowing final items of luggage and stores, and the ship dropped down to Gravesend in the evening. On the 25th the ship's husband paid his visit, and the crew received their wages in advance; on the 28th the *Hope* was anchored in the Downs; by the 30th she was at Spithead; on 25 February the purser arrived with the last dispatches from the India House; by 10 March the last of the passengers had come on board; on the 12th the signal was made for the convoy to sail; six weeks had been spent at Spithead alone. Delay of this kind was sometimes due to adverse winds, sometimes to the time wasted in assembling a convoy, and sometimes to the embarking of troops.

There is a record, fortunately, of the experiences of a passenger joining an Indiaman at Spithead. This is the diary of Mrs Sherwood, who sailed with her husband in the H.C.S. *Devonshire* in 1805. Captain Sherwood was in the 53rd Regiment. The convoy in which this unit embarked had the escort of Rear-Admiral Troubridge in the *Blenheim* (74). In running through the Needles, the flagship struck a rock, sustaining injuries the extent of which was not realised at the time. The Sherwoods embarked at the last moment in a crowded ship and experienced intense discomfort as a result.

...When Mr Sherwood hurried to the ship to make what preparations he could, every cabin was already taken with the exception of the carpenter's, and had he not been able to secure this I must have stayed behind.

No woman who has not made such a voyage in such a cabin as this can possibly know what real inconveniencies are. The cabin was in the centre of the ship, which is so far good, as there is less motion there than at either end. In our cabin was a porthole, but it was hardly ever open; a great gun ran through it, the mouth of which faced the porthole. Our hammock was slung over this gun, and was so near the top of the cabin that one could hardly sit up in bed. When the pumps were at work, the bilge water ran through this miserable place, this worse than dog-kennel, and, to finish the horrors of it, it was only separated by a canvas partition from the place in which the soldiers sat and, I believe, slept and dressed, so that it was absolutely necessary for me, in all weathers, to go down to this shocking place before any of the men were turned down for the night. But, wretched as this place was, I was not to have it till I could be truly thankful for it, for, according to some rule which I did not understand, the carpenter did not dare to let us have the use of it until the pilot had left us....

During the whole of that day our fellow-passengers were coming in. We had on board eleven of our officers, nineteen cadets, and several gentlemen of the Civil Service, Madras. There were in the state cabins two families—Colonel and Mrs Thornley and an infant, and Colonel and Mrs Carr. In the great cabin below were our officers on one side, and, on the other, partitioned off, three daughters of a well-known Dean of Bristol, Dr. L——.

I watched all these persons coming on as I sat on my gun-carriage, and thus that miserable day wore out. At night we got our cabin, not before I was thoroughly thankful for it. After a wretched night in our cot, which was slung over a gun, I awoke, as it were, to renewed misery....

Our cabin was just the width of one gun, with room beside for a small table and single chair. Our cot, slung cross-ways over the gun, as I have said, could not swing, there not being height sufficient. In entering the cabin (which, by the way, was formed only of canvas) we were forced to stoop under the cot, there not being one foot from the head or the foot of the cot to the partition. The ship was so light on the water that she heeled over with the wind so much we could not open our port, and we had no scuttle. We were therefore also in constant darkness. The water from the pump ran through this delectable cabin, and I as a young sailor, and otherwise not in the very best situation for encountering all these disagreeables, was violently sick for days and days, the nights only bringing an increase of suffering. The cabin could not be borne during the daytime....

When Mrs Sherwood became acquainted with the other lady passengers, she was given the use of their cabins, and this somewhat lessened the discomfort from which she suffered.

Soon after a ship sailed, it was the captain's business to issue rules and regulations applying to the passengers as well as the crew. We have seen that the male passengers were, to begin with, assigned action posts in the quarter-bill. Sir James Mackintosh, going out to Bombay in the H.C.S. *Winchelsea* in 1804, was not exempted from this duty by his position as recorder. His son and biographer describes how

...As the war then raged, and as the French Admiral, Linois, and his cruisers infested the Indian seas but too successfully, every person on board had some duty assigned to him, connected with the defence of the ship; and Sir James was placed at the head of a party of pikemen, composed chiefly of passengers, who were to oppose any attempt of the enemy to board. The alarm occasioned by the appearance of suspicious sails, summoned him repeatedly to his post at some periods of the voyage, particularly in running through the Mozambique channel.

Among the customs to be observed by passengers as well as seamen was that of saluting the quarter-deck. Every male passenger had to touch his hat when coming on to the quarter-deck, whether from the cuddy or from below, and 'a breach of this rule would be considered grossly insulting, and might induce a rebuke' from the captain or the officer of the watch. The weather side of the quarter-deck was, by a strict etiquette, reserved for the captain alone whenever he should be on deck. Twining remarks that 'it would have been considered an act of great ignorance or offensive presumption ...for any one to pass between the wind and his nobility'; and, indeed, when the captain was there, he 'seemed to require it all to himself'. A strict etiquette was maintained in the cuddy as well as an order of precedence. The captain's authority was absolute; he was responsible for the good conduct of the passengers. Hence Wallace could write that 'the greatest regularity is observed; no impropriety is allowed; no debauching or late seats are ever countenanced....' All lights were to be put out by 10.0 p.m. and the officers saw to it that this was done.

Some captains were overbearing in their manner and not a little apt to exceed their authority. One universal rule was that which forbade whistling, as being both disrespectful and unlucky. In 1818 there was a case of a young army officer who whistled on the quarter-deck and continued to do so after being told to desist. The captain put him in irons and, after his release, deprived him of his servant for three weeks. There was a lawsuit as soon as the ship reached Bombay and the captain, losing the case, had to pay Rs. 5000. It was seldom, however, that a captain was tempted to exceed his powers. Ordinarily, he was obeyed without question; and, at the worst, he could punish an offender by excluding him from the cuddy.

Meals on board an Indiaman began with breakfast at 8.0 a.m. This consisted of tea and perhaps coffee, biscuit and sometimes bread or rolls, with butter, potted or corned-beef and tongue, with boiled rice or curry for the Anglo-Indians. Many people, and especially ladies, found the meal uneatable. They said that the biscuit was too hard, the bread manufactured on board execrable, the butter rancid (which it usually must have been) and the tea nauseous. Sybarites would console themselves with 'biscuits, rusks, and preserved rounds of toast' out of hermetically sealed tin cases. Others, like Twining, found the tea disgusting and never appeared at breakfast for the rest of the voyage. Wathen, on the other hand, pronounced the tea excellent. Ladies seem usually to have thought otherwise, so that it was a meal at which they were seldom seen. 'At eight o'clock', Mrs Sherwood wrote, 'the gentlemen assembled for tea in absence of the ladies.' Her servant, or rather her husband's, apparently brought her something to eat. 'Miserable foraging it was', but she added that 'Bad as our breakfasts were in the dining-room, they were exquisite compared with what the soldiers got....'

The officers and passengers dined at 2.0 p.m.; or at least they did so as soon as the latter felt any inclination to dine at all. When the company was very numerous, the first-class passengers were divided, as we have seen, into two parties. Besides these, however, who dined in the cuddy, there were the young men who, paying rather less, dined in the steerage under the presidency of the third mate. According to the East India *Vade-Mecum*, they fared little worse than cuddy passengers:

> The third mate generally has a mess, in the expenses of which the fourth, fifth and sixth mates sometimes partake; the purser and surgeon being invariably at the captain's table. The captain's clerk, who is usually a midshipman, the surgeon's mate, when

there is one, and the second class of passengers, all mess with the third mate, who is allowed a certain space before the officers' cabins; which, being enclosed with canvas, makes a very tolerable berth, wherein the table is laid. Those of the mess who belong to the ship, subscribe to lay in such articles of provision, chandlery etc. as may suffice for their own consumption; the sums paid by passengers, who associate with them, being applied in due proportion towards the maintenance of the latter; any balances arising therein becoming the perquisite of the third mate. I have heard that, with the exception of so large a proportion of live stock as is destined for the captain's table, the mate's mess, in some ships, claims the palm in many respects. When so many passengers are ordered on board, as to render it impracticable for the captain to accommodate the whole at his table, the later applicants are consigned to the mate's mess during meals; but are admitted, so far as convenience can be extended, to a participation of the amusements and society of the round-house. On some occasions the mate's mess has, from the above cause, been able to boast of rather eminent characters.

It does not appear that the third mate ever made any considerable profit on his catering. Although, therefore, the cadets and others thus received full value for what they paid, the mess in the steerage had one disadvantage which Captain Williamson fails in the above passage to point out; namely, that the festive board was of necessity spread either by artificial light or else in almost complete darkness.

The various accounts which exist of the meals on board the Indiamen relate solely to the cuddy. The menu in the steerage must therefore be left to conjecture. The food served there was probably of the same kind but in less variety, while the wine may have been either of poor quality or small quantity. Whereas breakfast took place at the changing of the watch, there was no bell to announce the dinner-hour. The passengers and officers were therefore called together by beat of drum. It was a tuneless version of the well-known 'Roast-Beef of Old England' and, as such, seeming to raise hopes which could seldom be satisfied.

It being studied to take on board as much fresh meat as possible, at the time of sailing, some joints of good beef and mutton may be served up for the first week; after which the 'corned' (or slightly salted) meat comes into use. The ample supply of poultry, of all descriptions, fed in coops on the poop, and a small flock of sheep, perhaps from twenty-five to forty in number, maintained there on hay etc. enable the captain, for the most part, to exhibit fresh meat, of some sort, every day; which, added to the abundance of prime beef and pork, salted for his use, together with tongues, pickles, sauces of all kinds, potatoes, rice, pastry, olives etc. etc. form a tout ensemble, where even the most dainty may find something acceptable to the palate.

Captain Williamson, the author of the above account, had evidently been fortunate, on the whole, in his travels. Twining seems to have had even happier experience:

Upon leaving the Bay of Biscay I was able to take my place at the Captain's table, and to make up in some measure for my long absence, having as usual, after such a course of sea sickness, a particularly good appetite. The dinner exhibited an abundance and variety which surprised me, consisting of many joints of mutton and pork variously dressed, curries and pillaus, chickens, ducks, and on Sundays turkeys and hams. It was almost inconceivable where so many things could be stowed, and how they could be dressed and served up day after day. This generous prodigality was such as to call forth the friendly remonstrances of the passengers, without, however, checking the liberal profusion.

Wathen's comments, although equally favourable, apply only to the first few days of the voyage:

Dinner, about two o'clock, was announced by beat of drum; and at this time our bill of fare consisted of all kinds of fresh meat, exquisite curries, pies, tarts, puddings etc. prepared by a cook who knew his business.

Dinner in an Indiaman's cuddy was a ceremonious affair. Both ladies and gentlemen dressed beforehand as regularly as they would on shore. Mrs Sherwood commented a little enviously that 'those of our ladies who had had as many months perhaps to prepare for their voyage as I had had days, came out every day very elegantly and richly adorned...'.

When the company was seated according to a strict order of precedence, the captain, who presided, would both lead the conversation and exert his authority to preserve decorum. There were at least three courses, followed by dessert and coffee and accompanied by beer, spruce beer, wine, negus or punch. The quality of the cooking varied in different ships, but the general rule was that the standard of living deteriorated as time went on. While the livestock lasted, the fare might be called luxurious; but a single gale might dispose of all the poultry, and even when this did not happen the fowls became very tough and stringy after two or three weeks at sea. The pigs were less likely to perish, but the pork was sometimes tainted before it could be used. The mutton, too, was often in bad condition. The authoress of the account in the *Asiatic Journal* takes a gloomy view of the whole affair. Dealing with the period spent by a ship at Gravesend, she writes:

> The first meals eaten on board an outward-bound vessel are characterised by a rude kind of plenty, and a promiscuous assembly surrounding the board. Some apology is offered for any little remissness on the part of the cookery, on account of the vessel not being yet in order, and the passengers take their ill-concocted soup, queer-looking ragouts, and jelly of the colour of salt water, but not quite so clear, in the fallacious hope that these things will be amended in time. The whole affair, though conducted after a slovenly fashion, is not without pretension; the captain, in nine cases out of ten, takes his place with an air of conscious dignity, which is meant to be very imposing; the steward seems to be fully acquainted with the vast importance of his office, and the rest of the cuddy-servants look up to him with awe....

Something, perhaps, must be allowed here for the normal feminine attitude towards male domestic arrangements. All naval officers looked upon an Indiaman's table as the last word in luxury. A board where there might be champagne twice a week did not often come their way, nor did they often find themselves confronted with as many as thirty dishes to choose from.

Whatever the ordinary standard of cooking might be, a gale was quite enough to lower it considerably. Owing to the reform ordained in 1799 to make room for troops, the galley was on the upper deck, well forward under the forecastle. The galley floor was below the level of the deck so as to provide sufficient head room. While lessening the risk of setting the ship on fire, this transference of the galley from the middle deck had two unfortunate results. One was to remove a useful source of ventilation. The other was to expose the galley fire to extinction every time a sea was shipped:

> The dinner presented rather a melancholy spectacle, for...the fire had been quenched several times during the attempt to prepare for the repast. A sea-pie, a boiled leg of mutton, and two dishes of potatoes alone graced a board which had been hitherto distinguished for its ostentatious display, and even those, at least the mutton and potatoes, could not be kept in their respective dishes, but danced about, to the great diversion of some of the passengers, and the annoyance of others...a chair would occasionally start away from its position at the table, sidling out of the line in a most ludicrous manner, and carrying its occupant down the whole length of the cuddy, in most cases upsetting when it got to the bottom. After several disasters of the same kind, it was found expedient to erect stanchions or posts, at intervals down either side of the table, and even after this precaution had been taken, it became necessary, when all the company were seated, to have a rope passed round the chairs to secure each person in his place. There were swing-shelves for the glasses, and long rolls of cloth, entitled puddings, tied across the table, to prevent the plates and dishes from slipping.... [*Asiatic Journal.*]

In other ships, like the *Ponsborne* in which Twining sailed, the need for these arrangements in the cuddy was foreseen:

> The chairs round the table and the table itself were lashed down to iron staples driven into the deck. The dishes were kept in their places by means of long cushions of green baize stuffed with sawdust stretched across the table, and of smaller ones of a semi-circular form placed under each dish, thus both raising its leeward edge and preventing it from slipping....

Plate VII

Bosanquet describes what was liable to happen when the dining-table lacked these contrivances:

> Sometimes the weather was too bad for dressing our usual dinner, and sometimes, when dressed, the dishes would forsake their places on the table, and mutton, gravy and all, despite of every precaution, deposit itself in the lap of him who sat nearest it: whilst, on rising from the desolate meal, it was an even choice whether to retire to the dark, close, uneasy cabin, or to parade the deck in the midst of the spray....

The last word on the subject of dinner in an Indiaman's cuddy may be left to the authoress of the article in the *Asiatic Journal*. The final criticism of this uncharitable feminine critic is that there should have been less display:

> In fine weather, when no adverse circumstances occur to mar the efforts of the caterers, there is usually abundant room for improvement amid people who are slow to perceive that more would be achieved if less were attempted.

The ladies withdrew after the meal itself was over, usually to each other's cabins for conversation. Then, the cloth having been removed, the bottle was circulated two or three times 'according to the liberality of the commander'. With the last tour of the bottle, the captain rose and said 'good afternoon' pointedly. Whereupon, the gentlemen took the hint and withdrew.

Dinner was followed by tea, at 6.0 p.m., the end of the first dog-watch. Tea, as Mrs Sherwood remarks, was for 'those who chose it'. The water with which it was made, being 'strongly impregnated with filth', was usually passed through a filtering-stone before being boiled. By this tedious process, certain impurities were removed. The fecula left in the hollow of the drip-stone was found to be 'perfectly putrid'; and yet, even at the end of this process, the water was improved more in appearance than in odour. Tea made from it was, to many, undrinkable. Milk was usually obtainable during the lifetime of the cow or cows which all ships carried. If there was bread and butter to accompany the tea, the bread, as made on board, would be very bad, while the butter was sure to be in a liquid form even were its state no worse than that.

Supper was the last meal of the day and it took place at 9.0. It was, according to Williamson, 'little more than a matter of form':

> ... it consists chiefly of cheese and biscuits, rasped beef, sago soup, lobskous, which is a curious medley of various ingredients, forming something midway between water-gruel and peas-soup. One tour of the bottle, attended with 'good night', closes the operations of the day.

The rule which ordained the extinction of lights in the cabins by 10.0 had the effect of sending the passengers below almost immediately after supper. The object of this rule was partly to guard against fire, partly to ensure sobriety of conduct, and partly to enable the ship to escape the notice of enemies in the darkness. Even during the hours when candles were tolerated, the rule was in war-time that no such lights were to be visible 'to any vessel passing in the night'.

Except for the studious, life on board an Indiaman was intolerably dull. The passengers had, most of them, to spend six months in idleness and boredom, broken only by the discomfort of bad weather. Those sailing in April could not expect to arrive at Madras or Calcutta until September. And if there was any considerable delay during the earlier part of the passage, the Bay of Bengal might not be reached until after the north-east monsoon had begun; which would mean spending another month or six weeks afloat while the ship worked her way up to Balasore Roads. For the normal, as opposed to the studious passenger, the problem was to find occupation for from five to seven months of monotony. For soldiers especially, the problem often proved insoluble. Captain Marryat wrote that 'there are no classes of people who embark with more regret, or quit a ship with more pleasure, than military men...'. For the exceptionally intelligent young soldier, on the other hand, as for the civilian, the voyage was an opportunity to learn Persian, Hindustani or Portuguese. Colonel Arthur Wesley employed his time on board ship in reading history. But army officers were, in general, as little given to reading as they are to-day; and most of them did little but yawn, grumble, quarrel and look forward to their next chance of going ashore.

The first port at which an Indiaman was likely to call was Funchal, in Madeira. The object of this visit was to ship wine, together with some fresh vegetables, perhaps, and possibly some water. Passengers usually had the opportunity of visiting the island for just so long as sufficed for them to see and bewail the catholicism of the inhabitants. 'At Funchal, how could he witness the tawdry vanities and sickly superstitions of popery without a sigh?' wrote the biographer of the Rev. T. T. Thomason. In this mood of self-congratulation, the passenger could then look forward to noting the pleasing contrast at the strictly protestant Cape; that is, if we happened at the time to be at peace with Holland, or else in possession of the Dutch colonies. After the conquest of the Cape in 1806 this call became more common. If any considerable time was spent there, it was customary for the passengers to live on shore at their own expense. They boarded with respectable Dutch families, admired the local menagerie, and made expeditions to Constantia and Table Mountain. Ships bound for Bombay often made a further call at Johanna in the Comoro Islands, where there was some little trading with the natives. Those of the natives who were accustomed to come on board the Indiamen called themselves by the names which had been given them in jest, usually the names of such European statesmen as they seemed least to resemble. Ships bound for Bengal or Madras seem seldom to have called anywhere between the Cape and their destination. On the homeward voyage ships would sometimes call at St Helena for refreshments, chiefly in the form of vegetables and water. The stay there of a convoy was usually long enough to enable the passengers to go on shore. After 1816 this visit became more popular as it carried with it, for a few of the privileged, the chance of an introduction to Napoleon.

During long periods of fine weather, with no land in sight, the more intelligent passengers evolved a routine of employment for themselves. Lord Minto, for example, gave much of his time to literature, which meant chiefly Virgil and Cicero, with *Ossian*, Crabbe's *Borough* and *The Lady of the Lake* for occasional relaxation. Mrs Sherwood spent part of her leisure in teaching one of the soldiers' little boys, aged ten, to read:

> By the middle of May, when we passed St Lucia and St Vincent Islands, we on board had begun to understand each other, and to fall into little parties and societies. We had our little plots and under-plots, our likings and dislikings, our jealousies and small spites and real kindnesses, and I had formed my plans for spending my days. I arose early and got out of my horrid cabin, and came upon deck, and sat under the awning, by the wheel, at the door of the dining-room. I was now able to read and sew, and we were in the tropics; hence it was warm out of doors...with sewing, reading, or being read to, passed the time till it was necessary to dress for dinner....
>
> After dinner I was generally invited into Mrs Carr's cabin, or all the ladies went and took their tea on deck, and the gentlemen talked to them, and not unseldom there was a dance on deck.... ...It was necessary for me to go down to my miserable cabin long before other people retired, in order that I might be shut up in my cot before my neighbours on the other side of the canvas partition came down. Mr Sherwood often came down with me, and this was his hour for reading the bible to me....
>
> There was, I doubt not, much folly and much flirting on deck after I was gone down, which my presence might not perhaps have hindered, though it might have slightly checked it....
>
> The captain of an East India ship which carries passengers is always supposed to be the guardian for the time being of the ladies under his care. When they appear on deck he gives them his arm, and when they walk he walks with them. Everybody understands this, and no lady interprets these common attentions as meaning

anything. Poor Miss L——, however, did choose to place her private interpretation on the attentions of Captain Murray, and it was soon known to all our officers that the young lady had given him her heart; he at the same time favouring the opinion by increase of attentions. But whilst Miss L—— thus encouraged the captain, she was haughty in the extreme to every man whom she thought of inferior rank....

There were numerous ways in which passengers could get into mischief, but it was by flirting and quarrelling that duels, suicides and murders were occasionally brought about. It was the captain's business to maintain order and decorum. Responsible for the conduct of all on board, and interested financially in the ship's reputation, he had to exert his authority to prevent scandals.

...Notwithstanding the utmost vigilance on the part of the captain, attachments will spring up amongst the young people on board, and fortunate may it be considered when these are confined to the single of both sexes....

Under a weak captain both intrigues and quarrels might be carried to an extreme. If no sort of order was kept, gentlemen were apt to send each other formal notes on gilt-edged paper, requesting satisfaction as soon as there should be an opportunity of going ashore. How far this sort of thing could go may be gathered from Alexander Grieg's journal of the voyage and wreck of the *Blenden Hall* in 1821. It must be observed, however, that the *Blenden Hall* was not a regular Indiaman and that the passengers were of perhaps unusually low social origin. A regular ship would not, for instance, have carried the 'coloured' wife of an officer in the Bombay Marine. Even as things were, the passage money demanded may well have been a fantastically large sum. The wife of a merchant of Bombay for whose passage, according to Dalrymple, £5000 was paid, was in all probability a coloured woman. Apart from the Company's servants, whose position as such ensured a certain degree of respectability, the captain of an Indiaman could take or refuse whom he would. No ordinary ship of the period with which we are dealing would carry as mixed a company as did the *Blenden Hall*. Nevertheless, even the most select people could give a great deal of trouble. And a captain who interfered with his passengers was liable to receive a challenge himself. Captain T. R. Taylor, of the H.C.S. *Glory*, was killed in a duel by one of his passengers immediately on the arrival of his ship at Madras in 1804.

An interesting account of how General Sir John Malcolm spent his time on board ship is contained in one of the letters printed in his biography. It refers to his voyage out to Madras in 1817:

> ...I rise at half-past five, and every day, except Sundays, go through my exercises (gymnastics). I have from four to six scholars, some of whom have made great proficiency. I go to my cabin at seven, read in my flannel dress till eight, dress, breakfast at half-past eight, walk the deck till ten, return to my cabin, write....
>
> ...At twelve I break off for half an hour, when I commence work again, and leave off at half-past two; good dinner at three, break up at half-past four, walk the deck, read light books, or talk nonsense till six o'clock; drink tea; at seven go to cards—two whist tables for steady ladies and gentlemen and one for boys; leave off at ten, and all in bed by eleven. Next day the same course, except Sundays, when there are no gymnastics, no cards. If we have prayers upon deck, Captain C—— reads the service; I read lessons and sermon....

It is possible that, by 1817, the hour for dinner had become later under pressure from the fashionable world. But, during the period of the wars, if dinner was at three it was usually because the passengers were too numerous to dine simultaneously, so that half of them had to dine at one. Although the cuddy had its own cook, it does not appear that he had a separate galley; so that it was perhaps as well that the crew and the passengers did not have their principal meal at the same time.

Cards, music, conversation and dancing were the amusements ordinarily available for passengers. Deck-games do not seem to have been played, although they had been known in the seventeenth century. Most ships had a band of drums and fifes, which would play on fine evenings. The passengers, also, were often able to muster two or three violins among them; and sometimes a pianoforte. There might therefore be dancing, if the number of ladies allowed of it. The sailors disapproved of dancing. Like the crime of whistling, or the worse crime of appearing on deck in spurs, it was supposed to bring bad luck. Mrs Sherwood narrates how, when a fair wind died away, it was attributed by the seamen to the fact that there had been dancing on board.

Another occasional amusement was found in theatricals. Lady Nugent relates how the seamen of the H.C.S. *Baring* acted a translation of *Le Médecin malgré lui*. 'The performance', she writes, 'was very droll, and the poor soldiers and sailors, and the actors themselves, appeared highly amused.' On the same voyage the passengers produced *Macbeth* for the ship's company, the soldiers and sailors giving songs between the acts. A young writer on his way out to India rendered the part of Lady Macbeth in what was understood to be the manner of Mrs Siddons.

The ceremony of crossing the line was not at this time of very old standing, and there was another form of it besides that which has since become traditional. It was not even invariably held. The sailors could be very rough and Mrs Sherwood asserts that 'passengers have gone so far as to use pistols to protect themselves'. In 1802 a passenger in the *Scaleby Castle* brought an action against the captain on account of the rough treatment he had received. The captain was fined Rs. 400 by the court at Bombay. Whether 'Neptune's rites' were an occasion for harmless amusement or mere brutality depended on the ship's officers. Too often, the ceremony resulted in violent quarrels, especially between soldiers and sailors. Archibald Campbell, in his account of his voyage to China in 1806 on board the H.C.S. *Thames*, remarks that, in the passage to the Cape 'no incident occurred worthy of being recorded, not even the ordinary ceremonies upon crossing the line. We had a detachment of the 30th Regiment on board, the commanding officer of which did not chuse that the men should undergo the ducking usual upon that occasion.' This was not altogether unusual, and the decision was certainly a wise one when the relations between the troops and the seamen were already strained. Akin to the ceremony on crossing the line was the custom by which landsmen were tied to the topmast shrouds when first going above the main-top, and not released except on payment of a fine. This custom, however, had a good effect in discouraging boys from risking their necks.

As regards the hostility which was apt to arise between soldiers and seamen, Lady Nugent comments in her journal that 'the constant disagreements between the soldiers and sailors put Sir George to a great deal of trouble, to do justice and to keep order; for all the complaints of the poor recruits are brought to him, and there are generally so many faults on both sides, that it is very difficult to act'. Despite this impartial distribution of blame, it is probable that the seamen were more often at fault than the troops. They were not, to begin with, so well disciplined. And they were, again, more likely to be aggressive, as being on their own element, which the soldiers were not. The following narrative, from Lady Nugent's journal, shows to what a seaman's ideas of discipline could lead. It may be remarked that Captain Templar, of the *Baring*, had, earlier in the voyage, quarrelled with a certain Captain Midwinter. The latter had retired to his cabin, Templar subsequently refusing to allow him to resume his place. As a result of this unpleasantness, Lady Nugent had retired to *her* cabin, where she was joined by Lady Murray. The Captain Fraser who is, as it were, the hero of the story, was one of Sir George Nugent's aides-de-camp. Lady Nugent refers to him elsewhere as a 'growing boy'.

20th. A wretched day; for a most painful and distressing occurrence took place. One of the usual violent and distressing outrages was committed by Captain Templar, in knocking down one of the soldiers. Captain Fraser picked the man up, and remonstrated with Captain Templar, mentioning that the order given by Sir George was, that no soldier should be punished, without the complaint being made in a regular manner, and the punishment awarded by a court martial.—On this Captain Templar insulted poor Fraser, who took it most coolly; at the same time telling him, that such gross conduct should not remain unnoticed at a proper season.—Fraser's conduct met the approbation of every one on board, and all the gentlemen came forward, declaring they would no longer dine at the captain's table. He was so ashamed of his language and conduct himself, that he offered to dine in his own cabin the rest of the voyage; but, after much discussion, it was agreed, that Colonel and Lady C. Murray, Fortescue, Fraser, Sir George and myself, should have a separate table, and then the rest of the passengers, at last, consented to dine in the great cabin. Poor Fraser is so young, and just entering military life, that even Sir George thinks him right, in demanding satisfaction.... Captain Templar was ready to make any apology, but not publicly on the deck, where the offence had been given; in short all was unhappiness, and I have never left my cabin since.

This is now the 10th of January, 1812, and this morning we anchored opposite to Saugur Island. Immediately I heard boats lowered down, and I shuddered, guessing what was going forward.—I covered up my head, and would not leave my cot, till Fraser was conducted to my bedside, safe and well, and then my prayers for his safety were changed to thanksgivings, that all had ended so happily. It seems they both fired together, and then Captain Templar immediately begged Mr Fraser's pardon, and made the humblest apology for the outrage he had been guilty of.—This has been a most distressing business altogether, and the finale, although so repugnant to every feeling of religion and morality, I cannot now regret; as even Sir George assures me, any other termination might have been a lasting injury, and a most serious disadvantage, to poor Fraser, during the whole of his life as a military man; and so young as he now is, it would have been the ruin of his prospects.

Troubles between soldiers and sailors were often the characteristic of the passage to India. The homeward passage was seldom marred by such affairs, for there were then scarcely any soldiers, considerably fewer sailors and no great number of passengers. What disturbance there was came from the children, who might be numerous. The family of a wealthy official, going home on his retirement, might occupy nearly the whole of the accommodation in one ship. Charles Grant, returning home in the *Berrington* in 1790, had with him his wife, his five children, the child of a friend, two men-servants and three maid-servants. For these he required the whole round-house, both stern-galleries, and several cabins in the steerage. It would be interesting to know what he paid altogether. Major Price paid about £350 for a single small cabin in the H.C.S. *St Vincent* in 1805, on the passage from Bombay to England. Hickey, in 1807, paid £1000 for half the great cabin in the *Castle Eden*. What Grant must have paid can only be imagined. The Rev. J. Cordiner, who went home in the H.C.S. *Glory* in 1804, recorded the fact that there were in that ship eleven passengers, nine children, five invalid soldiers and a few invalid sailors. Of the passengers, four were invalided naval officers. This is a typical list; it throws light especially on the numbers of children a returning Indiaman might carry. Hickey wrote very bitterly on this subject, comparing their 'horrid screeches' when crying with their 'vociferous mirth' when playing. He had, as a fact, far less cause for complaint than Sir James Mackintosh, who, returning home in the *Caroline* in 1811, tried to occupy himself in the study of philosophy. This is from a letter:

> The round-house on the larboard side is occupied by Mr & Mrs Richards and their daughter. In front of them is a small cabin with Simon and William Campbell and Henry Stephenson. In

front of them, and immediately upon the quarter-deck, is my spacious apartment of nine feet square with one side port, two windows to the deck, and a sliding door; behind is a sofa convertible into a bed, above which is hung your picture. I sit at my desk placed on the old library-steps-table, fronting the deck; on my left is the wash-hand locker and a large camphor-wood trunk, with books and papers. The starboard side of the round-house is occupied by Forbes.

We are now nearly off Bancoot. We have a pleasant though not a perfectly fair breeze, and the thermometer is at 82. Thus much as an introduction, which I have written amidst as many noises and distractions as ever tried the presence of mind of Julius Caesar, always excepting those of battle. We have ten children on board....

Finished the first part of Stewart amidst the uproar of the mob of spoiled children on the quarter-deck. It is the severest test to which the power of attention of a student of philosophy was ever subjected. If I can acquire the art of studying metaphysics in the midst of this noise, I must not despair of being able to go through the most intricate reasonings of the 'Principia' on the hustings of Covent-garden.

On any voyage, outward or homeward, the routine of an Indiaman was liable to be upset by the sighting of a suspicious sail. In time of peace, it is true, the possibility of an attack by pirates was remote, even on the China voyage. But, in wartime, until after the capture of Mauritius in 1810, there was often real ground for alarm, both from cruisers and privateers. In nine cases out of ten the stranger would prove harmless. Occasionally he would turn out to be an enemy, and, still more occasionally, the encounter would end in an exchange of shots. Mrs Sherwood, in the *Devonshire*, was present at the action between the *Blenheim* and convoy with Admiral Linois in 1805. Her account is interesting as describing the skirmish from the non-combatant's point of view:

In a very short time after the enemy had been seen, one of the strangers lay to, whilst the other two came down, and, passing close to our rear, hoisted French colours almost before we had time to form our conjectures of what they were. The colours were no sooner up than they began to fire, and at the same crisis all hands were engaged on board our ship to clear for action. Every cabin which had been erected between the last gun and the fore-part of the ship was torn down, ours of course among the rest, and everything we possessed thrown in heaps into the hold or trampled under foot. All the women without respect of person were tumbled after the furniture of the cabins into the same dismal hole at the very bottom of the ship, and the guns prepared in the shortest possible time to return the compliment which the enemy had already paid us. One of the enemy's ships was a seventy-four, or eighty gun, the other a large frigate...their shot passed through our rigging....

It was quite dark when the contest ceased and we poor women were set at liberty. The hold was a dismal place, and there was no light but what came from above. There were six ladies and eight or ten soldiers' wives in it, besides a negro female servant of Mrs Carr, and one or two Madras ayahs. There were no children except little Master Durham, the boy whom I taught to read, and Maria Parker. The first thing which happened to me when I got down was to have little Maria popped into my arms, whilst her mother tried to collect our belongings, which had been scattered in the hold. Much as my mind was occupied at the time, I could not help wondering how the woman could possibly think of such matters. However, I had reason to thank her afterwards for her care. We were then considerably under water-mark, in darkness, and quite certain that if anything happened to the ship nothing could save us, for they had taken away the ladders, probably to keep us in our places. Our husbands and all our late companions were above, and we heard the roar of the guns, but had no means of learning what was going on. We were warned not to approach the opening lest a ball might roll in upon us, and there we were for some hours, not in the least knowing what was going on. There was, however, no fainting, screaming or folly amongst us; it is not on occasions of real trial that women in general behave weakly. As to myself, I can hardly say that I felt anything more than a sort of dull, dreamy insensibility, a kind of feeling which I have often experienced on very alarming occasions.

It was quite dark, though I know not the hour, when notice was given that all was over, and no mischief done in the Devonshire; and then ensued a strange ceremony, for the men began to hoist up the women instead of providing steps for us. They took the ladies up first, lifting them from one to another as if they had been so many bales of goods. There were larger and taller women amongst us than myself, but the men made no difficulty with any of us. We all repaired to Colonel Carr's cabin, where we congratulated each other on the happy termination of the affair, and much enjoyed some negus and biscuit....

After reading of all the discomforts and dangers to which passengers, and especially women, were exposed, it is strange to learn that there were some who enjoyed the voyage and were even sorry when it came to an end. Lady West, on a passage out to Bombay in 1822, during which she had only half a pint of water a day in which to wash, came in the end to like the life on board ship. In her journal she wrote 'little did I think I should be so reconciled to the walk on the deck of a ship as to like it'; and later she added 'it's odd, but I am not at all anxious to arrive...'. Knowing what she must have undergone, we can only agree that it was very odd indeed.

Chapter X

NAVAL PROTECTION

A useful chapter in naval history and tactics could be written on the defence of convoys, by which it might perhaps be made manifest, that a determined bearing, accompanied by a certain degree of force, and a vigorous resolution to exert that force to the utmost, would, in most cases, save the greater part of the convoy, even against powerful odds....

So writes Captain Basil Hall, with evident truth. But the chapter remains to be written. As regards the East India Company, however, the history of convoys presents no very great difficulty, as the Company's records exist to supplement those of the Admiralty.

The East India Company's ships were not compelled to accept convoy as many other ships were. The Act did not apply to them, as their heavy armament gave them something of the status of ships-of-war. They had the freedom which Letters of Marque conferred. At the same time, they were scarcely ever allowed to sail singly in war-time, and it was very rarely that they lacked naval protection. The Company could not afford to take risks. The ships, indeed, were nearly all hired; but those belonging to the Company itself were not insured. More important still, the outward-bound vessels often carried military stores on the safe arrival of which a campaign in India might turn. And the cargoes of homeward-bound ships, although insured, were a matter of national importance.

The East India Company's ships were fairly easily organised into convoys because, being all freighted by a single commercial interest, they had no occasion to compete with each other. Furthermore, their times of sailing were regulated in any case, to some extent, by the nature of things. Weather conditions in the Indian Ocean tended to confine the bulk, though not the whole, of the Company's shipping to certain periods of the year. For the China ships, an even more imperious necessity was the state of the tea crop. There was no object in arriving at Canton much before November when the tea was ready for shipment. So the time of year for sailing was settled according to the average length of time it took to perform the voyage. With India the case was different to this extent, that there were political considerations to be taken into account. It was essential to keep up a fairly continuous communication with India by sea, however unfavourable the climate might be to such a plan. Messages, it is true, could go by the overland route, but there was always an element of risk about it. A duplicate was always sent by sea, to make sure, and usually a triplicate by another ship, to provide against shipwreck. Besides, it was often necessary to send men instead of dispatches, and the overland route was not nearly safe enough for that, considering that the whole system might be upset by a change of policy at Teheran or Constantinople, if not by some petty brigand on the way. The monsoons could not be allowed to make the communications with India entirely seasonal.

The first sailings to arrange for in any given year were the ships for Bombay and China. These numbered about four and had to be dispatched early, having much farther to go than the other China ships and having nevertheless to arrive at the same time. The ships were chosen—or 'stationed', as it was called—at a Court held in the autumn of the previous year. Here is a typical announcement:

Sept. 20. A Court of Directors was held at the East India House, when the undermentioned Ships were taken up for the season 1799 and stationed as follows.

Bombay and China

Canton	1198 tons
Cirencester	1200 ,,
Ganges	1200 ,,
Earl Talbot	1200 ,,

These ships had to be afloat by 28 October. They were then to sail for Gravesend on 12 November, remain there for thirty days and be in the Downs by 18 December. The two Bombay and China ships for the season 1800 were similarly due in the Downs by 7 December. But the system was altered after the second outbreak of war, and for much of our period the ships for Bombay and China did not sail until about February of the following year. Thus the four ships stationed in the autumn of 1806, the *True Briton*, *Britannia*, *Nottingham* and *Scaleby Castle*, did not sail until 26 February 1807. This was apparently part of a scheme for reducing the number of convoys. The alteration made it possible to add other ships to this, the first convoy of the year. In 1807, for example, seven other ships sailed on 26 February; one for St Helena, Bencoolen and China, one for Bengal, two for 'Coast and Bay' and three for 'Coast and China'. 'The Coast' was, of course, the Coromandel Coast; which meant, as a rule, Madras. Here, then, was a group of eleven Indiamen sailing in company, none of which would be seen again much before July 1808. They would have naval protection for most of the voyage, but the ship calling at St Helena would have to separate from the rest in the Atlantic, while the remainder would split into two divisions sooner or later.

The convoy was produced by the amalgamation of what had been known as the 1st and 2nd divisions, sailing respectively in December and February. The former 3rd division, now the 2nd, remained much what it had been during the previous war. In 1799 there had been seven ships due to sail in March, five being bound for Coast and Bay. On 4 March 1807 seven ships sailed, four bound for Coast and

Plate VIII. An East Indiaman anchoring off Spithead.

From the lithograph by R. Dodd, dated 1797.

Bay—that is, for Madras and Calcutta. Of the three others, two were bound for St Helena and Madras, and one for Bombay. This division was made up solely of 800-ton ships until 1808, in which year the ships stationed for China direct, seven in number, sailed with the Coast and Bay ships on 5 March.

The 3rd and last division of the season, formerly the 4th, normally included those vessels bound for China by the direct route. The convoy sailed at the end of April 1799, with five of these China ships and two others. In 1807, on 18 April, thirteen ships sailed, of which number six were bound for China. Nine ships sailed on 15 April 1808, none of them for China.

The convoys sailing in May and June were for some reason regarded as belonging to a distinct season, the early season lasting apparently from December to April. In 1799 there were two divisions, one early in May and another at the end of June, with seven ships in each; in 1807 there was only one division, of five ships; in 1808 there were two divisions, one on 8 May, the other on 10 June, of eight and five ships respectively, all bound for India.

Following the sailings in June there was a slack period of some three months. Then, halfway through September, there used to sail the last convoy of the year. Nine ships sailed in 1807, all for India, and there were eight similarly bound on 17 September 1808. There were often one or two odd China ships among the May and June convoys, which brought the total number of the China fleet up to twelve or fourteen 1200-ton ships. There were fourteen in 1800, ten by the direct route, one via Bombay and three via Madras. The number was fifteen in 1807, eleven in 1808, ten in 1805.

The returning ships, both from India and China, were similarly grouped into convoys. The China fleet sometimes returned in two divisions, sometimes in one. In 1808 there were two divisions, one arriving in the Thames on 1 July, the other on 11 September. In 1804 there was only the one fleet. The ships from India were often collected at a rendezvous off Ceylon. In July 1799, for example, ten of the India ships arrived as a single convoy, some from each Presidency.

All these various convoys, both outward and homeward bound, had some degree of naval protection. Particularly after the taking of the Cape in 1806, the ships were escorted as far as St Helena or somewhere in that latitude by men-of-war which then returned to European waters, leaving the Indiamen to the protection of other ships from the squadron at the Cape. These would see them past the danger zone, until under the protection of the East Indies squadron. Frequently, a man-of-war would accompany a convoy throughout the whole voyage to India, but this was only, as a rule, when a third-rate or frigate happened to be bound for India. This was not infrequent, for the squadron in the East Indies was large and there was a continual relieving of the ships composing it, worn-out ships returning to England and fresh ships coming out to take their place. It was always arranged that these men-of-war should sail with convoy. There was also a long-standing rule that the Indiamen bound for China by the direct route should be accompanied by a ship of war all the way to Canton and back. This was necessary because these China ships, in their sweep to the southwards, went nowhere near any possible rendezvous where a fresh escort could meet them. The man-of-war accompanying them had no other task to perform and formed no part of the East Indies squadron, even when actually on the station.

Naval officers found the convoying of Indiamen a tedious, thankless task. But there was a right and wrong way of performing it, and lack of tact often made things worse than they need have been. What the naval officer was slow to grasp was the East India captain's claim to equality with himself. East of the Cape, at any rate, the commander of an

Indiaman was a person of some dignity. At Calcutta he would live ashore, perhaps own a house there and keep a carriage with footmen and runners. He was used to being treated with deference. He might not be the equal, in theory, of a captain in the Navy; but then he was a much richer, and sometimes a much older man. Some naval officers chose to treat the commanders of Indiamen exactly as they treated other Merchant captains; with contempt, that is to say, or else with condescension. The results were unfortunate, and especially so with regard to the convoy system. The captain of the escorting man-of-war had complete authority over the Indiamen, who were bound to obey his signals. It was for him to select the route the convoy should follow. Yet, often enough, he was entirely new to the Ocean he was crossing, whereas the men he was trying to guide had spent their whole lives traversing it. Naval officers who had been in India for a few years knew more about the Indian Ocean than the Company's officers, but the officer in charge of an outward bound convoy was almost of necessity a novice. Too often, the young naval commander began by insulting the East India captains, went on to earn their contempt by steering a bad course, badgered them with signals all day long, and ended by finding that they had all given him the slip in the dark. They could hardly be blamed for doing so; and yet the result was that the convoy went on without protection.

The best way for a naval officer to manage a convoy of Indiamen was obviously to begin by making friends with the commanders. If asked to dine and flattered a little and asked their opinion as to the best route to take, they soon became easy to handle. After that, more could be done by a hint in conversation than by any number of signals. Captain Hall, in describing his convoy duty in 1812, shows unconsciously how much conviviality had to do with the co-ordination of an East India fleet:

In fine weather there is naturally much agreeable intercourse between the different ships in such a fleet as ours; for East India Company's folks, whether of the land or sea service, understand right well the jolly art of good cheer wherever they go; be it on terra firma, or on the high seas, bivouacking on the lofty Himalayas, or feasting in the bungalows of the flat Delta of the Ganges, it is all one to them. So that during our whole voyage, there scarcely occurred a day on which, in the course of the morning, if the sea were tolerably smooth, and the wind not too strong, and the weather otherwise agreeable, the dinner invitation signal was not displayed from the commodore, or from some of his flock.... If it be the commodore who gives the dinner, he either heaves to, while the boats of the several captains come on board, or he edges down to the different ships in succession, passes them at the distance of a quarter of a cable's length, picks up his guests, and resumes his station....

Except when the best possible relations had been established over the dinner table, there was bound to be trouble over the rate of sailing. Indiamen were capable of speed, as we have already noted, but they were not given to hurry. A man-of-war, on the other hand, was always going its utmost speed. Even the good-tempered Captain Hall was not altogether sorry when he parted with his China ships. 'Alas!' he writes, 'many a good dinner we lost by that separation'; but he goes on to add that 'a smart frigate making a voyage with a dull-sailing convoy, reminds one of the child's story of the provoking journey made by the hare with a drove of oxen'. He hints at the torments of impatience a single 'haystack of a vessel' could inflict on the rest of the convoy; and he describes how a fast-sailing ship was sometimes detailed to take the straggler in tow 'and fairly lug her along'.

As typical of the naval officers to whom the convoying of Indiamen was a species of torture, we may take Rear-Admiral Sir Thomas Troubridge. A choleric middle-aged man of obscure social origin, he sailed for India on 24 April 1805, with the 3rd division of the season. It included the ships bound for China via Madras, and was essentially the same type of fleet convoyed by Captain Hall in 1812. There were eighteen sail of Indiamen, seven being bound for China. The China ships were the *Coutts*, *Hope*, *Exeter*, *Warley*, *Cumberland*, *Dorsetshire* and *Ganges*. The escort consisted of the flagship, which was the *Blenheim* (74), and the *Greyhound* frigate (32). Sailing from Spithead, Troubridge ran through the Needles, greatly to the annoyance both of the Admiralty and India House, and began his voyage to the southward. This was the time of the Trafalgar campaign, and Troubridge made a detour to the westward as soon as he heard that the Toulon fleet had passed the Straits of Gibraltar. He was in Lat. 49° 20′, Long. 9° 10′ W. on the 29th. By 7 May he was in Lat. 41° 07′, Long. 21° 15′, having had three days of foul winds, squalls, and a heavy swell from the westward. Two Indiamen had lost their fore-topmasts and jibbooms, and one her main-topsail yard. Irritated by this and subsequent causes of delay, the Admiral decided to issue a sharp reprimand to his charges:

Blenheim at Sea, May 30th 1805

General Memorandum.

The great negligence of many of the Convoy, particularly in the night, has been already a serious delay; The Admiral informs the Commanders of the several Ships, that the Conduct of such as have acted in this improper and inattentive manner is kept in a regular Journal to be transmitted to the East India Company; it therefore becomes their duty to caution their Officers to pay more attention, as the Captain is the person held responsible; The Admiral has also to notice the pointed neglect to Signal by many of the Ships by day, when the Commander is supposed and ought, to be on deck; of Course such neglect attaches to him.... The Ships which have dropped most, during the light, or baffling winds, have done so from unseamanlike management in not attending to keep their heads the right way....

It has also been noticed that Ships shorten Sail, as soon as it is dark, although the weather has been fine, and the wind moderate; Subject to these Omissions and Neglect, the Admiral has been particularly compelled to notice, the Metcalfe, Lady Castlereagh, and Earl Camden.

To the respective Commanders
of the Honble East India Compy's Ships
Under Convoy of His Maj: ship Blenheim.

N.B. The Blenheim will sometimes have occasion to burn a blue light, for the purpose of shewing her position, and to draw the attention of the Convoy.

(P.R.O. Ad. 1/176.)

Now, such a memorandum as this might have had some effect on naval officers. Commanders of Indiamen would almost certainly read it with derision. To begin with, the journal kept of their failings which was to be sent to India House can have had no terrors for them. Commanders of the East India Company's ships were not appointed or employed by the Company but by their owners. They were not removable, except for certain serious offences; and only then after a regular trial. There was, in short, not the least probability of the Company taking any notice whatever of Troubridge's complaints. The Admiral was himself in bad odour, incidentally, for taking the convoy through the Needles.

To tell the captain of an Indiaman when he ought to be on deck was not a particularly wise proceeding. The offender's retort might have been to offer the Admiral a few hints on tactics. As for the shortening sail at sunset, it was the universal custom in the East India fleet. The commanders were unlikely to alter the habits of a lifetime merely to please Sir Thomas Troubridge. The memorandum, in short, was far more likely to irritate than reform. It is not surprising that the Admiral had occasion to repeat his complaints with growing emphasis until the end of the voyage. Faults originally unintentional had very probably become deliberate.

On 14 July, Troubridge, having rounded the Cape, allowed the four ships bound for Bombay to part company.

The *Greyhound* escorted them through the Mozambique Channel and as far northward as 8° N.; then she had orders to leave them and head for Ceylon by the Eight or Nine Degree Channel. At the moment of parting with the Bombay ships, in Lat. 37° 03′ S. and Long. 25° 16′ E., Troubridge was reporting to the Admiralty that many of the Indiamen paid no attention to his signals, and that he was much delayed by 'the shameful Negligence and bad sailing of many of the Convoy'. With the departure of the Bombay division the Admiral lost three of the worst offenders; others, however, remained—or, rather, should have done so. On 27 July, in Lat. 36° 6′ S. and Long. 65° 52′ E., Troubridge had to report that the *Coutts*, *Warley* and *Dorsetshire* had all disappeared between the 16th and 21st, through negligence or, more probably, intention. The *Coutts* had the excuse of having lost her fore-topmast and main topgallant-mast—although that was due to pure negligence—but the others could have no such plea.

...As the Warley sails every way better than either the Blenheim or any of the Convoy, and is certainly the finest ship of the Convoy, (though it appears to me that neither her Commander or officers have the smallest Idea of managing her) she must have separated intentionally or from sheer neglect. To give their Lordships some faint idea of the want of skill and Seamanship in managing her, She is, in general, wore with the mizen and mizen Stay-sail Set, and Tacked with the Jib hoisted, and mizen brailed up. I mention these things as remarks made by the Officers of the Blenheim and myself, and in order that their Lordships may form a proper Judgement of the persons in charge of so valuable a Ship and Cargo.

The Anxiety and trouble which I have had with her, is beyond my power to describe; She attends to no Signal, has seldom any Topgallant yards up, and when the Signal has been made to get them up, they are crossed without the Sails being bent; in short, I feel no hesitation in saying, from the general observations I have made during the passage, that Captain Wilson is wholly unfit to command *any ship*, for, as I before noticed, though the Warley is the best sailing Ship of the convoy, she was continually astern for want of Sail, and by such repeated acts of misconduct has occasioned immense delay: I do most sincerely hope, for the benefit of the Company, and the Owners of the Convoy, that they will dismiss him the Service, for a Ship managed, as the Warley has been, by him, is a perfect nuisance....

I am
Sir
Your most obedient humble Ser't
T. Troubridge
(To Admiralty. P.R.O. Ad. 1/176.)

On the day following that on which the above was written, Troubridge wrote from Lat. 35° 5′ S., Long. 70° 02′ E. to say that the *General Steward* had parted company for a second time—probably by intention—and had not reappeared.

Blenheim at Sea, July 28th 1805

...If some example be not made by the Company, Convoy is only a covering to the Insurance made by Individuals, and of little, if any, benefit to the Company, for from the Ignorance of some, and Negligence of others, immense delays arise, which would not happen with proper attention on the part of the Commanders and Officers: I am sure to take India Ships under Convoy is the most unpleasant Service that can fall to the Lot of a Zealous officer, for he can never gain Credit by his care and attention, but will always be kept on the fret, by the gross ignorance and unseamanlike Conduct of the greater part of the Captains....

Some Indiamen may have been as incompetently managed as Troubridge states. But one cannot rid oneself of the impression that the Admiral was the victim of a practical joke. The *Warley* was not one of the ships originally complained of, and the literal obeying of a signal by crossing topgallant yards, and then omitting to bend sails on them, seems less a symptom of incompetence than of a sense of humour. The serious side to this kind of mischief—which was clearly the result, mainly, of the Admiral's irritable disposition—was that the missing ships were exposed to capture. Ten days after Troubridge wrote the above letter of complaint he was in action with the French Admiral Linois. It was mere chance that the French ships encountered the *Blenheim* instead of the *Coutts* and *Warley*.[*]

Instead of dropping astern during the night, some East Indiamen would repeatedly ask permission to part company, on the grounds that they were being taken out of their proper course. Admiral Drury had some experience of this in 1808, and wrote to point out to the Admiralty how awkward such requests could be:

> Their Lordships will perceive that my only motive for making this representation is to mark the impropriety of such applications being offered to the Officer charged with a Convoy, who must feel that, if he refuses reiterated applications, he immediately takes upon himself a responsibility which he ought not to bear: and in the event of complaints being preferred that the Ships have lost their season; he is not only liable to reprehension but the party contracting for such Ships exposed to a certain daily demurrage; and yet, by complying, he is conscious that Ships of immense value, as well as great national importance are in danger of being captured....

Convoys were often scattered, of course, by bad weather. It was very seldom that a gale would leave many ships in company with each other. Oddly enough, a dead calm had sometimes exactly the same effect. After a few hours of helpless drifting and twisting round, the ships were often miles apart from each other; a phenomenon less easy to understand than their tendency to collide should they happen to be near each other. The remedy for this occasional scattering of convoys lay in a system by which the next rendezvous was always known. Thus, stragglers might rejoin the convoy at Madeira, at the Cape, at Johanna in the Comoro Islands, or at various other anchorages.

The convoy system demanded above all things a high degree of tact and patience in the naval officer commanding the escort. These are not the qualities for which the Navy is particularly famed. Captain Hall evidently surpassed most other officers in this respect, yet it is clear that his patience was tried to the breaking point. And even he admits that the selection of a route was bound to cause difficulties. Not to ask the opinion of the Company's officers had its obvious dangers. To ask them lessened the authority of the naval officer in charge. Most officers were too tenacious of their authority to remain long in doubt as to which they would do. The result was a standing grievance, second only to that concerning impressment. The rancour of a whole generation of East India captains suddenly found an outlet in 1809, the object of their wrath being, as it happened, quite innocent of any special outrage against them. But for many of them the Navy had become in itself an object of dislike, embodying, as it were, all the arrogance, stupidity and ill-breeding they had endured while sailing with convoy.

Chapter XI

THE COUNTRY TRADE

THERE was an eighteenth-century proverb that he who would bring back the riches of the East must take the riches of the East with him. This was interpreted by Dr Johnson as meaning that the Merchant needed a stock to trade with. But there was another sense in which the proverb was true, more especially in the period with which we are dealing. For, although the English in India were making fortunes, most of their wealth came out of taxes paid, and to be paid, in England. This was a fact which few people observed at the time, and which fewer have remarked since; but it is one which may easily be ascertained from available statistics. The East India Company's affairs were being carried on at a loss, largely due to the extravagance of the Indian Governments. Instead of reducing expenses or admitting that there was no dividend to be paid, the Company's policy was to allow a huge debt to accumulate. This was partly in the hope that peace would bring prosperity again. But was there no other way of cancelling the debt? Surely, the far-seeing had already anticipated the eventual annexation of India by the Crown. And if any of the directors of the East India Company had this probability, or certainty, at the back of their minds, they were unlikely to worry very much about a debt which would ultimately be laid on the public. At least two men foresaw the fate of India and the India debt, and neither of them took much trouble to conceal his views. One was the Marquis Wellesley, and the other was William Cobbett. They differed only on the question as to whether India was worth the expense, and on this question disagreement is still possible.

If, however, all the friends of Lord Wellesley and all the readers of the *Political Register* were familiar with the possibility of India coming into public hands, it is scarcely credible that no rumour of it should have reached Leadenhall Street. As early as 1808, Cobbett was writing that 'there appears to be little doubt, that the whole of the *debts* of that Company, the individuals of which are gaining great *riches*, will finally, and, perhaps, very shortly, be thrown upon the nation...'. Indeed, he speaks as if the fact were notorious; which probably means that he had referred to it before. An expectation of this kind, which was evidently in the air, must be borne in mind when studying the Company's affairs.

Through the way, then, in which the debt was allowed to mount up in India, individuals were, as Cobbett says, gaining great riches. Care has been taken, at an earlier stage in this work, to indicate the scale on which the Company's servants were paid; from which it may be gathered that they were not allowed to starve, except perhaps in extreme youth. But, often as a result of an early period of indigence, their official salaries must be taken as forming a part only of what they received. As Burke admitted, there was nothing in the boys we sent to India worse than in the boys we were whipping at school. But the rulers of India were subject to peculiar temptations, not the least of which was the character of the people they were attempting to rule. The Duke of Wellington said that he had never met a Hindoo with a single good quality, and added that he thought the Mussulmans even worse. By his account there was 'more perjury in the town of Calcutta alone than...in all Europe taken together'. He may not have been especially sympathetic. Yet Indians were manifestly accustomed to be ruled by men who took bribes, and were merely bewildered by the spectacle of rulers who did not. Such an atmosphere was not good for young men who had been encouraged by circumstances to get into debt and then encouraged by opportunity to recoup themselves.

Apart from any bribes and perquisites which some may have taken, there were legitimate ways in which fortunes could be made. It was possible for Army officers to hold several posts at once, for example, and at the same time make large sums in prize money. When it was proposed to pension the family of Lord Lake, who left insufficient means for his son to support the title, an objection raised was that the General had been tolerably well rewarded in his lifetime. Mr Paull was able to demonstrate that Lord Lake and his son had, between them, made £300,000 during a period of six years spent in India. This scale of payment, if exceptional, seems at least to have attracted no particular attention at the time. The fortunes of other men, if not as great, were evidently comparable.

Now, fortunes made in India were not dissipated as quickly as they were made. Calcutta society was extravagant, we know, but it was not as wasteful as that. Large sums remained to be invested, at an Oriental rate of interest, and these sums were added to as long as the investor remained in the country. They were only withdrawn when he returned to England or died. There may have been some, like Thackeray's Colonel Newcome, who left their money in 'the Bundelcund Bank' even after their return home. These, however, were few; most men preferred the safety of landed property or Government stock. There was, then, at Calcutta, and to a lesser extent at the other Presidencies, a mass of capital to be invested. How was it to be invested? In what enterprise? Much of this wealth was undoubtedly left in the hands of native merchants and bankers. It lay behind much of the commercial activity of the 'black towns' which flourished at the gates of the three Forts. But many of these investors preferred to trust firms which at any rate took their names from the English, or more often Scotch, partners at their head. Hence there grew up a European mercantile community, both at Calcutta and Bombay. That at Madras was insignificant.

As far as one can judge, the British business men brought to their affairs neither capital, energy nor ability. They were certainly not in a position to teach the natives anything about business methods. They could introduce nothing novel in the way of banking, but they were white men and therefore able to inspire confidence in other white men, a confidence which they may or may not have deserved. With this advantage they were able at least partially to elbow the natives out of two particular types of business; shipowning and insurance.

The process by which Indian shipping came partly into the hands of British firms, or firms at least with British names, is very liable to be misunderstood. It was connected, of course, with the superseding, at an early period, of the native by the European type of ship. But this alteration in design, affecting only the larger vessels, is itself a matter requiring some explanation. For the obvious conclusion, that the European ship was a better ship, is more or less untenable. In many respects the European ship was no better than the ship it superseded; and the European ship that came from Europe, as opposed to the European ship built in India, was a great deal worse. Had it merely been a question of English-built vessels taking the place of Indian vessels, the case would have been one of bad ships superseding good ships. And there is another factor to notice about the advent of the European ship; namely, that it was not introduced by Europeans but by natives. It may safely be asserted that there was never an instance of a white carpenter standing over a native shipwright and telling him to build differently. The native shipwright had, in fact, no instruction of any kind; the proof of this being that his method of building remained unchanged, only the finished product being revolutionary. It was partly owing to this that his copy was so great an improvement on the original. What may seem the final puzzle is that he almost certainly introduced his imitation European ship without any conviction that it was a better ship than those his father had built; which indeed it may not have been.

To explain this extraordinary conduct of the native shipwrights it is only necessary to recall what part the Europeans were playing in the life of the East. They represented the Sword. They ruled not by skill but by courage. The great obstacle to trade in the Eastern Seas had always been piracy. It was not an obstacle to the Europeans. They first arrived in the sixteenth century in crank and leaky ships, vastly inferior to the Chinese junks, and a great deal smaller. In these ill-designed and ill-built vessels they made their way about the seas, and as they did so they were ravaged by diseases of which they died with amazing rapidity. But they did not die nearly so quickly as did anyone who tried to stop them. Their ships were bad, and they themselves did not even realise that the local ships were better, but they feared nothing under heaven. Had they feared anything they would never have rounded the Cape, least of all in such appalling craft. It was only by virtue of their courage that they were there at all. To men of this kind, running enormous risks daily, eternally on the verge of drowning or fatal illness, there was nothing frightening about piracy. They came to trade perhaps, but they came with swords, and some of them infinitely preferred fighting to trading.

After a few experiments the pirates of the East came to the conclusion that European ships were better left alone. It may have taken a generation or two before this opinion became general, but, once established, it became the golden rule of piracy. This must have been about the middle of the seventeenth century. By the end of that century the native builders at Surat were building ships made to look like European ships. The natives had found that, to sail the seas unmolested, it was merely necessary to look European. Henceforth they built all their larger vessels on European lines, altering them to suit European fashions. Eventually, they took to copying the English in particular, and there are places where they are still doing so. To this day the native craft built on Minicoy Island have the lines, it is said, of seventeenth-century ships, and are painted with a broad white band and black imitation gun ports at intervals, like English ships of the nineteenth century. The islanders have probably forgotten by now the object of this piece of camouflage, or even what the black squares are supposed to represent—if indeed they ever knew—but they have inherited the tradition that safety lies in looking English. They go on looking English long after the English themselves have ceased.

To understand the ships made at Surat, the ancient shipbuilding centre of India, in imitation of the European ships, it is essential to know something of the vessels previously built there. And the first thing to remark about them is that they had been built in the same way for a very long period; certainly since the thirteenth century, when Marco Polo saw and described them with great accuracy. Unfortunately, there is some doubt whether the vessels he described were actually Indian or whether they were Chinese craft trading to India. The shipbuilding methods, however, which he particularly noted were characteristic of Indian shipping at a later period. Allowing them to have had a Chinese origin, it is hardly to be supposed that no ships were built in India in the thirteenth century or that those then built there were without the features Marco Polo describes. Had there been any essential difference in construction between the Indian and Chinese vessels he would surely have remarked on it.

This resemblance, in construction, between the Indian and Chinese vessels is significant; for, whereas little is known about the early Indian craft, much is known about the Chinese junk. This type of vessel is still unchanged and we know her to be an exceptionally handy vessel. 'As an engine for carrying man and his commerce upon the high and stormy seas,' writes Mr H. Warington Smyth, 'it is doubtful if any class of vessel is more suited or better adapted to its purpose; and it is certain that for flatness of sail and for handiness the Chinese rig is unsurpassed.' He goes on to point out that in scientific fore-and-aft sailing and in the use of centre-boards, lee-boards, windlasses and labour-saving devices, the Chinese remained ahead of Europe until the middle of the nineteenth century. The larger five-masted junks of well over a thousand tons, such as used to trade with East Africa, seem to have disappeared for the same reason that the larger Indian vessels disappeared. It was found safer to entrust a large and valuable cargo to a ship that looked like an English ship. The safety thus attained was only relative, for, just as the Indian merchantmen began to model themselves on European merchantmen, so did the Mahratta pirates begin to model themselves on European pirates. Nevertheless, a good disguise always gave a sense of security.

Another type of vessel with which the ancient Indian vessels may have had points in common is the Arab dhow. This is another craft which has survived because of its evident fitness for its work. Although, by our period, it had become more or less confined to the Red Sea and the east coast of Africa, the dhow rig was evidently known to the builders of Surat. But the extent of its merits only became apparent to the English in the eighteen-thirties and forties when they were trying to suppress the slave trade. That its merits include that of speed became painfully obvious as time went on and the trade was not suppressed. What may seem still more remarkable is that the trade is not suppressed even now. There is evidently something to be said for a type of vessel we have been chasing without success for about a century. The late Mr Knight, journalist and yachtsman, has left an account of a race between two dhows in the Red Sea from which the reader gains an impression of the speed of which these craft are capable.

It is unnecessary to enter into any discussion of the merits of the junks, dhows, grabs, beglas, dingies, parias and other vessels which existed before the Europeans came. It is enough to realise that they had merits which the Europeans sometimes copied; and that some of them had merits in construction which were reproduced in the ships they copied from the Europeans.

The chief advantage, of course, enjoyed by the Indian builders was that they built in teak. This species of timber grows in the forests of Malabar, Coromandel, Pegu, Java, Sumatra and other parts of the East. It grows sometimes to a length of fifty feet long and twenty inches in diameter. Malabar teak was the best for shipbuilding, and it was in this wood that the Surat ships were built. Teak from Java or Coromandel was next in quality but could not be had in sufficient quantity. Teak from Pegu (Rangoon or Burman teak) was inferior to Malabar timber but was much cheaper to obtain and far more plentiful. The difficulty about the forests of Canara and Malabar was that the timber was difficult to transport. The trees grow too far away from any river suitable to float them down; and this was particularly true of the crooked trees. which were wanted for making knees and futtocks. The trees were there but they grew on high table-land, and the crooked ones chiefly on the highest slopes, farthest from the water. Burman teak was not so much more plentiful in growth, but it grew where it could be pushed into a river as soon as felled.

By our period Malabar teak was tending to be used only for keels and ribs, the planking being imported from Rangoon, while there was growing up a new shipbuilding industry at Calcutta, which was nearer to the Burman supplies. Nevertheless, the best ships still came from Surat or Bombay, and it was from Malabar that Calcutta derived its traditions of building. Surat, it may be well to observe, was not the only home of the art in Malabar. Tippoo Sultan used to construct teak-built ships and grabs at Onore, Mangalore, Todry and Sedashygur. It is worthy of note that what curved or crooked timber there was came mainly from the Mahratta country, so that the supply for Bombay ceased abruptly when the English were at war with the Mahrattas. Efforts were made to find what was wanted in Malabar and Travancore, so as to avoid dependence on the northern forests; but it may yet appear that the English persistence in those wars was not wholly unconnected with the timber supply.

Malabar teak was found to be too heavy for the upper-works of ships, and altogether unsuitable for making spars. Burman teak was sometimes used for masts, but the Malabar ships usually had masts and spars made from a wood called 'Poon' or 'Pohoon', which was obtained from Mangalore and elsewhere on the western side of India.

The great advantages of teak were that it was easy to work, strong, oily and without knots. It required no seasoning and had very little tendency to rot. Ships built of it, and especially those of Malabar teak, would last almost indefinitely. An oak-built ship used to last on an average some ten or twelve years. Teak-built ships frequently lasted eighty years and more. In 1811 it was pointed out that the Turkish flagship at Bussorah had been afloat in 1738, if not earlier, and was still perfectly sound. Stavorinus gives another instance of a ship which traded from Surat to Mocha and Jedda. She had been making this annual voyage, carrying pilgrims on their way to Mecca, ever since people could remember. She was so old that no one could tell when she was built. All that was known was that she was referred to in the records as 'the old ship' as early as 1702. She was not broken up until 1777. This vessel must have been one of the earliest imitation European ships. She was ship-rigged and two-decked and 130 or 135 feet long. Her cabin was said to be richly carved, so that 'not the least piece of wood was left without some foliage or imagery'. Supposing that she dated from the time of Charles II, when the English came to Bombay, this ship must have been afloat for a century. As for the teak-built ships built in the first years of the nineteenth century, one of them is said to be in use at the present day. Several, perhaps, may have survived long enough to be equipped with wireless apparatus.

Even when using their teak to build ships of a European appearance, the Indian builders clung to ancient usage in some respects. They would not, for example, launch a ship by the European method. The details of their building are best described by Stavorinus:

> They do not build their ships in the same manner as the Europeans; most of the timbers are fitted in after the planks have been put together. There was one built while I was at Surat, in what is called the English yard; it appeared to me to have about one hundred feet length of keel; it stood in a kind of graving dock, if a large excavation, closed towards the river by a dam, without a stone facing or any thing that resembled it, may deserve that appellation. They do not launch their ships, as we do, from slips; but, when sufficiently finished for floating, they dig through from the water to the sort of docks mentioned above, which they call cradles, where the ships are, as it were, dropped into the stream that is brought up to them.
>
> They do not put the planks together as we do, with flat edges towards each other, but rabbet them; and they make the parts fit into each other with the greatest exactness, bestowing much time and attention upon this operation; for this purpose, they smear the edges of the planks which are set up, with red lead, and those which are intended to be placed next, are put upon them, and pressed down, in order to be able to discern the inequalities, which are marked by the red lead, and afterwards taken away; they repeat this till the whole fits exactly; they then rub both edges with a sort of glue, which becomes, by age, as hard as iron, and they cover it with a thin layer of capoc, after which they unite the planks so firmly and closely with pegs, that the seam is scarcely visible, and the whole seems to form one entire piece of timber....
>
> Instead of bolts, they make use of pieces of iron, forged like spikes, the point of which is driven through, clenched on the inside, and again driven into the wood....

The term 'English yard' is interesting, as used here, for there was, very probably, nothing English about the yard except the appearance of the ships built there. Stavorinus wrote about 1770–5, by which period the natives would know something of the comparative ferocity of the European nations, and would naturally think the English best worth imitating. But there is reason to suppose that they grasped this by instinct at a much earlier period, perhaps as early as the seventeenth century. Grose wrote rather earlier than Stavorinus, and he makes it sufficiently clear which nation the natives were copying. 'At Surat too they excel in the art of ship-building', he writes: 'If their models were as fine as those of the English, of whom especially they prefer the imitation, there would be no exaggeration in averring, that they build incomparably the best ships in the world for duration, and that of any size....'

The vessels Marco Polo describes were without this 'rabbet-work' or interlocking planks; at least, he makes no mention of it. What most impressed him was the system of watertight bulkheads, which the Chinese retained but which these Surat builders had discarded or else never adopted. On the other hand, he paid great attention to two Indian usages which still survived at our period. One was the method of repairing ships. After observing that all vessels were sheathed or double-planked in the first place, he adds that, when a ship stood in need of repair, 'the practice is to give her a course of sheathing over the original boarding, forming a third course... and this, when she needs further repairs, is repeated even to the number of six layers...'. Nearly five hundred years later, Gabriel Snodgrass was urging the adoption of this system as a novelty, leaving the East India Company to suppose that he was the inventor of it. He also advocated 'rabbet-work', which was known to Marco Polo, although only, apparently, for internal bulkheads.

The other feature of Indian shipbuilding which the great Venetian noticed was the coating used for ships' bottoms:

...They are not coated with pitch, as the country does not produce that article, but the bottoms are smeared over with the following preparation. The people take quick-lime and hemp, which latter they cut small, and with these, when pounded together, they mix oil procured from a certain tree, making the whole a kind of unguent which retains its viscous properties more firmly, and is a better material than pitch.

Grose speaks of this coating merely as 'wood-oil', but it is clear that there must have been several distinct preparations which Europeans were apt to confuse. There is a description of 'dammer' in the *Naval Chronicle* for 1814, in which it is described as a kind of turpentine or resin obtained from a species of pine-tree growing in Sumatra and on the Malay Peninsula. Two kinds are mentioned, one being 'hard dark-coloured, brittle', the other 'soft and whitish, having the appearance and consistency of putty'; the best effect being obtained by mixing the two. The substances which Grandpré describes, on the other hand, seem to be quite different:

...This substance is a mixture of lime and fish-oil; it adheres so closely to the planks of the ship, that it fills all the crevices, and effectually prevents the water from penetrating. It is called by the Indians galgat.

They have another preparation, called sarangousti, which they spread over the heads of the nails and joints of the timbers. It is made of dry pitch and fish-oil, which are beaten together till the mixture assumes the consistency of a soft paste; in this state it is applied, and it gives such extraordinary hardness as to turn the edge of the best tempered instruments.

There is a composition in use in Indian dockyards to-day which is said to be a mixture of chunam or lime with a resinous oil, or with melted dammar. It is called 'gul-gul', which might be the same word as 'galgat'. Chunam is said to last twelve years, and all these compositions seem to have been effective; more effective, indeed, than copper sheathing. It was proposed occasionally to try them on English ships, but nothing came of it, if only because all the English ships were already coppered.

Not only was it needless to copper Indian ships; it was also needless to fasten them with copper bolts. Iron bolts always tended to corrode in an oak-built ship, especially if beneath the water-line. But teak is an oily wood which may safely be bolted with iron. As copper was expensive, this was a distinct argument in favour of teak.

The objections raised against Indian-built ships were mainly on two grounds. It was contended that they were clumsily built and therefore slow; and also that teak was unfit for fighting ships as it was too liable to splinter when struck by shot. This latter objection was made in a letter to the *Naval Chronicle* in 1813, and it seems to have been made in flat contradiction to known facts. Had it been true, teak would certainly have been less suitable for shipbuilding in days when most ships went armed and prepared for self-defence. But the fact evidently is that teak splits easily when struck endwise, which a ship's planks never were, but is much less liable to splinter than oak when struck against the grain. It was found in actual practice that a teak-built ship's side was almost impervious to cannon shot. This is the more credible in view of the fact that some teak-built ships had sides two feet thick.

On the other hand, this very solidity and strength of the teak-built ship goes to support the case against her on the grounds of clumsiness. Originally, no doubt, these vessels built of Malabar teak throughout, and calculated to last for a century, were but ill-designed for speed. Parias had a reputation for slowness to the end. But there grew up two schools of shipbuilding which, by a closer attention to European models, began to produce vessels with all the strength of the traditional Indian ship and with all the appearance and speed of English Indiamen. They were probably the finest ships in the world, and certainly the largest outside the Company's fleet and the Navies. The two schools of building were those of Bombay and Pegu, the latter school having an offshoot at Calcutta which imbibed something of the Bombay technique.

The Bombay tradition of shipbuilding was imported from Surat in the year 1735. That was the year in which a ship was built at Surat for the English East India Company; the first vessel built in the East for the use of the English. The foreman engaged in the work was a Parsee called Lowjee Nassurwanjee, and he was induced to migrate to Bombay. This was a triumph for Mr Dudley, the Master Attendant, and an important event in the history of that Presidency; indeed, it was perhaps *the* important event of its history. Work prospered and Lowjee brought two sons into the business, Monackjee and Bomanjee, who succeeded him on his death in 1774. The Master Builder's office was now purely hereditary, and when the sons died in 1790 and 1792, two grandsons, Framjee Monackjee and Jemsatjee Bomanjee, were left to carry on the work. In our period, the latter of these was the moving spirit.

The original business of the Company's dockyard at Bombay was the building and repairing of vessels for the Bombay Marine, together with the repairing of such East Indiamen as were crippled in the course of their voyage. Tentatively, the construction of Indiamen was undertaken as well, those built there being owned by the Company itself. From there it was only a step to building frigates and finally ships of the line for the Navy. During the period with which we are concerned, Jemsatjee Bomanjee and his son Nowrojee had a thousand workmen under them and a growing reputation for efficiency.

Their children were numerous and spread themselves over all the activities of the town. Those who took to trade, the more natural occupation of the Parsee, were a great deal richer than those who continued to build ships. The town was already filled, and largely owned, by other Parsees whose families had been there all along, however, so that some were left in the shipbuilding business from lack of opportunity if not from choice. Round the Company's yard therefore, as the centre of inspiration, and round the direct heirs of the Surat tradition, there grew up an industry of great importance. A fleet grew up of English ships built by Parsees out of local, or at least Indian, materials; officered by English seamen; manned by lascars; and owned either by English or Parsee firms.

Parallel with the Bombay school of shipbuilding, there grew up another building tradition on the other side of India. This had its roots in Pegu, the source of its timber supply. Ships had always been built there from the earliest times, and here also there must have been some Chinese influence. Parias had long been constructed for the trade in rice and salt, some with as great a burthen as six hundred tons, even before the Europeans came. Pegu teak, if less strong and durable, is lighter and more buoyant than that of Malabar, and this may have gone to make up for the absence of certain methods of building practised at Bombay. The famous system of rabbetting or mortising the planks, which Marco Polo described as 'incastrati', does not seem to have been known in Pegu. At Rangoon, as at Surat, the European type of ship superseded the larger native types by a process of imitative camouflage; traditional methods and material being used to produce vessels of alien design.

At Calcutta there grew up, after the middle of the eighteenth century, a shipbuilding industry dependent on Rangoon for skill and timber, not free from the influence of Bombay but producing vessels of a type greatly modified to suit local conditions and needs. The Calcutta yards grew up independently of Government and became established as early as 1760, in all probability; later, but not much later, than the establishment of the industry at Bombay. An improvement introduced at Calcutta was the use of certain other kinds of wood for planking, leaving only the ribs, keel and decks to be made of teak.

Between the vessels built at Bombay and those built at

Rangoon or Calcutta there were certain similarities and certain contrasts. The chief resemblance lay in their sailcloth, cordage and fittings. Both Bombay and Bengal produced canvas, the latter being thought the best. This was what is still known as dungaree. It was found to be not so strong and lasting as European canvas, Hollands duck or vitry, but more pliant and less liable to split. This, at least, was the general verdict. Messrs Kemp and Roberts, on the other hand, the manufacturers at Calcutta, were able to produce an 'unsolicited testimonial' in 1809 from an American captain in which a different opinion was given. Mr James Wilkinson, of the ship *Magdalen*, stated that he had found it unequalled alike 'for beauty and strength'. They thought about beauty in those days, and, as a fact, country or Indian sailcloth was more picturesque than any European canvas. 'Country ships', as vessels built in India were called, could be distinguished by their 'golden-hued' sails as well as by their yellow varnish, gilt mouldings, bamboo stunsail booms and coir rigging.

Coir rope is manufactured from the fibre of the coconut shell. In our period it was made and used throughout India, the fibre being mostly imported from Ceylon, the Maldives, Nicobars and elsewhere. For either running or standing rigging, coir cordage was not much esteemed among Europeans. It was said to be harsh, intractable and not very strong. For cables, on the other hand, it was thought excellent; and especially for cables of the largest diameter, from twelve to twenty inches. Captain Forrest, as one among many, praised the elasticity of coir cables. He said that ships riding to a coir cable a hundred and twenty fathoms long would give way as much as half their own length, and then shoot ahead after the squall had passed; this, under conditions when an unyielding hempen cable would have parted. As additional virtues, the coir cable would float, and was therefore less easily lost; and it was not liable to rot, except in fresh water.

India also produced what was called 'Sunn hemp'; or, to be exact, the Company spent large sums in encouraging its cultivation, in the hope of rendering England independent of supplies from the Baltic. Nothing came of this scheme beyond the production of a certain amount of cordage for the East Indies squadron. Country hemp was not bad in quality, but there never seems to have been enough of it. Manilla rope was already known, but it does not seem to have come into use until the end of our period, when intercourse was resumed with the Spanish colonies; and only then in small quantities.

Owing, then, to the deficiency or defectiveness of the local supplies, most of the best cordage in use was imported from Europe by the East India Company itself, this being one of the imports it monopolised. With the cordage came a variety of other ship fittings, comprising practically all metal parts. Anchors, guns, small-arms, shot, chains, copper; these, with bolts of canvas, formed the cargo of many of the smaller Indiamen. The cost of importation was heavy, owing to the high freight paid by the Company. Indeed, it was said that two-fifths of the outlay in building a country ship was spent in equipment. Owing to the expensiveness of these imported naval stores, most country ships must have shown mongrel leanings, each having a proportion of European sails and ropes and a proportion, which tended to increase, of dungaree and coir.

Resembling each other in equipment, the two groups of country shipping also resembled each other in the way in which they were owned and insured. That they were largely owned by British firms may seem, at first sight, the least explicable thing about them; the more so when it is realised how little energy the English merchants displayed. 'The European merchant', writes Grandpré, speaking more particularly of Madras, 'entirely neglects the minute details, and looks only at the abstract of the accounts given him by his dobachi: a negligence perfectly suited to the manner in which he lives, at a distance from the spot where his affairs are conducted, which he visits only once a day, and that not regularly, to bestow upon them two or three hours' attention.' And yet, despite this laxity, they had gained a large share in the ownership of shipping and something like a monopoly in marine insurance. The explanation is not obvious. There are, however, three possible causes which seem worth considering; all three, perhaps, having a certain effect.

In the first place, there is the willingness already alluded to of the wealthy English official to entrust his savings to an English or Scotch merchant, sitting in what looked like the office of an English firm. He was the more ready to do this when the merchant was a man he knew as a neighbour or had seen in church. And most of the merchants were men of some social standing—they had begun life, at any rate, with sufficient means to enable them to reach India. Those of lowest extraction were Scotch, but endowed with a provincial dialect which has always effectually prevented the English from 'placing' them socially. This may seem trivial. But it is certainly very much the reverse. The merchants of European birth were essentially camp-followers of the military. They depended for their success on their reception in official society.

The second factor in the shipping and insurance business is closely connected with the first. The shipping magnate who dined with the chief secretary to the Government had an immense advantage over the shipping magnate who did not; that is to say, the European had a great advantage over the native. Matters such as convoy, naval protection, intervention with native Powers, omitting to ask awkward questions and so forth—all these would arrange themselves over the dinner-table. A native merchant could have little hope of success in applying at an office. What is more, he probably underestimated such chances as he had. The Indian, and more especially the Parsee, is always apt to exaggerate the effect and scope of wire-pulling.

The third factor to consider is as little connected with business enterprise as the first two. The country ship was, as we have seen, trying to look like an Indiaman which was trying to look like a ship-of-war. She was therefore armed, and sometimes heavily armed for her size. She was sometimes expected to bluff and sometimes expected to fight. But to do either she required English officers. Lascars made fairly good seamen, particularly in a climate which could be depended upon, but were very little use at fighting. Sepoys could be carried to defend the ship, but they were none of them seamen by nature. Neither were they much disposed to take orders from the lascars. There had therefore to be an English captain. And, as he could not remain on deck all the time, there had to be one or two English mates. Three or four Englishmen all told were sufficient, but it was hopeless trying to do with less. It was, incidentally, extremely expensive to have any more. Now, it will presently be seen that everything in the country trade depended on the courage, energy, honesty and intelligence of the captain. To obtain the services of a good man was the first essential to success. Here, then, lay the third advantage of the European shipowner. English captains had a preference, on the whole, for European owners. And, what is even more important, a native owner could have little skill in judging the character of an English seaman. European firms were, by the nature of things, bound to have better officers.

The Bombay and Bengal ships, using these terms in the widest sense to include Surat and Rangoon vessels respectively, resembled each other to some extent in the materials of which they were built, the process by which they evolved and the way in which they were armed, equipped, officered, manned and owned. Where they differed was in size, shape, speed and in the character of their trade.

In describing separately the extent and importance of the two groups of shipping, it is necessary to point out that both were growing, and that allowance must be made for their growth. The total number of ships in the country trade was a hundred and twenty-eight in 1783, with a total tonnage of 44,865. In 1791 the number was five hundred and seventy-five, the tonnage 175,407. The growth was not as marked as that in the early years of the nineteenth century, and it was partly counteracted by capture. The Bombay shipping, which we shall consider first, was also somewhat reduced by purchase into the Navy, and may perhaps be considered as stationary. There were twenty-nine large ships trading from Bombay by the end of our period, nineteen of them measuring over six hundred tons. The leading firms were Forbes and Co., Bruce Fawcett and Co. and Briscoe and Beaufort. The first of these firms owned four ships, including the *Lowjee Family*, of 926 tons. The second firm had five ships, including the *Anna*, of 899 tons; and the third owned only two. There were some half-dozen other British owners of single ships, and the rest were owned by Parsees with names like Sorabjee, Bomanjee and Jamsetjee. Two of the leading native firms, each owning two ships, were Ardaseer Dady and Nasserwanjee Monackjee. A curious feature of these vessels is that many of them, built by a Framjee or Nowrojee, and owned by a Cowasjee or a Bomanjee, bore English names like *Minerva*, *Friendship*, *Milford*, *Alexander* and *Bombay Merchant*. Many of these had been built at Bombay or Surat, but others came from Dumaun, Cochin, Rangoon and even Calcutta. The total tonnage of these ships was 17,593.

The whole mercantile community of Bombay, including all who were interested in shipping, whether as owners, underwriters or merchants, numbered about forty-five. Of this number less than twenty were white men, and of these two or three were Spanish or Portuguese. The rest were natives; and it is worthy of remark that there were said to be Parsee partners in the European firms who had, in fact, provided the bulk of the capital. The House of Forbes seems to have had a sort of supremacy, but there were four other European Houses of Agency, Bruce, Fawcett and Co., Shotton and Co., John Leckie and S. Beaufort. Of the merchants, three were Portuguese, four Armenian, sixteen Hindoo, four Moslem. There were only six shipbuilders, all Parsees and all, very probably, members of the Lowjee clan. There were a number of individual underwriters, but the bulk of the shipping was insured by a single office, the Bombay Insurance Society.

In treating of the number and tonnage of the shipping, it must be remembered that not all the ships built at Bombay were owned there. It was not uncommon for Bombay builders to receive orders from Calcutta owners. The following notice dates from 1799:

> A very fine ship, of the burthen of 788 tons, called the Mysore, was launched in the month of October last, at Bombay, belonging to Messrs Lambert and Ross, of Calcutta, mounting 36 twelve and six-pounder carriage guns. The ship was built upon the improved principle of sailing upon a wind, and is to be added to the strength of the marine in India. Three other ships, of the same dimensions and force, are on the stocks at Bombay, and were expected to be launched in December.

It is very doubtful whether any country ship ever actually mounted as heavy a broadside as the *Mysore* is here credited with. It seems more probable that she was pierced for that number of guns and mounted a much smaller number. The following ships are more typical in this respect:

		Guns	European officers	Native crew
Scaleby Castle 1250 tons	Bruce, Fawcett & Co.	16	5	115
Shaw Ardiseer 870 tons	Alex. Adamson	8	4	130
Gangava 750 tons	Fromjee Monajee	12	4	75
Charlotte 672 tons	Forbes & Co.	14	4	75

Some of these ships might, very likely, have mounted a larger number of guns. But the naval officers on the station were apt to discourage merchantmen from carrying too heavy an armament. They may have carried more guns before the Peace of Amiens, and before Admiral Rainier began to question the expediency of the practice. It was in 1799, the year when the *Mysore* was completed, that he wrote to Lord Spencer on the subject:

> ...I cannot dispense remarking to your Lordship the prejudicial custom in the merchants in this country of arming their ships completely, having generally a tier of guns in their upper deck, with ammunition in proportion, to give them the appearance of ships of force, while they are only manned by natives who are seldom known to stand to their quarters; the mischief of which is, that when taken by the enemy they immediately become privateers fit for service.
>
> (*N.R.S.* vol. LIX, p. 202, 10th Dec., 1799.)

That phrase 'to give them the appearance of ships of force is the clue to what the country shipping interest was eternally aiming at. To look like an Indiaman was the first necessity for every country ship. That is probably one reason for their enormous size as compared with the shipping of Europe.

The chief business of these Bombay ships was to carry raw cotton to China. They also exported pepper, sandalwood, ivory, sharks' fins and precious stones. On the outward voyage they usually added to their cargo by purchases in the Straits of Malacca. They brought home in return, to India, tea, china-ware, nankeens, silks, satins, velvets, camphor and tutenague. This last import was a white metal akin to aluminium in its uses if not in its composition. The Chinese made it, using a great deal of imported tin for the purpose, and it served throughout the East as a sort of equivalent for pewter. In the late eighteenth century, before copper came into universal favour, there was a possibility of tutenague becoming the ordinary sheathing of European ships. There is a reference to it in Samuel Kelly's autobiography, disguised under the spelling 'tooth-and-egg', and its rejection is there attributed to its tendency to foul.

Several men of note were at one time or other in the Bombay trade, and their careers are of especial interest in that they serve to show the kind of way in which merchant seamen found their way to India in the first place. Eastwick, for example, narrates how he came out as a junior officer in an Indiaman, quitted the service at Bombay on learning 'that the country service in a merchant ship was amongst the best in the world', and became forthwith second mate of the *Hormuzeer*. He transferred to the Calcutta trade after a single voyage to China. More interesting is the career of James Horsburgh, afterwards F.R.S. and Hydrographer to the East India Company. He was born in 1762, of poor parents, in Fife, and served an apprenticeship in the North Sea coal trade. After a number of voyages between Newcastle, the Firth of Forth, Hamburg and Ostend, he was taken prisoner by the French in 1780. On his release he next went to the West Indies, eventually reaching Calcutta by unspecified means and becoming third mate of the *Nancy* country ship. In 1788 he was appointed second mate of the *Gunjavar* (also spelt *Ganjava*, etc.), a vessel described above, then recently completed and owned by a Moslem merchant called Chillaby, of Surat. After some years in the China trade, he entered the service of Messrs Bruce, Fawcett and Co. as chief mate successively of the *Anna* and the *Carron*, obtaining the command of the first-named ship in 1798. He finally returned to England in 1805 as a passenger in the Indiaman *Cirencester*. He was already noted for having charted the Straits of Macassar and the western side of the Philippines, while making two voyages to China by eastern passages. His 'Sailing Directions' gained him a reputation which enabled him to succeed Alexander Dalrymple as the East India Company's Hydrographer in 1810.

Without Horsburgh's eminence, Elmore gives a great deal

more information about the country trade than any other writer of the time. His account of himself, however, is disappointingly brief. He was in the Navy—he does not say in what capacity—until the Peace of 1783. He then became fourth mate of the East India Company's packet *Surprise*, which went out of the Company's service at Calcutta. He went into the country trade, in which he remained until 1796, when he was given the command of the Company's freighted ship *Varuna*. After a voyage to England and back to Calcutta, he apparently retired. Although chiefly conversant with the Calcutta trade, that of Bombay was not unknown to him.

These three careers seem to illustrate the connection there must always have been between the Company's service and the country trade. Officers in the country trade had often, no doubt, served at one time in an Indiaman; and Elmore's career shows that they were sometimes able to return to the service. The other connection between the Company's servants and the country trade was one of investment. The shipowners, both European and native, had charge of many fortunes derived from the revenues of India. Hence, the apparent rivalry between the Company and the private traders was not accompanied with much acrimony in India. It was in England that the Company's monopoly was most sternly upheld.

One art the officers of Bombay country ships had to master was the stowage of raw cotton. Elmore bears witness to their skill in this respect:

> ...The commanders and officers are the completest stevadores of this peculiar cargo I have ever met with, and so exceedingly quick and clever at it, that they will stow and screw from sixty to eighty tons of it in a ship's hold in one day; or from one hundred and twenty to one hundred and sixty bales, each bale containing from three to five hundred weight: and by their superior method of screwing this commodity, will put twelve hundred weight in the compass allowed for a merchant's ton (or forty cubic feet). Some of the larger ships, belonging to Bombay and Surat, will carry upwards of four thousand bales....

The country ships trading from Bombay to China usually sailed in April or early in May, and called in the Straits of Malacca for tin, pepper, betel-nut, rattans, sea-swallows and birds' nests. This last item must be classed with the sharks' fins exported from Malabar, as a luxury for which the Chinese would pay heavily. Both the fins and the nests were intended for the making of expensive and highly seasoned soups, which were (and are) valued in China as what Wathen calls 'stimulants of a particular nature'. It was while collecting cargo in seas infested with Malay pirates that country ships felt the benefit of their size. It was when caught in a gale on a lee shore that they felt the disadvantage of their size. For large ships laden with cotton tend to float high, exposing a great deal of top-hamper and having an insufficient grip of the water. Bombay ships were apt to make leeway and drive on shore.

Arriving at Macao in September or October, the Bombay ship would obtain a permit from the Mandarin there and so proceed to Whampoa. The captain would then give a manifest of his cargo to the Hong merchants, one of whom became security for his behaviour. The Hong merchants then fixed the price of the goods, their ruling being final in that no one else was allowed to bid. Cargo was unloaded into two hoppo, or custom-house boats, where it was weighed before being put into covered and locked boats and taken up to Canton. In this process it was discovered that 'the Chinese exceed greatly the watermen upon the Thames in filching and chicanery'; which was of course saying a great deal. A Compradore was appointed to each ship by the Hong merchants, and from him alone did the ship obtain its provisions. The country ships, like the Indiamen, had to be measured for tonnage by the Chinese method, as an assessment for taxation. The Tontiff who came down in state to perform this duty only measured the distance between the centre of the fore-mast and the centre of the mizen-mast, and also the extreme breadth at the gangway; so that it would be interesting to know whether this produced any alteration in the design of the ships. They apparently found it worth while to prepare for the visit by removing the after-wedges of the foremast and removing the stay so as to allow of wedging it close against the after part of the partners, simultaneously performing the opposite operation with the mizen-mast. According to Addison, the Chinese often insisted on measuring ships again despite their having been measured on a previous voyage, on the plea that 'ship make a changee; grow a littee more largee'. It seems possible that, with country ships, sheathed after the Bombay manner, this may actually have been the case.

The country ships which assembled in Canton River were by no means all from Bombay. In November and December 1808, when there were fourteen regular Indiamen at Whampoa, the country ships numbered twenty-eight. Fifteen of them were from Bombay, six from Bengal, five from Penang, one from Madras and one from Negapatam. In time of war the country ships usually availed themselves of the protection of the Indiamen on the return voyage, the whole fleet normally having a naval escort. They had, of course, to part company soon after passing the Straits of Sunda. It will be observed that it was the object of ships trading between Bombay and China to have the North-East Monsoon to take them down the Malabar Coast to Dondra Head, the South-West Monsoon to push them over to Achin and ultimately to Canton, the North-East Monsoon to bring them back into the Indian Ocean, and the South-West Monsoon to carry them back to Bombay. This ideal voyage may not always have been achieved, but it was the theory on which the voyage was based. Sometimes, however, ships which had sailed from Bombay to China returned to dispose of their cargoes at Calcutta.

Before quitting the subject of the country trade at Bombay, mention must be made of the trade from there to Persia and

Arabia. This seems to have been extensive but almost entirely in native hands. Bussorah and Muscat were the chief centres of the trade, and much of it was carried on in vessels belonging to the latter port. The articles of trade were too numerous to enter into here, but the cargoes were of sufficient value to require protection. Part of the business of the Bombay Marine was to escort this trade and check piracy in that part of the Eastern Seas. A few, perhaps, of the vessels sailing from the different parts of India for the Red Sea and Persian Gulf were of European rig and with British Officers; but few, if any, were owned by Europeans.

To turn now to the country trade on the other side of India, the first fact to notice is that it was far more extensive. The ships were more than twice as numerous, even if, on an average, somewhat smaller. Trade was also to a far greater extent in European hands; the effect, very possibly, of the number and wealth of the Company's servants at Fort William. There was already a certain amount of talk about English energy and business enterprise, but a list of the principal houses betrays the fact that comparatively few of the merchants were English. About the end of our period there were, in rough figures, fourteen Scotch, ten English and five foreign names among the list of merchants. And this is leaving out of account some twelve Armenian, six Portuguese and twenty-one native firms.

The great shipping firms were Fairlie, Fergusson and Co., Hogue, Davidson and Co., Hugh Atkins Reid, Palmer and Co., Edward Brightman, Johannes Sarkies and Shaik Gullum Hossain. The first three of these were the most notable. Fairlie, Fergusson & Co. owned nine ships, all over 400 tons; of these, four were over 700, one of 1100 tons. This firm must have been one of the largest in the world. Hogue, Davidson and Co. was a modest affair by comparison, with only five ships. Hugh Atkins Reid owned four ships, four other firms owning two each. Thirteen more ships owned by individuals brought the total number up to thirty-nine ships of over 300 tons' burthen. There were thirty-eight vessels registered at Calcutta of less than 300 tons, making a grand total of seventy-seven sail and 16,327 tons.

A peculiarity of the Calcutta mercantile world was the number of insurance companies. There were nine of them, some appearing merely as another aspect of certain shipping firms. The Calcutta Insurance Office, for example, had Messrs Fairlie, Fergusson and Co. as its agents. In the same way the India Insurance Co. was represented by Hogue, Davidson and Co. The system must have been for the small shipowners to insure with the large ones, and perhaps for the large firms to insure with each other. This would at least have the effect of spreading losses among them.

The ships owned and registered at Calcutta were nearly all built either there or in Pegu. Twenty-three of the vessels of over 300 tons' burthen had been built either at Calcutta or at Chittagong, and nine in the vicinity of Rangoon. The greater number, probably, of the smaller craft came from Pegu. It must be remembered that the list of vessels registered at Calcutta does not cover all the ships trading in the Bay of Bengal. Ships built in Pegu might equally be registered at Madras. There were several distinct and thriving trades, and it would be impossible to estimate the number of vessels engaged in them.

The general characteristics of the Calcutta country ships were somewhat different from those of the Bombay vessels. They tended to be rather smaller, the average ship being of about 400 tons rather than 600. They were not as heavily and strongly built. Many of them were designed for speed and many of them were heavily armed. There were, it is evident, two distinct types among them, intended for the two main branches of the trade. These branches can be described briefly as 'Rice' and 'Opium'; or else as 'West' and 'East'.

The rice trade depended on the fact that Madras was not self-supporting in the matter of food. It was a larger town than the surrounding district could feed. Rice had therefore to be brought there from Bengal, not as a temporary expedient but as a normal necessity; and there were occasional threats of famine, creating a need for additional supplies. On such occasions literally hundreds of ships might be engaged in the trade for a short time, as there must have been during the later famine at Bombay. Apart, however, from these emergencies, a set of vessels existed for the purpose of carrying rice. They were specially designed for the trade, it appears, and a peculiarity of their trade was its one-sidedness. Little or nothing could be sent to Bengal in exchange for the rice, so that the ships had to be suited alike for loading a heavy cargo and for sailing in ballast. The ideal ship, in fact, was one which could 'stand on its legs' without any kintledge at all. The ships had to be fast, for half the time spent at sea was profitless. It was only by making a series of rapid voyages that a ship could hold her own. This necessitated working against the monsoon and sailing in rough weather, so that the vessels had to be handy and seaworthy. As a final requirement, they had to be of sufficiently shallow draught to ascend the Hooghly, preferably as high as Calcutta itself.

The vessel produced by these conditions was a broad, low ship of some three or four hundred tons' burthen, drawing seventeen or eighteen feet of water when fully laden. A ship of this type could carry from seven to twelve thousand bags of rice, according to her size. She would load four cargoes of rice each year, making therefore eight passages, four probably in the teeth of the monsoon. The passage between Bengal and Madras took anything from a week to a month, as the weather dictated, but more time was spent in loading and unloading than in sailing. A ship that succeeded in making her four voyages a year, landing forty thousand bags of rice at a freight of two-and-a-half rupees, might bring her owners a profit of over nine thousand pounds annually, over and above her expenses.

The other branch of the Calcutta trade was the traffic in opium; or, perhaps it would be more exact to say that it was a traffic in which opium had a prominent place. The characteristics of the trade were risk and profit, both immense. Admiral Rainier said that the trade was one of 'bold speculations, requiring caution and secrecy in the execution'; and in moments of exasperation he called it 'mere buccaneering'. There was clearly a great deal of buccaneering about it, especially in peace-time. This was because much of the trade consisted in poaching on the Dutch preserves. The Dutch had long persisted in a policy of attempting to exclude all other Europeans from the spice trade; a policy which almost succeeded in the seventeenth century, but broke down to a certain extent in the course of the eighteenth. This exclusive spirit was foolish, if only because the Dutch lacked the force necessary to support their claims. Incidentally, a lot of energy was expended in maintaining a monopoly which might have been devoted more usefully to the development of the trade. The Dutch East India Company, for example, used to pay £3000 a year to the Kings of the Moluccas on condition that they should destroy all the spice-trees on islands other than those which the Dutch occupied. Detachments of troops were continually being sent round to see that this was done. And yet, after all this effort, the English interlopers were still there every year; which may have meant that there were a few islands the Dutch forgot to search, but more probably meant that the official spice-growing islands were being robbed by their own officers. Here is Grandpré's description of the trade and the ships engaged in it:

> Exclusively of the maritime trade between the coasts of India and that of China, the english merchants engage in smuggling adventures to the Moluccas. The profit of this trade is immense, and is proportioned to the dangers that are risked. The ships

employed in the voyage must be able to contend with a dutch sloop of eighteen guns, stationed as a guard-ship off those islands. On approaching the coast, the inhabitants, who are accustomed to this traffic, bring by stealth to the vessel under sail the spices which they have to dispose of, and which they barter at a very low rate. As no satisfaction could be obtained for any outrage they might attempt, and no application could be made to the dutch company for redress, the crews of the vessels employed in this trade never treat with the natives without being armed.

This kind of thing could degenerate very easily into piracy. How far it did so must remain conjectural. The period, however, with which we are dealing being mainly one of war with the Dutch, the potential pirate had acquired the status of a potential privateer. It was no longer necessary for officials at Fort William to look the other way whenever an obviously disreputable craft dropped down the river on its way to some doubtful destination. In an earlier age, and with a different foe, they would probably have come down to the waterside to acclaim a Protestant hero.

That maze of islands stretching from the Malay Peninsula down to New Holland itself formed in those days a world of mystery and complexity. There were several known highways by which China was reached, and every now and again someone like Horsburgh would publish a chart of Dampier's Strait or Pitt's Passage. But those who knew most about it, whether Dutch or English, had every motive for keeping their knowledge to themselves. Vast areas were unsurveyed, ill-surveyed, or even unexplored. And yet knowledge was essential to the navigation of these regions. No generalisation was possible. There were islands where the natives were friendly, some where they were hostile, others where they were treacherous. Some native rulers were in alliance with the Dutch, some were not. Some Dutch officials could be bribed at small expense, others required a heavy bribe, and there were even a few who would not be bribed at all. In such a world the trader was at once bold and guarded, jealous of his rivals and tenacious of his secrets. He was eternally watching for symptoms of treachery, both in his crew and among his customers. He was always ready to shoot, so as to be on the safe side. Sometimes he made a fortune and sometimes he was killed.

The ideal ship for the Eastern Voyage was of about four hundred tons burthen and pierced for eighteen or twenty guns. This was the size of the ship destined to finish her voyage at Canton, a size determined by the nature of the trade and the force of the Dutch guardships. There were smaller ships of a type intended only for trading among the Malay Archipelago. These were of two or three hundred tons. Both the large and small ships were designed for speed. Elmore begins his description of the ideal voyage with a few remarks on equipment, betraying therein a sober enthusiasm, a reflection of the adventures of his younger days:

> The ship, in addition to the necessary ammunition for her guns, musquets, and pistols, should have a box containing fifty hand granadoes in each top; together with an arm chest, containing musquets and ball cartridge: that if boarded by the Malays, or pirate Lanoons, and driven from the deck, your crew may be able, from the tops, to drive them off with their granadoes and musquets: the officers and people at the batteries below will prevent the enemy from getting possession of the inside of the ship....
>
> ...The commander ought to be well supplied with boats, viz. a good fast-sailing long-boat, as large as the ship could possibly stow; a second boat, or pinnace, to stow in her, also as large as possible; a third boat to turn bottom up over the former two; a yawl, to hang upon one quarter; a good paddling canoe, for dispatch, upon the other quarter; and a gig, or light fast rowing boat, to hang over the stern.
>
> The long-boat should carry two (at least) or four chambered swivels, of three pound calibre; the second boat two; and third boat one; with grape, canister, and langrage shot sufficient for them. Each boat should also be armed with a sufficient number of pikes, cutlasses, pistols, musquets, and bayonets, with an arm-chest to contain them; and a magazine for the necessary ammunition.

When the author goes on to explain that the ideal ship had to carry, in addition to the crew, one havildar (or sergeant), two naiks (or corporals), two drummers, a fifer, and twenty sepoys, a doubt begins to form itself in the reader's mind as to what exactly the ideal ship was setting forth to do.

> The British merchants resident in Calcutta [writes Milburn] are a respectable and enterprising class of men, many of whom are possessed of large and independent fortunes, in the acquisition of which they have displayed those mercantile talents, and that enterprising spirit, which are characteristic of the British nation.

No doubt; but a remark of that kind, taking us into the world of Smiles' 'Self Help' and the legend of the industrious apprentice, seems a little remote from all this talk about pikes, drums, and hand-grenades. In the guide-book we find a discreet reference to 'mercantile talents'; in the memoirs of the period we find nothing but tales of smuggling at the pistol point. Without questioning the necessity of all these arms, merely for purposes of self-protection while engaged in an illicit trade, it is easy to see how such voyages might end.

A significant fact about the opium ship, which was later to turn into the opium clipper, emerges from Elmore's description of how to deal with Malay pirates after they had boarded. He makes it clear that the ship was flush-decked, with all her guns on the main deck, under cover. Only in a flush-decked ship can one confine boarders to the upper deck. It would be interesting to know whether the flush-decked Indiaman, so rightly advocated by Snodgrass, was merely a copy of the Bengal country ship. Everything seems to point to the conclusion that it was. Snodgrass had not wasted his time spent at Calcutta, and there is evidently a trace of the rice ship in his demand for greater width. How far the rice ship and the opium ship were produced to suit the conditions of their trade, and how far they developed from the native types they superseded, this is a problem which only local knowledge could solve.

Opium was a difficult cargo to stow away, being perishable and liable to be ruined either by heat or damp. The opium ship had to be fitted with special compartments on the orlop deck, carefully ventilated by scuttles and windsails, and raised by battens running athwartships, to allow water to run clear. The opium itself was wrapped in poppy leaves, placed in chests, and the chests were covered with hides. There were four qualities of opium, Patna, Benares, Rungpore and Boggulpore, the first or 'Company's opium' being the best. The amount exported from Bengal was increasing during the early part of our period, steadying down after 1805. The great increase was in 1799, when the export more than doubled. It doubled again in the course of the period 1800–4, and then became fairly constant, the value of the annual export coming to about six million rupees, some three-fifths going to China and the rest to the Archipelago.

Elmore's ideal voyage begins, as all real voyages did, about the end of December or beginning of January. The Company's first sales of opium were about the middle of December, and a ship could not sail until the opium was on board. It formed only a small part of the cargo in bulk, some five hundred chests, each of about a hundred and sixty pounds, being all the largest ship would carry. The space in the hold was filled with rice, wheat and gram, as ballast; and the ship might also carry some piece goods and from twenty to forty thousand Spanish dollars in specie.

These opium ships always raced each other for an early market, and did all they could to impede each other. Those which succeeded in making an early start from Bengal scurried over the first part of their voyage so as to keep ahead of all rivals. Elmore describes the usual voyage in detail; Junkceylon, Penang, Salangore, Malacca, Lingin, Palambang, and so to Batavia. He is, of course, speaking of peace-time. At all these ports of call the ship would get rid of some of her cargo, taking tin, ivory and dollars in exchange. Any cargo left over was then disposed of on the west coast of Borneo, for gold, and the ship would then collect more tin, and pepper, and proceed to the Straits of Banca to meet the Company's China ships, due there about August. These would take on board much of the tin and pepper, on payment of freight, giving a loan of dollars in exchange. Paying in specie, the ship was then to buy more tin, pepper, rattans, wax and betel-nut, and then follow the China ships to Canton towards the end of September. It was necessary to discharge and load the return cargo with extraordinary speed in order to sail again early in November and reach Calcutta in the following month, ready to begin the voyage again. Elmore concludes that it is an active, busy and dangerous trade.

The danger is hinted at in such pieces of advice as this: 'While upon the coast of Borneo, be particularly cautious, and always ready to repel an attack, for your ship is never safe'; 'be careful of venturing on shore; and upon no account whatever be persuaded to take your ship into the river.' He explains how the natives tried to seize ships, kill the officers and share the cargoes. He advises the captains of small ships against going to Canton, as it will pay them better to entrust their goods to Indiamen and so avoid payment of the Chinese exactions.

Most interesting of all, Elmore gives a little advice about trading at Batavia. On arrival, the best thing was to petition the Council for permission to dispose of one's cargo. 'The Council will perhaps take all your opium at 500 rix dollars per chest, or may perhaps order you out of the roads; in this case recourse must be had to smuggling. While you are delivering your cargo you must sign a certificate for the behaviour of your officers and people, at the forfeit of your life, that you, nor none of your crew, will smuggle opium or spices, directly or indirectly; for which reason you are to follow these rules.' And he proceeds to give elaborate instructions as to how to smuggle without being caught; the essential thing being to gain the connivance of the Shabunder, or harbour-master, the Fiscal, the Boss at Onroost, 'the Chinaman that farms the duties and lives at the Boom', the Whipper-in at Edam or the Vizvis at Kyper's Island. Any of these, apparently, could be trusted. They would pay for the opium in specie, cinnamon, cloves, nutmegs and mace—the whole transaction being kept quite private.

Elmore was a respectable man, writing a book dedicated to the Court of Directors. He says not a word of anything that really disreputable captains might do. But what he does say is startling enough when taken from its calm and matter-of-fact context. To begin with, he states that Bengal exported a great deal of opium other than that sold by the East India Company. This was an infringement of a monopoly and a form of smuggling. He does not advise the purchase of it. He merely enumerates the different qualities and their acceptability in China. He goes on to describe how the opium, possibly smuggled out of Bengal, may be smuggled into Batavia immediately after the smuggler has sworn not to do so. It will be paid for very largely in spices, which are, of course, a monopoly of the Dutch Company which the smuggler has taken his oath to respect. The spices so obtained are to be loaded on an Indiaman to the profit of the commander, who thus exceeded his allowance of tonnage, breaking all the regulations of private trade. In return, a loan is made of specie, which belongs to the Company and is not the commander's to lend—let alone at 24 per cent. interest, an illegal rate of usury in itself. And the voyage may finally end up with landing opium in China, where it is contraband, while simultaneously trying to evade the Chinese tax on tonnage. The return to Bengal is uneventful, except for the possible smuggling of Japan copper and naval stores obtained by illicit traffic with bribed Dutch officials.

Eastwick's memoirs do not give so complete or scientific an account of the country trade as Elmore's book does. He does not, like Elmore, enter into the intricacies of several different branches of the trade. On the other hand, he relates actual experiences, not imaginary voyages of a typical or ideal character. He is particularly interesting on the subject of his own gains and losses. He was given his first command by a Parsee shipowner, Dorabjee Byramjee, of Rangoon. The ship was the *Rebecca*, of 1100 tons. 'This was', he writes, 'a brilliant appointment for a young man of twenty-one, and equal to at least £4000 a year, for in addition to pay of five hundred rupees per mensem, I received two and a half per centum commission on all freight, goods, and passengers consigned to my care....' This was probably the normal method of remunerating captains who also undertook the duties of supercargo. It is significant both as showing how much a captain could earn, and as indicating how enormous the gross receipts were; 2½ per cent. coming to well over £3000 a year, the total profit to the owners can be surmised. Eastwick mentions another ship so well provided with passengers that the passage money amounted at one time to £12,000. After this it is not surprising to learn that, after a few voyages between Rangoon, Calcutta, Madras and the Straits, he bought a ship of his own.

Eastwick made several fortunes, of £20,000 and upwards, losing them again by unwise investment with dishonest native bankers, and by his ship being captured when not insured. But one of his most interesting stories is of a fortune he failed to make:

> From the Pedir coast I sailed back to Penang, and whilst at this latter place the two annual Macao ships arrived and departed. Two days after they left, I was privately informed by a merchant of the place that they carried no less than half a million sterling on board for the purpose of buying opium at the Calcutta sales, which they were fearful of losing, having been delayed by bad weather. This information was worth a fortune, and having confidence in the smart sailing qualities of the Harington, I determined to follow with all speed, and endeavour to arrive before them.

Fortunately the north-east monsoon immediately broke in with a series of heavy gales, and by carrying on, whilst the great lumbering Portuguese vessels were hove to, afraid to proceed, I overtook and passed them, and reached Calcutta just in time for the sales....

The end of the story is as characteristic as the beginning. In trying to make his corner in opium, Eastwick was a shade too eager. His bidding attracted attention. Inquiries were made as to where he had come from. One or two brokers guessed what was afoot, and the price of opium soared. His nerve failing, he made nothing by his dash up the Bay. Two Armenians made their fortunes.

Opium was the parent of fast-sailing ships and reckless seamanship. It was a commodity in which one could speculate. Immensely valuable, it was apt to deteriorate in quality and fluctuate in price. Above all, it was the means of satisfying the irrational desires of mankind. As far as one can understand the subject, it seems that the opium consumer is torpid and miserable when deprived of the drug, only becoming his normal self when the craving is satisfied. Together with this fact there must be borne in mind the fact that opium is perishable. These two facts in conjunction explain why an early market was so desirable. Last season's opium being consumed or perished, those addicted to the drug would pay any price for the first supplies of the year. They would evidently bid high for an immediate satisfaction, despite the knowledge that larger quantities would soon arrive at a lower price. Once the immediate need was met, the consumer was himself again and in a mood to bargain. This is mere conjecture, of course, and quite possibly founded on error. If true, it is probably more applicable to the Malay Archipelago than to China, if only because the latter country has a colder climate in which the drug may be supposed to have lasted for a longer time. Whatever the truth of the matter may be, certain it is that gambling is most possible in luxury trades and in the supplying of goods to be classed either as rubbish or poison. Rational desires produce a predictable price. It is in such goods as opium that fortunes can be made.

The voyages just described, performed by Elmore and Eastwick, were by no means the only voyages open to the adventurer's choice. There were numerous islands and coasts where the merchant could trade. Elmore instances a number of alternative routes to take among the islands, and there were probably possibilities he did not care to mention. Country ships used to sail from Bengal victualled for twelve months. When at last they reappeared it was not always known exactly where they had been.

Next to opium, a principal article of trade was tin. And, as if to complete the picture of this mysterious and fantastic trade to the Eastwards, it appears that the value of tin depended not on its usefulness but on the religious customs of China and Japan. Tin was mined in the first instance by Chinese colonists in Sumatra and elsewhere. The Dutch obtained quantities of it in the form of tribute from the Sultan of Banee, the ruler at Balambangan. The English obtained other supplies in exchange for opium. It was then conveyed to China, by English and Dutch ships and, in smaller quantities, by Chinese junks. Some four thousand tons a year were transported in this manner, to which must be added another thousand tons, more or less, from the Cornish mines—this last traffic having begun about 1789, through the efforts of Mr George Unwin. All this effort was made, accompanied by we know not what degree of crime and oppression, subject alike to theft and piracy, and so the tin was brought to China. And the Chinese burnt it.

The merchants who bought the tin from the importer resold it to the gold-beaters, by whom it was manufactured into leaf. English tin could be beaten fairly thin—thirty-five square yards to the pound—but the Malayan tin was more valuable because it could be made thinner still. The leaf was pasted on to pieces of card, consecrated by the priests, and sold to the believers. The devout then burnt it morning and evening, in quantities proportioned to their piety.

Chapter XII

THE END OF MONOPOLY

THE first serious attack on the Company's monopoly came from the handful of merchants living in India under the Company's own protection. The story of the campaign for Free Trade begins with the effort of these merchants to obtain admission to the trade with Europe. The basis of their prosperity was, as we have seen, the wealth of the Company's servants at Calcutta and, to a lesser extent, at Bombay. In the later years of our period there were, Wathen points out,

> ...five houses of agency...in Calcutta, circulating through their many ramified channels the life-blood of commerce, and at once affording an employment for native capital, yielding a large interest of eight per cent. to such Company's servants as left the produce of their hard-earned labours to increase in their hands, and making at the same time the rapid and princely fortunes of many an enterprising merchant, who has returned to his native land a prince in revenue, himself the architect of his fortunes....

Some idea has already been given of the wealth made in India by individuals; and especially those in the Company's service. This wealth having been further increased by the type of investment Wathen describes, the problem arose as to how to send it to England when the time came for the owner to retire there. Originally, the transmission had been a very simple matter, for the fortunes acquired in India were neither numerous nor large. Before the days of the English power in that country, there had been no difficulty in sending home the wealth of individuals in the form of bills drawn on the Company. During the latter half of the eighteenth century, however, some other method had to be devised; and that for two reasons. In the first place, the Company placed limits on the amount to be transmitted in this way. And, in the second place, not all individuals were anxious that the Company should know how much they had made. Some other way, then, was needed, by which these fortunes could be sent to England. And yet some other method was not easy to find. It was absurd or impossible to send bullion to Europe, and the sending of goods was the Company's monopoly. A solution to the problem had to be found in the trade carried on by Portugal, Sweden, Denmark, and above all by the United States. It was to the ships of these countries that these individual fortunes were illegally entrusted in the form of goods. The goods so transmitted to Europe—tea, for instance—often ended up in England. Before the duties on tea were reduced there was a great deal of English capital behind the smuggling carried on from Hamburg and Dunkirk and other ports; and it was with English capital that the tea had been, in the first instance, purchased. This transmission of Anglo-Indian wealth from India to Europe in foreign, and chiefly American, ships was called the 'Clandestine Trade'. According to Joseph Cotton, it was a trade organised by 'a great commercial arrangement and combination...between houses in Copenhagen, or Hamburg, London, Philadelphia and India'.

The American ships had certain peculiar advantages in this traffic. They began to arrive immediately after the termination of the War of Independence, the first ship actually appearing in 1784. Major Shaw, the first American Consul at Canton, was installed during that year. No less than five American ships were at Canton in 1785–6. These ships all came across the Atlantic, and it was natural that they should call at Calcutta on their way to or from the Far East. So far from attempting to check this trade, it was the English policy to encourage it. In 1788 orders were issued that America should be treated as 'the most favoured nation'; and finally, in 1794, a treaty of amity, commerce and navigation was signed, by which the Americans were allowed to trade to India on payment of moderate duties, provided that they actually exported to the United States and not to Europe. This last provision was taken to mean that they had to call at an American port before going on to a European one. Other foreign nations were similarly privileged in some degree; at first to prevent them trading instead with the French and Dutch settlements, and later, by 1797, in order to keep on good terms with neutrals and allies.

At first the system was that foreigners put themselves in touch with English officials and merchants at Calcutta, to whom they tendered bills on Europe in exchange for money. With the money they purchased goods, on the sale of which they realised funds to cover their bills. The change from this system of paper remittance to a system by which the goods were bought by the inhabitants of Calcutta, and the foreign ships freighted by them, was inevitable. At first the foreigners had been compelled to bring specie, in default of goods, with which to buy their investments. But it soon became needless for them to bring anything. Devices were found for concealing the nature of the trade, which the Company found it impossible to check. The traffic was nevertheless a matter of common knowledge, and was bound to be so in that the foreigners were so manifestly taking out so much more than they brought in. That the foreign trade was carried on with British capital was obvious, but it was found impossible—or, more probably, unwise—to discover who exactly was involved in it. From the point of view of the Calcutta merchants, one convenience of the trade was that it enabled them to dispose of the goods which their own ships had brought in, spices, drugs, pepper and coffee. It was also an outlet for Indian goods like indigo, silk and sugar.

In 1793 an effort was made to rectify the abuse of the

foreign trade. An Act was passed by which the East India Company undertook to provide three thousand tons of shipping for the use of individuals, both in India and England; the latter provision in response to a clamour raised to the effect that the Company was not exporting all it might from the British Isles. This notion found its way into the writings of Adam Smith, owing to his having been brought up among the Glasgow merchants who considered themselves excluded. As might have been anticipated, however, little advantage was taken of the privilege of export. The demand for European goods in India was sufficiently met by the Company and by the officers of Indiamen. As the goods sent out were, moreover, in competition with the goods of the officers in private trade, it is not surprising that the latter proved a little obstructive when taking on board their rivals' exports. The officers had, in any case, a 10 per cent. advantage on the cost of freight. Imports by individuals, on the other hand, increased considerably from 1794 to 1803, when the trade began to decline somewhat owing to the limitation of the continental demand.

The appropriation of tonnage for the use of individuals was never a very effective device. The merchants complained that their trade was hampered by rules and regulations—which, indeed, it was—and the freight charged was much too high. Dundas, who was responsible for the measure, said afterwards that the Company had rendered it useless. There may have been something in this charge. Nevertheless, it is clear that the main obstacle was the high freight which the Company paid for its tonnage, and which it was accordingly compelled to charge. And this obstacle was the more formidable in war-time because the freights were increased so as to cover war-time rates of insurance which the neutral interloper had not to pay.

The dissatisfaction of the merchants with the facilities afforded them under the Act of 1793 found expression in their own complaints and in the support given them by Dundas and the Wellesleys. Perhaps the clearest, though not the most accurate, descriptions of the whole situation came from the pen of General Wellesley, afterwards Duke of Wellington. In his Memorandum on Bengal he pointed out that no imports could bear such a freight as the Company charged. Tonnage might clearly be had at a cheaper rate and 'there is no good reason why the people of Great Britain should pay the extravagant price of this tonnage for the Indian goods they consume, in addition to the price they pay for the mismanagement natural to an exclusive Company in all its commercial concerns'. Unless the trade was thrown open, or the Company compelled to furnish unlimited tonnage at a low rate, the clandestine trade would continue to increase.

Nothing has so far been said as to the amount of wealth which had to be transmitted every year. After 1800 the value of bills which the Company was legally allowed to accept stood at £650,000, exclusive of £5000 allowed in certificates to the commander and officers of each of the Company's ships. This was more than double the amount allowed under the Act of 1773; but, despite the low rate of exchange, the amount was habitually exceeded. The amount of the bills actually drawn between 1792 and 1813 averaged about £1,143,000 a year. Even so, there was still a great deal of wealth to transfer. The bills purchased annually from foreigners were supposed to amount to £1,000,000 a year as early as 1783. A decade later the amount had risen to a million and a half, by which time there were said to be thirty ships, totalling 13,000 tons, engaged in the trade. There was, moreover, a yearly increase. The American trade nearly doubled in 1799–1800, the Portuguese trade being quadrupled during the same period. And it was known that three-quarters of the foreigners' investment was with British capital.

The large share enjoyed by foreign ships in a trade from

which English shipping was excluded excited a great deal of criticism. The carrying trade between India and Europe was passing out of English hands, the port of London was losing its position as the sole market for Indian goods, and the revenue was being defrauded of the sums which might have been levied on goods destined for the Continent. The obvious remedy was to admit India-built shipping into the trade. When this was proposed, however, there was fervent opposition from the shipbuilders of the Thames, as also on behalf of the Company. The objections made were loud yet contradictory. Some asserted that no private traders could hope to compete with the Company. Others as firmly maintained that the Company would be ruined. The issue was, of course, confused by the fact that there were several different proposals under review, some desiring that the Company should hire its shipping in India and some thinking that the India-built ships should be allowed to trade on their own account. The chief pamphleteer on the side of the merchants in India was Mr Thomas Henchman, his chief opponent being Mr David Macpherson. But there were hosts of other disputants who left behind them a crop of ephemeral literature from which much information can be gained as to the shipping of the period.

The eagerness of the Calcutta merchants for admission to the trade with Europe was whetted by partial concessions, beginning with the Act of 1793. When seven of the largest Indiamen were taken into the Navy in 1795, and when the first importation of rice from India was ordered, twenty-seven India-built ships were taken up by the Indian Governments and dispatched to England, not only with rice but also with other goods on account of the merchants in India. They were permitted to bring back return cargoes of British goods. With the passing of the crisis, these ships went out of the service again, to the extreme annoyance of their owners.

When Lord Mornington arrived in India, as Governor-

General, in 1798, the case for India-built shipping was put before him forcibly by the merchants of Calcutta, and convincingly by his brother. He accordingly licensed some ships to proceed to London in 1799 and again in 1800. His letter justifying this step, and urging the policy of wresting the trade from the foreigner, was warmly endorsed by Mr Henry Dundas, then President of the Board of Control. Pamphlets multiplied, and it looked for the time as if the campaign on behalf of the India-built ships was likely to succeed.

The ultimate failure of the campaign at that time can be traced to three distinct causes. The first was the success of the country ships. Among those who opposed their admission to the trade some had held that they could not compete with the Company's ships. But this was a half-hearted opposition; for, were the contention just, it could do no harm to admit them. Actual experiment, however, showed that they could compete only too effectively; and this turned mere disparagement into active alarm. Had the *Scaleby Castle*, the *Carron* and the rest proved themselves slow and unseaworthy, they might have been admitted to the fullest privileges. But they turned out to be exceptionally fast. Having the bad taste to sail out of season, they ruined the trade of the Company's officers. Here is a paragraph dating from October 1802:

> The trade of the commanders and officers of the East India Company is gradually on the decline. The private ships, which, according to the arrangement lately made, are permitted to freight from India, return thither with an European consignment at all periods of the year, and thus the market is constantly kept overstocked. Within the last three months six ships of the above description have sailed for Bengal, and not one of the ships belonging to the East India Company, which are engaged this season, is yet afloat!

Not only did they sail out of season; they also wasted no time in loading and unloading. This had been the complaint about the American ships. 'The celerity with which they conduct their commercial operations is surprising', wrote Mr Udney in 1800. 'Instances occurred last season of several of their ships disposing of their imports, purchasing their export cargoes, and leaving the port in twenty and twenty-five days from the date of their arrival.' How, it was asked, could British seamen hope to compete? But British seamen were, as a matter of fact, competing quite successfully. James Horsburgh, when in command of Messrs Bruce, Fawcett and Co.'s ship *Anna*, of 899 tons, built at Bombay in 1790, made at least one passage of amazing speed, both in sailing and stowage. He left the Lizard on 20 April 1802 and anchored at Bombay on 31 July. He discharged 900 tons of European cargo, reloaded with cotton, and sailed again on 25 August. Arriving in Canton River on 30 September, he was there for about two months. He sailed with a heavy cargo on 3 December, anchored at Bombay on 11 January 1803, and cleared the ship in eight days. The whole voyage had taken only nine months.

Achievements such as this, showing how dangerous the rivalry of the India-built ships would be, gave the Court of Directors some real cause for alarm. The second factor weakening the case of the merchants in India was their own exclusive attitude towards merchants in England. At first there had been a combined assault on the Company, but then the attackers had quarrelled among themselves. The London merchants had wanted the trade thrown open to all ships sailing from the Thames. The merchants of Liverpool, and Adam Smith's friends at Glasgow, talked of the desirability of throwing the trade open to all British ships. The Liverpool merchants were especially convinced of the necessity of this because of the decline and ultimate disappearance of the two branches of enterprise in which they had been principally interested—slaving, that is to say, and privateering. It was when as yet unaware of what cotton could do for them that these merchants began to speak of Free Trade. The Manchester School was thus about to come into being. But the merchants in India had no trace of this spirit. They demanded that they alone should be admitted to the trade, to the utter exclusion of both Liverpool and enlightenment. And in doing so they lost potential or actual allies in England and Scotland. What was perhaps even worse, they charged as high a freight as the East India Company when it came to shipping goods for other people.

The third factor in their failure was their attempt to capture the Court of Proprietors. A number of them backed their claims through their London agents by the purchase of East India stock with a view to contesting their case in the General Court. This threat of forming a regular party among the qualified proprietors, accompanied by numerous pamphlets and appeals to the public, was regarded as an attempt to undermine the Court of Directors. There was a strong reaction and the claims of the merchants in India were rejected in 1801 by large majorities in the General Court; the grounds of rejection being that they had no better right to admission than the merchants in England, and that the throwing open of the trade to these would produce the most disastrous results. Among the consequences anticipated was the colonial settlement of India, accompanied by the ruin, oppression and eventual extirpation of the natives. Until 1813, then, the situation was that produced by the defeat of the Calcutta merchants. Meanwhile, however, the separate agitation conducted from Liverpool and Glasgow was leading up to the triumph of 1813 and the final abolition of the Company's monopoly. The foundations of Free Trade were being built upon the rock of tangible success.

NOTES

Note on East India Patronage (see p. 16)

The process by which an appointment was made, whether as cadet or writer, was a simple one and admirably suited for any corrupt purpose. The candidate, or his parents, had first to secure the favour of one of the directors. This might be done through the kind offices of some mutual friend, supposing that the candidate's relatives had no acquaintance in the direction. The director, having agreed to favour the young man's interests, filled in and signed a card of nomination. The candidate then presented the card at the East India House, and was directed to the Shipping Office. There he was laconically interviewed by a clerk, who asked him his name, questioned him briefly, filed the nomination card, and told him to return on a given day and at a specified time. Coming for this second interview, the candidate brought with him a birth certificate. He was shown into a waiting room, and ultimately brought before the Court of Directors. Someone asked him his age, and checked it by a glance at the birth certificate. Someone more important then asked him whether he had read the conditions, and whether he wished to go out to India as a cadet? Reassured on this point, the Court then appointed him, told him of the fact and had him shown out. Two minutes completed the business and the young man was free to begin ordering his tropical outfit.

In this casual method of appointment there were one or two glaring defects. One was the absence of any mechanism for ensuring that the boy interviewed and the boy appointed were one and the same. Another was the failure to insist on any qualification of any kind. Worse, however, than either of these was the complete reliance placed on the directors' honesty, perception and care. To work well, the system demanded that each and every director should be filled with a strong moral sense of his responsibility in making a nomination. Men are not like that. Inevitably, some directors were dishonest; inevitably, some were careless. Among the directors were to be found the good-natured and easy-going, the absent-minded, the trustful and the stupid; and with all these characteristics might mingle that slight laxity in principle which the nineteenth century had scarcely as yet learnt to condemn. It is easy to see what the results of such a system would be in the hands of any but the most austere.

Giving away anything from eight to fifteen appointments each year, a director could hardly have much personal knowledge of every candidate he nominated. He relied, necessarily, on the recommendations of his friends. From accepting the advice of a friend in such a matter it was but a step to giving the friend a signed nomination card and allowing him to fill in what name he chose. If the friend were unreliable, such a card was apt to get into circulation, change hands at a price, and end up with some complete stranger who had bought it through an agency. It was not easy in such a case to fix the blame on the director who signed the card. He might have been the original vendor, but then again he might as easily have been imposed upon. Money could not always be traced; nor was it always money that changed hands. Church livings, army commissions and seats in Parliament were also in the market, and patronage can be bartered as well as bought.

What evidence there is concerning the sale of writerships and cadetships is derived from the report of the Committee of Inquiry which sat in 1809. From this it would appear that the traffic was well-established before 1787, and so had presumably grown up during the period 1760–80. Its existence was so notorious that agents did not hesitate to advertise for cadetships in the newspapers. The first directors to inquire into the matter were David Scott and Charles Grant. They succeeded in tracing some advertisements to a certain Mr Shee, who used to advertise under the name of Calvert. He had, at different times, an office in 'Marybone Street', or else could be heard of 'at a grocer's shop on the right hand side of Wimpole-street going on to Marybone-lane'. He lodged near there, at a tailor's. One of his sons was in the Bank of England, and his son-in-law was a clerk in the Stamp Office. So much was discovered without much difficulty. This was in 1800. Fresh from their conflict with some of the other directors over the Shipping question, Scott and Grant were anxious to discover more. They would probably have welcomed any means of tracing corruption to its source, knowing very well which directors were likely to be implicated. With a little patience, and perhaps by employing an *agent provocateur*, they learnt the details of one of Shee's transactions. Chiefly with the object of obtaining further information, they made the East India Company prosecute. The principal witness for the prosecution was a young man called Kinnard, who had paid Shee in advance for a cadetship which had not, so far, materialised. On becoming aware of the plot against him, Shee sought this man with the object of repaying him. But Scott and Grant had expected this. Kinnard could not be found, for the good reason that he had been sent to Scotland by sea. Davison, a clerk in the Secretary's Office of the India House, kept Kinnard supplied with money and saw to it that he continued to travel backwards and forwards between London and Leith until the trial began. According to Shee, another witness of the name of Wright was sent out of the way and, for failing to appear in court, was given a pursership in an Indiaman for his son. The importance attached to Kinnard's absence before the trial was this: had Shee succeeded in repaying him, the only offence committed would have been an attempt to sell a cadetship—for which attempt the Company might perhaps have claimed damages. Were there no repayment, on the other hand, Shee could be prosecuted for selling what he did not possess, that is, for obtaining money under false pretences. Prosecuted he was, and the men who had instigated the prosecution saw to it that he did not escape. He was convicted at Clerkenwell and duly sentenced to twelve months' imprisonment in Newgate.

Although apparently successful, Scott and Grant failed to obtain the information they wanted. Shee made no disclosures in the course of the trial. In conversation with Davison, before the case came on, he remarked indeed that 'he had sold fourteen Cadets in the preceding year, and two or three Writers', but he implicated no one else and gave, in particular, no hint as to which of the directors were involved. After his conviction, he was promised a pardon if he would give full particulars of all his transactions. He refused to disclose anything. The prosecution was therefore, as regards its real object, a failure. All that remained to do was to reward Kinnard. On the recommendation of Mr Henry Smith, the Chairman appointed him to a cadetship at St Helena, on the grounds that no respectable cadet could be persuaded to go there.

Shee was convicted in 1800, and nothing further was done in the matter for some years. How exactly the scandal concerning Mr George Woodford Thellusson came to light is not very apparent. According to the evidence given before the Committee of Inquiry appointed by the House of Commons, Thellusson suddenly became aware in 1809 that his friends had been abusing his confidence, and went at once to the Court of Directors. It seems more probable that he was forced to do this by the persistence of rumours against him. His own story, for what it is worth, begins as follows:

> ...I believe it was somewhere about three weeks ago; I cannot recollect the day. I called at a friend's house in the city (Mr Battye) and conversing upon other matters, as I was going away, he said: 'I thought I had something to say to you, now I recollect it.' I returned back, and his words, as far as I can recollect, were 'I wish you Gentlemen Directors would be a little more careful of the distribution of your Patronage; not that I conceive that any is sold by the Directors, but I know of a Cadetship that has lately been sold, and for which a large sum of money was given.' I asked him what and how, and he told me: 'I know that £500 has been given for it.' I told him I believed he was wrong informed, because the utmost I had ever heard of these things going for was £300, and he must be mistaken. He told me, no, he was not; that he knew the person, and knew the young man's name. I asked him if he would allow me to mention this to my brother Directors....

In considering this tale, one had to ask oneself certain questions. Either Thellusson was familiar with the sale of cadetships, or else he was not. If the fact of cadetships being sold was known to him before, why should he rush off to inform the other directors? If he was so easily shocked, it would be reasonable to ask why he did not tell them when first he heard of the traffic. If, on the other hand, he had been ignorant of the practice, why should he reply, in effect—'Impossible! That is far above the market price.' There would seem to be another side to the story, which the Committee (perhaps deliberately) failed to discover.

What the Committee's discoveries amounted to was this: three writerships had been sold during the period 1806–8, all in the gift of Mr Thellusson. The prices paid were, respectively, £3500, 3500 guineas, and £3000 together with the presentation to the next vacancy in a Church living worth £300 a year. The first two were for Bengal, the last for Madras. There was no proof that Thellusson knew of the sale. It was furthermore found that at least eighteen cadetships had been sold during the period 1805–8, for sums varying from £150 to 500 guineas, and averaging at about £233. The directors who had made the various nominations were, besides Thellusson, Sir T. Metcalfe, Sir W. Fraser, Sir L. Darell, and Messrs Robinson, Thornton, Parry, Cotton, Toone, Manship, Devaynes and Bebb. There was no proof that any of these directors had been aware of any financial transaction. Others whose confidence had been similarly abused were Lord Castlereagh and H.R.H. the Duke of Clarence. To be proved guilty of carelessness in such good company was no very serious misfortune. Thellusson was the only one to lose his directorship as a result of the inquiry.

In the course of the Committee's investigations, Shee was questioned once more, being brought from the Fleet Prison for the purpose. It appeared that, although he had been resident for the last five or six years 'within the Rules of the Fleet', he had carried on his business through one of his sons, who was still at large. His evidence was somewhat unsatisfactory, and far less interesting than that of a friend of his called Robert Sharman.

Can you recollect any conversation that you at any time had with the elder Shee, relating to East India transactions, except those you have stated to the Committee?—He has said so much to me about East India appointments that I cannot state it all; he has said, that every Direction was worth six thousand a year and that he could prove it any day; but I always thought he was very extravagant in his way of talking about it, but so he has said repeatedly: I used to hear him say, though the East India Directors do not get the money, their Attornies do....

Among the curious stories heard by the Committee concerning East India patronage, the following is typical. Mr Stephen Lushington, LL.D., M.P., told of the individual who invaded his chambers one morning offering him 'a Seat in Parliament for Weobly, for seven years complete, independent of all obligation' in exchange for a writership. This transaction fell through when it was discovered that he who made this fair offer was not what he claimed to be—an emissary from the Marquis of Bath—but a mere adventurer of the most disreputable kind. Another remarkable story concerned the appointment of a man called Lewis to a cadetship. As he was a mulatto, he was not eligible for any such post. So he hired a young hatter called Phillips to impersonate him at the India House. Phillips performed this simple task in return for a fee of twenty guineas. He came before the Committee as the result of an attempt to blackmail Mr Toone when the inquiry began.

That the whole question of corrupt appointments was investigated so thoroughly may have been due, in part, to the fact that

Charles Grant was at this time in office as chairman. But the subsequent dismissal of the young men whose nominations had been sold them was something of a farce; for all, or nearly all, were immediately reappointed.

See 'The Debates held at the East India House on Wednesday, the 17th of December, 1800 and on Tuesday, January 20, 1801. On which latter Day the following Resolution was Moved: "That it be the opinion of this Court, that the Enquiry into the alledged abuse of Patronage ought to be continued."' Reported by William Woodfall. 1801. pp. 96.

Note on White Women in India (see p. 35)

White women going out to India were not very numerous. In 1810 it was estimated that the European women in Bengal could not number as many as two hundred and fifty. As the society of the Presidency must have included two or three thousand men of some social standing, not one in ten of them can have been married. As a matter of fact, only a small proportion of the gentlemen could afford it. It cost £500 to send a lady out to India. For her to live in comfort cost another £600 a year over and above the husband's previous expenditure—£300 a year being the very minimum on which she could live at all, without moving in society. To send a child to Europe cost about £150. As the domestic staff of even a bachelor establishment might number forty or fifty, and as a carriage was essential to the position of any of the higher officials, it is not to be wondered at that most of them preferred to keep a native mistress.

Supposing that British India contained altogether as many as five hundred white women, that number could be maintained only by the annual arrival of fifty or sixty new-comers. A proportion of these might be married before they sailed, either to Anglo-Indians home on leave or else to men of some rank going out for the first time. The remainder, the unmarried, would fall into two distinct categories; those who were going to join friends in India, and those who were not. Those in the first category were often young women of good position but small fortune, sent to India on the invitation of some married relative or friend already resident there. On arrival, they would be met and welcomed into a respectable home. Convention then demanded that the hostess should at once give a series of parties, to which all interested bachelors might come. These gatherings were a recognised institution, and little attempt was made to conceal their function. The young women were deliberately displayed and frankly inspected, often receiving instantaneous offers of marriage. Those not very soon married would not be married at all, for their chief attraction lay in a complexion which the climate would ruin in a few months.

The fate of the women who had no friends to join was one of almost inconceivable barbarity. Those in this second category might be middle-aged women staking their all on a final attempt to get married. These at least knew what they were about. More often, however, they were young girls whose parents or guardians saw fit to dispose of them in this way. Some might be illegitimate children, exiled to save their begetter an awkward explanation. One might be the eldest daughter of a clergyman, sent out in the hope that her marriage might benefit the younger children; another might be the unwanted child of parents living apart. Occasionally, too, a girl would be sent to join friends, only to find, on arrival, that her friends were dead. Whatever might be the reason, however, for a girl being friendless, her fate was much the same. She had to accept the first offer of marriage she received. Although taken from a novel, the following description comes very near the truth:

> ...A pilot brig soon approached the ship, and in the evening she was safely moored in Diamond Harbour. An express was immediately forwarded to Calcutta, giving an account of the arrival of the Tigris, and a particular description of the names, ages, and accomplishments of all the young adventurers who had come out to market for husbands.
>
> On the Tuesday following, a grand dinner was announced on board the Tigris. The young ladies were all recommended to put on their best apparel, and were most scientifically lectured by the Bibi Indigo and Captain Jessamy, upon their conduct on that auspicious day.
>
> The budgerows, with the rich sallow Europeans, arrived in due time; every Saib attended by his hookabedah. Fitzjohn and Jim stationed themselves on the gangway to observe the stateliness and self-complacency with which these "Counts Rupees" strutted up to Jessamy, who stood hat in hand to receive them.
>
> The young ladies had taken their stations on the cushions along and athwart the transom of the after cabin, leaving a space between each, for a gentleman to sit down. Bibi, Miss Jones, and three middle-aged tabbies, formed the first half-moon line in advance; so

that the dear petticoats appeared like the combined fleets at the battle of Trafalgar, each leaving an opening to pass through the first, to the second line.

As soon as the old boys had put on their well-washed jackets, the whole eleven, having broken through the first line, were introduced separately, and very deliberately, to the seven angels, which formed the second or transom line.

The young ladies had already been given to understand, that these were all men of considerable independence; and that the person who selected and sat down by them, would lead them to the dinner-table, and probably make them an offer of marriage before the dinner-cloth was removed....

Gentleman Jack, a Naval Story. W. Johnson Neale. London, 1837. 3 vols. Vol. II, pp. 310. See p. 150.

The author goes on to explain that the elderly suitors on such an occasion agreed with each other beforehand that no girl who refused one offer should receive another. Pressure was also brought to bear by the captain, who announced that 'every lady must leave the ship to-morrow'. To complete the scene, it need only be added that the girls were sometimes too young even to understand why they had been sent to India. There was apparently nothing in all this to offend the ethics of the time. Wrath was reserved for the child who fell in love with some other child in the course of the voyage.

Note on the arming of East Indiamen (see p. 160)

As an exception to the theory here propounded that an East Indiaman, armed for war, did not carry more than forty-eight guns, it may be mentioned that the *Royal George* was equipped in 1808 with sixty-two guns and five hundred men, including some troops acting as marines. The *Royal George*, successively under Captains Timins and Gribble, seems to have been the crack ship of the China fleet. In 1807 she performed the voyage from Portsmouth to Madras with over five hundred soldiers on board, making a total ship's company of six hundred and sixty. During a five months' passage there was little illness, no punishments, and only one death. On another occasion Admiral Sir Edward Pellew sent the ship a message: 'tell the captain if he had not his main topmast staysail in the brails, I should have taken his ship for a frigate'; a compliment as regards her smartness which would scarcely be applicable as regards her size. The *Royal George*, which made a passage of four months in 1823, was not the same ship, but her successor.

Note on the East Indiaman's speed (see p. 162)

Another factor affecting the Indiaman's speed after 1815 was the absence of any further need to sail in convoy. The act of keeping together ordinarily involved a good deal of delay. It was the cessation of the war, as well as the spur of competition, which allowed individual ships to make exceptionally fast passages. As an example of these one may quote the passage in 1829 of the H.C.S. *Marquis of Wellington* from England to Bengal in eighty-one days—a little under the time taken by H.M.S. *Medusa* in her record voyage of 1805–6. On the other hand, when the skill and recklessness of particular seamen is set on one side, it does not appear that the Indiamen themselves varied a great deal in their capacity for speed. In 1815, for instance, the twelve China ships separated off Java and yet all reached the Downs within a period of twenty-four hours. Thenceforward, Indiamen occasionally performed the passage from China to England in less than a hundred days, but the difference between one ship and another was never very great.

Note on the Shipping Interest (see p. 173)

An earlier period in the history of the Shipping Interest is well illustrated by the following passage from a pamphlet which appeared in 1778:

> By the appointment of a Committee of Proprietors in 1772, when, by a series of the most gross mismanagement, the Company had been brought to the verge of bankruptcy, the mysterious transactions of the Directors, until that time, in a great measure, impenetrable to any but the Elect, were laid fully open to those of the Committee who were inclined to undertake the examination of such voluminous proceedings; and among other matters that occurred on that occasion, their report of the enormous expences that attended the business of their shipping, had attracted the particular attention of the proprietors; and another Committee was appointed....
>
> It happened indeed, unluckily, that the Chairman of the Company, at that time, was too deeply concerned in the shipping business, and no one knew better how to avail himself of his station. He was

possessed of talents particularly well adapted to the governing principles, and politics of the times, at the India-House. He could not, in his own name at least, engage in the profitable business of ship husbandry, whilst he continued in the Direction, as being expressly contrary to the letter of the 9th bye-law; but it could be no legal objection to his brother's being a principal dealer in that branch; and although it had been also provided by the same law, 'That no ship should be hired, or freighted by the Directors, in which any Director was directly or indirectly concerned,' he had interest, and address sufficient, to persuade his brethren in the Direction, that being Rope-maker General to all the Blackwall Indiamen, which were by much the greater part of the Company's shipping, ought not to be considered as within the letter or spirit of that law. And however insignificant such a business might appear, he contrived by dexterity and good management in it, to amass as much wealth as many reputed Nabobs, but without the least tincture of their dissipating spirit; for he lived poor, and died rich.

From his intimate connection with a numerous shipping party, which had been firmly cemented by mutual interest, with but a scanty proportion of knowledge in other matters, and a liberal one of left-handed wisdom, he had acquired a considerable influence in the Direction; and contrived, by his management, to frustrate the honest endeavours of the Committee and disinterested Proprietors....

Considerations on the important benefits to be derived from the East-India Company's building and navigating their own ships. By the author of the essay *On the Rights of the East India Company.* London, 1778, pp. 37.

Note on John Wordsworth (see p. 186)

The John Wordsworth mentioned here as late commander of the H.C.S. *Earl of Abergavenny* was the younger brother of the poet, William Wordsworth. He first went to sea in 1787. After a voyage to Barbadoes, he joined the *Earl of Abergavenny* in 1789. He made several voyages to India in this ship, which was partly owned, apparently, by a relative. We hear of him staying with William and Dorothy Wordsworth at Grasmere in 1800. He made two more voyages, evidently as first or second mate, and succeeded to the command of the *Earl of Abergavenny* in 1805. He wrote to the poet from Portsmouth on 24 January of that year, telling him of a slight collision there had been in the Downs between his ship and the *Warren Hastings*. He sailed with convoy a week or ten days later, but, owing to an incompetent pilot (so it is said), his ship went aground off Portland Bill on 5 February and became a total wreck. John Wordsworth was drowned, with the greater part of his crew. The tragedy was the greater in that the *Earl of Abergavenny* had sailed with a crew of two hundred and another two hundred soldiers and passengers. In his last letter, Captain Wordsworth wrote: 'I shall have sufficient employment on my hands to keep all these people in order....' He is said to have died with exemplary courage, remaining at his post to the last. William Wordsworth wrote several poems concerning this catastrophe, notably one in which his brother figures as 'The happy warrior'.

Note on the Timins Family (see p. 195)

The close connection which existed between the Navy and the Maritime Service is well illustrated by the facts recorded of the Timins family. There were, apparently, four brothers. The eldest was in the Royal Marines, and was the senior officer of that corps at Trafalgar, living to hold the rank of Colonel. The second son, Captain Timins, was in the Company's service and commanded the *Royal George* at Pulo Aor in 1804. He had begun life in the Navy and was a midshipman in H.M.S. *Experiment* when she captured the famous French frigate *Belle Poule*. He later served under Captain Graeme at the action of the Dogger Bank. He was the real hero of the China fleet in 1804, and it was a very fortunate circumstance that he should have transferred to the Company's service. He came in the end to own the *Royal George*, putting his younger brother, Captain C. Timins, in command. This officer, the third son, had also served in the Navy. He had been a lieutenant in Sir Hyde Parker's flagship at Copenhagen; a fact which did him so little good that he forthwith left the service. Finally, there was the youngest of the family, George Timins, who was a lieutenant in the Navy, and who apparently so remained.

Note on the Maritime Service uniform (see p. 197)

The uniform worn by officers in the East India Company's maritime service is shown in a fashion plate by W. Alais in the *Gentleman's Magazine of Fashion*, Vol. II, 1829. The plate is reproduced in *Ships and Men*, David Hannay, 1910. It shows a captain and chief mate in consultation, the latter holding a speaking trumpet, the former leaning on his sword. By that date the full buttoned-back skirts of the coat had vanished, leaving a garment which the modern tail-coat closely resembles. The lapels, broader than now worn, were gold-embroidered. With coats very much the same, each officer wears a white or buff waistcoat, but whereas the captain wears breeches and stockings, the mate has a pair of blue trousers with white hosiery showing beneath. They both wear a 'fore-and-aft' cocked hat.

The seamen of an Indiaman, like those of the Navy, wore no uniform. Their typical outfit would probably, however, include the following items: Blue jacket, blue or flannel waistcoat, red or checked shirt, blue, or white trousers, kerchief, white stockings and shoes. A Guernsey or canvas frock, for bad weather, was the alternative garb, with possibly a canvas cap to match. Spare shirts, stockings and drawers, together with blankets and soap and personal belongings, were carried on board in a canvas kit-bag. To fit out the seaman, little more was needed apart from a knife, some twine, and a stock of chewing tobacco.

Note on maintaining discipline in the Maritime Service (see p. 198)

Although perhaps seldom worn in an Indiaman, the sidearms to which the officers were entitled had a certain usefulness. The sword was not yet a weapon of merely decorative value. Its chief function was in quelling mutinies. These were apt to occur, even in the Company's service. One of the most serious was that which took place in the H.C.S. *Belvidere* at Whampoa in 1787. It was put down by the chief mate (the captain being ashore, ill with dysentery) with the assistance of boats from the other Indiamen. The senior captain of the China fleet, Captain Dundas, held a Court of Inquiry—the Company's equivalent for a Court Martial—and sentenced the two ringleaders to be flogged round the fleet. Two other offenders received five dozen lashes each, three others, four dozen, and two others, two dozen. Dundas, brought to trial in England, had his legal expenses paid by the East India Company. He was fully acquitted, and complimented by the judges. There was a mutiny on board the *Royal George* in 1804, which Captain Timins quelled with a pistol. A sword, on the other hand, was used by Captain Kennard Smith in suppressing a mutiny in the H.C.S. *Minerva*. The same weapon sufficed Captain Mitchell, who had to deal with a mutiny in the H.C.S. *Bridgwater* in 1823. At the first act of disobedience, he fetched his sidearm. When a ringleader, whom he seized, made some resistance, Mitchell drew his sword and cut him down. Of the men who tried to interfere, he cut down one, wounded another, and seized the third. The rest fled and discipline was restored.

Indiamen seem occasionally to have carried letters of marque, presumably at their owners' desire, and perhaps especially when heavily armed with a view to sailing without convoy. A letter of marque carried with it the possibility of much greater severity towards mutineers. There was a case in point in 1798, when Mr Reid, second mate of the H.C.S. *King George*, assaulted his commander, Captain Colnett. Reid was tried by court martial on board H.M.S. *Stately* and sentenced to two years' imprisonment in the Marshalsea. Had the offence not taken place ashore at the Cape, the sentence would have been death.

Note on Captains' investments (see p. 201)

In the last letter written by Captain John Wordsworth to his brother, the poet, dated from Portsmouth, 24 January, 1805, the following passage occurs:

> My investment is well laid in, and my voyage thought by most persons the first of the season; and if we are so fortunate as to get safe and soon to Bengal,—I mean before any other ship of the season,—I have no doubt but that I shall make a very good voyage of it, if not a *very great* one. At least this is the general opinion. I have got my investment upon the best of terms, having paid ready money for a great part of it, which I was enabled to do by one gentleman lending me £5000. It amounts to about £20,000 in money.
>
> The passengers are all down, and we are anxiously expecting to sail. We shall muster at my table 36 or 38 persons. This must alone give me a great deal of trouble, to provide provisions etc. for them. I was obliged to apply to the Court of Directors to have some of the passengers turned out of the ship, which was granted. I thought at one time I should have had 45 persons at my table....

What we learn about this investment, unusually large as it must have been, throws some light on the way in which the capital to invest was almost invariably borrowed. Of the £20,000 here mentioned, John Wordsworth himself supplied only £3000. It was part of the sum of £8500 paid to the Wordsworth family by

Lord Lonsdale, in settlement of his father's debt. And, of this £3000, it seems that £1200 was a loan from William and Dorothy. It is probable that the investment was insured.

See *The Letters of the Wordsworth Family, from 1787 to 1855*. Collected and edited by William Knight. 3 vols. Boston, 1907.

Note on impressment and 'encouragements' (see p. 213)

You may talk o' the hardships of pressing—your man-hunting—and the likes of such lubberly prate; but if there's never no ent'ring, how the h—ll can you help it? Men-o'-war must be mann'd, as well as your marchanmen—marchanmen must have their regular convoys; for if they havn't, you know, then there's a stopper-over-all upon trade:—so take the concarn how you will—'by or large'—there's not a King's Bencher' among you can mend it. Bear up for Blackwall—ship aboard of an Ingee-man, and see how you will be badgered about, by a set o' your boheaing-hysun-mundungo-built beggars! Get hurt in their sarvice—lose a finger or fin by the chime of a cask in the hold—or fall from aloft, and fracture your pate—then see where's your pension or 'smart.' I'm none o' your arguficators—none o' your long-winded lawyers, like Paddy Quin the sweeper, or Collins the 'captain o' the head;' but d—n it, you know, there's never no working to wind'ard of truth.

The Naval Sketch-Book; or the Service afloat and ashore. By an officer of rank. 2 vols. 2nd ed. London, 1826, pp. 304. 'A galley story' (p. 28).

This may be taken to represent the contemporary naval view with regard to impressment. The character speaking, however, is made to do the East India Company an injustice in the matter of pensions and compensation for injury. The truth was that every Indiaman had a printed form displayed somewhere between her decks in which the following 'encouragements' were announced:

To the widow, children, father, or mother of every seaman that shall lose his life in defence of the ship, as aforesaid, thirty pounds. To every seaman that shall lose a leg or arm or both, in such defence, thirty pounds. To every seaman that shall receive any other wound, such sum of money as the said Court of Directors shall think fit, upon producing a certificate from their commander or superior officer touching their merits. That every seaman so wounded in defence of the ship shall be cured of his wounds at the charge of the said Company and owners.

There is here, it is true, no mention of compensation for accidental injuries; but the East India Company was usually generous in such matters, and the owners scarcely less so.

Note on the Navy and the Maritime Service (see p. 218)

In considering the comparative advantages of the Navy and the Company's service, the following extracts from Biden's work on Naval Discipline may be of interest:

> It is a favourite opinion among naval men, that merchant seamen are so discontented in *harbour*, that they frequently enter into His Majesty's ships. True, to a certain extent; but let us examine the cause. A man-of-war enters a foreign port, with but little other duty to perform but square the yards and water the ship. Mark the contrast.—An Indiaman in Bombay harbour, stowing and screwing cotton, the thermometer at 95, work going on from daylight till dusk. A West Indiaman, stowing sugar and rum etc. In a word, the most laborious duties of a merchant-ship are in harbour, while on board the man-of-war all is comparative ease....
>
> The scale of provisions on board a Company's ship is equally liberal with that under the direction of the Admiralty. If *less grog* is served out, our seamen have a larger proportion of *meat*; and every attention is scrupulously paid to the quality of provisions....
>
> Footnote: No one circumstance has operated so favourably in aid of the health and comfort of seamen as the improved mode of victualling ships in the Company's service since I entered it: tea or coffee for their breakfast, etc.; when, from 1803 to 1810, we had no such indulgence.
>
> An able and experienced officer, to whom the maritime interests of this country are much indebted, describes the condition of a seaman, on board a merchant-ship, as one of peculiar hardship and privation....I yield to his ideas about the superior comforts and ease of duty on board a King's ship; and could a seaman, when once he knew the true character of his officers, be sure of continuing to serve under them, his life would be far preferable to the merchant seaman's....But as another excellent author upon this subject observes, the man-of-war's man cannot forget 'that his happiness or misery, while in the service, solely depends on the personal character of a single individual, who may be repeatedly changed.'
>
> C. Biden, *Naval Discipline.* 1830.

However true it may have been that a man-of-war offered more comfort than a merchant ship, and certainly less work, it must not be forgotten that this advantage was outweighed in the East Indies by the length of time a man-of-war might be on the station. A man who joined, or was impressed into, a ship of the East Indies squadron had but a dubious chance of ever seeing England again. He might easily be kept in the East until he died. In almost every case an Indiaman would be paid off again within eighteen months.

Note on the regulations concerning recruits (see p. 229)

In the orders and instructions issued to the Commanders of ships in the Company's service in 1814, especial emphasis is laid on the need for preventing the escape of recruits, Lascars and Chinese. An allowance of five shillings was made for each recruit, to be spent on fresh provisions during the voyage. If no call was made at any port, that sum was to be paid to each recruit on landing in India. One provision laid down 'That you and your officers do take particular care of the Company's recruits, and not permit any person on board to beat or ill use them on any account'. The recruits' uniform consisted of red jackets with blue facings, white breeches and blue caps. If sailing at a cold time of year, these garments were actually worn when embarking and until a warm latitude was reached. But, whenever possible, the uniform was put away in a box and the boys issued with canvas frocks instead. If an enemy was encountered, the recruits were to be swiftly arrayed in their red jackets and stationed on the poop so as to impress the foe by an appearance of military alertness. They had no arms, however, and but little training. It was expected that they should make themselves useful about the ship, doing the work of 'waisters'. They were liable to be punished for any neglect, just as the sailors were.

Note on missionaries on board ship (see p. 243)

Besides the clergy employed by the East India Company, there were occasional missionaries sent out to India, both Anglican and and nonconformist. Charles Grant financed a small and not very successful effort of this kind; and Dr Carey went out as a missionary as early as 1793. 'In bad weather', he writes, 'you are not likely to find your fellow-passengers bland and courteous....' He seems, however, to have behaved with great sense and moderation, avoiding the 'enthusiastic' conduct likely to give offence.

Missionaries are generally allowed to conduct public religious exercises; though some captains have been, and still are, sufficiently prejudiced and absurd to prohibit them, judging that, if they take hold of the mind of a sailor, they disqualify in some way, they scarcely know how, for duty. Now and then, upon a very fine Sunday, they think it may do no harm to read the prayers of the Church of England. When that is done, they consider 'there is an end of it;' but what praying and preaching may lead to, is hard to tell.

Memoir of William Carey, D.D., late missionary to Bengal; Professor of Oriental languages in the College of Fort William, Calcutta. Eustace Carey. London, 1836, pp. 630, with frontispiece portrait.

In writing thus, Carey misjudged the commanders of the Company's ships. It was not hard for them to tell where revivalist religion might lead them. The problem of the 'psalm-singer' captain or officer was a familiar one in the Navy, and it was common knowledge that prayer-meetings among the men soon put an end to all discipline. Indiamen were not exempt from such experience. There were instances of a fanatic like Martyn causing no end of trouble, if only among the passengers.

Note on the instructions issued for troops on board ship (see p. 243)

The future Duke of Wellington's ideas were mostly embodied in the instructions issued in 1807 and 1808 to officers commanding troops 'embarked on board Ships belonging to the Honourable the East-India Company'. By these instructions, the officers in the Company's service were to take rank by seniority, but only after the Cape had been passed. There was to be a guard mounted, with sentries, and the troops were to be divided into watches.

The use of dumb-bells, and any diversion calculated for the purpose of bodily exercise, should be permitted as frequently as possible, as of the utmost consequence in maintaining the health and strength of the men....

Particular attention must be paid to the regulations of the ship with respect to lights, and no smoking be permitted between decks....

The strictest attention must be paid to prevent the men from sleeping on the deck in the warm weather, which they are very apt to do, and which is generally productive of fevers and fluxes.

The men are to wash their feet, and comb their hair with a small-tooth comb, every morning: they are to wash their bodies, shave, and put on clean linen twice at least a week, and to have the means of changing their clothes when wet....

The married people are not to be intermixed with the single men, but should have a part of the deck allotted particularly for their accommodation. They are not, however, to obstruct the circulation of the air by putting up blankets during the day time. The women, as well as the men, must rise at six in the morning, when all their partitions must be removed for the day.

The bedding being brought up, the men are to proceed in sweeping, scrubbing, and scraping the orlop deck, which must not be washed oftener than once a week, and then only when the weather is perfectly dry. Fumigation is strongly recommended, and should be resorted to as frequently as circumstances will permit....

The Officer of the Watch is always to be present, and to superintend the cleaning of the orlop deck, or that part of the ship allotted to the troops; and when properly cleaned and arranged, to report to the Commanding Officer that it is ready for his inspection.

At dinner time the Officer on duty is to attend to see that the men are regular at their messes, that their rum is mixed with at least three parts of water to one of spirit; and should he observe any circumstance of neglect in victualling the troops, he is to report the same to the Officer commanding, who, if necessary, will communicate it to the Commander of the ship....

The whole watch to be constantly on deck, except when the rain obliges them to go down for shelter. In fine weather, every man should be on duty the whole day.

It is advisable that soldiers, on embarking, should be provided with canvas frocks and trowsers, to wear while on board....

By command of His Royal Highness
the Commander in Chief

Horse Guards — Harry Calvert
24th May, 1807 — Adjutant General

The assumption in these orders is that the troops will swing their hammocks on the lower or orlop deck. This was doubtless the custom when the detachment was a large one, as when a whole regiment was going out at the same time. When the troops were less numerous, it is more probable that they slept on the main or gun-deck.

Note on the regulations concerning passengers (see p. 284)

Regulations for the Preservation of a good Order on board the Company's Ships:

At a

COURT OF DIRECTORS

held on

Thursday, the 17th January 1799

It having come to the knowledge of this Court, that the good order and wholesome practices, formerly observed in the Company's ships, have been laid aside, and late hours and the consequent mischiefs introduced, by which the ship has been endangered, and the decorum and propriety, which should be maintained, destroyed; they have thought proper to frame the following regulations on these points, to which the readiest acquiescence is expected; and any person offending against them will incur the Court's highest displeasure, viz.

Resolved, therefore, That in order to prevent any accident from the fire and lights being kept up beyond those hours usually observed in all proper disciplined ships, it is strictly enjoined, that no fire be kept up beyond eight at night, unless for the use of the sick, and then only in a stove, and that candles be extinguished by nine between decks, and ten, at latest, in the cabins; and that the utmost precaution be observed, to prevent their being visible to any vessel passing in the night.

That the hour for dinner be not later than two o'clock; and when the Commander of the ship retires from table, either after dinner or supper, the Passengers and Officers of the ship retire also.

That the Captain be strictly enjoined to pay due attention to the comfortable accommodation and liberal treatment of his Passengers, at the same time setting them an example of sobriety and decorum, as he values the pleasure of the Court.

That any excess or disorderly behaviour below, being equally repugnant to the good order and discipline of the ship, will on representation, be noticed by the Court of Directors, and not fail to incur their displeasure.

That any improper conduct of the Officers of the ship towards the Passengers or each other, shall be quietly made known to the Commander, who shall weigh the circumstances with impartiality, and if conciliation be ineffectual, decide according to the best of his judgement, and every person concerned be expected quietly to conform thereto; but should any one think himself aggrieved thereby, he may appeal to the Governor and Council of the first Settlement the ship arrives at; or if homeward-bound, to the Court of Directors.

The diversity of characters and dispositions which must meet on ship board makes some restraint upon all necessary; and any one offending against good manners, or known usages and customs, will, on representation to the Court, be severely noticed.

Resolved, That the said regulations be printed and delivered to every Passenger, proceeding to or from India or China, previous to their going on board; that they be enjoined a strict observance thereof; and that the Commanders have the most positive orders to conform thereto.

(Signed by the Order of the said Court)

James Cobb

Secretary

Note on the passenger's life on board ship (see p. 292)

Dislike for a sea voyage was not as universal among soldiers as Marryat supposed. The following extract from a journal of the period shows another aspect of the question:

> No situation can be more lively and agreeable than that of a young officer on board an Indiaman. Hope presents to his youthful mind a bright picture. The Captain and officers of the ship are generally attentive and gentlemanly, and a large party of ladies and brother passengers sit down every day to excellent cheer, and exhilarating wines, at the cuddy table, while the evenings are spent in dancing on the quarter-deck, either to an organ or the ship's band. At the same time, the lee-side is occupied by the soldiers and their wives, whose unsophisticated steps form a ludicrous contrast to the graceful movements on the other quarter. Time flies, and his flight is unheeded amidst the diversions found in music, books, drawing, backgammon, chess, and piquet. It is most to be dreaded, in such a situation, that quarrels should arise and disturb the harmony that ought to reign; but fortunately on this occasion there were so many old officers returning to their regiments, and such proper discipline exercised by the senior, who commanded the troops on board, that every aberration from concord was checked, and the whole kept in proper tune. Nothing was wanting but a few pretty girls, to make out a quadrille, or a love story; but it so happened that no Celia went to

the land of husbands at this time, and our young adventurer therefore had no opportunity of losing his heart.

Fifteen years in India; or sketches of a soldier's life. From the journal of [R. G. Wallace] an officer in his Majesty's service. London, 1822, pp. 540.

Note on East India captains and passengers (see p. 292)

The following account of a passenger's day dates from a later period than the one we are considering. Nevertheless, and though taken from a novel, it seems sufficiently authentic to deserve quotation.

> The mode of life on board an Indiaman is admirably adapted to ensure the greatest amount available of comfort and happiness, to a circle of people all, or nearly all of whom are rendered particularly fractious (to use a mild term) by their total lack of any occupation more serious than a search after—what Lady Blessington extols as 'Il dolce far niente', and if the party be, by nature, tolerably agreeable, time passes rapidly.
>
> Few passengers can sleep after five o'clock; at that hour the sailors begin to holy-stone the decks, and the noise occasioned by the operation is almost as effectual as a guilty conscience is said to be, in murdering sleep. The gentlemen parade the deck, *en robe-de-chambre* and sip coffee—the ladies very wisely remain in bed. At eight the gong sounds for breakfast. Tea is made in a huge barrel-like urn suspended in one corner of the cuddy, while chops, and cutlets, fresh salmon, red herrings, rice preserves, treacle, butter, biscuit, and hot rolls grace the long narrow table that extends from end to end of the cuddy or dining-room. This apartment is on the quarter-deck—usually aft of the mizen-mast—twelve or fourteen feet wide, and extending right 'athwart-ships'.
>
> At the centre of the table sits the captain—the first-mate is opposite to him—and the doctor and purser do the honours of the extremities. The passengers are seated most punctiliously according to rank, the captain's right hand being the post of honour; and during the whole voyage no one changes places.
>
> The morning is principally spent by all parties on deck, or in their own cabins, until half-past eleven (seven bells, in nautical phraseology), when the captain goes on deck to take the observations, surrounded by all the men and boys who rejoice in the possession of sextant or quadrant. At the instant the sun reaches its zenith, the chief mate is ordered to strike eight bells, which command he repeats to the midshipman of the watch; by this time, all the watches

and time-pieces on board are daily corrected—and as it must, of course, depend upon the ship's course, it sometimes happens that the day is nearly twenty-five hours long, or only twenty-three, according to her course, east or west, and the rate at which she has gone.

While the captain, in the retirement of his cabin, is engaged in working the observation, the same process being carried on in various other parts of the vessel by the other 'scientifics', a busy scene may be witnessed in the cuddy, when, attracted by the *strong* influence of *strong* waters, brandy, rum, Geneva, port, and sherry—to say nothing of biscuit, ginger-bread and cake, the passengers are all assembled, one hand tenaciously grasping food for the body, the other doing the mental by holding a chart, on which the eyes of the party are intently fixed—examining the course and progress of the vessel, as delineated in red ink. Presently the steward makes his appearance having a number of 'chits' (Anglicé 'notes') in his hand; one of which he presents to each lady.

They usually run something in the following style—

Madam

I am happy to inform you that we are in Lat. 30., 25 north—Long. 40., 0 west—Run, 130 miles.

I am

Madam

etc. etc.

And a sketch of some vessel frequently graces the vacant corner. Ostensibly, indeed, these notes are merely a little mark of courtesy—equally laconic to all—but I must admit that here, as elsewhere, appearances are sometimes deceitful. That trifling as is the space allotted, they do sometimes contain rather more interesting topics of discussion than mere Latitude and Longitude—that, in short, to a good-looking, agreeable captain, fond of flirtation, they form as pleasant a medium of communication as heart can desire—and did the fair *writees* ever *compare notes*, some curious histories would be developed.

En passant, I may as well remark that I know no situation in life which confers so many privileges on its possessor as are attached to the post of captain of an Indiaman—always provided that he be a *gentleman*, and a good-tempered, agreeable person. Talk of the power of an absolute sovereign! his Majesty of Prussia for instance! pshaw! Who would compare a reign of fear with one of love? who can measure dominion over lives, with sway over hearts! It is nothing, a mere drop in the bucket, compared with the absolute dominion of an East India Captain....

There is one particular, and very interesting class of his liege subjects who are more than any other under his protection and control. In plain terms, he usually has six, eight, or ten young ladies under his care (I *have* known the number extend to sixteen), with each, and all of whom it is his especial duty to walk, dance, play at chess or back-gammon, read and take wine, not to say anything of the long *têtes-à-têtes* absolutely necessary for giving advice—a duty incumbent, as we must all admit, even on a guardian *pro tem.*; some clever and accomplished men of my acquaintance formed their wards into classes, and whenever the duties of the ship did not require their presence on deck they occupied the vacant hours between breakfast and seven bells, by giving instruction in French, Italian, drawing, and painting, a practice which afforded quite as much amusement to a disinterested bystander like myself, as to either master or pupils. Oh, how would poor unhappy governesses bless themselves and their good fortune, did they ever meet with pupils so docile and attentive as those I have seen in the cuddy. Certainly, for eagerness to profit by instruction and attention to the instructor, they far eclipsed any set of young ladies or gentlemen I ever saw; although, from some cause which perhaps the parties themselves could best explain, there did not appear to me to be that rapid progress made, which from their apparent assiduity might have been anticipated.

The Court-Partial of 18– . *A tale of military life.* 2 vols. London, 1844.

Dating, as it does, from a later and doubtless degenerate period, this account illustrates some of the changes that took place between 1815 and, say, 1835. Besides the growth in the importance of breakfast (which improved, even for the seamen, after 1810), another change was in the hour for dinner. The new hour for dining was 4.0, a gong warning people to dress for dinner at 3.30. The author of *The Court-Partial* thought the meal 'a very wearisome affair, sauntered through with the view of finding it a little later than usual when the ladies rise from table'. On rising, the gentlemen 'joined the ladies' on the quarter-deck. There they might dance, promenade, or talk. After tea, parties were formed for whist, piquet, écarté, back-gammon and chess. In these games all would join 'except perhaps one or two pairs of moon-struck sentimentalists who still remain on deck....'

Note on music-lovers on board ship (see p. 297)

As regards the musical diversions of the passengers, the following passages may be of interest:

> The Ladies occupied the two round-house cabins, and a communication was left between them through the stern gallery which served for their drawing room. They were provided with a pianoforte, music, abundance of books and drawing materials; so that to those who knew how to employ it, time passed quickly....
>
> Those who made the slightest pretence to musical ability performed duets; oft times to the great annoyance of those who were so unfortunate as to be within hearing of their powerful effort. The multitude of musicians was at first a grievance, but the very energy with which they performed, went far to cure the evil. The violin strings could not stand the climate, and as they were expended, and some of the flutes cracked, the number of performers was reduced, for the comfort of the hearers, to those who knew the use of the instruments they undertook to handle....

Life in India; or the English at Calcutta. 3 vols. London, 1828. Vol. 1, pp. 259.

Note on ancient Indian shipping (see p. 322)

Regarding the size of the ancient Indian ships there is a great deal of evidence dating from the fourteenth and fifteenth centuries. Nicolo Conti, for example, states that 'The Natives of India build some ships larger than ours, capable of containing 2000 butts, and with five sails and as many masts. The lower part is constructed with triple planks, in order to withstand the force of the tempests to which they are much exposed. But some ships are so built in compartments that should one part be shattered, the other portion remaining entire may accomplish the voyage.' Chinese influence there may have been, but it is evident that vessels of this description were actually built at Surat and Calicut. Sir H. Middleton saw a Surat ship in 1612 which was 153 feet long, 42 feet broad, 31 feet deep, and said to have a burthen of 1500 tons. There can be no question but that ships of this size existed in the Indian Ocean from a very early age and were still to be found there in the seventeenth century. But neither Dr Vincent nor Prof. Mookerji has provided any distinct account of how these ships disappeared and were replaced by grabs and other craft of

European appearance; neither, curiously enough, does there seem to exist any satisfactory pictorial representation of these earlier vessels. Were such a picture in existence, and easily available, it is fair to assume that Prof. Mookerji would have reproduced it in his exceedingly able and interesting work on Indian Shipping. The vessels represented in the Sculptures of Borobudor are certainly interesting (and not least so in suggesting that the use of the compass was known in India as early as the sixth or seventh century A.D.), but they scarcely answer to the descriptions available of Indian shipping in the thirteenth–fifteenth centuries.

BIBLIOGRAPHY

LIST OF AUTHORITIES ARRANGED BY CHAPTERS

In the following list, which serves the purpose both of a general bibliography and of a guide to the sources of the present work, the same work is occasionally referred to more than once. Where this happens a full reference is given on the first occasion and a short title used subsequently. Most of the books mentioned are to be found in either the British Museum, Cambridge University Library, or the Library of the India Office.

CHAPTER I

THE INDIA HOUSE

AUBER, PETER. *An Analysis of the Constitution of the East-India Company*. London, 1826. pp. lxxii, 804.

BURKE, EDMUND. *The Works of the Right Honourable Edmund Burke*. 2 vols. London, 1855. pp. 538. See pp. 183, 195, 226, 233.

COBBETT, WILLIAM. *Mr Cobbett's Remarks on our Indian Empire and Company of Trading Sovereigns*. (Reprinted from the *Register* of from 1804 to 1822.) London, 1857. pp. 23.

FOSTER, Sir WILLIAM. *The East India House, its history and associations*. London, 1924. pp. 241, with 37 illustrations.

—— *John Company*. London, 1926. pp. 276, with 24 illustrations.

GRANT, ROBERT. *The expediency maintained of continuing the system by which the trade and government of India are now regulated*. London, 1813. pp. xix, 404. See pp. 271, 281, 322, 326, 340.

HOLZMAN, JAMES M. *The Nabobs in England: a study of the returned Anglo-Indian*, 1760–1785. New York, 1926. pp. 186, with 4 illustrations.

KAYE, JOHN WILLIAM. *The Administration of the East India Company*. London, 1853. pp. vi, 712.

LINDSAY, W. S. *History of Merchant Shipping and Ancient Commerce*. 4 vols. London, 1874. Vol. II, pp. 610, with a plan and illustrations. See p. 481.

MACPHERSON, DAVID. *The History of the European Commerce with India, to which is subjoined a review of the arguments for and against the trade with India and the management of it by a chartered Company*. London, 1812. pp. vi, 440, with a map. See pp. 244, 292, 362, 386.

McCULLOCH, J. R. *A Dictionary, practical, theoretical, and historical, of Commerce and Commercial Navigation*. New ed. London, 1854. First published, 1832. pp. 1484, with numerous maps and plans. See p. 650.

MILBURN, WILLIAM. *Oriental Commerce; containing a geographical description of the principal places in the East Indies...with their Produce, Manufactures and Trade....* 2 vols. London, 1813. pp. ciii, 413 and 581, with 12 maps and charts. See Vol. II, p. 191.

MILL, JAMES. *The History of British India*. (Continued by H. H. Wilson.) London, 1840–1845. Vols. VI and VII, pp. 683 and 608.

MORRIS, HENRY. *The Life of Charles Grant, sometime Member of Parliament for Inverness-shire and Director of the East India Company*. London, 1904. pp. xviii, 404, with 4 illustrations.

PARSHAD, I. DURGA. *Some Aspects of Indian Foreign Trade*. London, 1932. pp. 238. See p. 57.

SCOTT-WARING, Major. *Observations on the Present State of the East India Company*. 4th ed. London, 1808. pp. lxxvi, 76. See pp. 1, 13, 31, 63, 68.

SPEAR, T. G. P. *The Nabobs, a study of the social life of the English in eighteenth century India*. Oxford, 1932. pp. vii, 210.

TILBY, A. WYATT. *The English People Overseas*. Vol. II, *British India*, 1600–1828. 1911. pp. 286.

WISSETT, ROBERT. *A Compendium of East Indian Affairs, political and commercial*, collected and arranged for the use of the Court of Directors, by Robert Wissett, Clerk to the Committee of Warehouses. 2 vols. London, 1802.

WOODFALL, WILLIAM. *The Debates that have taken place at the East India House*.

CHAPTER II

BRITISH INDIA

A. GENERAL

BOSANQUET, AUGUSTUS H. *India seventy years ago*. By the Nephew of an East India Director. London, 1881. pp. viii, 311, with a portrait frontispiece.

CAREY, W. H. *The good old days of Honorable John Company*. 3 vols. Simla, 1882. pp. 292, 288, xxx and 166.

EAST INDIA COMPANY. *Report from the Committee of the Hon. House of Commons appointed to inquire into the existence of any abuses in the Disposal of the Patronage of the East-India Company*. Printed, by Order of the General Court. London, 1809. pp. 463.

FAY, Mrs ELIZA. *Original letters from India* (1779–1815), with an introduction by E. M. Forster. London, 1925. pp. 288, with frontispiece portrait.

HAMILTON, WALTER. *East India Gazetteer*. London, 1815. pp. 862.

HENCHMAN, THOMAS. *Observations on the Reports of the Directors of the East India Company, respecting the trade between India and Europe*. 2nd ed. London, 1802. pp. 461. See p. 100.

HICKEY, WILLIAM. *Memoirs*. Edited by Alfred Spencer. Vol. IV (1790–1809). London, 1925. pp. xii, 512, with 7 illustrations.

JOHNSON, J. *The Influence of Tropical Climates on European Constitutions.* 4th ed. London, 1827. pp. viii, 680. First published in 1813.

McCULLOCH, J. R. *A Dictionary of Commerce.* See p. 561.

MILBURN, WILLIAM. *Oriental Commerce.* Vol. II. See pp. 197, 203.

NEALE, W. JOHNSON. *Gentleman Jack,* a Naval Story. 3 vols. London, 1837. Vol. II, pp. 310. See p. 150.

OWEN, S. J. *A Selection from the Despatches, Memoranda, and other Papers relating to India, of the Marquess Wellesley, K.G., during his government of India.* Edited by S. J. Owen. Oxford, 1877. pp. cxi, 813, with 9 maps and plans. See Memorandum of General Stuart, p. 575; Memorandum on Bengal by Colonel Arthur Wesley, p. 773; and the Note on the policy of Sir George Barlow by T. C. Metcalfe on p. 804.

Parliamentary Papers. India Office. Volume for 1808–1813.

ROBERTS, P. E. *India under Wellesley.* London, 1929. pp. ix, 323, with a frontispiece and 4 maps.

SAMUELSON, JAMES. *India, past and present, historical, social and political.* London, 1890. pp. 390, with a map and 23 illustrations. The Bibliography by Sir W. W. Hunter.

WELLINGTON, Duke of. *Supplementary Despatches and Memoranda of Field-Marshal Arthur Duke of Wellington, K.G.* India, 1797–1805. Edited by his son the Duke of Wellington. 2 vols. London, 1858. Vol. I, pp. 592, with a map. See pp. 52, 88, 432–4.

WILLIAMSON, Captain THOMAS. *The East India Vade-Mecum; or complete guide to gentlemen intended for the civil, military, or naval service of the Hon. East India Company.* 2 vols. London, 1810. pp. xvi, 520 and vii, 506.

B. CALCUTTA

GRANDPRÉ, L. DE. *A Voyage in the Indian Ocean and to Bengal, undertaken in the years 1789 and 1790.* Translated from the French. 2 vols. London, 1803. pp. 278 and 303, with numerous illustrations. See Vol. I, p. 268; Vol. II, p. 17.

LONG, Rev. J. *Peeps into social life in Calcutta a century ago.* Calcutta, 1868. pp. 25.

MILBURN, WILLIAM. *Oriental Commerce.* See Vol. II, pp. 98, 107, 112, 123, 125.

Naval Chronicle. Vol. XVII, p. 495.

SETON-KARR, W. S. *Selections from Calcutta Gazettes of the years 1798–1805, showing the political and social condition of the English in India.* Vol. III. Calcutta, 1868. pp. xvi, 586.

C. Madras and the Coast

Barlow, Glyn. *The Story of Madras.* Madras, 1921. pp. vi, 117, with 22 illustrations.

Bradshaw, John. *Rulers of India. Sir Thomas Munro and the British settlement of the Madras Presidency.* Oxford, 1894. pp. 233, with a map.

Corrie, Rt. Rev. D. *Memoirs of the Right Rev. Daniel Corrie, LL.D., First Bishop of Madras.* Compiled chiefly from his own letters and journals, by his brothers. London, 1847. pp. 640, with a frontispiece.

Grandpré, L. de. *A Voyage in the Indian Ocean.* See Vol. I, pp. 211, 219, 226.

Johnson, J. *The Oriental Voyager; or descriptive sketches and cursory remarks on a voyage to India and China, in his Majesty's Ship Caroline, performed in the years* 1803–6. London, 1807. pp. xvi, 388, with a map. See Vol. I, p. 305.

McCulloch, J. R. *A Dictionary of Commerce.* See p. 828.

Milburn, William. *Oriental Commerce.* See Vol. II, pp. 3, 25, 32, 45, 68, 71.

Prior, James. *A Visit to Madras; being a sketch of the local and characteristic peculiarities of that Presidency in the year* 1811. London, 1821. pp. 35.

D. Bombay

Douglas, James. *Glimpses of old Bombay and Western India, with other papers.* London, 1900. pp. x, 334.

Drewitt, F. Dawtrey. *Bombay in the days of George IV: Memoirs of Sir Edward West.* London, 1907. Republished, 1935. pp. 342, with 7 illustrations. See p. 12.

Edwardes, S. M. *The Rise of Bombay. A retrospect.* Bombay, 1902. pp. 345, with plans and illustrations.

Graham, Maria. *A Journal of a Residence in India.* Edinburgh, 1812. pp. 211, with 16 illustrations. See p. 12.

Low, C. R. *History of the Indian Navy* (1613–1863). 2 vols. London, 1877. Vol. I, pp. xx, 541.

Marryat, Captain F., R.N., C.B. *Newton Forster; or, the Merchant Service.* London, 1838. pp. 383, with a frontispiece. See p. 293.

McCulloch, J. R. *A Dictionary of Commerce.* See p. 152.

Milburn, William. *Oriental Commerce.* See Vol. I, pp. 170, 236, 270.

Money, William T. *Observations on the expediency of Shipbuilding at Bombay for the service of His Majesty and of the East India Company.* London, 1811. pp. 73, with appendices. See p. 8.

RICHMOND, Admiral Sir H. W. *The Navy in India*, 1763–1783. London, 1931. pp. 430, with 16 diagrams and maps. Appendix I, Bombay Marine.

E. PENANG, MALACCA AND BENCOOLEN

ANON. *A short Account of the Prince of Wales's Island*. pp. 27.

EDGELL, T. C. P. *English Trade and Policy in Borneo and the adjacent Islands*, 1667–1786. Thesis, unpublished, in the Library of the University of London. Submitted, 1935. pp. 265, with a map.

EGERTON, HUGH E. *Sir Stamford Raffles: England in the Far East*. London, 1900. pp. 290, with a frontispiece and 2 maps. See p. 6.

JOHNSON, J. *The Oriental Voyager*. See p. 221.

MACPHERSON, DAVID. *The History of the European Commerce with India*. See pp. 230, 238.

MILBURN, WILLIAM. *Oriental Commerce*. See Vol. II, p. 297.

POPHAM, Sir HOME. *A Description of Prince of Wales Island, in the Streights of Malacca: with its real and probable advantages and sources to recommend it as a marine establishment*. London, 1805. pp. 72. See pp. 8, 26.

SWETTENHAM, F. *British Malaya*. London, 1910. pp. xi, 354, with 50 illustrations.

WELLINGTON, Duke of. *Supplementary Despatches*. Memorandum on Pulo Penang, 1798. See Vol. I, p. 24.

F. CANTON

ADDISON, THOMAS. *The Naval Miscellany*, Vol. I. Navy Records Society publication. Vol. xx, edited by J. K. Laughton. 1902. pp. 462, with 8 illustrations and maps. See p. 333. Extracts from the Journals of Thomas Addison, 1801–1830.

HALL, Captain BASIL, R.N. *Narrative of a Voyage to Java, China, and the great Loo-Choo Island*. London, 1840. pp. 81, with two charts. See p. 73.

LINDSAY, Lord. *Lives of the Lindsays*. Wigan, 1840. Vol. IV, pp. 295. "An adventure in China" (p. 281), by the Hon. Hugh Lindsay.

MEARES, JOHN. *Voyages made in the years 1788 and 1789, from China to the North West Coast of America*. London, 1790. pp. 372, xcv, with appendices, numerous illustrations and charts. See pp. lxxv, lxxxvii.

WATHEN, JAMES. *Journal of a Voyage in 1811 and 1812, to Madras and China*. London, 1814. pp. xx, 246, with 24 illustrations. See p. 185.

G. Ceylon

LORD, WALTER FREWEN. *Sir Thomas Maitland, the mastery of the Mediterranean.* London, 1897. pp. 301, with a portrait and 2 maps. See pp. 72 and 96.

MILBURN, WILLIAM. *Oriental Commerce.* See Vol. I, p. 352.

PERCIVAL, ROBERT. *An Account of the Island of Ceylon.* London, 1803. pp. 420, with a map and 2 charts.

WELLINGTON, Duke of. *Supplementary Despatches.* Colonel Arthur Wesley's Memorandum on Trincomalee. See Vol. II, p. 343.

CHAPTER III

TRADE TO THE EAST

ANON. *Case of the British Cotton Spinners and Manufacturers of Piece Goods, similar to the importations from the East Indies,* 1790.

CUNNINGHAM, W. *The Growth of English Industry and Commerce in Modern Times.* 3 vols. Cambridge, 1912. Vol. III (*Modern Times,* Part II). pp. 1039.

EAMES, J. B. *The English in China; being an account of the intercourse between England and China from the year* 1600 *to the year* 1843. London, 1909. pp. 662, with 2 maps and 7 illustrations.

HENCHMAN, THOMAS. *Observations on the Reports of the Directors of the East India Company, respecting the trade between India and Europe.* 2nd ed. London, 1802. pp. 461. See Appendix III.

LINDSAY, W. S. *History of Merchant Shipping and Ancient Commerce.* See Vol. II, p. 432.

MACPHERSON, DAVID. *Annals of Commerce.* 4 vols. London, 1805. Vol. IV, pp. 550, with appendices, gazetteer, etc.

—— *The History of the European Commerce with India.* See pp. 162, 292, 389, 402; also Appendices V, VII, VIII.

MCCULLOCH, J. R. *A Dictionary of Commerce.* See pp. 1131, 1291.

—— *The Literature of Political Economy; a classified catalogue of select publications in the different departments of that science.* London, 1845.

MILBURN, WILLIAM. *Oriental Commerce.*

MONTEFIORE, J. *A Commercial Dictionary; containing the present state of Mercantile Law, practice and custom.* London, 1803.

MORSE, H. B. *The Chronicles of the East India Company trading to China,* 1633–1834. 4 vols. Oxford, 1926. Vol. III, pp. 388, with 6 illustrations and a map.

MORTIMER, THOMAS. *A General Dictionary of Commerce, Trade, and Manufactures; exhibiting their present state in every part of the World.* London, 1810.

—— *Universal Commerce, or the Commerce of all the mercantile cities and towns of the world.* By the editors of *Mortimer's Commercial Dictionary.* London, 1818.

Naval Chronicle. Vol. XVIII, pp. 87, 351.

PARSHAD, I. DURGA. *Some Aspects of Indian Foreign Trade.* See pp. 75, 100, 111.

ROBINSON, F. P. *The Trade of the East India Company from* 1709 *to* 1813. Cambridge, 1912. pp. 186.

SMITH, ADAM, LL.D. *An Inquiry into the Nature and Causes of the Wealth of Nations.* Edited by J. R. McCulloch, Esq. Edinburgh, 1839. pp. 648.

STEVENS, ROBERT. *The Complete Guide to the East-India Trade, addressed to all Commanders, Officers, Factors, etc. in the Honourable East India Company's Service.* Robert Stevens, Merchant in Bombay. London, 1766. pp. 157.

VALENTIA, GEORGE, Viscount. *Voyages and Travels to India, Ceylon, the Red Sea, etc. in the years* 1802–1806. 4 vols. London, 1811. Vol. I, pp. 439. See p. 43.

WELLINGTON, Duke of. *Despatches.* Edited by S. J. Owen. Memorandum on Penang, 1797, p. 487. Also p. 658.

CHAPTER IV

THE EASTERN SEAS

CAPPER, JAMES. *Observations on the winds and monsoons; illustrated by a chart and accompanied with notes, geographical and meteorological.* London, 1801. pp. xxvii, 234.

DUNN, SAMUEL. *A New Directory for the East-Indies. A Work originally begun upon the plan of the Oriental Neptune, augmented and improved by W. Herbert, W. Nichelson, now... further enlarged by Samuel Dunn.* 5th ed. London, 1780. pp. 554, with a frontispiece.

ELMORE, H. M. *The British Mariner's directory and guide to the trade and navigation of the Indian and China Seas.* London, 1802. pp. 342.

FLINDERS, MATTHEW. *A Voyage to Terra Australis; undertaken for the purpose of completing the discovery of that vast country.* By Matthew Flinders, Commander of the *Investigator.* 2 vols, with atlas. London, 1814. pp. cciv, 269 and 613, with numerous illustrations.

FORREST, Captain THOMAS. *A Treatise on the Monsoons in East India.* Calcutta, 1782. pp. vii, 51.

GRANT, CHARLES, Viscount DE VAUX. *The History of Mauritius or the Isle of France, and the neighbouring islands; from their first discovery to the present time.* London, 1801. pp. xxi, 571, with 3 maps and plans. See pp. 309, 338, 346, 351, 474.

GROSE, J. H. *A Voyage to the East Indies.* 2 vols. New ed. London, 1772. pp. 343, 478, with plans and illustrations. See p. 34.

HALL, Captain BASIL, R.N. *Fragments of Voyages and Travels.* Second Series. 2nd ed. London, 1840. pp. 160. See pp. 23, 25, 37, 83, 89.

—— *Narrative of a Voyage to Java, China, and the great Loo-Choo Island.* See p. 1.

HALL, Commander W. H. *Narratives of the Voyages and Services of the Nemesis, from* 1834 *to* 1840, *and of the combined naval and military operations in China*, from notes of Commander W. H. Hall, R.N., with personal observations by W. D. Gribble, Esq. 2nd ed. London, 1844. pp. 488, with 15 charts, plans, diagrams and illustrations.

HORSBURGH, JAMES. *Directions for Sailing to and from the East Indies, China, New Holland, Cape of Good Hope, etc.* 2 vols. London, 1809–11. pp. 397, 518.

HOSKINS, H. L. *British Routes to India.* New York, 1928. pp. 494, with 11 illustrations.

IRVING, B. A. *The Commerce of India, being a view of the routes successively taken by the commerce between Europe and the East.* London, 1858. pp. xii, 271.

JOHNSON, J. *The Oriental Voyager.* See pp. 63, 78, 118.

MEARES, JOHN. *Voyages made in the years* 1788 *and* 1789, *from China to the North West Coast of America.* See p. 47.

M'LEOD, JOHN, M.D. *Voyage of his Majesty's Ship Alceste, to China, Corea, and the island of Lewchew, with an account of her shipwreck.* 3rd ed. London, 1819. pp. 339, with 7 illustrations. See p. 18.

Naval Chronicle. Vols. I, p. 68; II, pp. 51, 61, 131; XXVI, Correspondence throughout relating to the Indiamen lost in 1807–9; XXIX, pp. 304, 312; XXX, p. 213; XXXIII, p. 414.

PRIOR, JAMES. *Voyage along the Eastern Coast of Africa to Mosambique, Johanna, and Quiloa; to St Helena, etc. in the Nisus Frigate.* London, 1819. pp. 114, with 1 illustration.

—— *Voyage in the Indian Seas in the Nisus Frigate,* 1810 *and* 1811. London, 1820. pp. 114, with a chart, 2 plans and one illustration.

SMYTH, Captain W. H. *The Life and Services of Captain Philip Beaver,*

late of His Majesty's Ship Nisus. London, 1829. pp. 339. See pp. 222, 226, 231, 234, 250, 283.
STEVENSON, WILLIAM. *Historical Sketch of the progress of discovery, navigation, and commerce, from the earliest records to the beginning of the nineteenth century*. Edinburgh, 1824. pp. 654. See p. 529; Catalogue of Voyages and Travels (100 pp.).

CHAPTER V

EAST INDIAMEN

ANON. *Remarks on the Calumnies published in the 'Quarterly Review' on the English Ship-builders*. London, 1814. pp. 44. (See below, under *Quarterly Review*.)
CHATTERTON, E. KEBLE. *Ships and Ways of other Days*. London, 1913. pp. 292, with 130 illustrations.
—— *The Ship under Sail*. London, 1926. pp. 224, with 36 illustrations.
—— *The Old East Indiaman*. 2nd ed. London, 1933. pp. 308, with 15 illustrations.
EAST INDIA COMPANY. India Office MS. Brief Historical Sketch of the Shipping Concerns of the East India Company, *circa* 1796.
—— Printed Proceedings. *Marine Miscellanies*.
—— Proceedings relative to Ships tendered. Vols. I–VI.
FLETCHER, R. A. *In the Days of the Tall Ships*. London, 1928. pp. 348, with 30 illustrations.
GREEN, H. and WIGRAM, R. *Chronicles of Blackwall Yard*. London, 1881. pp. 69, with 9 illustrations and 2 maps.
GROSE, JOHN HENRY. *A Voyage to the East Indies*.
HANNAY, DAVID. *The Sea Trader, his Friends and Enemies*. London, 1912. pp. 388, with 22 illustrations.
HARDY, CHARLES. *Register of Ships employed in the Service of the Honorable the United East India Company, from the union of the two companies, in 1707, to the year 1760...to which is added from the latter period to the present time*. London, 1799. pp. 280, with a chart.
HARDY, H. C. *A Register of Ships employed in the Service of the Honorable the United East India Company from the year 1760 to 1812*. Revised by H. C. Hardy. London, 1813. pp. 308, with indexes and appendices.
LINDSAY, W. S. *History of Merchant Shipping and Ancient Commerce*. Vol. II.

 26-2

LUBBOCK, BASIL. *The Blackwall Frigates.* 2nd ed. Glasgow, 1924. pp. 332, with 72 illustrations, maps and appendices. See pp. 25, 34, 64 and illustrations.

MILBURN, WILLIAM. *Oriental Commerce.* See Vol. I, pp. XC, XCVII.

Naval Chronicle. Vols. II, p. 310; III, pp. 239, 345, 418; V, pp. 129, 227, 231, 321; VI, pp. 76, 427; IX, p. 71; XXII, p. 472; XXIII, pp. 97, 448; XXIV, pp. 76, 366; XXVI, pp. 214, 308, 314, 401, 470; XXXI, pp. 185, 446; XXXVIII, pp. 189, 304.

NEWTE, T. *Observations on the Importance of the East India Fleet to the Company and the Nation.* 1795.

Parliamentary Papers. India Office. Volume for 1808–1813. *Minutes of the evidence taken before the select committee of the House of Commons on petitions relating to East-India-built shipping.* Ordered, by the House of Commons, to be printed. 1814. pp. 666.

POLO, MARCO. *The Travels of Marco Polo the Venetian,* with an introduction by John Masefield. London, 1907. pp. xvi, 461.

Quarterly Review. Vols. X, October 1813; XI, April 1814.

RICHMOND, Admiral Sir H. W. *The Navy in India,* 1763–1783. See p. 384.

STAPLETON, Commander G. *The Blue Peter,* Vol. XIV, No. 151, October, 1934. Article on Minicoy.

STEEL, DAVID. *Elements and Practice of Naval Architecture.* Illustrated with a series of thirty-eight large draughts and numerous smaller engravings. London, 1805. 2 vols. with atlas of illustrations. Also another edition, 1822, revised by John Knowles, pp. 438, with appendices, plates, etc. See Plate XX.

WHALL, W. B. *The Romance of Navigation.* London, n.d. pp. 292, with 33 illustrations.

CHAPTER VI

THE SHIPPING INTEREST

ANON. *Dangers and Disadvantages to the Public and East India Company from that Company building and navigating its own ships.* London, 1778.

—— *Considerations on the important benefits to be derived from the East India Company's building and navigating their own ships.* By the author of the essay *On the Rights of the East-India Company.* London, 1778. pp. 37.

—— *An Olio, as prepared and dressed on board an East Indiaman. The Ingredients by the Directors, Husbands, Messrs Baring, Brough, Dalrymple and others.* London, 1786.

ANON. *Letter to the Proprietors of East India Stock in behalf of the Present Owners of East Indian shipping.* A proprietor. London, 1795.

—— *Two letters on East India Shipping*, which appeared in the *Morning Chronicle* of the 13th and 20th of January, 1803. Reprinted, London, 1803. pp. 24.

BROUGH, A. *Considerations on the Necessity of Lowering the exorbitant Freight of Ships employed in the Service of the East India Company.* London, 1786.

CANNAN, D. *A Statement of Facts relative to the conduct of Capt. W. Hope, commander of the Herefordshire... towards Messrs Card and Cannan, managing owners of that ship.*

COTTON, JOSEPH. *A Review of the Shipping System of the East India Company; with suggestions for its improvement, etc.* 1799. pp. 59.

DALRYMPLE, A. *A Fair State of the Case between the East India Company, and the Owners of Ships now in their Service. To which are added Considerations on Mr. Brough's Pamphlet concerning the East India Company's Shipping.* London, 1786. pp. 54.

EAST INDIA COMPANY. *Proceedings relative to Ships tendered.* Vols. I, 1780–1791; II, 1791–1796; III, 1796–1799; IV, 1800–1803; V, 1803–1806; VI, 1806–1809.

FAYLE, C. ERNEST. *A Short History of the World's Shipping Industry.* London, 1933. pp. 320, with 8 illustrations.

FIOTT, J. *Three Addresses to the Proprietors of East India Stock, and the Publick, on the subject of the Shipping Concerns of the Company.* Mr J. Fiott, merchant, of London. London, 1795. pp. 322.

[SMITH, Captain NATHANIEL.] *An Address to the Proprietors of East India Stock in consequence of the Errors and Mistakes in some late Publications, relative to their Shipping.* London, 1778. pp. 122.

SUTHERLAND, LUCY STUART. *A London Merchant*, 1695–1774. Oxford, 1933.

WALSBY, Captain JOHN. *The Ship's Husband, A Narrative.* London, 1791.

CHAPTER VII

THE MARITIME SERVICE

ADDISON, THOMAS. *Journals.* Edited by J. K. Laughton. *Naval Miscellany*, Vol. I. Navy Records Society publication, Vol. XX, 1902. pp. 462, with 8 illustrations and maps. See p. 235.

TRADE IN THE EASTERN SEAS

ANON. *Papers respecting the Trade between India and Europe.* Printed by order of the Court of Directors. London, 1802. pp. 190. See p. 167.

—— *Service Afloat: comprising the personal narrative of a naval officer employed during the late war; and the Journal of an officer engaged in the late surveying expedition under the command of Captain Owen, on the Western Coast of Africa.* 2 vols. London, 1833. pp. 303 and 322.

—— *An Appeal to his Majesty's Government and the Honorable East India Company, for justice to the claims of the Hon. East India Company's Maritime Service, to Compensation.* By an Officer of the Service. London, 1834. pp. 84.

—— *Memorial of the Committee of the East India Company's Maritime Service, presented to the Honorable the Court of Directors, July 30th,* 1834. London, 1834. pp. 23.

—— *The East India Company and the Maritime Service.* London, 1834. pp. 27.

—— *The Saucy Jack, and the Indiaman.* By a Blue Jacket. (A novel.) 2 vols. London, 1840. pp. 242 and 271.

BIDEN, CHRISTOPHER. *Naval Discipline...or a view of the necessity for passing a law establishing an efficient naval discipline on board ships in the Merchant Service.* Christopher Biden, late Commander of the Honourable East-India Company's Ships *Royal George* and *Princess Charlotte.* London, 1830. pp. 392. See pp. 64, 86, 159, 165, 215, etc.

CAMPBELL, A. *A Voyage round the World, from* 1806 *to* 1812. Edinburgh, 1816. pp. 288, with a chart. See p. 21.

CHATTERTON, E. KEBLE. *The old East Indiaman.*

DEWAR, DOUGLAS. *Bygone Days in India.* London, 1922. pp. 287, with 18 illustrations.

EAST INDIA COMPANY. *Orders and Instructions given by the Court of Directors of the United Company of Merchants of England, trading to the East Indies, to the Commanders of Ships in the Company's Service.* London, 1814. With appendices, pp. 232.

EASTWICK, R. W. *A Master Mariner. Being the life and adventures of Captain Robert William Eastwick.* Edited by H. Compton. London, 1891. pp. 351, with 6 illustrations. See pp. 44, 60.

FLETCHER, R. A. *In the Days of the Tall Ships.* See p. 47.

GRIBBLE, CHARLES B. *A brief statement shewing the equitable and moral claims of the Maritime Officers of the Honourable East India Company for Compensation.* London, 1834. pp. 24.

HALL, Captain B. *Fragments of Voyages and Travels.* Second Series. See p. 22.

HANNAY, DAVID. *Ships and Men.* Edinburgh, 1910. pp. 324, with 12 illustrations. See p. 131.

HARDY, CHARLES. *Register of Ships.* The East India Company's regulations for the Maritime Service.

JAMES, SILAS. *Narrative of a Voyage to Arabia, India, etc.... Performed in the Years* 1781–1784. London, 1797. pp. 232, with frontispiece.

LINDSAY, W. S. *History of Merchant Shipping and ancient Commerce.* See Vol. II, pp. 466 and 470.

MACPHERSON, DAVID. *Annals of Commerce.* See Vol. IV, p. 151.

—— *The History of the European Commerce with India.* See p. 235.

MARRYAT, Captain F. *Newton Forster.*

MILBURN, WILLIAM. *Oriental Commerce.* See Vol. I, p. lxxx; Vol. II, p. 126.

Naval Chronicle. Vols. II, p. 355; VII, p. 345; IX, p. 263; XXXII, p. 196.

PARISH, Captain A. *The Sea Officer's Manual; being a Compendium of the Duties of a Commander; First, Second, Third and Fourth Officer; Officer of the Watch; and midshipman in the Mercantile Navy.* Captain A. Parish, of the East India Merchant Service.

WELLESLEY, the Marquess. *Despatches.* Memorandum by Colonel Arthur Wesley on India-built shipping. See p. 773.

CHAPTER VIII

THE VOYAGE

ANON. *Asiatic Journal and monthly Register for British and Foreign India.* Vol. XVIII. London, 1835. pp. 316. Article on p. 195 entitled 'Outward Bound'.

AUBER, PETER. *An Analysis of the Constitution of the East-India Company.* See p. 321.

BOSANQUET, AUGUSTUS H. *India Seventy Years Ago.*

CARTER, GEORGE. *A narrative of the loss of the Grosvenor...* 1782. London, 1791.

CHATTERTON, E. KEBLE. *Ships and Ways of other Days.* See p. 285.

CUPPLES, GEORGE. *The Green Hand. Adventures of a naval Lieutenant.* London, 1900. First published in 1849. pp. xi, 413.

EAST INDIA COMPANY. *Orders and instructions given by the Court of Directors of the United Company of Merchants of England, trading to the East Indies, to the Commanders of Ships in the Company's Service.* London, 1814. With appendices. pp. 234.

HARDY, H. C. *A Register of Ships,* 1813.

HOTHAM, RICHARD. *Instructions etc. given by Owners of the good Ship called the [Royal Admiral] in the Service of the Honourable United Company of Merchants of England, trading to the East Indies.* 1778. Rd. Hotham to Captain Edward Berrow.

LINDSAY, W. S. *History of Merchant Shipping and ancient Commerce.* See Vol. II, pp. 421, 477.

LUBBOCK, BASIL. *The Blackwall Frigates.* See p. 71.

MACPHERSON, DAVID. *The History of the European Commerce with India.*

MARRYAT, Captain F. *Newton Forster.* See pp. 203, 215, 293.

MILBURN, WILLIAM. *Oriental Commerce.* See Vol. I, p. lxxxvii, and pp. 259, 261.

MINTO, Countess of. *Life and Letters of Gilbert Elliot, First Earl of Minto, from 1807 to 1814, while Governor-General of India.* Edited by the Countess of Minto. London, 1880. pp. 403, with a map. See p. 251.

Naval Chronicle. Vol. I, pp. 171 and 445.

STEVENSON, WILLIAM. *Historical Sketch of the progress of discovery, navigation, and commerce, from the earliest records to the beginning of the Nineteenth Century.* Edinburgh, 1824. pp. 654. Catalogue of Voyages and Travels, pp. 529–628.

VAUGHAN, WILLIAM, F.R.S. *Tracts on docks and commerce, printed between the years 1793 and 1800, and now first collected; with an introduction, memoir, and miscellaneous pieces.* London, 1839.

WATHEN, JAMES. *Journal of a Voyage in 1811 and 1812.*

WELLINGTON, Duke of. *Supplementary despatches and memoranda. Regimental orders for troops on board ship, 1797.* See Vol. I, pp. 19, 50; Vol. II, p. 309.

WISE, HENRY. *An Analysis of one hundred Voyages to and from India, China, etc., performed by Ships in the Hon'ble East India Company's service.* Henry Wise, late Chief Officer of the Honourable Company's Ship *Edinburgh.* London, 1839. pp. 120, with frontispiece and 3 diagrams.

CHAPTER IX

PASSENGERS

ANON. *Life in India; or the English at Calcutta.* 3 vols. London, 1828. Vol. I, pp. 259. See pp. 10, 19, 31.

—— *The English in India.* By the author of *Pandurang Hari* and *The Zenana.* 3 vols. London, 1828. Vol. I, pp. 328.

ANON. *The Asiatic Journal and monthly Register for British and Foreign India.* Vol. XVIII, 1835. See p. 195.

—— *The Court-Partial of* 18—. *A tale of military life.* 2 vols. London, 1844. Vol. I, pp. 336. See pp. 79, 93, etc.

BOSANQUET, A. H. *India Seventy Years Ago.* See p. 24.

CAREY, EUSTACE. *Memoir of William Carey, D.D., late missionary to Bengal; Professor of Oriental languages in the College of Fort William, Calcutta.* London, 1836. pp. 630, with a frontispiece portrait. See p. 105.

CORDINER, Rev. JAMES. *A Voyage to India.* Aberdeen, 1820. pp. xi, 315, with a portrait frontispiece. See pp. 21, 286.

DEWAR, DOUGLAS. *In the Days of the Company.* Calcutta, 1920. pp. 210. See pp. 4, 7, 12.

—— *Bygone Days in India.* See pp. 50, 64.

DOUGLAS, JAMES. *Glimpses of old Bombay and Western India, with other papers.* See pp. 7, 30.

DREWITT, F. DAWTREY. *Bombay in the Days of George IV: Memoirs of Sir Edward West.* See pp. 33, 37.

EAST INDIA COMPANY. *Orders and Instructions...to the Commanders of Ships in the Company's Service.* See Appendix No. X.

FORBES, JAMES. *Oriental Memoirs: A narrative of seventeen years' residence in India.* 2 vols. 2nd ed. London, 1834. pp. xix, 550 and viii, 552, with a frontispiece to each volume. See Vol. I, p. 7; Vol. II, p. 479.

GRAND, G. F. *The narrative of the life of a gentleman long resident in India.* First published, Cape of Good Hope, 1814. New ed., edited by W. K. Firminger, Calcutta, 1910. pp. xix, 333, with 14 illustrations. See p. 6.

HERVEY, Captain ALBERT. *Ten Years in India; or the life of a young officer.* London, 1850. 3 vols. Vol. I, pp. xvi, 358.

HICKEY, WILLIAM. *Memoirs.* Edited by Alfred Spencer. 4 vols. Vol. IV (1790–1809). London, 1925. pp. xii, 512, with 7 illustrations. See pp. 357, 366, 369, 376, 381, 410.

JOHNSON, GEORGE W. *The Stranger in India; or three years in Calcutta.* London, 1843. 2 vols. pp. viii, 304 and vi, 294. See pp. 1, 9, 13.

LOCKHART, J. C. *Blenden Hall.* London, 1930. pp. 232, with a map and 8 illustrations. See pp. 28, 34, 53.

MACKINTOSH, Rt. Hon. Sir JAMES. *Memoirs.* Edited by his son, Robert James Mackintosh. London, 1835. 2 vols. pp. vii, 527 and vii, 516, with a frontispiece to each volume. See vol. I, pp. 203, 205; Vol. II, p. 144.

MALCOLM, Sir JOHN. *The Life and Correspondence of Major-General Sir John Malcolm, G.C.B., late Envoy to Persia, and Governor of*

Bombay. 2 vols. London, 1856. pp. xii, 538 and vi, 631, with a frontispiece to each volume. See Vol. II, p. 144.

MINTO, Countess of. *Lord Minto in India*. See p. 251.

NEALE, W. JOHNSON. *Gentleman Jack, a Naval Story*. 3 vols. London, 1837. Vol. II, pp. 310. See p. 150.

NUGENT, Lady MARIA. *A Journal from the year* 1811 *till the year* 1815, *including a voyage to and residence in India*. 2 vols. London, 1839. Vol. I, pp. xii, 428. See pp. 20–67.

ROBERTS, EMMA. *The East India Voyager, or the Outward Bound*. London, 1845. pp. lxiii, 263.

SARGENT, Rev. J. *The Life of the Rev. T. T. Thomason, M.A., late Chaplain to the Honourable East India Company*. London, 1833. pp. xi, 344, with a frontispiece.

SHERWOOD, Mrs. *The Life and Times of Mrs Sherwood* (1775–1851) *from the diaries of Captain and Mrs Sherwood*. Edited by F. J. Harvey Darton. London, 1910. pp. xiv, 519, with 11 illustrations. See pp. 228–50.

TWINING, THOMAS. *Travels in India a hundred years ago...being notes and reminiscences by Thomas Twining*. Edited by the Rev. William H. C. Twining. London, 1893. pp. xii, 537, with portrait and map. See pp. 1, 5, 10, 14, 49.

WALLACE, JAMES. *A Voyage to India: containing reflections on a voyage to Madras and Bengal, in* 1821, *in the ship Lonach; instructions for the preservation of health in Indian climates; and hints to surgeons and owners of private trading-ships*. London, 1824. pp. vi, 166. See pp. 11, 104, 159.

[WALLACE, R. G.] *Fifteen years in India; or sketches of a soldier's life*. From the journal of an officer in his Majesty's service. London, 1822. pp. 540. See p. 45.

WATHEN, JAMES. *Journal of a Voyage in* 1811 *and* 1812.

WILLIAMSON, Captain THOMAS. *The East India Vade-Mecum*. See Vol. I, pp. 22, 45, 52.

CHAPTER X

NAVAL PROTECTION

ADMIRALTY RECORDS. Public Record Office, Ad. 1/180 and Ad. 1/181.

HALL, Captain B. *Voyages and Travels*. Second Series. See pp. 22, 37, 83.

HARDY, CHARLES. *Register of Ships*, 1799.

HARDY, H. C. *A Register of Ships*, 1813.

JOHNSON, J. *The Oriental Voyager.* See pp. 116, 126, 135.

Naval Chronicle. Vol. XXVI, p. 309.

RICHMOND, Admiral Sir H. W. *Private Papers of George, second Earl Spencer, First Lord of the Admiralty,* 1794–1801. Navy Records Society publication, 1924. Vol. IV. See p. 202.

STEEL, DAVID. *The Ship-Master's Assistant and Owner's Manual.* 10th edition, very considerably improved and enlarged. London, 1803. pp. 450, with 168 pp. of appendices. See p. 433.

CHAPTER XI

THE COUNTRY TRADE

CHILDERS, Colonel SPENCER. *A Mariner of England. An account of the career of William Richardson...*[1780–1819] *as told by himself.* London, 1908. pp. 317.

COATES, W. H. *The old 'Country Trade' of the East Indies.* W. H. Coates, F.R.G.S., Commander, R.N.R. (retired). London, 1911. pp. ix, 205, with chart and 9 illustrations.

EASTWICK, R. W. *A Master Mariner. Being the life and adventures of Captain Robert William Eastwick.*

ELMORE, H. M. *The British Mariner's directory and guide to the trade and navigation of the Indian and China Seas.* See pp. 128, 162, 167, 219, 227, 275, 282, 286, 311.

GRANDPRÉ, L. DE. *A Voyage in the Indian Ocean.* See Vol. I, p. 107.

GROSE, J. H. *A Voyage to the East Indies.* See Vol. I, p. 107.

HENCHMAN, THOMAS. *Observations.* See Appendices I, V, IX, XI, XII.

IRVING, B. A. *The Commerce of India, being a view of the routes successively taken by the commerce between Europe and the East.* London, 1858. pp. 271.

LINDSAY, W. S. *History of Merchant Shipping and ancient Commerce.* See Vol. II, p. 454.

MACCAULY, THOMAS. *The Indian Trader's Complete Guide; being a correct account of coins, weights, measures etc. etc. at the different settlements of India and...Asia.* Calcutta, 1816. pp. 116.

MACKONOCHIE, ALEXANDER. *Theory and Practice of Naval Architecture....Comparative State of Naval Architecture in Great Britain and India.* (Prospectus announced in 1803. The work, however, if ever published, appears to be unobtainable.)

MACPHERSON, DAVID. *The History of the European Commerce with India.* See pp. 230, 378.

MILBURN, WILLIAM. *Oriental Commerce.* See Vol. I, p. 236; Vol. II, pp. 125, 147, 170, 172, 220.

MOOKERJI, RADHAKUMUD. *Indian Shipping: A history of the sea-borne trade and maritime activity of the Indians from the earliest times.* Bombay, 1912. pp. 283, with 23 illustrations.

Naval Chronicle. Vols. II, pp. 51, 60, 136; XXII, pp. 362, 422; XXV, pp. 148, 299; XXVII, p. 399; XXVIII, p. 411.

Parliamentary Papers. *Minutes of the evidence taken before the select committee of the House of Commons on petitions relating to East-India-built shipping.* Ordered, by the House of Commons, to be printed. 1814. pp. 666.

PHIPPS, JOHN. *A Guide to the Commerce of Bengal, for the use of merchants, ship owners, commanders, officers, pursers and others resorting to the East Indies...containing a view of the shipping and external commerce of Bengal.* Calcutta, 1823. pp. xviii, 489.

—— *A Practical Treatise on the China and Eastern Trade; comprising the Commerce of Great Britain and India, particularly Bengal and Singapore, with China and the Eastern Islands.* Calcutta, 1835. pp. v, 338. Appendices, lxvi pp.

—— *A Collection of Papers relative to Ship Building in India.* Calcutta, 1840. pp. 264, with appendices.

POLO, MARCO. *The Travels of Marco Polo the Venetian.* See Book III, p. 321.

RICHMOND, Admiral Sir H. W. *Private Papers of George, second Earl Spencer.* Vol. IV. See p. 202.

SMYTH, H. WARINGTON. *Mast and Sail in Europe and Asia.* London, 1906. pp. 448, with numerous illustrations.

WELLESLEY, the Marquess. *Despatches,* p. 630. Memorandum on Bengal by Col. Arthur Wesley, p. 773.

CHAPTER XII

THE END OF MONOPOLY

ADOLPHUS, JOHN. *The substance of the speech of John Adolphus, Esq. before a Select Committee of the House of Commons, in summing up the case of the English ship-builders, on their petitions respecting ships built in India.* London, 1814. pp. 46.

ANON. *Papers respecting the trade between India and Europe.* Printed by order of the Court of Directors. London, 1802. pp. 190.

—— *Considerations upon the trade with India; and the policy of continuing the Company's monopoly.* London, 1807. pp. 190.

BIBLIOGRAPHY

ANON. *Memorial to the Board of Trade, from the Ship-builders in the Port of London, on the ruinous consequences which will result from the Employment of Indian built Ships in the Service of the East India Company, etc. etc. Dated 28th Jan.* 1809. Signed by Wells, Wigram & Green, Samuel & Daniel Brent, Thomas Pitcher & Son, Francis Barnard, Son, & Roberts, John Dudman & Son, Curling, Cox & Co.

—— *Hints for an answer to the Letter of the Chairman and Deputy Chairman of the East India Company to the Right Hon. Robert Dundas, dated 13th January*, 1809. London, 1812. pp. 75.

—— *General thoughts contained in a letter on the subject of the renewal of the East India Company's Charter.* London, 1812. pp. 54.

—— *Free Trade; or an Inquiry into the pretensions of the Directors of the East India Company, to the exclusive trade of the Indian and China Seas.* London, 1812. pp. xi, 70.

—— *The Question as to the renewal of the East India Company's Monopoly examined.* Edinburgh, 1812. pp. 117.

—— *A short conversation on the present crisis of the important trade with the East-Indies.* London, 1813.

—— *Remarks on the Charter of the East India Company.* Cambridge, 1813. pp. 60.

—— *The present system of our East India Government and Commerce considered; in which are exposed the fallacy, the incompatibility and the injustice of a political and despotic power possessing a commercial situation also within the countries subject to its dominion.* London, 1813. pp. 68.

—— *Some facts relative to the China Trade; shewing its importance to this country, and the inexpediency of its remaining exclusively in the hands of the East India Company.* Edinburgh, 1813. pp. 44.

—— *Free Trade with India. An Enquiry into the true state of the question at issue between His Majesty's Ministers, the Honorable East India Company and the public at large.* By 'Common Sense'. London, 1813. pp. 23.

DALLAS, Sir GEORGE, Bart. *A Letter to Sir William Pulteney, Bart., on the subject of the trade between India and Europe.* London, 1802. pp. 102.

GRANT, ROBERT. *The expediency maintained of continuing the system by which the trade and government of India are now regulated.*

HARRISON, W. *The substance of the speech of William Harrison Esq. before the select committee of the House of Commons on East India-built Shipping on Monday, April* 18, 1814. Sir Robert Peel in the chair. London, 1814. pp. 23.

—— *The substance of the reply of William Harrison Esq. before the select committee of the House of Commons on East India-built Shipping, on Tuesday, June* 28, 1814. London, 1814.

HENCHMAN, THOMAS. *Observations on the reports of the Directors of the East India Company, respecting the trade between India and Europe.*

LAUDERDALE, Earl of. *An Inquiry into the practical merits of the system for the government of India, under the superintendence of the Board of Controul.* Edinburgh, 1809. pp. 260, with a map.

LAURIE, DAVID. *Hints regarding the East India Monopoly; respectfully submitted to the British Legislature.* Glascow, 1813. pp. 66.

LESTER, W. *The Happy Era to one hundred millions of the human race; or the Merchant, Manufacturer, and Englishman's recognised Right to an unlimited Trade with India.* London, 1813. pp. 48.

MACLEAN, CHARLES. *A view of the consequences of laying open the trade to India, to private ships; with some remarks on the Nature of the East India Company's Rights.* 1812. pp. 55.

—— *Remarks on the evidence delivered before both Houses of Parliament on the East India Company's affairs.* 1813.

Pamphleteer, The. Various tracts. See Vol. I, *Letters of Gracchus on the East India Question,* reprinted from the *Morning Post.* 1813. pp. 60. Also, *Letters of Probus on the East India Question,* reprinted from the *Morning Post.* 1813. pp. 15. See also Vol. II, *Considerations on...British Commerce.*

Parliamentary Papers. *Reports and Minutes of Evidence taken before the Committee of the Whole House, and the Select Committee on the affairs of the East India Company.* Ordered, by the House of Commons, to be printed. 1813. pp. 591.

—— *Minutes of the evidence taken before the select committee of the House of Commons on petitions relating to East-India-built shipping.* Ordered, by the House of Commons, to be printed, 1814. pp. 666.

RENNY, ROBERT. *A Demonstration of the Necessity and Advantages of a Free Trade to the East Indies etc.* 2nd ed. London; 1807.

INDEX

[NOTE: FOR NAMES OF VESSELS, SEE UNDER 'SHIPS'.]

INDEX